Small Business Experts Love the Book

"It takes a brave woman to start, build, and run a business. For all those women out there who keep saying to themselves, 'I think I can, I think I can!,' with this excellent book, now they can!"

—Nell Merlino, Founder and CEO, Count Me In for Women's Economic Independence, and Author, *Stepping Out of Line: Lessons for Women Who Want It Their Way in Life, in Love, and at Work*

"More and more women are making business ownership their career choice. Peri Pakroo has created a superb resource for any woman entrepreneur to get her business off the ground successfully."

—Connie Evans, CEO of the Association of Enterprise Opportunity, Public Member of the U.S. Delegation to the United Nations 54th Session of the Commission on the Status of Women

"This no-nonsense guide is an essential road map for any woman considering entrepreneurship. It's packed with how-to information and real-life examples that will help save significant time and money in getting a venture started. Highly recommended."

—Sara Gould, former President and CEO, Ms. Foundation for Women

"What a great, practical and readable resource! This is not your typical 'motivational' business start-up book, but a detailed guide to all the steps of actually getting started, including specific tips and resources for women entrepreneurs. Peri's book clearly details all the nuts and bolts of starting a business so often lacking in how-to books. A must-read before you launch."

—Lindsey Johnson, former National Director, SBA Office of Women's Business Ownership

"A good read all around, Peri provides a practical guide that is useful and helpful for women starting and growing their businesses—love the real-life examples, too! This is a great book!"

—Wendy K. Baumann, President, The Wisconsin Women's Business Initiative Corporation

"This is a detailed resource for business. Instead of reading it like a regular book, go through the table of contents and find the areas where you need the most help. Read through and then take notes of what you remembered in that chapter. You'll be feeling well-versed and confident in business in no time!"

—Lisa Fetterman, Co-Founder of Nomiku, Kickstarter-funded cookware company

"The Women's Small Business Start-Up Kit is a must-read for any woman thinking about starting a business. As a Director of a Women's Business Center for nearly 20 years, this is the first book I've read which provides a realistic road map on how to make it happen. In spite of the remarkable accomplishments that self-employed women have made, let's face it, women continue to be the primary nurturers who hold American families together, a fact which makes starting and growing a successful woman-owned business fraught with challenges and sweet with its rewards."

—Agnes Noonan, Executive Director, Women's Economic Self-Sufficiency Team (WESST)

"Don't even think about starting a business without reading this book. Approachable, easy to understand and totally straightforward, Peri has done a service to all future entrepreneurs by giving solid advice to set you up for sustainable success."

—Amy Swift Crosby, Founder, SMARTY, A Resource for Entrepreneurial Women

"This book on small business start-ups is certainly a valuable tool that will assist women in making sound and sustainable decisions when beginning a new business venture. Peri's many years in the business consulting and training trenches gives her advice and information a high value of credibility. She has enormous experience and insight to share, and this book and kit is a must read for the aspiring entrepreneur."

—Patricia Harris, Executive Director & CEO, The Edge Connection, Women's Business Center at Kennesaw State University, Coles College of Business

GIFT RECEIPT

Barnes & Noble Booksellers #2780
1441 West Webster Avenue
Chicago, IL 60614
773-371-3610

STR:2780 REG:002 TRN:9684 CSHR:Caitlin R

Women's Small Business Start-Up Kit: A S
9781413322750   T1
(1 @ VH.HH)   VH.HH G

Connect with us on Social

Facebook- @BNClybourn
Instagram- @bnclybourn
Twitter- @BNClybourn

101.42A   12/24/2016 01:14PM

CUSTOMER COPY

Opened music CDs, DVDs, vinyl records, audio books may not be returned, and can be exchanged only for the same title and only if defective. NOOKs purchased from other retailers or sellers are returnable only to the retailer or seller from which they are purchased, pursuant to such retailer's or seller's return policy. Magazines, newspapers, eBooks, digital downloads, and used books are not returnable or exchangeable. Defective NOOKs may be exchanged at the store in accordance with the applicable warranty.

Returns or exchanges will not be permitted (i) after 14 days or without receipt or (ii) for product not carried by Barnes & Noble or Barnes & Noble.com.

Policy on receipt may appear in two sections.

Return Policy

With a sales receipt or Barnes & Noble.com packing slip, a full refund in the original form of payment will be issued from any Barnes & Noble Booksellers store for returns of undamaged NOOKs, new and unread books, and unopened and undamaged music CDs, DVDs, vinyl records, toys/games and audio books made within 14 days of purchase from a Barnes & Noble Booksellers store or Barnes & Noble.com with the below exceptions:

A store credit for the purchase price will be issued (i) for purchases made by check less than 7 days prior to the date of return, (ii) when a gift receipt is presented within 60 days of purchase, (iii) for textbooks, (iv) when the original tender is PayPal, or (v) for products purchased at Barnes & Noble College bookstores that are listed for sale in the Barnes & Noble Booksellers inventory management system.

Opened music CDs, DVDs, vinyl records, audio books may not be returned, and can be exchanged only for

4th Edition

The Women's Small Business Start-Up Kit

A Step-by-Step Legal Guide

Peri Pakroo, J.D.

FOURTH EDITION	MAY 2016
Editor	MARCIA STEWART
Production	SUSAN PUTNEY
Proofreading	ROBERT WELLS
Index	JANET MAZEFSKY
Printing	BANG PRINTING

Names: Pakroo, Peri, author.
Title: The women's small business start-up kit : step-by-step legal guide /
   Peri Pakroo, J.D.
Description: 4th Edition. | Berkeley, CA : Nolo, 2016. | Revised edition of the
   author's The women's small business start-up kit, 2014. | Includes index.
Identifiers: LCCN 2015049049 (print) | LCCN 2016000836 (ebook) | ISBN
   9781413322750 (pbk.) | ISBN 9781413322767 (epub)
Subjects: LCSH: Businesswomen. | Small business--Law and legislation. | Small
   business--Handbooks, manuals, etc.
Classification: LCC HD6053 .P35 2016 (print) | LCC HD6053 (ebook) | DDC
   658.1/1082--dc23
LC record available at http://lccn.loc.gov/2015049049

Please note

We believe accurate, plain-English legal information should help you solve
many of your own legal problems. But this text is not a substitute for
personalized advice from a knowledgeable lawyer. If you want the help of a
trained professional—and we'll always point out situations in which we think
that's a good idea—consult an attorney licensed to practice in your state.

Dedication

For Jila and Jasper

Acknowledgments

Update for the 4th Edition
In addition to the original Acknowledgments for the first edition
(see below), I have a few more thanks to give. In the few years
since this book was originally published in 2010, a number of
people have entered my life who have helped me in important
ways with their support, friendship, creativity, and just all-around
awesomeness. Sage Harrington, thank you for everything:
child care, research help, podcast jingles, tiny dogs, playing and
singing, and just being you. You have been a lifeline through
some very tough times; thank you. Matt Corson, thank you for
your awesome songs and for pushing me to learn new things.
It's a joy to be in your band and I'm glad you can out-boss me
(sometimes). Chris Burnett, thank you for roping me into your
podcasting kingdom; it has been a super-fun ride! Huge thanks to
everyone involved with Pyragraph.com, especially Lex Gjurasic,
Eva Avenue, Adam Rubinstein, David Dabney, and Turtle
O'Toole. I'm incredibly proud of what we've accomplished, and
all of it was under insane circumstances. Immeasurable thanks
to the many doctors and nurses who have helped my girl and my
family during a very intense medical experience over the past
year-plus: Dr. Mark Unverzagt, Dr. Michael Grimley, Kathleen
Novak, Dr. David Margolis, Lynette Anderson, Dr. John
Bucuvalas, Jennifer Willoughby, and Dr. Lucille McLoughlin,
among many others. Debbie Weissman, you have also been an
absolute lifesaver with your love, friendship, and support; thank
you. Endless love and thanks to my entire family, especially
Turtle, Jila, and Jasper. Your love keeps me going.

—PHP 2016

Acknowledgments for the 1st Edition

My previous books were all written in my child-free days, so when I started this one I fretted mightily about how on earth I would get it done with a three-year-old daughter in the picture. Then, a couple months into the project, I was simultaneously thrilled and terrified to learn I had another baby on the way, due three months before my final deadline. How could I possibly make this work?

My salvation came in the form of many usual suspects, plus some new ones. My husband, Turtle O'Toole, put in nothing short of heroic efforts to care for our family while I was up to my eyeballs in the book, then pregnancy, then a newborn. Thanks aren't enough, but thank you, Turtle. Thanks also to my dad for flying out here (twice) to help out, and to my mom and sister for relinquishing him. Jila, my amazing girl, thank you for believing me when I told you month after month I'd eventually be done with the book. And Jasper, you brought magic with you when you were born. Somehow all the cuddling and nursing and baby smiles gave me energy and sustained me while finishing the book, instead of the opposite. (Your sleeping at night was pretty great too.)

I feel incredibly lucky to have had Marcia Stewart as my editor. Besides doing an amazing job of actually editing the book, she gave me the perfect balance of encouragement, deadline pressure, and empathy to help me stay not only sane, but productive. Thank you so much Marcia.

Thanks also to all the editorial, production, marketing and applications development folks who make Nolo books so outstanding. Stan Jacobsen was a huge help in providing research and statistics. Terri Hearsh made the layout clean and the content easy to understand— no small thing with all this information. And big thanks to Andrea Burnett, Jackie Thompson, Wendy Jacobson, Helena Brantley, Colleen McHugh, Sigrid Metson, Jennifer Balaco, Simone Odom, and Michelle McKenzie for all their efforts to get the word out about the book. Finally, thanks again to Jake Warner for roping me into being an author many years ago. I'm really glad and grateful you did.

Thanks to all the amazing women who let me interview them and ask nosy questions about their businesses for this book. Shout outs go to Lauren Bacon, Kim Blueher, Elissa Breitbard, Jennifer Cantrell, Isabel Walcott Draves, Emily Esterson, Nicola Freegard, Leila Johnson, Lisa Kurtz, Emira Mears, Rebecca Pearcy, Sabrina Habib Williams, and Kyle Zimmerman—the information you shared is incredibly valuable; thank you. Thanks also to Clare Zurawski, Agnes Noonan, and the rest of the team at WESST in Albuquerque. I so enjoy teaching at and working with your awesome organization.

I couldn't have kept all the balls in the air this last year without the help of David Dabney and Damian Taggart. Thank you for everything; I'm so glad to have you on my extended team.

Finally, big love to Zz Pakroo, Parisha Pakroo, Stacey Strickler, Laura Taylor, Carolyn Nelson, Inga Muscio, and Samantha Campostrini-Medeiros. Also to Debbie Weissman and Kayte Blanke, our extended family here in New Mexico, and Emily Cooney for all your help and wonderful spirit. Thanks also to Bea Perez for all you do for us. And my fellow Moist Towelettes, Jeff Rutherford, Brent Templeton, Scott Batherson, and my main man, Turtle. Thanks for keeping the joy and good stuff flowing.

About the Author

Peri Pakroo (www.peripakroo.com) is a business author and coach, specializing in creative and smart strategies for self-employment and small business. She has started, participated in, and consulted with start-up businesses for more than 20 years. She is the founder, publisher, and editor of Pyragraph (www.pyragraph.com), an online career magazine for artists, musicians, designers, filmmakers, writers, and other creative workers worldwide.

Peri received her law degree from the University of New Mexico School of Law in 1995, and a year later began editing and writing for Nolo, specializing in small business and intellectual property issues. She is the author of the top-selling Nolo titles *The Women's Small Business Start-Up Kit, The Small Business Start-Up Kit* (national and California editions), and *Starting and Building a Nonprofit*, and has been featured in numerous national and local publications including *Entrepreneur, Real Simple, Investor's Business Daily*, and *BusinessWeek*. For several years Peri taught adult education courses at WESST (www.wesst.org) in Albuquerque, a nonprofit whose mission is to facilitate entrepreneurship among women and minorities in the state of New Mexico. She is active in supporting local, independent businesses and is a cofounder of the Albuquerque Independent Business Alliance.

About the Women Entrepreneur Contributors

I've learned an incredible amount from teaching, consulting, and just being friends with scores of women business owners for the past several years. The entrepreneurs listed below were particularly helpful in lending their insights and perspectives for this book. The businesses started by these creative and savvy women range from consulting practices and technology firms, to day spas and photography studios—as well as retail operations both online and off.

I interviewed these women in 2009, and since then several of them have moved on, some to new ventures, some to new jobs, some to take time off for parenting or other pursuits. The info that they shared, and I included in this book, should be viewed as a snapshot of their experiences at the time of our interviews.

I myself have started a new business since the first edition of this book, an online career magazine for creative folks, called Pyragraph. We launched in early 2013 and have been growing steadily ever since. Watch www.pyragraph.com to see how we develop, and I'll definitely share my lessons learned in future editions of this book.

Having experienced the ups and downs, in various measure, of being entrepreneurs, all of the women below have generously (and bravely!) shared their experiences with me, along with the valuable lessons they've learned. Their quotes appear throughout the book, adding a real-life component to the business start-up information I provide

You'll find full interviews with the women entrepreneurs profiled here on this book's companion page (see the end of the table of contents for information on this dedicated page on Nolo.com).

Lauren Bacon and Emira Mears are the founders and owners of Raised Eyebrow Web Studio Inc. (www.raisedeyebrow.com), a Vancouver-based Web development firm focused on providing strategic, beautiful, and effective online communications for clients in the nonprofit, government, and progressive business sectors. Lauren and Emira launched Raised Eyebrow in early 2000 and grew the business together until Lauren moved on in 2012; Emira continues to run Raised Eyebrow as Lead Strategist. Lauren and Emira also share their excellent insights about small business in their book, *The Boss of You: Everything A Woman Needs to Know to Start, Run, and Maintain Her Own Business* (Seal Press).

Elissa Breitbard launched Betty's Bath & Day Spa (www.bettysbath.com) in Albuquerque, New Mexico, after a decade in teaching. Repeatedly named as "Best Spa" in several local publications and websites, Betty's offers hot tubs, massage, facials, and restorative spa treatments, as well as retail products including natural bath and body products and jewelry. Betty's employs approximately 50 part- and full-time staff in a zen-like space in a rustic stretch of Albuquerque's north valley. In 2001, a year after launching Betty's, Elissa received the Emerging Entrepreneur of the Year award as part of the Public Service Co. of New Mexico's Entrepreneurial Leadership Awards. She is the founder and past president of the New Mexico Spa Association. She also cofounded and served as president of the Albuquerque Independent Business Alliance. Elissa sold Betty's in 2015 and successfully transitioned the business to new ownership. She is thrilled to see Betty's continue to thrive

Jennifer Cantrell is a certified public accountant with a long roster of entrepreneur clients and more than three decades of experience with small business issues. She began her practice from her garage when her children were toddlers. She and her husband have bought and sold several small businesses over the last 30 years.

She is board member of the WESST loan review committee, which specializes in microlending for small businesses. Jennifer especially enjoys working with other entrepreneurs.

Isabel Walcott Draves (www.isabeldraves.com) is an Internet start-up consultant and an expert in strategic Internet marketing, social media, user-generated content, and creating communities online and off. She has worked with entities large and small, including PinkArmy. org, VentureBeat, GreenHome.com, Linden Lab (SecondLife), SheSpeaks.com, Communispace.com, Digitas, Edelman PR, Gartner, and Bertelsmann. She is the founder of Leaders in Software and Art, a monthly salon in New York City. Isabel started the first online community written by teenage girls for teenage girls, SmartGirl.org, where she was CEO from 1996 until its acquisition in 2001 by the Institute for Research on Women and Gender at the University of Michigan.

Emily Esterson (www.e-squarededit.com) is a freelance writer, editor,author, and writing coach. Before striking out on her own in 2005, Emily was editor-in-chief at the *New Mexico Business Weekly* for six years. She was an associate editor at *Inc.* magazine in Boston, where she wrote about growth companies and technology. As a freelancer, she has written for *Business Week, Fortune Small Business,* and dozens of other trade publications. In 2009, she launched E-Squared Editorial Services, a custom publishing company focused on the horse industry—a lifelong passion. Emily has also authored *The Adult Longeing Guide* and *The Ultimate Book of Horse Bits.* She regularly contributes to several horse publications, and blogs at MyHorse.com. She lives on a farm near the Rio Grande in North Central New Mexico with three horses and other assorted animals.

 **Nicola Freegard** cofounded Vy&Elle, an eco-conscious fashion label headquartered in Tucson, Arizona, that made handbags from recycled vinyl billboards. Her interest in environmental design and recycling was born in the 1980s while working in the film industry as a music producer, and seeing the enormous amounts of waste involved in film production. In the early 1990s, she founded an eco-textiles company which created bedding and other soft home goods with fabrics imported from Nepal, Tibet, and Guatemala, as well as sustainable fabrics like hemp. Turning her focus to industrial waste, Nicola teamed with two friends who had been involved in recycled furniture and architectural salvage, to launch Vy&Elle (a play on the word vinyl) in 2002. By 2009, Vy&Elle's average annual revenue was $2 million and it had recycled about 200 tons of vinyl otherwise destined for landfills. In 2009, Nicola folded the billboard bag concept in with another eco-conscious label, Blowfish Shoes.

 **Leila Johnson** is vice president and co-owner of VelaMira, Inc., dba Data-Scribe® (www.data-scribe.com), a full-service Web firm. She founded her business in 2003 along with her husband, Brett. In 2007, they also founded the first association for entrepreneurial couples, the Couples in Business Network (www.copreneursociety.org). Leila has ten years of experience in information technology, quality assurance, customer service, communications, and business operations. She was a winner of the *New Mexico Business Weekly's* 2007 "40 Under 40" award and the NAWBO Northern New Mexico Chapter's 2005 "Up and Coming Business Owner" award, and has been interviewed by *Home Business Magazine, Entrepreneur* magazine's *Home Based Biz Show,* and many other publications. She is the author of *Driving to Success: Let Your Spirit Take the Wheel,* which focuses on taking a spiritual approach to your professional life. Leila resides in New Mexico.

 **Catherine Oddenino** is the owner of Luca & Bosco (http://lucaandbosco.com), an ice cream company based in New York City. She is a graduate of the University of Virginia's McIntire School of Business with a concentration in Marketing. Catherine spent 13 years working as a marketing, ad sales, and business development executive for media companies in New York City. She was a founding member of the New Products Group at Turner Broadcasting, launching several new products and media brands. Catherine led business development for the digital food, home, and travel brands at Time Inc., including *Real Simple, Cooking Light*, and *Sunset*, and led gluten-free holiday content development for MyRecipes.com. Catherine's entrepreneurial spirit is reflected in both her career and her personal endeavors. She has a food blog, *A Gluten-Free Guide* (http://aglutenfreeguide.com), which has led to freelance travel writing and food photography projects. Her interest in ice cream was sparked after tasting a magical combination of homemade banana ice cream with her candied bacon topping. Catherine wanted to be able to buy it, and when she couldn't find it anywhere in New York City she knew there was a place in the market for a new ice cream offering.

 **Rebecca Pearcy** is the founder and owner of Queen Bee Creations and Chickpea Baby (www.queenbee-creations.com), which manufacture and distribute a variety of handmade bags, wallets, panniers, diaper bags, and accessories to retail and wholesale customers around the world. Rebecca founded Queen Bee in 1996 in Olympia, Washington, as a one-woman operation, doing all the stitching, selling, and everything in between. The business moved to Portland, Oregon, in 2002 and has grown to about a dozen employees (including Rebecca). All items are handmade in the Queen Bee studio (a.k.a. the Hive) in North Portland, which is open to the public seven days a week. Queen Bee also has a significant online operation, including an online store and a strong presence across a wide swath of social media.

Sabrina Habib Williams cofounded JS Photography in Gainesville, Florida, with her husband, Jeff in 2002. Sabrina and Jeff worked for other photographers before starting their own photography business, first at home, and later moving into a high-profile storefront studio. Sabrina continues to do photography and fine art projects with Jeff, and in 2013 began teaching university courses in communication and visual production.

Kyle Zimmerman opened her Albuquerque photography studio, Kyle Zimmerman Photography, in 1996 after more than 25 years of national and international experience in fashion, advertising, and commercial photography. Her business and her photographs have received numerous awards, including a City of Albuquerque Public Art Award to create images and capture the life, people, and happenings of one of the city's major thoroughfares, Mountain Road, for the City of Albuquerque's Public Art Program. Kyle's energy and big heart made her one of the most sought-after photographers in Albuquerque and beyond. In 2015, Kyle decided to close her photography studio in order to focus on more personal creative and photographic work, while also pursuing a career in real estate. She continues to work with a select few clients.

Table of Contents

5 Understanding and Choosing a Legal Structure 143

6 Your Business Location: Working From Home or Renting Space 183

7 Dealing With Start-Up Requirements and Bureaucratic Hurdles 225

13 **Lawyers and Accountants:**
Building Your Family of Professionals.. 477

A **How to Use the Interactive Forms on the Nolo Website**... 491

Get Updates, Forms, Spreadsheets, Interview Transcripts, and More on This Book's Companion Page at Nolo.com

You can download any of the forms, worksheets, and calculators in this book at:

www.nolo.com/back-of-book/WBIZ.html

When there are important changes to the information in this book, we'll post updates on this same dedicated page (what we call this book's companion page). You'll find other useful information on this page, too, such as author blogs and podcasts.

In addition, this book's companion page includes the full transcripts of interviews with women entrepreneurs who were interviewed for this book. You'll find quotes from these women sprinkled in sidebars throughout the text, but the full interviews provide a richer perspective on what it's like for women to start and run a small business. See "About the Women Entrepreneur Contributors" at the beginning of this book for bios on the women contributors.

The Women's Small Business Start-Up Companion

'm excited every time I hear about a small business start-up. Whether it's a one-person consulting firm, a small retail shop with a few employees, or a software company that aims to become a technology empire, it always gives me a thrill to see people put their ideas and dreams into action. And I'm particularly happy when I see women at the helm of new business ventures. As more women take the leap into entrepreneurship, more of us get to taste the rewards that come when we control our own destinies. With women-owned businesses launching at nearly twice the rate of start-ups overall (a trend that has persisted for a couple decades), entrepreneurship is thankfully no longer the overwhelmingly male-dominated domain it used to be.

Women become entrepreneurs for all sorts of reasons. Some are tired of the glass ceiling and want more control over their careers, including the power to implement their own ideas. Others want more freedom and flexibility for personal or family time. Some women are nearing retirement and want to finally pursue a dream they've harbored for years. Still others are finally ready to take a passion or hobby to the next level and pursue it as an actual business.

These days, another powerful motivator has come to the forefront: Many women recognize that self-employment is a smart survival strategy. Being able to work for yourself is sometimes a critical factor helping women stay afloat in between jobs, during personal upheavals like divorce, or for extended periods of unemployment. In an economy where no job is safe, having the skills and know-how to go it on your own provides security that no one can take away from you.

It's key to remember that being your own boss can mean a lot of different things, from being a solo freelancer to running a multimillion-dollar international empire. The beauty is, none of these are more valid or objectively better than any other—there's no single "right" way to work for yourself. Some businesses involve a relatively high level of risk and commitment, along with the potential for major profits; others may offer more modest financial rewards but allow much more personal freedom. The key (as described in Chapter 1) is to make a point of clarifying your goals, then planning your business so it helps you meet them.

No matter what type of business you want to start, there's no question that working for yourself provides an excellent opportunity to live a more satisfying, authentic life on your own terms. This book explains all the considerations and steps you need to take to make your unique vision a reality. You'll learn everything from developing a profitable idea, to choosing a legal structure, to marketing the business and managing its finances—and a lot more.

The book also includes useful forms such as a sample partnership agreement, and interactive calculators and worksheets to help you do financial projections, such as a break-even analysis and a cash flow projection. You can download all of the forms, worksheets, and calculators in this book (listed at the end of the main table of contents) at the Nolo website. See the appendix for a link to the forms in this book.

Some of you may already be dabbling in freelancing, maybe on a small scale or part time, and want to learn how to transform your microenterprise into more of a full-fledged business. All the information you need to take your business to the next level is included in this book.

Do women entrepreneurs need their own book?

Some of you may be wondering why women business owners need their own start-up book. In some ways, they really don't. The elements of business success are the same for women and men: a profitable market, strong financial management, and marketing savvy, for instance. And—with the exception of the process of becoming certified as a woman-owned business in order to qualify for government contracting preferences—all the bureaucratic start-up steps and tasks are gender-neutral.

But starting and running a business involves more than spreadsheets and bureaucracies. Women quite simply have a different experience running businesses than men do. Despite the huge diversity of businesses that women entrepreneurs run, there are common threads and themes in the experiences women report, such as the challenge of keeping work and personal life in balance, and the difficulty of obtaining start-up or expansion financing.

This book addresses these issues and concerns, in addition to all the business basics that apply to men and women alike, such as writing a business plan, managing your finances, or launching a website. It also covers women-specific topics such as how to become certified as a woman-owned business, how to pursue government contracting opportunities for women, and what resources are available for women entrepreneurs, such as Women's Business Centers and microlenders. In addition, I've included a substantial amount of advice and guidance from a wide variety of women entrepreneurs whom I interviewed for the book. They offer valuable real-world perspectives that supplement and balance all the how-to information in these pages.

What you won't find in this book

If you've been shopping around for women's business books, you've likely seen many that emphasize inspiration and pep talks. If that's what you're looking for, this book may not be for you. You won't find lengthy discussions to help convince you that "you can do it." In this book, "you can do it" is assumed. My focus will be on the actual nuts and bolts of *how* to do it—how to start a business that has a real shot at success. And if confidence is an issue for you, I happen to think that arming yourself with practical, detailed information is the best way to build it.

I also wince every time I see a business writer try to appeal to women entrepreneurs through silly stereotypes. Not every businesswoman wears high heels, lives to shop, has 100 colors of lipstick, or likes to be called a "sassy diva." This persistent imagery paints a picture that excludes tons of women business owners (including me). I'll assume you readers are as diverse as the world of entrepreneurs that I have worked with over the years, including high-powered executives; visionary artists; buttoned-down worker bees; genius intellectuals; earthy health and wellness enthusiasts; brainy technology ninjas; hipster crafters; and everyone in between.

Women's Business Organizations

As women-owned businesses have proliferated, so have women's business organizations. These groups provide resources for women entrepreneurs (such as help writing a business plan or seeking financing), promote their interests, and provide opportunities for them to interact and learn from each other. The organizations below are nationally based (there may also be local groups of women business owners in your city or region):

- The SBA's **Office of Women's Business Ownership (OWBO)** exists to establish and oversee a national network of Women's Business Centers (WBCs). The SBA's website changes often, so go to the main SBA site at www.sba.gov, then search the site for the term "women." You'll find a list of Women's Business Centers, information on government contracts for women-owned small businesses, and more on the SBA site. To find the nearest Women's Business Center, you can also check the list published by the Association of Women's Business Centers at www.awbc.org.

- The **National Association of Women Business Owners (NAWBO)** is a dues-based organization that advocates for the interests of women entrepreneurs in all industries. See www.nawbo.org.

- **Count Me in for Women's Economic Independence** offers resources, business education, and community support for women entrepreneurs seeking to grow micro businesses to million-dollar enterprises. See www.countmein.org.

- **WomanOwned.com** is an online resource with a wide range of information for women business owners, including in-depth information about government contracting. See www.womanowned.com.

- The **National Women's Business Council (NWBC)** is a nonpartisan federal advisory council concerned with economic issues important to women business owners. See www.nwbc.gov.

- The **Women's Business Enterprise National Council (WBENC)** offers WBE certification for women-owned businesses that is accepted by many government agencies and U.S. corporations. See www.wbenc.org.

- The **National Women's Business Owners Corporation (NWBOC)** is a private organization that offers a national certification program for women-owned and controlled businesses. See www.nwboc.org.

Go forth and prosper

As a consultant and teacher on small business start-up issues, it's incredibly satisfying to play even a tiny role in helping women (and men) make their business ideas a reality. I feel the same way about writing business books. I deeply hope the information in this book helps you and your ideas take flight.

Women-Owned Businesses Are a Major Economic Force

There are over 9.4 million women-owned businesses in the United States generating over $1.5 trillion in revenues and employing nearly 7.9 million people. The number of women-owned businesses has been growing at a rate of one-and-a-half times the national average: Between 1997 and 2015, when the number of businesses in the United States increased by 51%, the number of women-owned firms increased by 74%. (Source: The 2015 State of Women-Owned Businesses Report, commissioned by American Express OPEN.)

Choosing the Right Business for You

Pop quiz: What life do you envision for yourself as a business owner? I'm not talking about the business you see yourself running, but the life you want to lead. If you haven't thought much about this, now is the time. Assuming that you want your business to serve your life instead of the other way around, you need to include big-picture life goals in your planning process. Self-employment takes many different forms and supports a wide range of lifestyles; it's up to you to decide what goals are most important to you and plan your business accordingly.

It's all too easy for new entrepreneurs to be seduced by traditional notions of business success without thinking about the lifestyle implications or considering alternatives. The "success" stories we always hear about in business magazines and other mainstream media constantly focus on big dollars and rapid growth—and the classic depiction of the business owner who works 18 hours a day. If you leap into starting a business without taking the time to define your own vision for your life as a small business owner, you might find yourself among the many entrepreneurs who complain they've become slaves to their businesses—much like they felt like slaves to their jobs.

The truth is, business success can take many different forms, from major retail empires to microbusinesses with modest incomes. If you take care to explore your unique vision of success early in your business planning, you'll be much more likely to build a business—big or small—that truly makes you happy.

This chapter looks at big-picture lifestyle questions new entrepreneurs should consider when in the early planning stages of a venture. I'll focus on developing a realistic picture of what it's like to run a small business and help you understand how to approach your planning efforts so that the business fits in well with your personality and lifestyle choices. We'll cover:

- the realities of working for yourself, including what personality traits and skills are important when you're self-employed
- practical tips for maintaining a healthy work/life balance, including choosing the right type of business and engaging in healthy work habits

- the importance of implementing systems within your business to ensure that it runs smoothly, especially when you're not around and/or if you have staff, and
- what's involved in the role of the business owner, separate from other roles you might play in the business, such as leading a sales team, providing professional services, or handling tasks like bookkeeping.

By the end of this chapter, you'll have a good idea of the personal considerations you should address in order to ensure the business you start fits well with your ideal life. You'll then be in a good position to start the "business" side of your business planning as covered in upcoming chapters, when you'll focus on developing a winning idea (Chapter 2) and fleshing it out in a solid business plan (Chapter 4).

What's the best part of running a business?

"Getting to do exactly what I want, how I want to ... and not working for someone else."

— Kyle Zimmerman

"The fact that I work in the field of my choice doing what I love, with freedom to be creative. The ability to model the business philosophy exactly to my standards and beliefs is something I would never have working for someone else."

— Sabrina Habib Williams

"Being self-employed is pretty ideal for becoming a parent. I can decide what kind of a schedule I need (within reason) and be more in control of my life than if I worked for someone else."

— Rebecca Pearcy

"Getting to call the shots—nothing quite compares to having the autonomy to decide which projects you want to take on, and when and how you want to work. Even when things are rough, it's reassuring to know that if you want things to change, it's in your power to change them."

— Lauren Bacon and Emira Mears

What's the best part of running a business? (continued)

"The constant newness, change. There are always new issues and challenges, and this suits my personality. For example, just last week we decided to launch an entirely new brand/branch within Betty's—Betty's To Go, which will be off-site massage geared toward the film industry. Now we have this new focus to keep things fresh. It's also true that I now cannot imagine working for someone else."

— **Elissa Breitbard**

"The best part of running a business is the flexibility of my schedule. I realized how important this was when I was pregnant and after having my daughter."

— **Leila Johnson**

"The challenge and the learning are the best parts of this business owner puzzle. After failing at other businesses, I have rejoiced in understanding that my failures have been my best lesson. I have no fear of thought-through risk, and have built a tremendous amount of confidence from this."

— **Nicola Freegard**

"When you're a consultant, people really are turning to you for advice. Having the intellectual freedom to speak my mind and being able to substantially influence the direction of a business entity are probably the benefits I appreciate most about the choice I've made."

— **Isabel Walcott Draves**

The Realities of Entrepreneurship

While teaching business start-up courses for the past several years, I have met scores of would-be entrepreneurs with boundless energy, passion, and fabulous ideas for new businesses—including many with seriously misguided ideas about what it's like to own and run a business. If the idea of being your own boss conjures images of sleeping late, enjoying fancy lunches with clients, or a swank corner office with panoramic views, think again. Starting a business is rarely so glamorous, especially in the early days when you may find yourself fantasizing about simple things like an afternoon off or a quiet homemade dinner.

Even if you think you have a pretty realistic vision of starting a business, it's worth stepping back in the early days of planning your business and examining your motivations and assumptions to make sure entrepreneurship is really right for you. Here's a quick list of practical realities.

- **Business owners need to be comfortable making decisions on their own.** From big strategy decisions, such as what type of business entity to form, to details such as how much to pay an administrative assistant, a business owner makes lots of decisions every day. Even if you hire a manager for your flower shop or restaurant, ultimately the buck stops with you. If decision making isn't one of your strong suits or stresses you out, think twice about being your own boss.
- **Pessimists need not apply.** Most entrepreneurs are eternal optimists who see opportunities instead of barriers. If you immediately think of ten or 100 reasons why an idea might fail, you'll likely have a hard time making it far in business.

 RESOURCE

To nurture your inner optimist, read *The Art of Possibility: Transforming Professional and Personal Life,* by Rosamund Stone Zander and Benjamin Zander (Penguin). The book opens with a story about two marketing scouts from a shoe factory traveling to Africa to explore business opportunities. The first scout sends a telegram back to the factory, "Situation hopeless ... no one wears shoes." But the second sends the message, "Glorious business opportunity ... no one wears shoes." The more you can cultivate the latter attitude, the more attuned you'll be to opportunities all around you.

- **You'll need a thick skin.** The most successful business owners are unafraid (or at least willing) to boldly promote themselves, their businesses, their products, and their services. You'll need to be able to handle rejection from potential customers or challenge from competitors, so if you are easily wounded or prone to giving up when faced with obstacles, entrepreneurship may not be the best route for you.

- **Running a business can be lonely.** Many entrepreneurs are surprised to find how isolating it is to run a business. Working alone, late at night after the kids have gone to bed can really make you feel alienated from the world. It's a common issue for solo operators, but even those with employees often bemoan their lack of peers. You may have to spend extra energy developing friendships and a social circle. Note that if you take the advice we offer throughout this book and regularly engage in networking, you'll feel less isolated while simultaneously boosting your business's chances of success.

- **A great business idea is no guarantee of success.** I can't count how many people I have met who say they have a fabulous business idea—in many cases, it actually is fabulous—but seem to think that this killer idea will just magically transform into a profitable business. The truth is, an idea is just the starting point. Even the best idea requires work and money to start the business, market the product or service, and guide the venture to success.

- **Being organized will help lower the stress of running your business.** Below we discuss the importance of organizational skills such as keeping a schedule for yourself and developing methodical systems to run your business. In general, being organized helps save time and reduce stress, two major factors in how much you're likely to enjoy your life as a business owner.

- **Without a boss, your motivation and discipline will need to come from within.** For some people, it's a struggle to find the motivation to put in long hours and do tasks they loathe (for many, this includes bookkeeping). If you need a boss to keep the fire under you, self-employment may not be a good fit.

- **You should love what you do—and remember to treat it like a business.** I've never been a fan of choosing a business idea purely based on what's hot and profitable at the moment. Going with what you know and love is always a better bet. But just because you pursue a passion doesn't mean you should be any less businesslike. If your business is making jewelry, doing photography, freelance writing, or any other creative pursuit, it's important to treat your work like a business, not a hobby.

The many different aspects of doing this—business planning, conquering the bureaucracy, keeping your books, and more—are the prime subjects of this book.

Top Considerations for Developing Your Business

Besides getting real about what life as an entrepreneur might look and feel like, you should also take into account some specific considerations regarding your own strengths and weaknesses, as well as of the team you're considering putting together. Let's look at some of the most important things to think about as you push your business idea forward.

Honestly Evaluate Your Small Business Skills

When deciding what business to start, it's important to evaluate your ideas in terms of what skills may be particularly important. For a business to succeed, many skills come into play—not just the expertise at the heart of the business. In addition to that expertise (for instance, graphic design experience if you want to start a graphic design firm, or knowledge of pet products and services if you want to open a pet supply shop), a successful business relies on more general skills. For example, every business regardless of industry needs to manage its money, engage in marketing, and, if the business has staff, manage employees or subcontractors.

New entrepreneurs are often surprised to discover that the success of their venture may depend on skills they didn't expect would be important—and that they may not possess. For example, some businesses may be heavily dependent on technology, or may require sophisticated financial management. By evaluating the skills required for your business and your own strengths or weaknesses in those skills, you'll develop a realistic picture of how well suited you are for running that business.

A common scenario is for an entrepreneur to have plenty of skills in the core aspect of the business but not in administrative or financial areas. This is especially true for creative entrepreneurs. For example, a master knitter who wants to start a business teaching knitting classes may have no trouble at all in defining how she'll run the classes, what techniques she'll cover, what supplies she'll need, and the like. But when it comes to doing bookkeeping, managing finances, or marketing the business, she may feel clueless. I meet entrepreneurs like this all the time—caterers, craftspeople, photographers, and writers who are great at providing their products or services but who lack skills and confidence in the more "business-y" aspects of the business.

> EXAMPLE: Simone wants to start a wedding planning website that will offer information and local resources for brides (and to a lesser extent, grooms). She has been a buyer at a bridal store for nearly ten years and knows the industry well. Based upon other websites she's evaluated, Simone believes her website can earn revenue through online advertising and affiliate agreements with local wedding-related businesses, such as florists. For example, Simone's site could earn commissions when site visitors click through to and/or make purchases at florists listed at her site. In researching her idea, Simone talks with a couple of contacts of hers who have experience in online publishing. Both her contacts help Simone understand that the success of her business idea will heavily rely on how successfully she can negotiate affiliate agreements with other wedding-related businesses. Simone's in-depth knowledge of bridal fashions and trends, while helpful, won't be the key to the business succeeding. Simone is disheartened to hear this advice since she has little to no sales experience outside the realm of buying dresses for her shop—and she was never very comfortable with the negotiating aspect of her job. She reluctantly realizes that her idea may not be a good fit for her skills, and that she might be better off with a slightly different type of business, such as being a wedding consultant or planner.

The good news is that gaps in your skills and experience can be filled, either by hiring employees or contractors, or taking on co-owners. Most entrepreneurs aren't experts in every aspect of running a business, and sometimes they may simply loathe certain tasks such as bookkeeping or marketing. The key is to recognize those gaps and fill them with other key people. Hiring staff is discussed in Chapter 12. We discuss taking on co-owners in the next section.

The many hats of entrepreneurship

"Even though I had already worked for someone else as an apprentice, I think I still had the naive notion that to be a photographer I'm going to be doing something that I love and something creative all the time, and that it's going to be great and I'm going to have all this fun. I didn't know I was going to have to learn to be a bookkeeper and take accounting classes; I didn't know I was going to have to learn about all these laws related to taxes and how to write them off; I didn't know I was going to have to learn to be a salesperson; I didn't know I was going to have to learn marketing and branding and go home and rack my brain and think of the next marketing campaign that suits our business the best, or the most creative way to network that somebody hasn't done yet, to keep myself innovative. I thought I was going to have to be innovative with my imagery, and my photography. I didn't know I was going to have to be creative and innovative with branding and marketing. Branding and marketing were words that didn't pertain to my life. So, being able to wear every hat and any hat—and many hats at any time and all times. Juggling 30 things at once. It's basically getting over that overwhelming part of it. Now I feel that we can handle it and it just comes naturally to us."

— **Sabrina Habib Williams**

Consider Co-Owners Carefully

Starting a business with other co-owners (either partners, LLC owners, or corporate shareholders) can be easier in many ways than going it alone. At the most basic level, it can be a huge relief to have other motivated owners to share the burdens of starting and running the business, instead of being responsible for everything yourself. This is true not only with regard to the hard work involved, but also the start-up money needed—co-owners can be an important source of funding. In addition, as discussed earlier, co-owners may bring important skills to the table that you may lack, such as experience with financial management or legal knowledge.

There are potential drawbacks to starting with co-owners, however. One is that there are more complexities involved in starting and running a business with multiple owners. You'll need to hammer out important details, such as ownership shares, work responsibilities, salaries and other compensation, and buyout provisions, among others, and execute an agreement outlining all key terms (for partners, a partnership agreement; for LLC owners, an operating agreement). Assuming the co-owners will actively work in the business (as opposed to being silent investors), you'll need some level of management structure to ensure the co-owners work together efficiently, fulfill their job descriptions, and put in the hours they've committed to. In comparison, being the only owner is considerably simpler.

Besides complexity, the existence of multiple owners introduces the possibility of conflict. This can happen even when everyone is working hard and has the best intentions—even well-meaning, reasonable people can disagree (sometimes vehemently). All sorts of issues can be fodder for conflict: fundamental business strategy, hiring decisions, marketing and branding choices, and pricing are just a few examples. Conflict becomes even more likely when one or more owners don't live up to their responsibilities or make poor choices. When a co-owner fails to keep the books up to date or makes a habit of missing important meetings, discord is sure to follow.

To avoid problems like these, the most basic advice is to be very careful in choosing your co-owners. As tempting as it may be to jump into business with your best friend, it's critical to evaluate the situation and relationship first. Do you essentially trust the person's judgment in general? Besides common sense, does your potential co-owner have good business instincts? On a personal level, do you have an easy rapport that facilitates getting things done and resolving conflict when it inevitably arises? And perhaps most important, do you trust this person is honest and ethical? If you have any serious doubts about any of these, co-ownership may not be wise. Trust your instincts and don't dismiss any nagging unease. As many business consultants note, going into business with someone is much like getting married. Don't make the mistake of finding yourself in bed with an unreliable or untrustworthy partner.

RELATED TOPIC

Partnerships, LLCs, and corporations are discussed in Chapter 5.
That chapter offers details on the legal and tax characteristics of these business
types and what differentiates them from one another. The bureaucratic steps
involved in starting various business entities are covered in Chapter 7.

Use Caution When Working With Your Spouse or Relatives

If your vision includes your spouse or other relatives as part of the
business (either as co-owners or employees), make sure you've thought
through the details and potential pitfalls of this set-up. At a minimum,
make sure that your family members are qualified for the jobs you're
planning for them. As Chapter 12 describes in more detail, you should
approach the hiring process methodically, draft clear job descriptions,
and pay wages regularly as you would with any hire.

Even if your spouse, brother, cousin, or other family member is
perfect for the job, ask yourself: Are you really sure you want to mix
business with family? Conflicts are common in day-to-day business, and
the start-up period is particularly stressful. Be honest about whether
you think your family relationships can handle the stress. This can be a
particular concern when working with your spouse   obviously, this is a
relationship you want to protect and nurture. Some spouses work really
well together, even in stressful, grueling situations. Other relationships
do better with more space. Evaluate your relationships carefully before
bringing family members into the business.

RELATED TOPIC

**Working with your spouse raises issues related to your business
structure and taxes.** Chapter 5 discusses the question of which legal entity
is most beneficial and appropriate when working with your spouse, and the
tax implications of which entity you use. Small business taxes are discussed in
Chapter 11.

When your business partner is your spouse

"Because my partner Jeff is also my husband, our communication is fantastic. I mean, we can talk through anything. And we work really well as a team. And we have a good time together. Because we often work long hours it's nice to be able to spend that time together. You know, as opposed to working long hours away from each other. If I'm having a hard day I'm able to get a nice hug in the middle of the day if I need to. And we can have lunch together and all these things that are all perks. The hardest things are not to bring work home or into our relationship. If we have a baby- sitter and we have a movie-and-dinner date, we're very likely to sit and talk about business through our whole dinner, which is supposed to be our time together. So there are no boundaries, we talk about business laying in bed before going to sleep, and that kind of stuff. That to me is the lowest, the worst drawback, and it's really hard to separate."

— Sabrina Habib Williams

Assess Your Tolerance for Risk

While starting a business is generally a riskier life choice than being employed in a regular job, some businesses definitely involve more risk than others. In a nutshell, the more money you need to start a business, the more risk is involved. If you're putting significant savings into the business, they might be lost. If you obtain a start-up loan and the business fails, you may need to take an unsavory job to pay off the loan. For many entrepreneurs, these risks are worth the potential to turn a profit.

But don't buy into the myth that you need to be a high-rolling risk junkie to be an entrepreneur. If you're not comfortable with putting lots of money on the line, there are plenty of businesses that cost very little to start or run. You may be able to start a service business like a design consulting, house painting, or gardening business with very little initial outlay, especially if you already own many of the tools you'll need.

Often, but not always, increased risk corresponds with higher profit potential. Examine your own risk tolerance and how important money is to you in order to pick a business that fits with your comfort level.

Keep Networking at the Top of Your To-Do List

One of the biggest keys to success for any business venture is maintaining a network of useful contacts and associates. As described in more detail in Chapter 8, networking and cultivating key relationships is a critical ongoing activity for every business owner.

If you're naturally gregarious and find yourself easily chatting with all sorts of people, you might do this without even thinking. If you're more reserved, you may need to push yourself a little to flex your networking muscle. Without forging relationships within your local business community, your industry, your target customers, or whatever group is appropriate for your specific circumstances, you're almost assured of missing out on opportunities that could mean the difference between success and failure.

Networking is also a great way to find key vendors, suppliers, collaborators, staff, professionals (lawyers, accountants, and Web developers), and others who can be major factors—sometimes, *the* major factor—in your business's success.

Lots of folks new to the world of business fear that successful networking requires unsavory schmoozing or pandering. Not so. In fact, if you adopt a sleazy, wheeler-dealer approach, you risk alienating the very people whom you want to make your allies. Instead, successful networking is little more than sincere communication with others about what you do.

Elissa Breitbard, founder of Betty's Bath and Day Spa, is a study in the power of networking. Not content merely to engage in networking opportunities, Elissa made a point of creating them. Not long after she launched Betty's Bath and Day Spa, she founded the New Mexico Spa Association. "Our view is that boosting the spa industry in general just helps us," she explained. "In starting the New Mexico Spa Association I really reached out to all the spa owners and directors throughout the state, because I believe that to work together will better the entire industry. Plus I learn so much from others." Networking also played a big role in getting her business off the ground. Lacking any experience in the spa industry, Elissa had a lot to learn. "Some information was really hard to get," she said, "which is why I started networking with other spa owners at the I-Spa conferences, the big professional organization. I really recommend that to women: to get involved with networking in their professional organizations. Just networking in general is one of the golden keys of a successful business, and it has been for me."

You can take this same networking approach on a smaller level—much like forming a book club, except that your group is focused on similar business issues, not literary tastes. For example, women who own a certain type of business—whether it involves IT, health care services, retail clothing, Web development, or jewelry design—could form a networking group that meets once a month for lunch, happy hour, or dinner to talk shop. Networking is discussed in more detail in Chapter 8, but just remember to keep an eye out for local groups, such as a local restaurant or neighborhood merchants' association.

Maintaining Work/Life Balance

One issue that comes up over and over again for women entrepreneurs is the challenge of balancing the duties of running a business with their personal lives. Consistently, women report this is one of the most stubborn challenges they face as business owners. For many women, a business that allows flexibility and freedom is essential so they can care for a family (this might include caring for children or for aging parents), and spend time with a spouse or partner. Other women may want to preserve time in their lives for pursuing other interests such as creative work, travel, sports, or any number of activities. Still other women may simply be committed to not being workaholics and want plenty of down time in their personal lives. The bottom line is that for all these reasons and more, flexibility and work/life balance are recurring themes in what women entrepreneurs report as important concerns.

So what's the best way to go about pursuing this elusive state of balance? First, it's worth stating the obvious, that balance is fluid and there's no such thing as achieving it with any finality. Maintaining a healthy balance between running your business and enjoying your life is an ongoing pursuit—more of a habit than something to strike off your "to do" list—so the trick is to adopt strategies and practices that will tend to bring you back to a happy state of equilibrium when things inevitably get out of whack.

Another reality to keep in mind is that no small business runs itself, and it's a mistake to underestimate the time commitment your venture will require. I've met plenty of prospective entrepreneurs who seem to think that their great business ideas will just blossom into success of their own volition. Unfortunately, this completely wrongheaded expectation is a dangerous set-up for the business owner to become quickly overwhelmed and burned out when she realizes that every business—even those based on brilliant ideas—requires a lot of work to get off the ground. Having realistic expectations from the get-go is critical in helping you maintain your energy and passion, and pacing yourself mentally and physically in your business's crazy early days.

The good news is that it is possible to be a business owner and maintain flexibility and freedom in your life. First, clarify for yourself what "success" looks like. There's no universal rule that you must strive to build a huge multimillion-dollar empire like the entrepreneurs you read about in business magazines (not that there's anything wrong with that). Being clear about your own definition of success will help you choose the right type of business and aim for a scale and structure that don't require more management than you want to provide. Also, be vigilant about developing healthy habits, such as taking certain days off or putting away your laptop after a certain hour, and taking time for personal, social, and family activities.

The following sections take a closer look at each of these.

How do you achieve work-life balance?

"Oi! I'm working on it all the time, 'working' on keeping a balance with massages, art, dreams, and friends. And I make myself not do anything that's 'work' on Sunday, ever."

— **Kyle Zimmerman**

"Our hours are set to optimize personal and family time. We also opened a storefront studio; before that we were working from home, which meant we never left work. Having to leave everything behind at the end of the day makes a huge difference in our lives."

— **Sabrina Habib Williams**

"I spend as much time as I can with my family and my eight-year-old son, Eden, when I'm not at my studio. We paint, draw, read, write and tell stories. I have a close community of dear friends I've known for many years too. They keep me grounded and support me for who I am, not because of what I do. Keeping life simple has been the best balance."

— **Nicola Freegard**

"Honestly, this is a perennial struggle. It's made much easier when you've got a business partner, like we do—we encourage each other to take time off when we need it, make sure we take the vacation time we're supposed to, and leave work at a decent hour as often as possible. Of course we don't always achieve balance—but who does?"

— **Lauren Bacon and Emira Mears**

"I delegate most of the front-end operations of Betty's to our managers, so that I can work less, be with my family, and do other things that feed my soul. I work 18 to 20 hours a week, and am hands-on when I'm here, but then let others run the business when I'm away."

— **Elissa Breitbard**

"I have a great team of people that works with us on projects, which helps me to manage my time. I can remember the early years in our business where I felt like the evenings and weekends were just the second shift of our business. Now, I have true off-hours where I can just focus on my personal interests."

— **Leila Johnson**

> *How do you achieve work-life balance?* (continued)
>
> *"Finding balance is especially hard when your business is such an extension of your creativity and expression in the world. It helped me to really begin treating Queen Bee as a proper business and to get some perspective about it. At the end of the day, what I do is not life or death—we make and sell bags. So, it can be helpful to keep that in mind!"*
>
> — **Rebecca Pearcy**

Define "Success" on Your Own Terms

Your personal goals and unique vision of success should guide you when choosing and developing a business idea. While some might define success as making millions of dollars and establishing an international empire, for you success might mean earning a comfortable income that allows you to save enough for your children's education and have a month or two of vacation time every year. Or you might define success not in financial terms but in terms of personal or creative freedom— simply being able to cover business and personal expenses may be enough, as long as you are able to define your own schedule (being home with the kids after school or taking yoga classes a few mornings a week), pursue your passion (be it creative work or a personal cause), or travel freely (or all of the above).

When your planning process includes a conscious consideration of your own definition of success, it's more likely that your business will help you meet those goals. For example, people often assume that a bigger business is better—but larger businesses generally require a heavier commitment to run and manage. While you may make more money with a larger operation (and even that isn't guaranteed), you'll also be putting in a lot more effort. If your vision of success doesn't include working more than 40 hours per week, a big business with employees might not be the best solution for you. There's nothing wrong with modest goals or planning a business that is truly small in order to maximize your personal freedom. Don't let business consultants, other entrepreneurs, or misleading stereotypes convince you otherwise.

Of course, your ideas about success may change over time—just as your business might. For instance, maybe a couple years down the line you'll find yourself wanting to devote more time to your business and grow it in size or income. Don't worry—you can always adapt your business strategies as your goals evolve.

Business success is ...

"It's gone from in the past looking at the percentage of revenue growth annually, to the present, appreciating that we have low to no turnover of staff and a good reputation as being a community-minded business."

— **Elissa Breitbard**

"At first, achieving amazing images and outdoing myself as a photographer was the only measure of success, but I quickly learned that the bottom line (finances) strongly dictate the measure for success. Without good finances there won't be any opportunities to produce images."

— **Sabrina Habib Williams**

"Success for me is having a business that provides enough money to take care of my basic needs and some of my wants, and allows me to have enough time for myself and with my family. I used to think it was all about having big-name clients, winning awards, and having lots of employees. I soon found that this definition did not match with my personal values and goals."

— **Leila Johnson**

"The way we've always defined success is to do meaningful work for great clients; to make a good living doing it; and to have a happy and healthy work environment. What's changed is that rather than just wanting that for ourselves, these days we're very inspired to help that vision of success materialize for our entire staff."

— **Lauren Bacon and Emira Mears**

"Before, I thought it was about offering a product that is unique. Now I think it's all about consistency."

— **Kyle Zimmerman**

Business success is ... (continued)

"When I was young, I used to think success was defined by fame and fortune. Over the years, I have realized that true success is being able to do what I love every day, and support my husband and child in a way that gives us a positive and happy life. To live gratefully. This is true success for me."

— **Nicola Freegard**

"Letting go of control is one of the hardest things to do when your business is your own creation. I always keep in mind something that my business counselor said: that it's great when you let go of control of some aspect of the business, and the person taking on that role does it better than you did! That is success."

— **Rebecca Pearcy**

Pick the Right Business Structure and Size

The type of business you start and its size can definitely affect how much work it will take for you to run it. If maximum freedom and flexibility are important to you, one good approach is to start a business that uses a freelancer or independent contractor model, in which you can do most of the work yourself with few or no employees or contract staff. (I often use the term "freelancer" and "independent contractor" interchangeably; there's no meaningful difference between the two.) Of course doing all the work on your own often means you'll be very busy, but the upside is that you'll often be able to do the work on your own time, according to your own schedule (subject, of course, to your clients' needs).

Freelancers often struggle with whether it makes sense to hire a few workers or assistants to help boost productivity and income. While doing so might help you be somewhat more productive, the burdens of managing these helpers often (though not always) outweighs any reduction in your workload. Some freelancers find a happy balance with one or two key assistants (usually contractors rather than employees), and find that hiring any more than that results in too many management commitments.

On the flip side, operating as a freelancer will limit your growth and ultimately prevent you from following the somewhat traditional arc of business development, in which an entrepreneur gradually shifts out of the day-to-day operations of the business. If you eventually want the business to run without you, you'll of course need to hire other people who, through training and experience, will manage the business independently. This is quite a different scenario from being a freelancer, so it's important that you clarify your long-term goals when developing your vision of your business.

Ask yourself, do you envision doing the hands-on work of the business for the long haul, or do you see yourself evolving to a more strategic position, overseeing the growth of your company that runs under your direction? For example, if you have graphic design skills, you could start a graphic design firm with a staff of ten, or you could take the route of working as a freelancer, taking on clients and projects only when they fit your schedule. Starting a firm will undoubtedly take more work (and start-up money) from the outset, but in a few short years you may get the payoff of having a well-oiled machine of a firm that allows you to take five months off. Starting as a freelancer is usually simpler but it doesn't offer a structure that allows you to take time off while the business continues to run.

Bear in mind that you can always start as a freelancer and expand down the road. A few years later when the kids are in school, for example, you could take the leap and launch a fully staffed firm—with the advantage of having some crucial experience under your belt, not to mention loyal clientele.

In short, working as a freelancer provides short-term flexibility and freedom, but will limit how much you'll be able to get away from the business in the long term. Starting a slightly larger firm with staff will tether you to the business more in the short term, but the long-term payoff (if you manage things well) is that you'll be able to reap the benefits of owning the business (as in, profits) with fewer day-to-day duties. The choice is up to you—and *now* is the time to think about your long-term vision.

Blurring Lines Between Freelancing and Running a Firm

A short generation or so ago, starting even a small business involved significant cost barriers. Today, it's a different story. Armed with relatively affordable computer and software systems, legions of enterprising souls have taken the leap into self-employment. Home-based businesses, Internet businesses, professional consultants, and freelancers of all stripes have never been so plentiful.

Along with this boom in small, micro-type businesses, the line between freelancer and firm has become blurred. Freelancers and independent contractors are now able to operate much more like small firms, thanks in large part to technological innovations, such as the ability to collaborate remotely via the Internet. You may become one of the growing number of freelancers to hire freelancers on a project-by-project basis in order to take on bigger, more complex, and more profitable projects without committing to overhead such as employees or physical office space. You might call this new model of business a freelancer-firm, reflecting the fact that you might essentially be a freelancer, but operate like a firm in that you hire other freelancers to get the jobs done.

But with the opportunities to reap greater profits afforded by this trend, there are challenges too. You may feel pressure to grow into an actual firm with permanent employees and office space. Is growth always the right way to go, or is it possible to aim for a longer-term existence in the space between being a high-performing freelancer or a small firm?

The answer depends on your goals and circumstances. If flexibility is a priority, it might make sense to pursue the delicate balancing act of the freelancer-firm model. But if you're open to a greater commitment, hiring employees will give you more control over projects, both in terms of costs and the services you can offer. If in doubt, start with the more flexible model and don't commit to lots of overhead. If and when you have the fortunate problem of having more work than you can handle with this approach, you can reevaluate whether you're ready for a bigger commitment and more of a true firm.

Develop Healthy Work Habits

Amidst the many, many details you need to take care of when starting and running a business, don't neglect to take care of yourself. Stress and burnout are real dangers for entrepreneurs, especially in the start-up days. Virtually everyone who has started a business has gone through a period of just constant work—and when not working, of thinking about (and often stressing over) work. This may be inevitable in limited stretches, but when it becomes chronic, it can have a serious negative impact on your health, life, and business.

One of the best ways to prevent the business from consuming your personal life is to be organized. Create a schedule and stick to it as best you can. Specify which days and times you'll work on specific aspects of the business—and, importantly, which days you'll take off. Don't flirt with burnout by becoming a work zombie. Take the time to recharge mentally and physically by taking well-deserved time off.

> EXAMPLE: Patrice, who is starting a one-woman advertising agency, drafts a schedule for herself. She plans to work from Tuesday to Saturday; she'll answer emails from 8 a.m. to 9 a.m., do billable client work from 9 a.m. to 3 p.m. (with an hour for lunch), do another hour of email between 3 p.m. and 4 p.m., and organize bills, contracts, and other paperwork at the end of the day, from 4 p.m. to 5 p.m. Patrice establishes Tuesday and Thursday afternoons for running errands when necessary (like getting office supplies or going to the post office); Sundays for catching up when necessary, and Mondays as her day off. Of course, in reality, she'll likely deviate from this schedule somewhat—for example, she may have to work some nights when under a tight deadline for a client's ad campaign. But having the schedule in place will help Patrice keep her life much more organized than having no schedule at all and winging it each day.

Besides implementing a schedule, try to establish consistent, methodical practices—in other words, systems—for the things your business does over and over again, such as client intake, doing the morning open and set-up for a retail store, bookkeeping entry, or doing inventory. As described in more detail in the next section, the more that you can create and use systems in your business, the more it will run consistently and efficiently. Systems are essential for businesses with more than a couple employees; without them chaos will reign, and it becomes very difficult to take time off since employees will need you around to manage things. But systems are also incredibly helpful for businesses as small as one person; they'll save you valuable time and mental energy—two resources no entrepreneur wants to waste.

Here are some more tips for maintaining balance in your life:

- **Live a healthy lifestyle, including eating well and exercising regularly.** This can be hard to do when you're chronically pressed for time—but don't succumb to the evils of fast food and inactivity. Personal wellness will pay off big time in terms of more physical energy and mental clarity, which in turn will benefit your business. And you'll likely be less prone to illness that can rob you of precious work days—getting sick can be a real nightmare for the self-employed. For all these reasons, a healthy lifestyle can truly and positively impact your business and your life.

- **Watch out for substance abuse issues that can creep up on the self-employed.** If you're prone to drinking too much, smoking a lot of marijuana, or even abusing harder drugs, self-employment can open the door to these problems gaining real traction in your life. Since self-employed people often have flexible hours and aren't subject to a boss's supervision, they can more easily slip into alcohol and drug abuse and addiction. If this is a concern for you, take it seriously and consider getting professional help even before you have a full-fledged problem. Proactive counseling (in other words, before you have a problem) can help you develop strategies to stay healthy and sober in your newly unstructured life of self-employment.

- **Create boundaries and rules to protect your private life.** For example, don't take work calls or check work-related email around the clock. While it's important to be responsive and professional, don't set up unrealistic expectations with your business contacts that you'll available 24/7 by phone and email.

- **Schedule dates with yourself.** If you're inclined not to take your personal time seriously, it's a great idea to put your leisure activities into your calendar just as if they were any other obligation or appointment. Doing this helps change your mindset and increase the chances you'll actually follow through. For example, if you've been dying to catch up on your pleasure reading, put "Reading" in your calendar for a specified day and time—and don't stand yourself up! It may seem strange to do this, but until you've developed a good habit of taking time for yourself, it's a very helpful trick.

Nurture Personal Relationships

It may go without saying, but when you start a business it's important to find time for your family and friends. Launching a start-up can be pretty brutal on family and social life, which can be especially hard to swallow if you were drawn to self-employment by the desire to spend more time with your family or friends. When you feel like you're up to your eyeballs in the business, you'll need to make a conscious effort to create space for quality time with your loved ones.

Similar to my advice above about scheduling dates with yourself, I recommend making specific plans with your friends and family and putting them in the calendar. This may sound obvious, but in the pitch and sway of running a business you may find yourself backing off from committing to social plans or family activities. The next time you find yourself wanting to say "Hey, let's get together soon," instead make a point to pick a date and make a plan. And treat your commitments seriously—including ones you make to your family. For some reason, maybe because we assume our families will be understanding, it seems that people are more cavalier about changing or cancelling family activities than plans with friends. Your family relationships will surely suffer if this becomes a habit. When you make a hiking date with friends, a brunch date with your spouse, or an afternoon at the zoo with your kids, commit to it just like your other business commitments.

If making time for personal relationships doesn't come naturally to you, following these tips will help you develop a habit of enjoying your time off and doing the things you love to do outside of work.

Mixing Business and Kids

While you might think it's impossible or just plain nuts to start a small business when you're pregnant or with small children in the house, it can be done—and without necessarily being Super Mom. And I'm talking about legitimate business ventures here, not the ubiquitous "work from home" schemes often targeted at women by sleazy scam artists. (Chapter 2 includes advice on identifying and avoiding these shady fake opportunities.)

If you have kids or are planning to have them, evaluate your priorities and choose a type and size of business accordingly. For many mom entrepreneurs, top priority is flexibility to spend time with the kids. If this is true for you, choose a business that has flexible hours, allows you to work from home, and can be scaled down easily if necessary. For example, a small freelance business is often a good option since you can work whenever and wherever you want, and you can downsize the business simply by choosing to take on fewer clients. (This is exactly how I handled having my first child: As soon as I got pregnant I started thinning my client list to the minimum that was financially feasible. I scaled back up starting when my daughter was about three months old.) Web-based businesses can also work because you won't necessarily need to be available during regular business hours. (But be sure that you have at least a minimum level of reliable phone and/or email customer support.)

But just because there are kids in your picture doesn't mean you need to start small. Perhaps your spouse is the primary caregiver, or you have a full-time nanny, and you want to make a real go of it with your business idea. It's definitely possible to launch a larger business even if you're pregnant or have young kids, particularly if you collaborate with co-owners or with high-level managers who can be trusted to get things up and running without you. This route requires a heavier commitment than the options described above, and usually more start-up money since multiple people will need either to be paid or to share profits. If you need to take time off to have a baby or care for your toddlers (if, for example, your spouse or nanny becomes sick), your collaborators will likely expect you to be back in action as soon as you can to be an active participant in guiding the business to success.

Most parents—moms and dads alike—hate being away from their little ones, so there's definitely a downside to taking this approach. But unlike a freelance business, a larger business may more or less run by itself in a couple years or so. The payoff of running a larger business is that in time, if the business succeeds, you can reap the rewards of the business without having to do very much hands-on work. You'll have to decide for yourself whether the possible rewards are worth sacrificing precious time with your little kids, especially considering there's no guarantee the venture will succeed.

Whatever type or size of business you choose, it's very likely that you'll need at least occasional child care help. See Chapter 3 for tips on finding affordable child care, Chapter 6 on handling child care when you work at home, and Chapter 11 on the tax implications of money you spend on child care.

Developing Business Systems

A common element among successful businesses is the implementation and use of systems. It's useful to view any business as a set of interrelated systems that together, make the business work. Understanding and embracing this early on is a major step in building a business that fits within your personal goals and doesn't stealthily overtake your life.

A system is essentially a well-defined process to get things done. The more that you can organize your business's essential tasks into systems, the smoother your business will run. Even microbusinesses benefit greatly from having some basic systems in place, like well-organized bookkeeping records and procedures for entering financial information. For larger businesses, especially those with employees, systems are essential. (Chapter 12 offers more detailed information on implementing systems within businesses that have staff.)

Balancing parenting with business management

"I've known for a very long time that I wanted to be a mom. So I've actively built and grown my business to enable me to step away and leave it in good hands so that I could focus on becoming a mom. I'm now able to be absent from the daily operations for a couple of months without having a detrimental impact to the function of the business."

— **Rebecca Pearcy**

"Becoming a parent, I don't have the time to dedicate 24/7 to my career anymore, and I admit I see men and childless women outpacing me and that doesn't make me happy. But that's a trade-off I'm so glad I made—I just have to remind myself of it from time to time."

— **Isabel Walcott Draves**

"When I had my child he would come to the office in a basket and I would breastfeed him while I was having phone meetings with people in New York, and he would be sleeping and I would try and make it work. That lasted about six months and then I finally decided he needed better care! So it's been a challenge. But my son really appreciates what I'm doing. I think it's a really great lesson for him to understand that you can run and choose your life on your own terms."

— **Nicola Freegard**

"We have a two-and-a-half-year-old and a nine-month-old. Little ones. We found a babysitter that we love. She's like family, and we drop the kids off at her house, and they eat her home cooking, and interact with her ten-year-old daughter. For us it was important to find somebody to take care of our kids that felt very much like a family member. Another important part was that she has the flexible hours that we have. Because sometimes we have to stay till 7:00 or 7:30, and sometimes we work on Saturdays. So the flexibility of having somebody to deal with the crazy schedule of a business owner— that was a huge deal for us."

— **Sabrina Habib Williams**

Though there are many different ways to break a business down into systems (business schools and consultants theorize on this topic incessantly), typical systems include:

- **Operations:** The specific activities and logistics involved in actually providing the product or service.
- **Supply chain management:** The system of managing relationships between a company and its vendors and suppliers, aiming to streamline the process of creating products for sale to end users.
- **Finances:** The system of tracking income and expenses, and generating reports to manage the company's finances.
- **Marketing:** The activities related to promoting the business, its brand, and its products and services among target customers.
- **Customer relationship management:** The systems involved in tracking and managing relationships with existing customers and prospects.
- **Human resources management:** The tasks related to finding qualified candidates, hiring, reviewing, and terminating staff, plus managing benefits if they are offered.

When you break down a business into systems, it's easier to see in a concrete way how certain skills contribute to the business. For example, bookkeeping or accounting skills obviously relate to financial systems, communication skills (say, graphic design or writing) would be part of marketing systems, negotiating skills would relate to supply chain systems as well as sales, and so on.

When in the early planning stages of your business, consider how it breaks down into systems and whether the participants in your vision (either partners, employees, or subcontractors) are equipped to handle them. If you are planning to start the business with a number of partners, ideally they will have well-dispersed and complementary skills to cover most of the critical areas. If you're planning to start on your own, you may well have to enlist the help of other key players, either as employees or subcontractors (or, you may find that you need to offer a partnership to someone who offers particularly critical skills).

In Chapter 12 we talk more about hiring staff, including the importance of defining tasks and drafting job descriptions. For now, just focus on a higher-level view of your business and assess whether your broad-strokes idea fits well with the skills you and any collaborators have to offer.

Achieving balance through business systems

"For me, systems are completely interconnected with the question of how running a business has changed since having children. For mom entrepreneurs, to keep a balance between work life and other life, the way is through systems. And hiring amazing people. And you also need to be someone who's willing to let go—which I'm blessed with being able to do. I'm not a workaholic. I worked really hard for three years, but I work part-time now. I'm really here half-time. And that means 20 hours or less. This is over a million-dollar company run successfully with me being here 20 hours or less, and that is because of the systems in place and the staff we've hired. I have one operations manager who has been with us nine years. And two or three other managers, and they know what they're doing. They know it's not just lip service—they know that I trust them to run the business."

— Elissa Breitbard

"When I mentor other younger freelancers I tell them that they absolutely, positively have to run their business like a business—they have to be professional, they have to have an invoicing program, they have to have a CPA, they have to have the administrative part in line, they have to have the latest software, I mean they absolutely have to run it like a business. And I can't say that I started out that way! It was all learned, and I still have problems keeping track of projects, but I do have really intact systems in place now."

— Emily Esterson

The Role of Business Owner

Small business owners are often heavily involved with several (or sometimes all) aspects of running the business, such as doing the bookkeeping, designing marketing materials, managing staff or contractors, or providing services to clients, to name just a few. While this can be entirely normal and acceptable—especially in the start-up days—it's vitally important to realize that none of these tasks are truly part of the role of business owner.

A distinction that is lost on many entrepreneurs is that the real job of the business owner is to guide the ship, so to speak; this includes defining strategy for the business, evaluating the market for opportunities and threats, assessing whether the business is meeting its goals, and generally acting as chief strategist and decision maker. In the real world, business owners often get swamped with "making the donuts"—in other words, with the hands-on work and operational tasks of the business—and they fail to fully embrace their role as business owner.

But for any business that wants to grow, finding time to put on the "business owner hat" is essential. Developing solid systems is an important way to do this. Putting procedures and policies in writing is one way to define a system—for example, having a bookkeeping manual or written procedures for hiring, reviewing, and terminating employees. Besides having written documentation of systems, training staff is also essential. The more that systems are established in writing and reinforced through training and review sessions, the more that you'll be able to let your staff run the show, allowing you breathing room to perform your role as business owner and help guide the business at a higher level.

Note that some business owners may not have a business model in mind that aims for growth in terms of employees or operations. For example, a certified arborist may go into business for herself with no plans ever to hire employees or assistants. Ditto for all sorts of freelancers or consultants; many of these types of microbusinesses operate perfectly well with the business owner doing all the work of the business. The important point to understand is that if you want your business to grow beyond just yourself, you'll need to be able to eventually pull yourself out of the trenches to some degree so that you can do the important strategic work of growing a business.

Targeting a Profitable Market With a Winning Idea

A major factor in whether a business will succeed boils down to a simple question: Is the business idea a good one? Execution matters too, of course, but the idea itself can make or break the venture. The tricky part in answering this question is that lots of entrepreneurs are in love with their ideas—even when it's not warranted. The graveyard of small business failures is full of ventures that from day one were questionable at best.

Don't make the mistake of letting your enthusiasm (or intuition) get in the way of examining your business concept thoroughly. Your passion counts for a lot in starting a successful business. And I'm not saying never to follow your intuition—by all means intuition can be a powerful instinct for an entrepreneur. But like every entrepreneur, you should back up your intuition with a solid, objective look at your business idea to figure out whether it's likely to be a success. For example, say you have the skills to run an employee wellness service for small business owners. You know that you would love doing this kind of work and that it would provide the flexible schedule you crave, and you believe that many businesses could benefit from your service. But all this aside, you need to analyze the market first before quitting your day job and running out and printing brochures for your new business.

Some of you may be at an earlier stage and still trying to decide what kind of business to start. While many people find success by staying within their zone of expertise, others have done very well starting companies in entirely new fields. Plenty of entrepreneurs who felt burned out in their careers have scrapped it all, shifted gears entirely, and pursued their passions to find success. The truth is that when it comes to what type of business you should start, there's no one-size-fits-all approach.

We'll start this chapter with a look at the pros and cons of starting a business in a field you know well, versus starting fresh in an area that's new to you. Then we'll turn to the question of how to evaluate your business idea to determine if it's ripe for success. As described in detail below, this involves learning about and analyzing the market, which includes potential customers, your competition, and the broader industry. I'll explain why it's usually a good strategy for businesses to target a specific market segment or "niche," and describe some simple, effective approaches for doing market research. We'll end with a section on a special niche that some women business owners may find it worth pursuing: marketing your services or products to government agencies.

Just Say No to Work-at-Home Scams

Fraudulent work-at-home schemes are as annoying as they are ubiquitous. You'll commonly see these solicitations as spam email, but you'll still find them in the old-school places, in classified ads (including online classifieds) and flyers. These aren't job offers; they are so-called "business opportunities" that typically require those who respond to send money for some sort of kit or equipment necessary to start the "business."

While I'm sure none of you savvy readers would fall for these shady schemes, allow me to offer a quick list of warning signs that a business opportunity may be less than legitimate.

- **If it's an offer in an unsolicited email (spam),** forget it and throw the email in the trash. It's a scam.
- **If it promises thousands of dollars a week or more, in a short amount of time,** it's almost certainly a fraud.
- **If you are asked to pay any money for any reason**—for an informational guide, equipment, or a "start-up kit"—it's probably not legit.
- **If the primary focus is recruiting new people and/or soliciting other people for money,** it's probably a scam, specifically a pyramid scheme. Note that there may be a fine line between an illegal pyramid scheme and a multilevel marketing business (technically legitimate but still often somewhat shady), which also focuses on recruiting new people. In a pyramid scheme, however, the emphasis is on recruiting people—not on actually selling a product.
- **If the work-at-home business involves assembling products, stuffing envelopes, or doing medical claims billing,** it's most likely a fraud.

If you come across a business opportunity that you're not sure about, you can always call the Better Business Bureau (www.bbb.org), the Federal Trade Commission (www.ftc.gov), or do research online such as at www.scam.com.

TIP
Even if you already know what type of business you want to start, keep reading. No business concept is ready to go out of the box—you'll always need to prod and test it, usually involving at least some research and refinement. This chapter will help you understand the process of developing your idea to increase its potential for success.

Choose the Right Business Idea

New entrepreneurs often get conflicting messages about how to choose a field. On one hand, there are endless books and articles with titles like, "10 Best Businesses to Start" or "101 Hottest Start-Up Ideas." But on the other hand, there's the "Do what you love and the money will follow" philosophy (actually, a book by the same title by Marsha Sinetar) that emphasizes passion as an essential element to business success.

These competing approaches may leave you confused—should you pick a business idea in a hot industry that you may know or care little about, or an idea in an industry you know well and involves products or services you are passionate about? Which approach is right?

The short answer is that most people will find it easier to start a business in a field they know well, either via experience, education or both. However, plenty of entrepreneurs have found success by switching fields entirely. Below I discuss both these approaches and describe a middle road that works for many entrepreneurs.

Starting a Business in Your Current Field

Starting a business in a field you know has definite advantages. It will help you run the business with less learning and ramp-up time, and perhaps even more importantly, it provides a crucial head start in figuring out a business plan. That's because you'll already know a lot of the basic information you'll need to determine whether the business will be profitable. (I'll talk in depth about drafting a business plan in Chapter 4.) Unlike those who've never worked in the field, you'll know at least a little something about who your target customers will be, how your business will operate, and how you'll market the business.

If you're considering opening a vintage clothing store, for example, and previously worked as a manager in a similar store, you'll be familiar with important issues, such as where to get the best inventory at the best prices, how much inventory to maintain, where to find the best purses from the 1930s and '40s, how much to mark up hats versus shoes, how many salespeople to have on the floor, and so on.

Starting a business in a familiar field is also a good idea if it's a field you truly enjoy and are good at. Passion is an excellent motivator and will definitely help you clear the inevitable bumps and hurdles—and plain old fatigue—along the way of becoming your own boss.

Different approaches to starting and choosing a business

"I grew up doing arts and crafts with my artist mom. We were always making something, and I loved all of it. I started making really fun and wacky clothing for myself in high school and then started creating fashions to sell later in high school and into college. So, I was entrepreneurial from a young age—I even made and sold Cabbage Patch Doll knockoffs at my elementary school bazaar! There wasn't really a moment when I realized that I could form a business from my interests—it was like I was doing it all along and it really evolved out of what I was already doing. Both of my parents are self-employed so I think that also had something to do with it. And I was always encouraged to do what I wanted to do."

— **Rebecca Pearcy**

"I had a little experience in the fashion industry. I have a sister who's a very experienced fashion designer, and she very kindly gave me a contact to talk to regarding factories and working with brokers. And with my own experience of shipping fabrics in from Nepal and India (during a previous business selling eco-bedding products, called EarthWorks), I felt very confident that I could work it out."

— **Nicola Freegard**

Different approaches to starting and choosing a business (continued)

"I was a teacher for ten years before starting this business. Back then (in 2000), you couldn't buy a book on how to start a spa. So, it was a really high learning curve for everything from the business side of it to the practical, 'How do I even order a massage table?' to 'How do I figure out how to interview my massage therapists?' The way I handled a lot of the newness of it was to meet at least once with other spa owners. And I started going to professional conferences in the spa industry two years before I started Betty's, so I started networking with other spa professionals, to really help me answer some of those nuts and bolts questions."

— **Elissa Breitbard**

"In my mid-twenties, I launched SmartGirl.org—the first website written 100% by teenage girls for the teen girl audience. After running SmartGirl for five years I transferred the company to the University of Michigan and took a series of full-time jobs. Nothing was as freeing and inspiring as SmartGirl, and I kept being disappointed by my roles. Between full-time jobs I would do consulting gigs to support myself. Eventually it just sort of became obvious that the consulting gigs were more fun, I was more successful at them, and I much preferred the independence consulting added to my schedule. It happened over about seven years, but I eventually figured out I should just be a consultant and stop looking for the perfect 'job'—because I had found it."

— **Isabel Walcott Draves**

Choosing a New Field

On the flip side, some enterprising types find success in a new field. Now may be your opportunity to do something completely different and start a business in an area that you have long dreamed about, or one that's newly "hot" and offers the possibility of healthy profits and growth.

The downside to this approach is an obvious one: Starting a business in a new field requires you to make up for your lack of experience and will involve a steeper learning curve. Practically speaking, it will take more work to develop your business plan and figure out whether the business can make a profit, and you may need to rely more heavily on others to help get your enterprise off the ground. For example, if you're new to the vintage clothes industry, you might not know the best sources of vintage clothing and accessories, optimal pricing strategies, or the best ways of marketing the business—all things a more experienced owner would know. And if you've never owned a clothing store (or even worked in retail) you're at a special disadvantage. If you're starting a new business, you will have to spend more time doing research (I'll discuss market research further below) and may need to rely more heavily on others to help get your enterprise off the ground.

Starting a business in a new field works best for people who aren't afraid of research, and who have a well-developed understanding of the common systems that exist in just about any business (operations, finances, customer service, marketing, and human resources management, for example). Because of the hurdles involved in learning about a new industry, this approach tends to be best for people with a business education or previous experience running a business.

 CAUTION

Don't let fantasy obscure the realities of how a business operates. For example, many people who love to cook dream of starting restaurants. But if you have never worked in the restaurant industry, or you have no experience with business strategy and planning (or even worse, you lack either type of experience), you may have no idea what it takes to run a profitable restaurant. Many novice restaurateurs are deeply disappointed to learn that running a restaurant mostly entails managing vendors and staff, detailed bookkeeping, and other management tasks. Whether you're starting a restaurant, a children's clothing store, or a tax preparation business, do your research to really understand what you're getting into.

While it's somewhat riskier to start a business in a new field, the hurdles are not insurmountable. Savvy entrepreneurs minimize the risks of going into a new field by recognizing their weaknesses and compensating for them in some way. If you dream of starting a business in an area that you're not familiar with, it's essential that you recognize any important gaps in your experience or knowledge and fill them—either by doing careful research yourself, or by bringing in experienced partners or high-level managers who know the field well.

Finding the Right Business Idea

In general, read widely to become familiar with trends and opportunities. Read national and local newspapers, business magazines (*Fast Company* is especially good for entrepreneurs), and the many, many blogs and websites offering small business news. Many of these are the online versions of traditional publications, such as the Small Business section of *The New York Times*' website (www.nytimes.com), or *Inc.* magazine's website (www.inc.com). Besides that general advice, here are some particularly useful resources and approaches for helping develop your business idea.

If you want help figuring out what business might suit you best:

Read a book. Two of the best are *Wishcraft: How to Get What You Really Want*, by Barbara Sher, or *The Pathfinder: How to Choose or Change Your Career for a Lifetime of Satisfaction and Success*, by Nicholas Lore.

Hire a life coach. Ask friends and colleagues for recommendations for coaches who have relevant experience, training, and certification, such as with the Coaches Training Institute (www.thecoaches.com). Since much of life coaching takes place on the phone and through email, be sure you can communicate well this way.

Attend a class or seminar. Local colleges, Ys, or other places often offer career development courses.

If you want to learn more about a particular field:

Check out books on the particular business type, be it a restaurant or green business. *Entrepreneur Press* has lots of business-specific titles (see www.entrepreneurpress.com).

Take a course or seminar. Many local colleges and universities have great continuing education programs, on topics such as interior design or human resources management.

If you want first-hand experience in a particular business:

Consider volunteering. The website www.volunteermatch.org is a great place to start if you don't have a specific business in mind.

Finding the Right Business Idea (continued)

Investigate apprenticeship opportunities. You can set this up on your own, or plug into one of the many programs—from health care to information technology—organized by the U.S. Department of Labor's Apprenticeship USA (www.dol.gov/apprentiship).

If you want to sell online at Etsy, Amazon, or eBay:

Go to the source. Check out the details on their websites, or read one of the several books that cover these types of online stores. (Chapter 9 covers e-business in detail.)

Finding the Best of Both Worlds

For most typical entrepreneurs (if there is such a thing), the best way to choose a business is to take a middle road: Start a business in a field you know, but tweak your business idea so that it capitalizes on profitable trends or emerging markets. This approach minimizes the research you need to do in order to adequately plan your business, and incorporates flexibility for you to refine your business idea to best meet the needs of a profitable customer base.

Finding a profitable market segment—often called a niche—is one of the best ways for small businesses to gain a foothold in a competitive economy dominated by megastores, national chains, and discount online businesses. A small specialty shop can often succeed by offering products that are more tailored for its select audience than the products available at bigger chain stores. I'll explain more about defining a profitable niche below.

Target a Profitable Market

Once you have an idea of what type of business you want to start, the essential next steps are (1) defining the market for this idea, and (2) determining whether or not that market will prove to be a profitable one.

No matter what field you choose for your new business and whether or not you have experience in it, you won't be likely to succeed if there's not a solid market for your idea.

Often, the term "market" is used as shorthand for your customer base. But understanding your market also means knowing who your competition is and what the trends are in your industry. When you have a clear vision and understanding of all three—customers, competition, and industry—you'll be well positioned not only to tailor your business to a profitable customer base, but also to reach that customer base with effective marketing strategies (We discuss cost-effective marketing in Chapter 8.) The following subsections look at each component of the market—customers, competition, and industry—in a bit more detail, and examine why carving out a niche, or narrow market segment, is a successful strategy for so many small businesses.

Identify Your Target Customers

When evaluating and refining your business idea, one of the first questions you need to ask yourself is whether there are enough potential customers to support the business you're envisioning. A big part of answering this question involves determining exactly who you expect your customers to be. Without having a clear vision of your desired customer base, you will seriously diminish your business's chances of success for a number of reasons:

- You may fail to realize there are not enough potential customers for your business (in other words, there is not enough demand for your products or services).
- You may miss opportunities to tailor your products or services, or to tweak your business idea to better meet the needs of a profitable customer base.
- You won't know how to reach your most promising prospects, which is another way of saying you won't know where and how to target your marketing efforts (online, through publicity, or word of mouth).

- You won't be able to craft your marketing messages appropriately —using the right tone, language, and attitude to appeal to your best prospects.

In a nutshell, defining your target customers means identifying specific characteristics of the people or businesses who you believe are most likely to actually buy your products or services. These characteristics are sometimes called a demographic profile.

Common characteristics used to classify customers include:

- age
- gender
- education
- income level
- buying habits (amounts spent, products/services purchased, online vs. in-store shopping, and the like)
- occupation or industry
- marital status
- sexual orientation
- family status (children or no children)
- geographic location
- ethnic group
- level of technology and Internet use
- political affiliations or leanings, and
- hobbies and interests.

Use these criteria to draw a profile of your most promising potential customers: those who have a real need or desire for your products or services. A women's clothing store specializing in professional wear, for example, may identify its target customers as 25-to-40-year-old women in the legal, financial, and real estate industries, living or working within a ten-mile radius of the store. A photography business with a focus on children and family might define its target customers as 25-to-40-year-old married women with kids living in the metro area. An online camping and outdoor gear store might target 18-to-30-year-old childless women and men in the New England, Rocky Mountain, and Pacific Northwest regions.

Targeting Businesses

Instead of selling your products or services to individuals, your business may cater to other businesses (sometimes called B2B, for "business to business"). This can be lucrative because businesses usually buy in larger quantities than individuals. For example, a specialty soap manufacturer might sell 50 bars of soap to individual customers via its website in a given month, but could sell 500 bars in just one sale to a hotel. An information technology (IT) consulting firm would likely want to be hired by companies with complex and ongoing technology needs, instead of individuals who may have minor, occasional problems for the IT consultants to solve.

Having businesses as your clients also may insulate you somewhat from economic downturns. Often businesses are more reluctant to scale back on key products and services than individual consumers. For example, if you run a landscaping company, a recession may force many of your residential clients to cut back on your services. For your business clients, on the other hand, maintaining a professional image will be a higher priority and letting their landscaping go unmaintained may just not be an option.

If your business is targeting other businesses, you should still define your target customer, using characteristics such as:

- **Industry.** A document storage business could target law firms, hospitals, or insurance companies, for example.
- **Size, by number of employees or annual sales.** A human resources consulting firm could target local businesses with 50 to 200 employees.
- **Geographic location.** A laundry service could target restaurants within its metropolitan area.

Deciding how narrowly to define your target customer is more of an art than a science, but in general it helps to err on the side of being more specific. (Businesses that focus on a particularly narrow customer base are called niche businesses; we discuss them below.) It's far more common for business owners to make the mistake of envisioning their customer base too broadly, making it difficult to make realistic assessments about the size and habits of that market. And, as we discuss further in Chapter 8, a well-defined target serves as a foundation for all your marketing activities. The more carefully you've defined your target market, the more likely your marketing efforts—even simple, low-cost methods—will bear fruit.

New entrepreneurs sometimes resist defining a target customer base, thinking that it will limit the business or reduce the number of potential customers. This is a misconception. Solidly establishing your business with a well-defined target audience certainly won't prevent you from taking customers who fall outside of your target profile. What it does accomplish is help your business stand out from the pack and develop a loyal clientele—an essential stepping-stone toward growth into new markets. Small businesses actually increase their chances of success by focusing on a specific market segment, marketing to that audience, and meeting their needs better than anyone else.

EXAMPLE: Lucia has made handcrafted furniture for years, and is ready to leave her day job and make furniture full time. As she plans out what types of furniture she'll make, she realizes that not everyone can afford her products, so she starts brainstorming what items she could add to her product line that anyone could afford. She gets on a roll, excited about all her great new ideas, and pretty soon she has a lengthy list of handcrafted wood items including candlesticks, napkin rings, picture frames, and jewelry boxes.

By the time Lucia starts thinking about making children's toys, her excitement gives way to feeling overwhelmed and lost. She calls up her friend Molly who owns a small natural fiber knitting shop, and asks for advice. Molly, who opened her shop ten years ago and has enjoyed moderate and steady profits consistently, tells Lucia she's trying to be too many things to too many people. "Pick a target audience," says Molly, "and focus on their needs. Don't worry about everybody else."

Lucia finds this advice to be a huge relief! She really wants to make the furniture that she's made for years—dining tables and chairs, primarily— and while it was exciting for a short time to think of a line of new products, that's not where her strengths lie. Based on Molly's advice, Lucia drafts a profile of her typical customer: 35-to-50-year-old married couples with annual income above $100,000 with a rustic design aesthetic. She bases her business plan on this profile and puts careful thought into how she can reach and satisfy this target market. Within a year, Lucia develops a reputation as an amazing designer and builder of dining sets, and makes decent sales. She knows that she will eventually need to expand her products since her existing customers won't buy new dining sets every year, but she realizes that keeping her efforts focused at the beginning helped provide her a foundation from which to grow.

Evaluate the Competition

Evaluating your market also includes learning about your competition: the other businesses that are trying to sell similar products or services to roughly the same customers you are planning to target. The more that another business targets your customer base, the more important it is for you to develop compelling reasons for customers to choose your business instead of theirs.

When evaluating your competition, start with the businesses that are your closest, most direct competitors—the ones that target the same customers that you would target. Remember, if your product or service isn't very specialized, you can expect lots of competition—for products like books, shoes, or a host of others, competition online is intense. Assuming you will focus on a specific target audience, you'll need to know whether other businesses are doing the same thing. If so, there may not be room for another business and you may want to find a different angle.

Keep in mind that a profitable market that has little or no competition will likely not stay that way for long—others will see the opportunity to make a profit. Sometimes, in fact, being the first business in a profitable market isn't an advantage. Other businesses can observe and learn from the experiences of a "pioneer" business and improve upon the business model, sometimes beating out the original pioneer. The moral here is that profitable markets will either already have competition or will develop competition in the future. To keep your competitive edge, you'll need to stay current on what customers want and what the competition is offering. In addition, you'll want to know about industry trends, which we'll discuss next.

Know the Industry

Learning about an industry is not the same as researching competition—rather, the industry is the broad world of businesses that operate in your field, some of which may be competitors. Learning about industry trends will help you define your business's competitive edge by incorporating hot new ideas. It also helps you avoid trouble by knowing what trends pose a threat to your business.

For example, if you're considering opening a restaurant in Salt Lake City, you should learn about trends in the restaurant industry, including what is happening in cutting-edge areas like New York and Los Angeles. The restaurants in New York and Los Angeles aren't competitors, but their practices and experiences help you learn valuable information about the restaurant industry. A trend such as text-message ordering for take-out might be happening in New York and getting positive reactions from diners, but not happening at all in the Salt Lake City area. By learning about the industry trend, you could be the first in your region to offer a text-message ordering system and reap valuable positive publicity.

Some trends can threaten entire industries, so being aware of them might be essential because you can adapt to accommodate them. For example, the low-carb trend of the last several years was a serious blow to bakeries and others serving or manufacturing carbohydrate products. Smart businesses adapted their business strategies to account for this. Many restaurants began making rice or pasta optional in certain dishes, or offering gluten-free buns for their burgers. Bakeries offered other products like expanded coffee and tea menus or deli items heavy on meat and cheese. Others responded with marketing messages designed to convince customers that not all carbs are bad. Whatever the strategy, the key was to recognize the trend in the first place and respond in time, rather than be blindsided by it.

Look for trends—and follow your instincts

"I think eco-conscious businesses have really become a part of the norm now, but when I started 15 years ago, I was kind of a laugh. I started with a hemp store, and I remember people coming in making jokes, and now it seems very mainstream. So we've really seen a huge curve towards 'eco' and consumer awareness."

— **Nicola Freegard**

TIP

General economic conditions are important, too. Economic forecasts for your city or region can give you an idea of whether upturns or downturns are on the horizon. The health of other key industries may also have a big effect on your business. For example, if you are planning to open a cafe near a major corporation that is facing huge layoffs, that would certainly impact your business.

Find a Niche

A niche business is one that focuses on a relatively narrow or specialized market within a certain field—for example, a maternity clothing boutique specializing in corporate/professional wear, a human resources consulting business specializing in the hospitality industry, a law firm that specializes in immigration cases, or an IT firm serving government clients (the topic of government contracts is discussed at the end of this chapter). In a crowded marketplace, a niche serves the critical function of distinguishing you from your competitors.

Focusing on a niche is an effective and profitable strategy for small businesses because it is often too difficult and costly to try to cater to very broad audiences. Instead of trying to appeal to everyone, a small business usually will do better to develop a specialty in an area that is not being fully served by other businesses, and exploit that niche with cost-effective marketing strategies. Think of a niche as a hook that will help you reel in the potential customers that you have identified as the most profitable and likely prospects for your business.

For retailers, pursuing a niche is often the best way (and sometimes the only way) to compete with the national chain behemoths who will always be able to undercut you on price and offer a wider selection. Instead, successful niche businesses offer customers a product or service that is not offered by the big guys.

There are two aspects of defining a niche: an operational aspect and a marketing aspect. Operationally, you'll have to decide to what degree your business will tailor its products or services for the target customer base. This is separate from the question of how you'll market your business to this target market. Targeting a niche usually involves both, to varying degrees—tailoring your products or services for a specific market segment, and actively reaching out to this segment with your marketing efforts—and it's up to you how you balance the two aspects.

For example, a vegan catering business is an example of a business that is heavy on the operational component of defining its niche: Its services (providing vegan meals) are completely dictated by its aim to appeal to the vegan market. Of course, it will also focus its marketing efforts on outreach to vegans. In contrast, consider a spa that mostly caters to local residents, but that recognizes an opportunity to boost business from the sizable number of tourists that come to its city. Though the spa's massage and other services might not be highly specialized for tourists, it could focus its marketing efforts on this niche by reaching out to the city's hotels, tour group companies, and travel agents. While its operations might not be wholly dictated by its goal of attracting tourists, it might make small operational tweaks, such as offering on-site massage services at local hotels or including maps of local tourist attractions in its lobby area.

The point to understand here is that marketing to a niche usually involves some combination of operational adjustments to appeal to a target audience, along with focusing your marketing outreach to this audience. When you do both well, you'll be on your way to carving out a niche for your business. Niches are by definition narrow, but not so narrow that they don't contain enough customers to sustain your business. The key to defining a profitable niche is to find an area where there is an unmet demand, and to fill that need with your products or services.

> ### *Distinguishing yourself from the competition*
>
> *"You need to know what you're selling. If a new photographer were to come to me and say 'I want to start a studio,' I'd say, 'What's different? What are you doing? You want to take good pictures? That's great—now what? How are you going to make sure that there's a reason to come to you?' For me, the reason I want people to come to me—and I tell them this all the time—is not because I'm so talented with my camera, but it's because I have access to my heart."*
>
> **—Kyle Zimmerman**

 TIP

A profitable niche may exist in bucking a trend. For example, if you're the only electronics shop in town that fixes or sells turntables, you may have a profitable niche with little competition, even though turntables and vinyl records are hardly a growing industry (though it is seeing a resurgence among audiophiles). Technology businesses are particularly vulnerable to trends and market changes, which could open a possible niche of serving the few customers who continue to use the obsolete technology. As with any niche, the trick is to make sure it's big enough.

Do Your Homework: Market Research

Before you launch any business—even before you write a business plan—you'll need to gather information and do research to demonstrate that your idea will be successful. All too often, many entrepreneurs get stalled at this point, not knowing how to go about the task of doing market research to test their assumptions about their customer base, competition, and industry. The term "market research" tends to scare business owners who think it means hiring pricey firms and conducting complicated demographic studies. In fact, market research can be much simpler and just as effective.

Most prospective entrepreneurs can do their own market research with a very limited budget. If you're planning a large business venture involving significant start-up capital, you might consider hiring a firm to do more extensive market research studies, but doing it yourself usually makes more sense for small to medium businesses.

As you research and learn about the market you may come to realize some flaws in your original idea—and you will likely see some ways to tweak and refine it. Of course, it's also possible that you may decide the market is poor or nonexistent, leading you to abandon your idea altogether. If so, your efforts have done their job by preventing you from pursuing a business idea with little or no likelihood of success.

> EXAMPLE: Stacey wants to start a cupcake shop, driven equally by her love of cupcakes and the surge in their popularity. There's only one bakery in her city that specializes in cupcakes, which is way across town from where Stacey wants to open her shop, leading Stacey to believe it's a good market with little competition for her. However, upon doing market research, she learns that the profit margin on cupcakes is awfully small (a business article in *The New York Times* stated the per-cupcake margin for several cupcake shops across the country). She also learns that the cupcake craze is dying down, based on surveys published in restaurant trade journals in which many respondents said they used to buy cupcakes during the heyday of the trend, but now make them at home for significantly less money. These and other research results lead Stacey to change her concept toward a more full-featured bakery with higher-margin items like custom cakes, with cupcakes featured less prominently in her product offerings.

As discussed further below, market research can include primary and secondary research. Primary research involves doing surveys and other inquiries with potential customers to find out how they feel about your product or service ideas and your competitors' offerings, and to answer a myriad of other questions about their shopping habits and preferences. Secondary research involves studying what others have learned about your market; typically this involves reading trade journals, other business publications, or reports generated from studies that others have commissioned. Another way to look at the distinction is this: With primary research, you collect information *from* your target customers. With secondary research, you collect information *about* them.

Small businesses often focus on secondary research because they find primary research intimidating. But as described below, small businesses can easily and inexpensively tackle primary research—and there's no substitute for the information you get directly from your target prospects.

Market Research Questions and Methods by Subject		
Subject	**Questions to Answer**	**Methods**
Customers	Who are your target customers?	Surveys and questionnaires
	What products/services do they need or want?	Focus groups
	Where/how do they buy products/services?	One-on-one interviews or inquiries of trusted contacts
	What do they typically pay for your type of products/services?	Magazine or trade journal articles
		Reports from previously conducted studies
		Online resources
Competition	What do they offer?	Direct sources (the competition's marketing materials and websites; site visits; and the like)
	What do they charge?	
	How do they provide the products/services?	Trade shows
	Who are their customers?	Networking
	What is their competitive edge?	Magazine or trade journal articles
	How do they market themselves?	
Industry	What are standard practices?	Magazine or trade journal articles
	What are the latest trends?	
	What does the future hold?	Trade shows
		Books

Clarify Your Research Objectives

The first step in doing market research is figuring out what questions you want answered: What specifically do you want to learn about your market? A very helpful way to go about this is to approach each aspect of your market—potential customers, competition, and industry—separately. For each of these, make a list of the questions you need answered to get your business started.

The table "Market Research Questions and Methods by Subject" offers a breakdown of the types of questions and research methods that would be appropriate for each group. It's not an exhaustive list, but is meant to illustrate how your inquiry will shift depending on what you're researching and what you're trying to answer. With a clear outline of what questions you want answered, you'll be in a good position to choose the best research methods.

The best approach is to conduct both primary and secondary research—getting information from actual prospects (primary) and reading what others have learned about your market (secondary). (But it's usually best to do this in reverse order: secondary research first, then primary research.) The answers you come up with will help you figure out whether your business makes sense or if you need to tweak it (a little or a lot) and maybe even consider doing something entirely different.

Do Secondary Research

Despite the name, it's often best to do secondary research before primary research. For one, secondary research is generally simpler to do. And secondary research will often get you on the right track by answering fundamental questions and raising other, more specific questions that you can then examine further using primary research tools.

Doing secondary research is generally as easy as reading trade journals, business publications, newspapers, blogs, and any other media outlets that may offer relevant information about your market. Blogs can be particularly valuable sources of information, especially if they allow comments which will provide a window into the perspectives of the general public, not just the blogger. Most industries have at least one trade publication (many have several); identify the ones most relevant for you and read them as often as you can. Note that trade magazines do tend to be expensive, so read them at your local library if it's not in your budget. (Reference librarians can be amazingly helpful in tracking down information and steering you to obscure-yet-helpful reference materials.) Also, particularly if your business will mostly have local customers, read your local newspapers and other media to keep an eye on your local economy.

> **TIP**
> **Read beyond the business pages.** Valuable business-related information is often found in other sections of your local newspaper. For instance, if you run a garden supply company, the home and garden section will have lots of information on trends and may feature other companies in your market. And an owner of a clothing store might find out about interesting fashion trends in the arts and culture section.

> **TIP**
> **Check with your city resources.** Chambers of commerce and city planning departments can be great sources of information for anyone considering starting a local retail shop or restaurant. They can tell you the history of similar places in the neighborhoods you're interested in and provide advice on what has seemed to work and what hasn't.

Do Primary Research

Though primary research may not be quite as easy as reading a trade magazine, it's very doable and will generally yield much more valuable information because it comes directly from the individuals you hope will be your customers. How you'll get the information you need will depend on your type of business and the product or service you're offering, but in general you have three options: surveys and questionnaires, interviews, or focus groups. None are inherently difficult to do and, when used creatively, can yield immensely valuable information about your market.

Using Surveys and Questionnaires

Distributing surveys or questionnaires to individuals who fit within your target customer profile is a great way to compile a lot of valuable information with a relatively small investment of time or money. The trick is to make sure you ask the right people the right questions that will yield valuable and useful information.

Start by identifying exactly what you want to learn; you can call these your research questions. Based on these research questions, you'll draft the actual survey questions themselves. Keep in mind that your research questions are not exactly the same as the survey questions: The survey questions are the ones that you'll pose to the survey recipients. You'll want them to be very specific, and crafted so they yield results that will help you answer your more general research questions.

> **EXAMPLE:** Roxy plans to open a hair salon in San Francisco. Of the many details she's exploring, one is what neighborhood to choose. She's inclined to open the salon in Noe Valley because she thinks this neighborhood will appeal to her target customer base: 25-to-40-year-old working women with young children. However she's concerned that the limited parking in that neighborhood might deter customers. She does some initial market research by visiting salons similar to the one she wants to start (her potential competition), visiting their websites, and searching the online archives of local business media for any relevant info she can find. To get information directly from prospective customers, Roxy creates a survey she'll distribute via email to her contacts who fit her target customer profile. To address the location question, Roxy's research question is: "Is Noe Valley a good location for a hair salon?" To help her answer this fairly general and subjective question, Roxy drafts specific questions for the survey, such as:
> - "What hair salon(s) do you currently use, and how often? Where are they located?"
> - "What do you like and not like about the hair salon(s) you currently use?"
> - "What are the ideal times of day for you to schedule a hair appointment?"
> - "Do you consider parking in Noe Valley to be a problem?"
> - "What hair salon services are currently lacking in Noe Valley?"
> - "What would be the ideal neighborhood for you to get hair salon services?"

The survey responses indicate that there is a great desire for a hair salon in Noe Valley, and only mild concern about parking. The primary complaint about the existing hair salons is that their hours don't accommodate the schedules of busy working moms. The survey results solidify Roxy's decision to open her salon in Noe Valley, and help her tailor the services (particularly with expanded hours) to her target audience.

You can send surveys in hard copy via mail, in plain text format via email, or—even better—by using a Web-based service, many of which are free. At sites such as SurveyMonkey (www.surveymonkey.com), you can create professional-looking online surveys, invite your prospects by email, and tabulate the results in useful ways, all for free. Even more features are available if you upgrade to a paying account. (We discuss developing your distribution list below in "Getting Your Research Started: A Basic Approach.")

Learning and adapting are key in defining a niche

"When we started the business in 2000, it was the only women-owned Web design firm in town, as far as we knew. (There were some female freelancers, but no all-women operations.) So we figured we'd be a shoo-in when it came to the women entrepreneurs market. However, we quickly learned that our prospective clients were far more interested in our expertise with nonprofits than they were in the fact we wore skirts. So we refocused our energy on the nonprofit, government, and progressive business sectors (all of which we had extensive experience working with) and never looked back. In the end, the best market research we did was to jump in and find out what our clients were looking for, face to face."

—Lauren Bacon and Emira Mears

Interviewing Prospects One-on-One

There are a few different ways to approach individuals and ask them for information. Here are some ideas.

Set up interviews with people whom you trust and who may have relevant opinions. For example, if you want to start a child care referral service, you could meet with people you know who have young children and ask them about their experiences, or talk with pediatricians or HR managers at large corporations. Or if you're considering starting a software company that will focus on data management for construction companies, set up lunch meetings with people you know in the construction business and pick their brains about their data management challenges.

"Cold call" any prime prospects with whom you don't have any connection. You'll generally get a lower response rate from cold calls, but if you approach prospects professionally and persuasively, it can be effective.

Interview people at locations where you are likely to encounter your target profile. A good example is going to a trade show related to your industry, standing in a high-traffic area, and asking people if they could answer a few short questions. The key here is to have just a few short questions that passersby can answer quickly and concisely ("yes" or "no" or a numerical answer, for example) that you can easily record on a clipboard or laptop computer. To encourage participation, provide a bottle of water or packaged mints (always appreciated at trade shows). Other locations might include special events that appeal to your target audience, such as a film festival, concert, or sporting event. You can even just stand on a street in the neighborhood where you want to start a business and ask passersby.

Working With Focus Groups

A focus group is simply an event at which you provide a presentation or demonstration to potential customers and solicit their feedback (typically using a survey or questionnaire you prepared in advance). Feedback may also be obtained though oral question-and-answer sessions and discussions among the group that are recorded by someone taking careful notes. Examples of focus groups might include:

- a food manufacturer holding taste tests of a new salsa, asking participants to rate flavor and texture and to compare the new salsa to the competitors' versions
- a software company having users test their new time-management application, asking them to rate it on ease of use and timing them on how long it takes to complete certain tasks with the software, or

- a nail salon demonstrating its signature pedicure on focus group participants, asking them for feedback on their experience during the pedicure and on the results.

While there's nothing inherently complex or expensive about conducting a focus group, it will require at least a nominal commitment of your time. You'll need to develop the agenda for the event, invite appropriate participants, and handle all the logistics of actually executing the event, including preparing the surveys for the participants. If you don't have access to retail or other space and need to have a gathering larger than your living room can accommodate, you may need to rent an appropriate venue. If you have a budget for it, you can hire a focus group consultant to handle many or all of these tasks for you; of course, going this route can get quite expensive.

Because of the preparation and possible expense involved, be sure to start the invitation process early enough to ensure that you get enough confirmed participants to justify the time and expense of doing the focus group. Use your networking skills (discussed further in Chapter 1) to get the word out to the right people. And offer something to draw people there—free food is one of the surest ways to boost attendance— or something related to your business, such as a coupon to the store you plan to open.

Getting Your Research Started: A Basic Approach

Now that you have an overview of primary research tools, here's a simple approach to help get you started:

1. **Identify your research questions.** In other words, specify exactly what you want to learn. For example, an online retailer start-up might be particularly interested in what features to include on its site or whether potential customers are satisfied with the usability of competitors' products. A furniture manufacturing business may want to know the price sensitivity of its target market of college students.

2. **Decide the best way to get those questions answered.** As described above, the basic methods include surveys, interviews, and focus groups (usually in conjunction with a survey or questionnaire).

The methods you choose will largely depend on the types of questions you want answered and the nature of your product or service. For example, if your main concern is whether your product is tasty, or easy to use, then you'll need to have some sort of focus group to allow participants to actually try out your product. On the other hand, if your questions have to do more with price sensitivity or your prospects' current buying habits, an emailed survey would likely suffice.

3. **If you'll be using a survey or questionnaire, draft the questions.** Your goal is to craft questions that will yield responses that will help you answer your research questions.

4. **Identify and invite your study's participants.** An easy approach is to start with your address book of contacts and associates, and include people who fit your target customer profile. You can build and expand this list by asking trusted contacts to suggest others who would be appropriate. Perhaps you know another business with a similar audience that's not a competitor. You may be surprised at how extensive a list you can develop with simple networking. If you'll be targeting other businesses, scan other directories for their contact information. Alternatively, if you have a budget for it, you can hire a mailing list firm and pay a fee for a list.

5. **After conducting the study, compile the results.** Remember, doing market research is all about obtaining data, so don't neglect the essential task of assembling and analyzing your results. Once this is done, you'll be poised to make business decisions based on the information you've learned.

Research Your Competition

Beyond reading trade journals and other secondary research sources to scope out your competition, you'll also want to dig a little deeper to learn as much as you can about key aspects of their operations. An easy way to start is to visit their websites and visit them in person (if they have storefronts open to the public) to find out basics such as details on what products or services they offer, what they charge, how many staff they have, and their hours of operation, for example. When visiting in person, note what you like and don't like about their operation. Similarly, evaluate what seems to work or not work for the business.

Resources on Market Research

Assuming you don't plan to hire a pricey market research firm, but want some help figuring out how to do your own market research, here are some ideas.

Read a book. There are dozens of market research books available, some very broad, others focused on one particular aspect, such as survey design. A good entry-level guide is *The Market Research Toolbox: A Concise Guide for Beginners*, by Edward F. McQuarrie (SAGE Publications, Inc.). Another quality book is *Strategic Market Research: A Guide to Conducting Research that Drives Businesses*, by Anne Beall (IUniverse). Your public librarian should also have some good ideas.

Get an intern's help. If there's a business school nearby, see if they have any intern programs in which their students may work for school credit, so they can help with your market research project for free.

Take a market research course. Check out course listings at a local community college or continuing education program.

Contact a Women's Business Center for market research help. They may offer free or reduced-rate services, such as consulting or classes. For the closest Center, check the list published by the Association of Women's Business Centers at www.awbc.org.

Check out SCORE (www.score.org), a program of the U.S. Small Business Administration. SCORE personal business coaches provide all kinds of help, including online and onsite mentoring and business advice; workshops for business start-ups on topics such as marketing your business; and volunteer mentors who can help with a wide range of expertise, including market research and business plan development.

Don't forget the U.S. Small Business Administration (www.sba.gov). Its nationwide network of Small Business Development Centers (SBDCs) have lots of resources, including free online training as well as one-on-one help.

When available, obtain copies of any brochures or other marketing materials your competition has created, and use them to figure out their marketing strategies. The same goes for any ads you see in print media, on TV or radio, or elsewhere such as billboards or buses. Use all of these to determine, as best you can, what customers are being targeted by your competition and what competitive edge they are trying to leverage.

The more you know about how your competitors are trying to position themselves, the better you can position your business accordingly. Sometimes, this might mean going head-to-head with another business—for example, if a competing florist is trying to get hired by all the restaurants to do arrangements and you had already started pursuing this niche, you may want to compete aggressively and try to come out on top. Or, you might decide you don't really care about the restaurant niche and switch your efforts to hotels.

TIP

Stay ethical when researching your competition. It's not uncommon for new businesses to spy on their potential competition in a variety of ways—and sometimes it goes too far. Going into a rival business to check out their stock and their prices is one thing; posing as a supplier to obtain sensitive price information from the rival's manager is venturing into sleazy (and possibly illegal) territory. In general, it's fine to browse the offerings of a competitor as if you were a customer. Asking some basic questions of the staff might be okay, but not if you start wasting too much of their valuable time. A good way to gauge how far is too far is to think about how you would feel if a competitor did it to you.

Also consider that once in business, you may have to interact with the competitor—and in many cases, collegial relationships between competitors can be mutually beneficial. It's not at all uncommon for a business to refer a customer to a competitor if, for whatever reason, the business can't accommodate their needs at that time. (I myself do this all the time with Web development and graphic design clients.)

Working with competition can advance mutual interests

"I started going to professional conferences in the spa industry two years before I started Betty's, so I started networking with other spa professionals to really help me answer some of my nuts-and-bolts questions. Our view of competition is different than a lot of business owners. I believe that to work together will better the entire industry. Plus I learn so much from others. So that's my view of so-called 'competition.' We had everything to learn, and I'm also at the extreme of, 'Share, tell all, be really open about how I run the business.' And that's only served me well."

— **Elissa Breitbard**

Government Contracting Opportunities for Women

So far, this chapter has assumed that your customers will be individuals or other businesses. Another possibility is to market your services to the government, from federal departments down to local agencies. Getting government contracts can be extremely profitable; one major contract could represent a year's worth of income or more. But government contracting—particularly at the federal level—is not for the squeamish. The process of registering with the government as a vendor, obtaining certifications that may apply to you, and finding opportunities can be major work.

I'm including this section last because the government market is quite radically different from private markets. The hurdles involved in getting government contracts are high—not insurmountable, but high enough that the government market may simply not be a good fit for your business. Pursuing government contracts (also called government procurement) really only makes sense if selling to the government is part of your business plan, and you're willing to commit to the considerable work involved.

The commitment required for government contracting

"For new entrepreneurs, it takes an investment of time and money if you are serious about getting government contracts. To compete with others in your industry, you need to make the government a key part of your marketing efforts: researching their needs, meeting the buyers, attending and even having a booth at events. Keep in mind that you are not only competing with other companies in your state, but with any other vendor in the country that receives notice of current opportunities. I would recommend starting by bidding on low-dollar, smaller requests for services or products for your local city, county, state, or federal government agencies first so that you can get your feet wet."

— **Leila Johnson**

Along these lines, let me dispel a myth right up front: There's no magic shortcut to getting government contracts just by being a women-owned business, even if you are certified as such. The processes and benefits of becoming certified as a women-owned business are complicated, often less beneficial than you might think, and offer no guarantee of actually getting a government contract. If you harbor any notion that contracts will come flowing in because you have a women-owned business, you'll be in for a rude awakening. With government contracting, there's definitely no free lunch.

This section describes the realities involved in the government market—particularly for women-owned businesses—so you can decide whether it's one you might want to target in the first place. In case it is, I'll include some of the key steps in the process of seeking government contracts such as registration tasks and certifications you may obtain, including being certified as a women-owned business. By the end of this section you should have a good sense of whether or not government contracting seems like something you want to pursue, and if so, how to get started.

Government Contracts in a Nutshell

There's a simple reason why many businesses are so interested in getting government contracts: Governments spend an awful lot of money. The federal government alone spends more than $500 billion each year on just about every product and service imaginable, from paper clips to aircraft engines, cleaning services to nanotechnology consultants. State and local governments spend billions more. If your business can get a contract with one or more agencies to buy your products or services, you can reap major profits.

Here are the downsides:

- **Governments tend to have complex and burdensome rules governing how they must go about making purchases, particularly for purchasing services (as opposed to products).** You'll generally need to go through a somewhat complicated registration process just to be able to bid for a government contract (in other words, to become a government vendor), plus the processes to obtain any certifications you're entitled to which may improve your chances of winning a contract.

- **Besides these procedural requirements, most government agencies— especially at the federal level—give contracts only to businesses that meet high performance standards.** You probably won't get a contract unless you've been in business with positive cash flow for at least two years. And your business will need to be "contract ready"—government contracting lingo that basically means your administrative and financial management systems (accounting in particular) are sophisticated enough to satisfy government requirements.

- **Finally, most government agencies, especially at the federal level, have "past performance" requirements, and will only hire firms that have a track record of working for the government.** Subcontracting to another business that acts as the prime contractor for a government contract will establish this track record, even though you're not directly working for the government as the prime contractor. (As described further below, subcontracting is a highly recommended strategy for breaking into government contracting.)

Considering how much work is involved in pursuing contracts—not to mention the significant rewards possible—maximizing your chances of success is the name of the game. This is where preference programs and certifications come in.

Federal Preferences, SBA Programs, and Certifications

One of the reasons you may be interested in government contracting is that you've heard that women-owned businesses can get preferential treatment in contract awards. Here's some background.

Through various pieces of federal legislation, the U.S. Congress has established goals and preferences to support certain types of businesses in federal contracting. To support and achieve these goals, the Small Business Administration has created a number of procurement assistance programs such as the Women-Owned Small Business (WOSB) Federal Contract Program, and the 8(a) and HUBZone programs (more on these below). Each program has different eligibility requirements and varying levels of benefits.

Some programs have formal processes to become certified; others allow businesses to "self-certify." Generally speaking, the programs with formal certification processes offer more benefits than those with self-certification. The certification process can be fairly intense (and remember, this is in addition to the process of registering as a government vendor), but it can really pay off by boosting your chances of getting a federal contract. In particular, if you can get certified for a program that offers set-asides, sole-source contracts, restricted competition, and/or price preferences, you'll have a real leg up in getting a federal contract. Here's what those terms mean:

- A **set-aside** means that the government reserves certain contracts just for that category. For example, the federal government may set aside a contract for construction services for WOSBs, which means that only certified WOSBs will be allowed to bid on the contract.
- A **sole-source contract** is a contract that is awarded to the only business that bid on the contract. Sole-sourcing is generally disfavored in federal contracting, but is allowed in some programs like the 8(a) Program.

- **Restricted competition** means the purchasing agency allows only certain firms to bid on a contract. Sometimes agencies choose to use restricted competition to achieve goals of contracting to certain groups; other times the restricted competition may be because the contract was part of a set-aside.
- A **price preference** means that a bid by an eligible business may be considered to be lower than others even if it is a certain amount higher. For example, a bid by a WOSB business may be considered to be lower than non-WOSB businesses as long as it is no more than 10% higher than the rest.

SBA programs vary in how they use these preference mechanisms, and the way they may be used within a program is often subject to complex rules. Further complicating things, changes in federal legislation and SBA program rules are common, and even the programs themselves may be suspended or new ones may be introduced. For these reasons, you'll need to check with the SBA or with the resources we offer at the end of this section to find out the latest programs and rules that may offer opportunities for your business.

With that in mind, let's look at how women-owned businesses fit into the picture and how to take advantage of the opportunities out there.

TIP

Contracting with state and local governments can also be quite profitable, but you'll need to learn the ins and outs of each government's contracting programs. They'll generally be similar to the federal programs, but preference categories and criteria may differ. Note that some states and local governments may have specific preference programs for women-owned businesses, unlike the federal government. Check with your state and local government websites for details; look for a "Doing Business With" link, or "Office of Small Business" or something similar.

The Women-Owned Small Business Federal Contract Program

Prior to 2011, the federal government had established a goal that 5% of federal contracting dollars would be awarded to women-owned small businesses (WOSBs)—but the goal was purely that: a goal, with no set-asides or mandatory incentives. (Note that the federal government uses the term "women-owned small business" while others may use "women-owned business" or WOB.) Since Congress established the 5% goal in 1994 it has never been achieved; according to the National Women's Business Council only 4.32% of federal contracting dollars went to WOSBs in fiscal year 2013 (see www.nwbc.gov).

A welcome change came in 2011, when the SBA authorized the Women-Owned Small Business Federal Contract Program. This program for the first time allowed contracting officers to set aside specific contracts for certified WOSBs and economically disadvantaged women-owned small businesses (EDWOSBs). Even better, changes to the program that became effective October 14, 2015 now allow contracting officers to award sole-source contracts to WOSBs and EDWOSBs. There are some significant limitations, the biggest being that only some industries are eligible for these sole-source contracts. Nonetheless, these new programs and rules offer great promise for federal agencies to finally meet the 5% WOSB contracting goal.

To be eligible, a firm must:

- be at least 51% owned and controlled by one or more women, and
- be primarily managed by one or more women.

In addition, the women must be U.S. citizens, and the firm must be "small" according to SBA's size standards for its industry. In order for a WOSB to be deemed "economically disadvantaged," its owners must meet specific financial criteria as set out in the program's rules.

Firms that wish to be considered as WOSBs must either self-certify (basically, fill out and upload an SBA form) or be certified as a WOSB by an approved third-party certifier; these include: El Paso Hispano Chamber of Commerce, National Women Business Owners

Corporation, U.S. Women's Chamber of Commerce, and Women's Business Enterprise National Council.

For more details on the WOSB program, see www.sba.gov/wosb.

Tips for WOSB Contracting Success

Selling your business to federal agencies on the basis of its status as a women-owned business takes some homework. You'll want to target agencies that are falling short of the 5% goal. To find out how specific agencies have done toward this goal in previous years, download the Federal Procurement Report from the Federal Procurement Data System's website at www.fpds.gov.

Once you know what agencies you'll target, you'll want to contact the right person in that agency. Most federal agencies have designated a person to be a point of contact for WOSBs. You can simply call the office and ask who that contact person is. Or, a good resource for finding the offices within federal agencies that deal with small businesses and procurement is the Federal Office of Small and Disadvantaged Business Utilization Directors Interagency Council (OSDBU Council). Its website is www.osdbu.gov; find the list of offices by searching the site for "offices." If you're interested in a specific agency, you can Google the name of the agency along with the term "small business services."

When pitching a federal agency on your self-certified WOSB, it's definitely okay to address their record of awarding contracts to WOSBs and that hiring your firm will help them meet the 5% goal. Don't be accusatory, but use a helpful tone. Emphasize the specific reasons why you're the best firm for the job, and that your status as a WOSB is a bonus. Ask if they'd consider restricted competition (which by law they have the discretion to use) in order to help them improve their procurement record with WOSBs.

The SBA 8(a) Program

The 8(a) Business Development Program is not specifically aimed at women-owned businesses, but aims to help socially and economically disadvantaged firms gain access to the federal procurement market. A common source of confusion is that a women-owned business can obtain federal contracting preferences through the 8(a) program. This is totally separate from being certified as a WOSB as described above. It's also separate from any set-aside programs for WOSBs. Here's the lowdown.

To be certified for the 8(a) program, a business must be owned and controlled by a socially and economically disadvantaged individual. African Americans, Hispanic Americans, Asian Pacific Americans, Native Americans, and Subcontinent Asian Americans are presumed to be socially and economically disadvantaged. Other individuals can qualify for 8(a) certification if they show through a "preponderance of the evidence" that they are disadvantaged because of gender, race, or other status. In other words, to qualify as an 8(a) disadvantaged small business on the basis of gender, you have to show by a preponderance of the evidence that discrimination, based on your gender, has hindered your ability to grow a business. There are other requirements to qualify as an 8(a) business including having a net worth of less than $250,000, excluding the value of the business and personal residence.

Obtaining 8(a) certification is particularly desirable since program participants are eligible for sole-source contracts, set-asides, limited competition, and other benefits.

HUBZone and Other SBA Programs

Finally, keep in mind that you may qualify for other, non-gender-related federal preferences. For all the programs listed below, get more detailed information from the SBA; see www.sba.gov.

- **Self-certifying as a small business.** The federal government has a goal of awarding 23% of all federal contracts to small businesses. To qualify as a small business you must meet the SBA's size requirements for your industry. You self-certify when registering as a government vendor.
- **The HUBZone ("Historically Underutilized Business Zone") Program** helps small businesses in urban and rural communities gain

preferential access to federal procurement opportunities. If you have a principal office in a HUBZone, or employ staff who live in a HUBZone, you may be able to obtain HUBZone certification.

- **Self-certifying as a service-disabled veteran.** Businesses owned by veterans who incurred or aggravated disabilities in the line of duty are eligible for sole-source contracts and set-asides.

Steps to Obtain Government Contracts

Registering as a federal vendor is a somewhat involved process. As we mentioned at the beginning of this section, make sure that government contracting is a reasonable part of your business plan before wading into these waters. Government contracting can be really lucrative for businesses that are prepared and committed to this market; if you're not ready, it will only waste a lot of your valuable time.

Here's a general outline of the steps involved in getting started.

1. **Find out your NAICS code(s).** The NAICS (for North American Industry Classification System) code is a five-digit code identifying your type of business. It's not uncommon to have multiple codes for the different business activities; some businesses might have 20 or more codes. You'll need to know your NAICS code(s) before you can register as a federal vendor. You'll find a list of NAICS codes at www.census.gov, or Google "naics codes" to find your code(s).

2. **Get a DUNS number.** Again, you'll need this before you can register as a federal vendor. A DUNS number is a unique nine-digit identification number assigned to each physical location of a business. These numbers are issued for free by Dun & Bradstreet; go to www.dnb.com to get yours.

3. **Register at the U.S. Federal Contractor Registration database (www.uscontractorregistration.com).** This is the database of federal vendors, now called System for Award Management or SAM. If you're not in the SAM database, you basically don't exist to the federal government.

4. **Apply for any certifications for which you are eligible.** You'll indicate self-certifications when entering your business into the SAM. Other certifications such as WOSB 8(a) certification are completed at the SBA or other organizations.

5. **Look for contracting opportunities.** This sounds obvious but it can be one of the hardest parts of government contracting. There are many different resources you can use here. A primary one is to sign up for FedBizOpps (www.fbo.gov), which will notify you of contract solicitations and requests for proposals. Also, as described above, research individual agencies and their record of hiring WOSBs. This may be a consideration in which agencies you want to target.

6. **Look for subcontracting and partnering opportunities.** Government agencies generally require past government contracting work before they'll hire you. The best way to get this experience is through subcontracting, working for the businesses that have the government contracts (called the "prime contractor"). Research which firms have government contracts and market your business to them. Note that prime contractors often use contracting preferences like the federal government does, so you can market your business to a prime contractor who is falling short of its 5% goal of contracting with WOSBs.

Resources for Government Contracts

As you can probably tell, government contracting can be pretty complicated. If you're considering dipping a toe into these waters, you'll definitely need more detailed information than is provided here. There are lots of resources online which are worth checking out; even better, get assistance from a Small Business Development Center or other program in your area. Here are the best resources out there.

- The **Small Business Administration (SBA)** administers federal preferences programs. For information straight from the horse's mouth, go to the SBA website at www.sba.gov.

- **Procurement Technical Assistance Centers (PTACs)** exist nationwide to help businesses understand and prepare for government contracting and navigate the processes of becoming a vendor. For more information, search PTAC on www.sba.gov.
- The SBA's **Office of Women's Business Ownership (OWBO)** exists to establish and oversee a network of Women's Business Centers (WBCs) throughout the United States and its territories. The SBA's website changes often, so the best way to find this site is to go to the main SBA site at www.sba.gov, then search the site for OWBO.
- Your local **Small Business Development Center** may offer consulting and assistance with questions about government contracting. Some PTACs are located within SBDCs. For more information, search SBDC on www.sba.gov.
- **FedBizOpps.gov** is an online database and notification service of opportunities with the federal government.
- Local **Women's Business Centers, microlenders, and other nonprofits** may offer consulting, classes, or other procurement assistance services.
- **WomanOwned.com** is an online resource with a wide range of information for women business owners, including lots of in-depth information about government contracting. See www.womanowned.com.
- The **Women's Business Enterprise National Council (WBENC)** offers WBE certification for women-owned businesses. WBENC certification is accepted by many state and local government agencies, as well as hundreds of U.S. corporations. See www.wbenc.org.
- The **National Women's Business Owners Corporation (NWBOC)** is a private organization that offers a national certification program for women-owned and controlled businesses. See www.nwboc.org.

Making the Financial Transition to Self-Employment

P robably the most common snag that delays or thwarts small business start-ups is the financial reality that comes with starting a new venture. Most businesses require at least a moderate infusion of cash—sometimes, a lot of cash—at the beginning which is typically followed by at least a few months of low revenues. If you're leaving a job and a salary behind, it can be quite a financial shock to your system. Child care costs may be an expensive new necessity for you if you're transitioning to self-employment from being your kids' primary caretaker. If you're leaving a job that provided health benefits, you'll need to cover health insurance costs on your own—a sobering prospect. There's no question, clearing the financial hurdles of starting a business can be a major challenge.

This chapter provides a financial reality check while you're still in the early stages of developing your business idea. We'll help you develop a realistic picture of the costs you'll need to cover while getting your business off the ground—both in terms of business start-up costs and your personal living expenses. Like many entrepreneurs, you may realize you'll need start-up funds to survive. The last section of this chapter introduces you to the best sources of small business funding, especially for first-time entrepreneurs.

The next chapter on drafting a business plan walks you through the details of making financial estimates and projections to determine whether your business will succeed. There's no substitute for doing those projections, or for carefully managing cash flow once you're in business to make sure your business can stay afloat. For now, let's focus on the big-picture financial realities of starting a business and strategies for surviving your start-up days.

Business Start-Up Costs

A fundamental money issue you need to consider early on is how much money it will take to get your business off the ground. We'll go through the specifics of business planning and making detailed financial projections in the next chapter, but let's look at some broader considerations here.

Every business is different in terms of what kind of initial investment is necessary to launch successfully. Some businesses do fine on a shoe-string—think of a graphic designer who works on a computer at home and has a slew of clients right from the start. Other businesses need a lot more cash to get started—for example, a bakery owner who needs to rent and furnish a commercial space, buy baking supplies and equipment, hire staff, and do some local advertising. And despite what some people think, Web-based businesses aren't necessarily cheap to run. If your business model relies heavily on sales generated online, you may well need to spend tens or even hundreds of thousands of dollars on your online operation.

Early in your planning stages, put careful thought into the level of start-up investment your business will require, and be realistic. Starting a business without enough cash (called being undercapitalized) puts you at real risk of failure. You'll need enough money to do things right, which varies from business to business—it may be essential to furnish your office professionally, or buy high-end inventory, or develop a robust website. Shortchanging these may mean the difference between success and failure. And you'll need some padding to weather the start-up days, which typically have lower income. Otherwise, you may suddenly be unable to pay suppliers or pay your taxes, which could mean closing shop is your only option.

Generally speaking, you'll want to start your business with enough money to survive for a minimum of six months of slow to very slow sales. In a slow economy, you may have to go longer before sales pick up. At a minimum, you'll need to cover your business's key expenses during this time just to stay alive. In addition, you'll need to cover your living expenses, which we discuss next.

TIP

It always helps to be frugal in the start-up days. In particular, watch out for the dangerous combination of high start-up costs and low projected profits, because it will take you far too long to recover your initial investment, leaving you little cash to live on or reinvest in the business. The bottom line is to spend wisely, saving your start-up funds for things that are essential or that you are confident will directly help generate income.

Be realistic about what time and resources you can commit

"I'm often asked for advice on starting a business, and the answer I give is to really think about your commitment to it. How much time are you going to be able to commit? I'm a mother of a young child, and I'm fortunate that I have a husband who is able to help me raise my child and to be there when I'm at trade shows, or traveling for meetings. It's a lot of time, it's a lot of energy, it's a huge commitment. And it's a financial commitment too. So be smart, and don't go in big—start very small and build it. That is my key advice."

— **Nicola Freegard**

"Start small, and then grow your business slowly. We renovated half of our 6,000-square-foot building first, then renovated the additional 3,000 square feet four years after opening. Similarly, we started out with two retail items and now have an entire store's worth of products. The point is to start within your means. Keep your overhead low."

— **Elissa Breitbard**

Personal Costs of Living

Besides the difficulty of keeping your business afloat during the early days, you'll also need enough personal income to keep your living expenses covered. If you don't plan for this, you could find yourself unable to pay your mortgage or your car insurance payments, which could spell doom for the business just as much as the business's being unable to pay its suppliers or workers. Don't forget to include a reasonable salary for yourself in your business plan financials, sufficient to cover your essential personal costs. (Lots of small solo operators just take out periodic withdrawals, called "draws," instead of having a regular salary; We'll just use the term "salary" here for simplicity's sake.)

If you already have a clear idea of the minimum amount you'll need to cover your costs, great. For example, if you're leaving a job and you were just barely able to survive on your salary, you'll know that the business will need to pay you at least that much. If, for whatever reason, you don't have a good sense of what your monthly costs are, it's important to take the time early on to figure it out.

When drafting the financials of a business plan, many business owners are tempted to minimize a salary for themselves, or even entirely leave it out in order to achieve profitable financial projections. On a practical level, obviously this strategy can work only if you can live off your savings or other sources of income such as a spouse's salary. If so, nixing a salary for yourself might be an acceptable way of minimizing expenses in the start-up days to keep your numbers in the black. But you should only do this as a way of overcoming a cash shortage that is clearly related to your start-up expenses. If your projected earnings from the regular operations of your business don't consistently exceed your projected regular expenses, then denying yourself a salary is just putting off the inevitable.

Instead of leaving out a salary for yourself in the early days of the business, a much safer approach is to include a salary, but keep it as low as possible in the first year or so. A good way to figure out what the salary should be is to cost out your personal life—essentially tally up all your essential expenses to determine a rock-bottom amount that you must be paid in order to stay personally afloat. The sample Personal Living Expenses Worksheet shown below itemizes common personal costs; make one of your own to help figure out your personal bottom line.

Since health insurance and child care are two major expenses for many women starting their own business, I've covered them separately, below.

The costs of running a business

"The most common mistake made by start-ups? Underestimating the costs of running a business. Period. I mean I can elaborate on that, but you can put that in bold capital letters. Especially taxes."

— **Sabrina Habib Williams**

Personal Living Expenses Worksheet

Expense	Monthly Cost
Household Expenses	
Rent/mortgage payment	_____
Homeowners' insurance	_____
Home maintenance	_____
Auto payment	_____
Auto insurance	_____
Auto maintenance	_____
Furniture/appliances/electronics	_____
Association dues	_____
Miscellaneous	_____
Subtotal:	_____
Utilities/Services	
Telephone	_____
Internet service	_____
Cable/dish fees	_____
Electricity	_____
Gas	_____
Water	_____
Trash	_____
Miscellaneous	_____
Subtotal:	_____

Expense	Monthly Cost
Personal Expenses	
Health insurance/dental care premiums	_____
Health care out-of-pocket costs (co-payments, coinsurance, medications, dental care)	_____
Child care	_____
Groceries/food	_____
Personal care/health/beauty products	_____
Clothing	_____
Auto fuel	_____
Public transportation/auto toll fees	_____
Gifts	_____
Dining out	_____
Movies/entertainment	_____
Pet expenses (food, vet bills)	_____
Travel/vacations	_____
Credit card payments	_____
Loan payments	_____
Personal savings	_____
Miscellaneous	_____
Subtotal:	_____
Education	
Tuition/fees	_____
Books	_____
Supplies	_____
Miscellaneous	_____
Subtotal:	_____
Total:	_____

Health Insurance and the Affordable Care Act

For many people, leaving a job means more than leaving a paycheck—any health insurance, sick leave, and retirement benefits included in employment will also terminate, which are sometimes worth practically as much as the wages earned. Unless you are one of the lucky few for whom money isn't an issue, you'll need to carefully consider how these issues may affect your transition and how you will handle them.

A huge issue for countless small business owners is the question of how to handle health insurance for themselves and their families. (We're talking about coverage for the business owner and any dependents here, not creating a health plan for employees; see Chapter 12 for an overview of paying employee benefits.) For many new entrepreneurs, starting a business means leaving a job that may have offered health benefits such as a group plan paid for in part or—for some particularly fortunate employees—in full by their employer. While some of you venturing into entrepreneurship may be able to get health insurance under a spouse or domestic partner's plan, this isn't an option for everyone (such as those who don't have a spouse/partner, or whose spouse/partner doesn't have a plan that will cover you).

The good news is that the Affordable Care Act (ACA) has made it significantly easier for individuals to purchase health insurance on their own, without an employer. Let's take a look at some of the most important rules for those starting self-employment.

How the Affordable Care Act Affects Small Business Start-Ups

Here's the super-simplified version of how the Affordable Care Act changes things:

- **Guaranteed issue and renewal.** Under the ACA, individuals can no longer be denied coverage based on preexisting conditions, which is a huge improvement from the old status quo. In the pre-ACA days, only group plans offered guaranteed coverage, and if you didn't have employer-based insurance, you often couldn't get into a group plan. Now, with individual plans also offering guaranteed coverage, you don't need employer-based group coverage to get that protection.

- **Transparent choices and lower prices.** While the health insurance market under the ACA will likely be in flux for some time, the ACA's promises of broad options with lower premiums and out-of-pocket costs for most people has largely been fulfilled. The ACA approached the costs conundrum by (1) requiring states to create exchanges (and creating a federal exchange for residents of states that opted not to create an exchange), and (2) making coverage mandatory, which should create large enough pools of enrollees to spread risks efficiently and bring premium prices down. As of late 2015, most reports show costs to be lower than the pre-ACA days. Note that some bare-bones catastrophic plans may have been cheaper than the plans offered now, but this is largely because the ACA requires plans to have a higher level of minimum benefits. In other words, the super-cheap plans are no longer offered because they don't offer the minimum level of benefits required by the ACA.

- **Subsidies and tax credits.** Besides aiming to use market forces to lower the cost of premiums as described above, the ACA offers subsidies for individuals, based on income levels and family size that can lower the costs of premiums and out-of-pocket expenses. Some of these subsidies are offered as "advance tax credits" that can be used to lower premium costs right away. For small businesses, those with fewer than 25 employees, making an average of about $50,000 a year or less may qualify for a small business tax credit of up to 50% to offset the cost of health insurance. The smaller the business, the bigger the credit.

- **COBRA rendered largely obsolete.** A federal law, the Consolidated Omnibus Budget Reconciliation Act, or COBRA, requires employers to allow departing employees to remain covered by the company's group policy for up to 18 months, with the employee paying 100% of the premium, plus a 2% administrative fee. COBRA continuation coverage offered an easy, if not cheap, solution to keeping your health insurance from a previous employer. However, with the availability of affordable, comprehensive coverage under the ACA, COBRA is somewhat unnecessary and obsolete. The ACA did not affect COBRA in any way, and as of this writing, COBRA is still fully in effect, so if you leave a job and want to keep your existing coverage you can do so under COBRA. But choosing that option will likely be significantly more expensive than buying a plan through your state or the federal exchange. Many consultants predict COBRA will eventually be eliminated, but no one knows for sure.

No question, the new health insurance landscape created by the ACA dramatically affects your options as you transition into self-employment. For most people, the changes are largely positive.

Where to Learn More About Health Insurance and the Affordable Care Act

For objective information on health insurance, see the National Coalition on Health Care at www.nchc.org. Other useful sites include Insure.com (www.insure.com) and eHealth (www.ehealthinsurance.com); even though they both are portals for purchasing insurance, they include lots of practical information on how to understand your options. Finally, an excellent site offering state-by-state rules and regulations on health insurance is State Health Facts (www.statehealthfacts.org), maintained by the Henry J. Kaiser Family Foundation.

For more information on the Affordable Care Act, including income subsidies and tax credits, see HealthCare.gov, a federal government website managed by the U.S. Department of Health & Human Services. Another informative resource is a website maintained by the Henry J. Kaiser Family Foundation, Health Reform Source (http://healthreform.kff.org).

Child Care

If you have young children—especially if they haven't started school yet—you'll probably have to arrange for child care of some sort to allow you time to run your business. If you think you'll be able to care for your baby or preschooler at your office (or, for home businesses, at home) while also running the business, think again. It's true that owning your own business does provide flexibility so that caring for your kids while you're at work will sometimes be an option—but only sometimes. If you plan to work anything close to full time, child care will be a necessity, at least in your start-up days.

RELATED TOPIC

See "Balancing Family, Kids, and Home Businesses" in Chapter 6 for advice on managing child care when you work at home.

If your business model includes employees who will do most of the hands-on aspects of the business, you may be able to scale back your hours once the business is up and running—say, in a year or two—and spend more time with your kids. Remember, if you want to transition out of the day to day work of the business, you'll need to plan for it and implement solid systems to ensure the business will run smoothly without you. But even when you've carefully planned systems before launching the business, you'll need to be closely involved in the early days to get the business on solid ground. It's just unrealistic to expect to be able to care for your children while also caring for your newborn business.

You may already have child care covered if you're transitioning to self-employment from a full-time job. But if you've been the primary caretaker and regular child care is new for your family, don't underestimate the time it takes to find suitable arrangements. And, of course, don't forget the cost. According to a 2014 report by Child Care Aware of America (http://usa. childcareaware.org), the average cost of full-time day care can easily exceed $10,000. (You can find the full report at www.naccrra.org.)

Depending on your family situation, your spouse could help with child care instead of working at a job. But for this to work, your start-up will need to support the whole family, or you'll need other resources, like savings or other income (say, from rental properties), to stay afloat. If that's not realistic, you'll need to bite the bullet and pay for child care. Your options generally fall into a few categories: day care centers and preschools, home day care, and care in your home (either a nanny or babysitter). In-home care provides the most flexibility, but it's costly: Sitters and nannies generally charge a minimum of $10-$15 per hour (or more), so depending on how much time you need, this solution can easily cost hundreds of dollars a week. Sharing a nanny can be a cost-effective way to go; the trick is to find a good fit with another family in terms of where and when your kids will be cared for. (For more on shared child care options, see the child care resources listed below.)

If you've never had anyone outside of your family care for your kids before, finding an arrangement that you feel safe with can be really stressful (even if you find a great nanny and your child is at home in familiar surroundings). And leaving your child on that first day is sure to be emotional and even scary. But rest assured, it gets easier. Lots of moms (myself included) find out, to their amazement, that their kids really enjoy day care or preschool. There's no better feeling in those early days than going to pick up your child and finding that he or she is having such a good time that they don't want to leave.

To find a facility, home-based center, or caregiver you trust, start by asking other parents. Just as helpful as networking is for your business, it's also essential with important decisions like child care. Parents naturally talk a lot about their kids' preschools and day care providers, and what aspects are great or not so great, so it's easy to get a lot of helpful information this way.

When it comes to in-home caregivers like babysitters and nannies, be aware that some parents might be reluctant to share the names of their favorite caregivers. No parent wants their favorite sitter to suddenly be booked with other families, so they tend to guard their favorites jealously. But don't let this stop you from asking around. Family situations often change; for instance, a family might no longer need their wonderful nanny once their kids start school, so the nanny might be available to you.

TIP

Start your search early. It takes time to make calls, talk with the right people, and set up meetings and interviews. And, of course, you need to account for dreaded waiting lists. In some big cities—and these days, even not-so-big cities—desirable facilities are often full. In some cities, spots might not open up for a year or more. (In Albuquerque, we had to wait a year and a half to get our little one into the neighborhood Montessori. It was worth it because now we can walk her to school.) If you're looking for in-home care, finding the right fit can often take a while. Give yourself a minimum of six months' lead time, or longer if your area has a shortage of good facilities.

RESOURCE

Resources on finding child care. Child Care Aware of America (http://usa.childcareaware.org) has useful articles and state resources on choosing child care providers; understanding licensing rules; how to run background checks; finding child care for children with special needs; and much more. The website www.babycenter.com is also a useful resource on how to choose among the different types of child care.

Unfortunately, the money you spend on child care is not deductible as a business expense. But you can claim a credit for child care expenses on your federal personal tax return. (See Chapter 11 for details.) Another option—a considerably more expensive one—is to operate a child care center at your business that you and employees can use. Employers are entitled to a federal tax credit for the costs of qualified child care expenses, which include the costs of constructing and operating a child care center or paying an outside facility to provide child care services for company employees (including yourself). (Chapter 12 provides more details.) While most start-ups aren't in the position to do this, it's something to consider if you're launching a larger, well-capitalized (in other words, you have plenty of start-up money) company with employees.

Be flexible to control child care costs

"Because it's more expensive of course to leave kids with a babysitter rather than with day care (like way more, almost double the price), we manage the cost of that by me staying home two days a week. Implementing systems to accommodate me being home was part of the solution to be able to run our business and manage child care."

— **Sabrina Habib Williams**

Funding Sources

When you've realistically assessed your money needs to start your business, you may well conclude that you'll need to obtain start-up funds. Even before you start writing a business plan, it's smart to get to know what funding sources are available. As we describe below, some funders like Women's Business Centers may even help you write your business plan, so be sure to look into your local resources early on.

So how hard is it to raise start-up funds? Let's start with a reality check. It has never been easy for first-time entrepreneurs without a track record of success to get start-up loans from banks or interest from investors. And in an economic downturn, your chances of getting a loan or an investment are even slimmer. Add to this grim picture the fact that women have historically found it more difficult to obtain small business financing, and it's clear that raising start-up funds can be a real challenge.

Now for the good news. There *is* money out there for businesses with market potential. If your idea is in fact a good one and you've done a diligent job of planning it out, you'll be well positioned to get the start-up funds you need. The key is to be creative and reach beyond just the usual suspects, such as banks and venture capital firms; most regions have Women's Business Centers and other nonprofit lenders that can be very supportive of small start-ups. Finally, be professional and be persistent. Being rejected for funding is a rite of passage for every entrepreneur.

The sections below explain key concepts you need to understand regarding business financing and outline various sources of funds. While seeking funding can be difficult, your chances will be improved by understanding some basics about how financing works and by knowing nontraditional funding sources, such as microlenders and Women's Business Centers.

Debt vs. Equity Financing

Before you start your quest for cash, make sure you've got a good handle on the basics. One fundamental distinction is the difference between debt financing and equity financing. The concepts are simple. With debt financing, you borrow money that needs to be repaid; equity financing involves receiving money in exchange for an ownership share, or equity, in your business. Debt financing involves a repayable loan; equity financing means acquiring new owners who invest cash in your business.

Unless you originally planned to get money by acquiring investors, chances are that a business loan is a more practical option for your business. Not only will bringing new owners into your business involve potentially complicated issues related to the legal structure of your business, but it will dilute the shares that you and any other original partners own. This means your share of business profits will be reduced, and— potentially even more troubling—you may have to share management control and decision-making authority with the new owners, raising the distinct possibility of conflict.

One way to avoid this is to bring on investors as limited ("silent") partners who will have no authority over business decisions. (See "Partnerships" in Chapter 5 for more on this arrangement.) Even with a silent partner, however, equity financing involves more structural complexities than raising money via a loan.

Bank Loans and Lines of Credit

As mentioned earlier, banks are notoriously reluctant to lend start-up funds to first-time entrepreneurs. But don't let me underestimate your powers of persuasion. If you are fortunate enough to find a lender willing to finance your start-up, you should understand the basics of how typical loans operate. Here's a primer.

Loans can be secured or unsecured. When you obtain a secured loan, you give the creditor an interest in some kind of asset—such as business equipment, real estate, inventory, or receivables—in case you default on the loan. An asset used to secure a loan is called collateral. Lenders tend to be conservative when appraising the value of the collateral, and will only lend a percentage of that value. The loan amount compared to the value of the collateral is called a loan-to-value ratio. An unsecured loan is one that is not backed by any collateral.

Because a strong credit history or an established cash flow is essential in obtaining an unsecured loan, most start-ups aren't in a good position to obtain one. Also, banks usually require start-up business owners to personally guarantee the loan, which puts your personal assets at risk—even if you are incorporated or have formed an LLC. A personal guarantee can sometimes be avoided if you put up sufficient collateral, but personal guarantees are a necessity for most loans to start-up businesses.

Certain details regarding your loan are obviously crucial, such as how much money you need to borrow, the length of time over which you'll pay it off (the term), the interest rate, and any fees you'll need to pay. Most small business loans are short-term, from one to three years. As with most other loans, the longer the loan term, the higher the interest rate. Interest rates can be variable or fixed, usually a little higher for a fixed rate. In addition, you may have to pay points or other fees for various aspects of the application process, such as document reviews or credit checks. Find out if there will be any additional fees for prepayment of the loan.

Related to loans are lines of credit, which also are typically offered by banks. Unlike a typical bank loan, with a line of credit you don't take a lump sum of money all at once. Instead, assuming you're approved, you'll have access to a set amount of money that you can draw on and pay back much like a credit card. Rates are higher than traditional loans, but you'll pay interest only on the amount you've drawn and not yet paid back, not on the whole amount for which you've been approved. The advantage offered by lines of credit over credit cards is that they offer better cash advance terms. Interest rates for lines of credit are typically significantly lower than credit card cash advance rates and don't involve extra fees.

TIP
Establish a relationship with a bank. Even though first-time entrepreneurs typically have a low success rate in seeking loans from banks, it's still a good idea to establish a relationship with a bank early in the life of your business. Open an account and use the services it offers to small business owners

to establish your business as a trustworthy and reputable customer. With a solid relationship in place, you'll be in a better position to apply for funding down the road, either as a line of credit or a traditional loan, when your business is growing and needs money to expand.

Fewer Women Use Bank Loans Than Do Men

A Chamber of Commerce report asked business owners to report where they obtained start-up funding. Most were owners of small businesses, with 95% of respondents having fewer than 100 employees. Among other criteria, the results were reported by gender. Men and women used most funding types at similar rates, though there was a marked difference in the numbers that used bank loans: 23.4% of men reported using bank loans, compared to just 13.3% of women.

Source of funds used to initially start business, by gender

	Total, both genders	Men	Women
Revolving credit	3.1%	3.2%	3.0%
SBA loan	3.4%	3.0%	3.0%
Home equity loan	8.3%	9.0%	7.4%
Friend/family loan	14.8%	16.2%	13.9%
Credit card	15.1%	16.0%	14.8%
Bank loan	18.2%	23.4%	13.3%
Personal savings	80.9%	80.0%	81.5%

Source: "Access to Capital: What Funding Sources Work for You?" published by the U.S. Chamber of Commerce Statistics and Research Center, 2005.

Available for download at www.uschamber.com.

Alternative Sources of Funding

Instead of focusing on the traditional types of funders like banks (and stressing out over your low likelihood of success with them), the best approach for start-ups is to be creative when looking for funds. Alternative funding sources, such as microlenders and small business incubators—including many that specifically focus on assisting women entrepreneurs—tend to be incredibly helpful, since they give not only money, but also support and expertise to nurture your fledgling business. If these types of resources are available in your region they are definitely worth exploring.

The following sections cover some of the most promising sources for start-up funds.

Women's Business Centers

One of the first places you should look for assistance with start-up funding is a Women's Business Center. These nonprofits exist all over the country in both cities and rural areas; their mission is to help support women entrepreneurs with financing and other helpful support services such as classes and one-on-one consulting. Many of these organizations obtain their lending dollars from the federal government, so their lending programs are less affected by bad economic conditions than commercial banks.

Since Women's Business Centers are dedicated to helping women succeed, you'll have a much higher chance of getting the start-up funds you need—as well as support to improve your chances of success. At the very least, you won't likely be outright rejected as you might with a big commercial bank. If your business idea has flaws or your business plan needs development, there's a good chance that a Women's Business Center will work with you to tweak your idea or plan so that it does qualify for a loan. Of course, a Women's Business Center won't fund just any harebrained idea a woman brings in, but if you're serious about your venture you'll likely get valuable support.

Some Women's Business Centers even help you write your business plan from start to finish. Many of these centers offer intensive, multi-week classes and workshops that guide you through the business planning process, with the goal of completing a business plan by the end of the sessions. They may provide additional support through one-on-one consulting, providing feedback to your business plan drafts.

For example, the organization that I worked with for several years, WESST (for Women's Economic Self-Sufficiency Team), offers loans up to $10,000 for start-ups, and up to $50,000 for existing businesses. In addition, it offers a wide range of classes on business topics such as a six-week business plan workshop. Other classes cover basic computer skills, using bookkeeping software, marketing, start-up strategy, and more. Fees are extremely affordable, often in the $25-per-class range. WESST also offers one-on-one consulting to help new entrepreneurs with specific issues, as well as a business incubator that leases office and manufacturing space to small businesses at affordable rates, in a beautiful green-certified building. In some cases, loans are contingent on an entrepreneur's taking certain classes.

RESOURCE

For help in finding a Women's Business Center near you, go to the Association of Women's Business Centers website at www.awbc.org. You'll find a list of Women's Business Centers nationwide.

Use Community Resources—and Persistence— in Seeking Start-Up Funds

Like so many entrepreneurs, Elissa Breitbard learned that persistence is key when seeking funding to start her business. She developed her business plan for Betty's Bath & Day Spa with the help of WESST, a Woman's Business Center in Albuquerque, then approached banks of all sizes—and received a slew of rejections. Finally, on her ninth try, she was approved for a loan of just under $200,000 from a small community bank. Elissa supplemented this loan with smaller loans from WESST and from her friends and family to buy and renovate a building.

Microlenders

Besides Women's Business Centers, there are thousands of institutions nationwide that specialize in lending to specific communities and populations. If there's not a Women's Business Center in your region, perhaps you can find a microlender with a different focus. There are a number of different types and names of these institutions including community development banks (CDBs), community development loan funds (CDLFs), and credit unions. Some have been certified by the U.S. Treasury as community development financial institutions (CDFIs). In a nutshell, these are nonprofit lenders that are aimed at community development via small business lending and support services.

Microlenders can be especially helpful for start-ups, businesses with poor credit, and businesses seeking relatively small loans, generally up to $100,000. As with Women's Business Centers, most microlenders offer guidance and expertise to your business in addition to financing, which will help your chances of success.

RESOURCE

For help in finding a local community development financial institution, go to the CDFI Fund website at www.cdfifund.gov and click "Are You an Individual or Business Seeking a Loan?" From that page you will be directed to the lists and databases of certified CDFIs.

Small Business Administration Programs

The Small Business Administration, or SBA, has developed programs to help solve the problem of banks' being reluctant to lend to small businesses. The SBA does not provide loans itself, but helps businesses secure loans from banks by guaranteeing them—in other words, the SBA promises to repay the loan (up to a certain limit) if the business defaults. As with traditional bank loans, you'll often need collateral or a personal guarantee for an SBA loan.

RESOURCE

To find out about the SBA's guarantee programs and the application process, contact your local SBA office or visit the SBA online at www.sba.gov. The SBA site has lots of info on its own programs and other sources of start-up financing.

Thinking Locally

Besides using the SBA programs to help secure funding from banks, start-up owners should be savvy about which banks offer the best chances of success. Local community banks that have a vested interest in the health of the local economy tend to be much more supportive of local businesses than big chain banks. And often, the application processes and criteria are softer at the smaller banks. For information on community banks, see the Independent Community Bankers of America website at www.icba.org.

Similarly, be sure to look into credit unions, savings and loans, and other financial institutions in your area that may have financing programs for small businesses.

Loans from Family, Friends, and Associates

Since start-ups are so commonly turned down by banks and other traditional funders, entrepreneurs often turn to friends and family for an injection of cash. If you're lucky enough to be related to or friends with people with money, by all means explore this route. Also consider people whom you know professionally such as colleagues or business associates who may be interested in your venture. People with whom you have a positive working relationship and good reputation may be good candidates for a loan.

As you surely know, you must be careful when mixing money, blood, and friendship. The best way to proceed is to be as businesslike as possible when asking for and getting money from family or friends. Draft a promissory note outlining the amount of the loan, the interest rate, and its repayment terms. Make it clear to the person who is lending you the money that you will treat the loan just like a commercial loan from a bank. Follow through with that promise by generating financial reports at least quarterly—and paying back the loan according to the agreed-upon terms.

Check Out Social Lending Networks

Online networks, such as www.prosper.com and www.lendingclub.com, allow creditworthy business start-ups to post loan requests. Depending on the amount and purpose of your loan, these peer-to-peer lending sites may be an option for your business.

Venture Capital Firms, Equity Financing, or Angel Investors

While most of you reading this book are probably planning a small to midsize venture, some of you may have a larger business in the works. If so—and if you are serious about your business plan—venture capital might be an option to consider.

Venture capital (VC) firms invest money in businesses in exchange for ownership shares, usually at least 20%. Each individual deal will vary in terms of how much management control the venture capital firm wants, but it's safe to say that all VC firms will want a significant return on their investments. For this reason, VC firms are usually interested only in relatively large start-ups and aim to invest at least $2 million or more. Typically, VC firms invest in technology companies that can be scaled up quickly and go public at some point.

If you're planning a smaller business for which you'd like to find an investor, a more likely route is what's called an "angel investor": essentially an individual with lots of money (this may or may not be someone you know). Whether you can find an angel investor is a hit-or-miss proposition, but the more serious you are about your business plan, the better your chances of persuading an angel to invest in your company. As with any equity financing, remember that you'll be giving up some ownership of your business, so it's critical that you are comfortable with all the terms, including how much management control the angel wants.

TIP

You'll need professional help structuring an equity investment. For more information on angel investors, see the Angel Resource Institute at www.angelresourceinstitute.org (look at the "Entrepreneurs" section and the "Women First Enterprise" program).

Crowdfunding and Social Media

Crowdfunding refers to a specific method of raising money online that harnesses the power of social media to spread the word about your business or project. For the uninitiated, social media sites allow users to connect with others online and form networks of contacts variously called "friends," "followers," "circles," and so on. Users—who can be individuals or entities like businesses or nonprofits—interact and share things with their social media networks, usually by posting text, photos, videos, or links. Facebook and Twitter are two of the most high-profile social media sites, but there are tons of others: LinkedIn, Instagram, YouTube, and Pinterest, to name just a few.

Crowdfunding sites are essentially social media sites that are geared toward enabling users to raise money for various types of projects (more on that in a moment) from other folks online. Here's how they work.

Will Crowdfunding Work for Your Business Start-Up?

To raise money through crowdfunding, you typically choose a crowd-funding site (such as one of those listed below), create a campaign with information about your project and why it needs funding, set a dollar amount goal and a deadline, and promote your campaign using social media and email outreach. The site will typically keep a percentage of the funding raised, generally 5% to 10%.

The most prominent crowdfunding site is Kickstarter (www.kickstarter.com). Other sites like Indiegogo (www.indiegogo.com) and Crowdrise (www.crowdrise.com) are more geared specifically toward nonprofits.

When choosing which crowdfunding site to use, besides knowing which types of projects are allowed, be sure you understand whether the site is an "all-or-nothing" model or a "keep what you raise" model. For example, Kickstarter uses an all-or-nothing model, so if you don't meet your fundraising goal by the deadline, then your backers don't pay and you don't get anything. Indiegogo, on the other hand, offers a "flexible funding" option that allows you to keep what you raise, even if you fall short of your fundraising goal. Whether or not you meet your goal, you'll be charged a 5% fee of the total raised.

Crowdfunding typically works best for businesses and people who already have a strong social media presence. If your business (or an embryonic version of it) has hundreds or thousands of followers on Facebook and interacts with them daily, you'll be likely to get a lot of mileage from a crowdfunding campaign that you promote appropriately on Facebook. If, on the other hand, your business rarely uses social media, it will be harder to get traction with a crowdfunding campaign, even one that's well crafted and compelling.

Tips for Raising Money Online

Here are some general tips for using social media to raise money for your start-up.

- **Be thoughtful about your rewards.** Instead of asking folks simply to support your project out of the goodness of their hearts, make your rewards attractive enough that they essentially sell themselves. And just as important, plan carefully so you can follow through and fulfill those rewards orders. Don't overpromise and underdeliver, or you are sure to receive bad press even before your grand opening.

- **Use social media in combination with other traditional outreach tools.** Social media is great for spreading the word about off-line events or sharing links to press coverage or other information (for details, see Chapter 9). When used as a component of a multichannel promotional push (which may or may not include a crowdfunding campaign), social media can dramatically expand the reach and exposure of your message.

- **What's hot might not be effective, and what's effective one day may be old news the next.** Kickstarter and Indiegogo are hot crowdfunding options today, but in a year or two they may have fallen out of favor. The bottom line is that you have to constantly stay on the lookout for what's new, innovative, and effective in social media crowdfunding, and be ready to switch courses if your methods become outdated.

- **As with networking in the real world, the payoff from networking online isn't usually immediate or direct.** Keep a broader, longer-term perspective when engaging in social media. Networking isn't the same as direct solicitation, and you shouldn't expect every "friend" to rain funds on your project. But over time, the exposure, relationships, and goodwill you generate through your social media efforts will undoubtedly pay off in some measure.

Personal Financing: Credit Cards, Lines of Credit, and Home Equity Loans

If all other options have failed, many tenacious entrepreneurs turn to credit cards and home equity loans to get their ventures off the ground. This route may work, but you must watch for serious potential pitfalls. Credit cards often charge much higher interest rates than business loans—especially if you're taking cash advances, which are subject to high interest rates and fees and may not have a grace period. Credit card minimum payments are set at such a level that it could take decades to pay off your debt. If you keep high balances on the credit cards and pay just the minimum, your debt can quickly spiral out of control. If you must go this route, a personal line of credit is almost always a better option than a credit card.

Another issue is that a business owner who resorts to credit cards to finance the business may not be as disciplined in managing the debt and spending. While bank lenders typically require financial reports and other proof of solid financial management, credit cards do not—potentially allowing you to get sloppy with your finances. Don't make this mistake. If you use credit cards as start-up funding, be just as serious about your bookkeeping and financial management as if you had a big bank looking over your shoulder.

With home equity loans or lines of credit, your house serves as collateral for the debt. These types of loans will usually offer better interest rates than credit cards, but, of course, they require you to put your home at risk. If your business fails and you are unable to pay your home loan, you may face foreclosure. Be sure you evaluate this sobering possibility before taking out a loan against your home to finance your new business.

TIP
Business plan competitions can be a source of funds. See Chapter 4 on business planning for more information.

Drafting an Effective Business Plan

A rmed with what seems like a brilliant business idea, you may be anxious to jump into action and launch your venture while the iron is hot. But before you start buying inventory, soliciting clients, or otherwise doing business, you need to spend a little time planning the details of your empire. One of the most important steps you take should be drafting a basic business plan.

Boiled down to its core, a business plan is a document that describes with words (a narrative) why your business will be a success, and includes numbers (financial data) that show exactly how you'll turn a profit. A business plan is essential because it helps you see whether your business has a reasonable likelihood of success before you pour your efforts and money into the business. Having a business plan is also a must in order to convince potential investors or lenders (if any) that your business is a solid investment proposition.

SKIP AHEAD

If you've already written a business plan, you may want to skip this chapter—although you may find reviewing this material useful to evaluate the work you've already done.

Unfortunately, entrepreneurs sometimes procrastinate at or make short shrift of the business planning process because they don't know where to start or have an overblown idea of what a business plan is. But business plans don't have to be complicated or filled with business school jargon. What is important is that you take the time to flesh out key details and draft a basic outline of the fundamental elements of your business, most of which you've probably thought a lot about already.

In this chapter, I'll offer a simple approach to writing a business plan —no business degree or any specialized skills required. We'll walk step-by-step through drafting the narrative and financial portions of the business plan, including the subsections and reports that are typically included.

Like many entrepreneurs, you may feel insecure about tackling the business planning process on your own, especially if you lack business experience. There's nothing wrong with seeking help in drafting your business plan—especially if you're looking for major funding and you want to make sure your plan is solid in both substance and design. "Business Planning Resources," below, offers a list of resources for support and guidance in business planning, particularly with preparing the financial sections of your plan.

> **TIP**
>
> **Drafting a business plan and starting to crunch numbers can be inspiring.** When new entrepreneurs start making financial projections, they often find it to be much simpler than they feared. In fact, many find this activity to be quite exciting, as it helps them see how the business will actually work and grow. If you haven't played with numbers yet, you'll likely find that it makes the business feel a whole lot more real and may help stoke the fire under you to really get it rolling.

Why Write a Business Plan?

There are several good reasons to write a business plan, and virtually no good reasons not to. (Being too busy is not a good reason.) Traditionally, entrepreneurs write business plans to get financing from lenders or investors. Funders want to see that they're likely to make money from their investment or loan (or at least not lose money), and a business plan provides a snapshot of the likelihood of a business's success. If you plan to seek start-up funds from a bank or an outside investor, you'll most certainly need a business plan even to get in the door. If you're borrowing start-up money from family or friends, as many entrepreneurs do, a solid business plan will convince them of the seriousness of your effort.

Similarly, if you want to persuade a partner to join you, or to recruit a key management employee, a business plan may be essential. Collaborators, like co-owners or high-level managers, will likely be reluctant to take on the risk inherent in starting a new venture unless they feel confident that the business has a reasonable chance of success. A business plan is the best way to prove this and to pave the way for partners or employees to commit to joining forces with you.

But creating a business plan is important even if you don't need to raise start-up money or attract collaborators. As you wrangle through the details of how your business will operate, the process often brings up issues and potential problems that you may not have thought of before. Drafting a business plan provides an essential opportunity for you to tweak or refine your business strategy to improve efficiency and maximize your competitive edge, before you even get started. If you skip doing a business plan, this is a major opportunity lost.

Besides merely improving your odds of success, a business plan—particularly the financial sections—will also help you avoid starting a business that is destined to fail. Financial projections, such as a break-even analysis and a profit and loss forecast, will help you decide whether your business is really worth starting, or whether you need to rethink some of your key assumptions. Some business ideas don't have a chance to make a solid profit from the beginning, and drafting a business plan will help you discover that up front. If you can't find a way to make adjustments that result in a profitable business forecast, you'll know to go with another opportunity or idea. As any experienced businessperson will tell you, the business you decide not to start (often because its business plan doesn't pencil out) can play a greater role in your long-term success than the one on which you bet your economic future.

 TIP
Business plan competitions can be a source of start-up funds.
Universities, nonprofits, government agencies and other entities award millions of dollars in these competitions every year. Prizes can be substantial, usually starting at around $10,000 and sometimes going into six figures. A good list that is continually updated can be found at www.bizplancompetitions.com.

Finally, a business plan teaches you skills you'll continue to use as you guide the business toward success. Every business owner needs to engage in the strategic thinking and financial analysis involved in business planning, not only at the start of the business but on an ongoing basis. From refining your operations to maximize efficiency, to evaluating your business's financial performance, to monitoring market conditions, a business owner needs to engage in planning-type activities throughout the life of the business. While the document that results from your planning is important, the planning process itself has independent value, as you learn skills that help you control your business's destiny.

A strong foundation in a solid business plan

"Our business plan bridged the chasm between the dream phase and a reality-based vision. In particular, churning out our first break-even analysis and cash flow statements was momentous, for the statements revealed the feasibility of our spa business. Even though the numbers weren't totally accurate, the important thing was to play with different scenarios and numbers and see that the business was, in fact, viable. The business plan helped us secure funding (not only from the bank, but also from family and friends) and provided me with a base of confidence—a concrete way to address some of the fears and issues that arise with taking a risk. There's always talk about how many businesses fail; less discussed is the fact that the owners who have taken time to methodically set their business intentions in writing have a high rate of 'making it.'"

— Elissa Breitbard

How Detailed Should a Business Plan Be?

Business plans vary greatly in their level of detail. Before starting your plan, it's wise to set some general goals regarding how detailed and extensive yours will be. In large part, your goals here will depend on how you intend to use the plan.

If you will use your business plan to borrow money or interest investors (a topic covered in Chapter 3), your plan should be fairly detailed and very persuasive. Funders will want to see in-depth analysis of your market and evidence of solid research, and you'll want to do what you can to encourage them to see your business as a winning proposition. Also keep in mind that the amount of funding you're seeking will affect how much information to present in your plan. If you're trying to raise $2 million in venture capital, your plan should be considerably more detailed than a plan used to seek a $50,000 loan from a microlender.

Business Planning Resources

Depending on the type and amount of help you need with your business plan, there are lots of useful resources available. Here are some of the best. Aside from the first two resources, which focus on business plans, many of the organizations listed here offer help with other start-up issues, such as raising money and marketing your business.

- *How to Write a Business Plan,* by Mike McKeever (Nolo). This comprehensive book covers how to evaluate the profitability of your business idea; estimate operating expenses; determine assets, liabilities, and net worth; and find potential sources of financing.

- *LivePlan* and *Business Plan Pro* (Palo Alto Software). These two applications, published by Palo Alto Software, are loaded with features and tools to help you write a business plan, generate financial projections, format the document professionally, and more. *LivePlan* is an online application with monthly fees (approximately $20/month), while *Business Plan Pro* is software that you install on your own computer (Windows only); it costs about $100. Both applications include more than 500 sample business plans covering a wide range of industries (beauty salons, bed and breakfasts, professional services such as graphic design, and more) and are of much higher quality than the vast majority of free business plan templates found online. For details, see www.bplans.com.

- **Women's Business Centers and other microlenders.** There are many nonprofits that help support entrepreneurship, either for women only or for specific populations and communities. Besides offering lending services (a topic covered in Chapter 3), these organizations typically provide a wide range of assistance with developing business plans, including multiweek classes, workshops, and one-on-one consulting help. To find a Women's Business Center in your community, check the list published by the Association of Women's Business Centers at www.awbc.org. Microlenders certified by the U.S. Department of Treasury as community development financial institutions are listed at www.cdfifund.gov.

Business Planning Resources (continued)

- **The U.S. Small Business Administration (SBA).** The SBA website (www.sba.gov) includes several resources to help you write a business plan, including a step-by-step online business planning workshop. You'll find these resources in the "Starting & Managing" section of the SBA site; alternatively, search the SBA website for "write a business plan."
- **Small Business Development Centers (SBDCs).** The SBA offers a nationwide network of SBDCs that provide valuable and free assistance to small businesses on a range of issues, from permit and license questions to financing and business planning. Counselors are typically available for one-on-one help with the process of developing a business plan. To find a local SBDC near you, visit the SBA website at www.sba.gov and look in the "Starting & Managing" section; alternatively, search the SBA site for "SBDC locator."
- **SCORE.** Originally, the Service Corps of Retired Executives (though the spelled-out version has essentially been abandoned), SCORE is another SBA partner program. SCORE (www.score.org) offers templates of financial tools and a start-up business plan. SCORE also offers a free online workshop on developing a business plan and one-on-one counseling for entrepreneurs. Contact your local office (listed at www.score.org) to set up a meeting.
- **Private business consultants, or possibly a bookkeeper or an accountant.** These professionals may be able to help with the financial portions of your business plan.

If your business plan will primarily be for your own use—that is, if you don't need to raise money—you'll still want to cover important details on market analysis and financial projections, but you can dial down the persuasive material. For example, sections establishing your business credentials could be minimized or eliminated entirely, because you won't need to sell anyone on your business acumen.

The length of a business plan also varies widely. Those developed primarily for personal use typically range from five to 15 pages, while plans used to raise funds might range from 15 to 30 pages or so, and may include appendixes with supplementary information such as market research data, detailed product specifications, or other supporting material. While some consultants insist no plan should exceed 20 pages, or that 50 pages is the optimal page count, we don't feel there are any truly hard rules here. Generally speaking, let the specifics of your business and your intentions for the plan be the ultimate determinant of its length.

RESOURCE

Where to find sample business plans. Seeing an example of a business plan can be immensely helpful in understanding how to put one together yourself. An awesome resource is the website affiliated with Business Plan Pro software (described in "Business Planning Resources" above), at www.bplans.com. This site offers literally hundreds of quality sample plans in dozens of different industries. Reviewing them will help you develop a feel for what kind of information to provide, how much detail to include, and typical ways to format your plan.

The Narrative Sections of a Business Plan: Describing Your Business and Yourself

The narrative sections of a business plan describe exactly what the business will do, how it will do it, what its market is, and why it will be a success. This includes a detailed explanation of the ins and outs of providing your products or services, as well as who your target customers are; an analysis of your competition, and what your competitive edge will be; how you plan to market the business; and why you (and any other co-owners) are well-suited to guide the business to success.

TIP

Be specific! One of the most common mistakes is to write a business plan that's too vague. It's critical to be specific enough to show that you've thought through all important details such as who your key suppliers or vendors will be, how you will handle quality control when manufacturing abroad, how your customers will make their purchases (such as online or in a retail store), or how you'll handle returns and customer service.

We recommend that you break the narrative section of your business plan into several subsections, as described below. However, these are not written in stone. If slightly different sections or titles work better for you, make the appropriate adjustments.

Business Purpose

In this section, you should offer a broad description of the nature of your business and—most importantly—why there is a need for the products or services that you'll offer. For example, if you're planning to open a children's educational toy store focusing on products for developmentally disabled children, you'd use this section to explain what unique products your business will offer and discuss the growing demand for educational products for children with special needs. You'll provide more specific details in later sections of your business plan; here, just focus on offering a compelling vision of the big picture.

A statement of business purpose doesn't need to be complicated or lengthy. In fact, some of the best simply state the obvious. If the need for your business will be clear to lenders or investors (for example, a sandwich shop in a fast-growing office area), one paragraph may be all you need. But if the value of your business idea isn't so readily apparent (for example, an innovative software company), you will want to say more. Show how your business will solve a real problem or fill an actual need. And explain why customers will pay you to accomplish the task.

At this point, early in the business plan, you need to quickly, concisely, and powerfully make a case for your business idea. This is especially important if you're trying to persuade lenders or investors. Here are a few examples of persuasive approaches (you'll get other ideas by doing your own market research, as discussed in Chapter 2).

- **Similar businesses have been successful.** For example, if several fitness clubs with business service centers (WiFi access, computers, and fax machines) are all the rage in Los Angeles, you might point to this as a good indication that your similar business would succeed in Chicago, where the market is currently dominated by more traditional gyms.
- **Marketing surveys or demographic reports point to a growing need for your product or service.** For instance, to buttress your contention that there will be a need for your new line of paralegal training materials, point to U.S. government reports listing paralegals as one of the fastest-growing occupations.
- **Media reports confirm the popularity of and demand for your business.** For example, include newspaper clips or transcripts of television news reports on the surge of demand for antibacterial air fresheners as evidence that your germ-killing Sani-Scent will sell.

Description of Products or Services

Once you've stated the need that your business will fill, describe how you'll go about filling it. This isn't a place for fluffy text about the brilliance of your entrepreneurial idea. Instead, outline in detail exactly how your business will operate. You may want to have a separate paragraph or list of bullet points for dealing with each of these points.

Include specifics such as:

- how you will provide the product or service
- details about the online aspects of your business, assuming you'll at least have a basic website, or possibly more extensive online operations (Chapter 9 covers e-business in depth)
- what key equipment and supplies you will need and where you will buy them

- who your customers will be and how they will pay you
- how many employees you will have, and what they will do
- your hours of operation, and
- your business location (if possible, include details about how your customers will find you—this is especially important if you are an online-only business).

Keep in mind that even the smallest, simplest business involves a swarm of pesky details. While you're describing your products or services, don't assume there's anything obvious about your business, even if it's a tiny one-person operation. For example, if you plan to start a pet-grooming business, how many different types of services will you offer: Shampooing? Flea bathing? Nail cutting? Hair trimming? Teeth cleaning? Will you charge separately for each individual service, sell them in packages, or both? How will you attract customers and regularly stay in touch with the best ones? How will you accommodate animals with special needs, such as allergies, or behavioral problems, such as aggressiveness? How will people drop off and pick up their pets? Will your business need insurance in case an animal is injured or dies while in your care? As you can see, this is where you'll need to answer the bulk of logistical questions about your business.

TIP

There's such a thing as too much detail. Earlier, we strongly encouraged you to be specific when writing your business plan. However, it's also true that your plan shouldn't devolve into minutiae. When it comes to day-to-day details, such as procedures for stocking and taking inventory, or opening and closing tasks, these are best covered in operations manuals. We discuss developing your business's systems in Chapter 12, including the importance of putting policies and procedures in writing—a particular necessity for businesses with employees.

Describing your products or services will probably take the most editing and revision, too, as you change or refine your business idea. This gives you an opportunity to fill in the gaps before you actually open for business. And even if you discover a flaw so big that you decide not to start the business after all, your business plan has done its job. While undoubtedly disappointing, it's far better for your business to fail on paper than in real life.

Market Analysis

In this section, you'll define and analyze your market, including target customers, competition, and your industry. It's often a good idea to cover these aspects in separate subsections. (Again, refer back to Chapter 2 for advice on targeting your customers and market.)

Target Customers

Who will buy your product or service? Even the most innovative business will fail if it doesn't quickly find enough customers to make a profit. Clearly identifying your target customers is essential to proper marketing and crucial for your own success, so make sure to include this important information in your plan even if you won't be using it to raise funds. If you will be presenting the plan to potential financers, they will definitely want to see this information, so it will be even more important to include.

The better you can show that you know exactly who your target customer is, the more confident you will be that you can actually find these people and sell to them. For example, if you're opening a bar with live entertainment, you might identify your target as primarily childless, urban professional 21-to-35-year-olds, who tend to have more disposable income and leisure time than others. If you can show there are plenty of those folks around, you're on the right track.

Besides defining your target customer base, include information about your potential customers' buying habits and preferences, to demonstrate there is an actual demand for your product or service among this group. Use market data, news reports, trade journal articles, or whatever other data you can get your hands on. As described in Chapter 2, surveying your target customers is a great way to get powerful information, and you could include these results in your business plan. For example, if you will run a business repairing and reconditioning acoustic guitars and similar stringed instruments, you might include results of a survey of guitarists and other musicians in the area on what kind of repair services they need, as well as quotes from them saying that they'd use your services.

RELATED TOPIC

Is the government a target customer? Government contracts can be extremely profitable, but involve a lot of hurdles. If you plan on targeting this market, make sure you understand everything that's involved. See Chapter 2 for advice.

Competition and Industry

Competition is a fact of life for every business. If you happen to be lucky enough to have developed a solid business idea with clear demand and little or no competition, count on that situation to change. In this section of your business plan, provide an analysis of what competition exists for your business and how you will deal with it. If they're out there, focus on your direct competitors—not just businesses in the same general field, but those focused on the same target market. Identify what will make your business stand apart—in other words, what your competitive edge will be. Don't be shy about detailing competitors' strengths and weaknesses as part of showing that you understand the market and know why your business will better meet customers' needs.

In discussing the competition, put yourself in the shoes of a customer who is comparing your business to a competitor's. From the customer's perspective, what factors are most important in choosing which business to patronize? Some obvious considerations are quality and selection of products or services, customer service, convenience (access), reliability, and price. Your competitors will probably excel in some of these areas and be weaker in others. The same will probably be true of your business. The trick is for you to find a spot, or niche, among the competition, and offer a combination of elements—such as unique product choices and educated, attentive staff—that no one else offers.

CAUTION

Think twice before competing on price. If your main competitive advantage is price, it will be hard to maintain—eventually, there will almost always be someone who will charge less, especially if you have a product a big box retailer can sell. Far better to look for another edge that's harder to replicate, such as superior quality, unique products, or exceptional customer service.

Marketing Strategy

Once you have a clear idea of who your customers will be and why they will buy your product or service from you instead of from your competitors, you'll need to go a step further and describe your strategy for reaching your customers in a cost-effective way. In other words, how will you market your business?

RELATED TOPIC

Read Chapter 8 to learn how to develop a cost-efficient marketing plan. For the purposes of your business plan, you'll just need a summary description of your marketing approach. Some businesses may want to go a step further and draft a separate marketing plan; even if you don't go that far, Chapter 8 will help you decide on the most cost-efficient marketing strategies for your business. Also, be sure to read Chapter 9 which focuses on the e-commerce part of your business.

Small businesses that don't have much of a marketing budget shouldn't be shy about their smaller-scale plans. Even if you don't plan to spend much (if any) hard cash on marketing or advertising, you should have a plan for how you'll reach your first customers. In your business plan, simply describe what this strategy is. Explain what methods you will use (and the costs), such as holding special events or workshops; media relations; online marketing (such as search engine optimization (SEO) or networking on social media sites); directory listings (such as trade directories or the yellow pages); or advertising (print, television, radio), to name a few. If you plan to use nontraditional guerrilla marketing tactics, such as putting up posters all around town or staging publicity stunts, explain exactly what you plan to do. And no matter what kind of marketing strategy you outline, be sure to explain why you think it will work.

Management and Staff Structure

Use this section to describe who will be working for your business and in what capacity. Obviously, include yourself and any co-owners (you'll provide details on your business accomplishments in the next section). Also, describe how many employees you plan to have, their duties and job descriptions, how much each employee will cost, and how any departments or lines of authority will be structured. Also include job descriptions and costs of any regular contractors you plan to hire. We'll discuss how to hire and manage staff in detail in Chapter 12, but in short, a little structure goes a long way in creating an efficient operation. If you will use your business plan to raise money, your funders will definitely want to see a well-organized plan for day-to-day management of the business.

Business Accomplishments

In addition to showing what a great, profitable business you will be running, you need to show why you (and your partner(s), if any) are the right person(s) to run it. This is particularly important if you will use your business plan to raise money. Do this by including a section that highlights your business accomplishments. This information is often presented as a résumé, but it can be presented as a basic narrative, written like a biography.

If you have never run a business before, don't worry; just focus on your accomplishments, training, or experience that are relevant to the business and the role you will play in the business. For example, if you have managed budgets, done sales, or supervised staff while working for another company, include that information to show that you will be able to do the same with your own business. Be sure to include specific accomplishments or results you were responsible for, such as doubling sales in a certain period of time or managing the addition of a significant number of new employees. In a nutshell, include any personal information likely to inspire confidence in you as a business person.

Prospective lenders and investors will want to know a number of things about you, such as:

- **Do you understand the business?** Lack of hands-on experience will be a red flag to investors, who know a nonexpert boss can't roll up her sleeves and help out in emergencies. If you don't have experience in the field, explain why the skills you do have will help your business succeed.

- **Can you manage people?** All sorts of organizations, including small businesses, fail because their leaders—no matter how technically competent—can't work well with others. If you have successfully worked with others, and preferably led, supervised, or managed in the past, you should emphasize this experience.

- **Do you understand money?** To be successful, you will need to know how to manage—and make—money. If you don't have money management skills, make sure someone you're working with does (and can help you get the details into the plan). If you have money management experience, emphasize it, even if it is in another industry or field.

Putting the Narrative All Together

Most of you should be able to handle writing the narrative portions of your business plan. Simple, straightforward language always works better than complicated business jargon. If writing is not your forte, and especially if you're going to use your business plan to seek funding, the writing quality, tone, and overall professionalism of the plan will be very important. Resources like Women's Business Centers, microlenders, and small business development centers often offer business plan assistance, so check to see if you have any such resources in your area to help you finalize your plan. (See "Business Planning Resources" above.) Or consider hiring a freelance writer with business savvy to help you develop, edit, and polish it.

A business plan doesn't have to be dullsville

"Lauren was a bit compulsive about wanting to write a proper business plan, while Emira felt more confident that so long as we had done the basic homework, we didn't need to go through all the formalities of putting all our thoughts down in written form. We met somewhere in the middle, with a half-formed business plan that went in-depth on all the bits that were really important to our business, and skimmed over the stuff that was less mission critical, or that we felt we had already considered carefully. We found the business plan writing process rather dry and clinical. What was more fun for us was to take a less stuffy approach and get creative with some of the same questions that are typically set out in a business plan, i.e., What are you selling? Who's buying? etc. We developed wildly detailed target market profiles, brainstormed lists of our dream clients, toyed with name ideas— and crunched numbers in between those fun-filled excursions."

— **Lauren Bacon and Emira Mears**

Financial Projections: Showing Your Business Will Profit

After persuasively describing how your business will work, you'll need to do some number crunching to show that it will, in fact, make enough money to pay the bills and turn a profit. All the rosy descriptions in the world won't make your business a success if the numbers turn up red.

Projecting the finances of your business may seem intimidating or difficult, but in reality it's not terribly complex. Basically, it consists of making educated guesses about how much money you'll need to spend and how much you'll take in, then using these estimates to calculate whether your business will be sufficiently profitable.

It's important to be as realistic and accurate as possible about your projected profitability, regardless of whether you intend to use your business plan to raise money. Even if you'll just be using the business plan as an internal management document, you'll still want to make a convincing case to yourself (and any dependent family members) that your business idea will fly. Realistic figures are even more important if you present the plan to lenders or investors; they'll likely call you out on any overly optimistic projections. For example, if you project your knitting supply business will turn millions in the first year, potential lenders or investors may dismiss you outright.

On the other hand, don't get too hung up with worry that your estimates won't be accurate. Of course your estimates won't be 100% on target, but it's essential that you do take a stab so you at least have initial versions of financial projections that can be refined over time. With some common sense and, when necessary, research (as discussed in Chapter 2), your estimates are likely to be at least in the ballpark. If your first projections show your business losing money, you'll have an opportunity while still in the planning stage to make sensible adjustments, such as raising your prices or cutting costs. And, of course, if your numbers turn out to be even better than you had hoped, you can move forward with confidence that your plan is indeed a good one.

To demonstrate sound financials, a business plan should include at least the following financial projections, all of which are discussed in detail in the rest of this chapter:

- **A break-even analysis.** Here you use income and expense estimates for a year or more to see whether, at least in theory, your business will be able to turn a profit.

- **A profit/loss forecast.** Here you'll refine the sales and expense estimates that you used for your break-even analysis to create a formal, month-by-month projection of your business's net profit for at least the first year of operations.

- **A start-up cost estimate.** As the name suggests, this is simply the total of all the expenses you'll incur before your business opens. These costs should be included in your business plan to give a true picture of how much money you'll need to get your business off the ground.

- **A cash flow projection.** Even if your profit/loss forecast tells you that your business will have higher revenues than expenses, that doesn't mean that you'll always have enough cash available on key dates, such as when rent is due or when you need to buy more inventory. A cash flow projection lays out how much cash you'll have—or how much you'll be short—month by month, so you can plan for adequate funding. This lets you know if you'll need to get a credit line or set up other arrangements to make sure funds are available.

We'll go through each of these in the sections below. First, however, let's review some basics to make sure you're up to speed with some of the fundamental concepts involved in the reports and projections discussed in this chapter. (Of course, if you have an MBA or experience with small business money management, feel free to jump ahead to the specific discussions of each financial projection.)

RESOURCE

Recommended reading on small business finances. If you feel out of your depth with the numbers and money aspects of your business, you're not alone. Entrepreneurs commonly report feeling insecure and anxious about handling financial matters—especially related to the start-up business plan, since it's the first financial-related task that faces new business owners. Besides getting outside help from Women's Business Centers and other resources described earlier in this chapter, another way to educate yourself is to do further reading about small business money management and the financial aspects of business planning. *How to Write a Business Plan*, by Mike McKeever (Nolo), is especially good at explaining various financial tools and financial planning tasks in considerable detail. Another good (although older) resource for understanding business finances is *Small Time Operator*, by Bernard Kamoroff (Taylor Trade Publishing).

Get to Know Your Numbers

The main reason people get confused is not that they're bad at math—it's that they don't understand what the numbers mean. It pays off to take some time early on to learn what your key financial numbers are, and how they relate to one another. One big-picture formula that's helpful to keep in mind is:

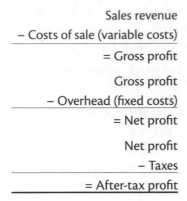

With this very basic formula as a foundation, let's take a closer look at some key financial concepts. It's important that you understand these fundamentals before we dive into the financial reports and projections recommended for your business plan.

Dealing With the Numbers Is Essential

Kim Blueher is the director of lending and teaches business planning classes at WESST, a Woman's Business Center in Albuquerque, New Mexico. Here's what she tells WESST clients to help them understand the importance of having control over the financial aspect of their businesses:

"Your business is like your baby—it is a living entity that you put your blood, sweat, and tears into. The financial part of your business can be like changing the dirty diapers of your baby: something no one wants to do, but is essential to the health of the baby. Having a good understanding of the financial part of your business is essential to its health as well. Many businesses fail because their owners didn't want to deal with this critical area."

Sales Revenues

If you haven't projected sales numbers before, the task can be daunting —but of course, it's fundamental to developing meaningful financial projections. One good way to estimate how much money you'll be bringing in is to compare your business to similar ones. Retail businesses, for example, often measure annual sales revenue per square foot of retail space. If you plan to open a pet supply store in a 1,000-square-foot space, for example, you can base your estimated revenue on the revenue per square foot of other pet supply shops. (You'll usually adjust downward to account for the fact that your store will be new and unknown for at least a few months or more.)

You may have to do some creative research to find this kind of info; of course direct competitors probably won't share their financials with you. If you've worked in a similar business, perhaps you know what daily or monthly sales were like. Or maybe you have a friend in a similar business who's privy to sales information. Industry publications or business journals (including business sections of general interest publications like *The New York Times*) often offer sales information about specific businesses or industries. Attending trade shows where you can meet and talk with people who own similar businesses in other parts of the country is another good way to gather valuable information.

If you're planning a service-based business, your estimate of sales revenue will depend on how many billable sales you'll be able to make each month—that is, the total number of hours you'll be able to charge clients for your (or an employee's) time. Remember, even if you plan to work full time, you won't be providing billable services every hour you're at work. For example, if you run a landscaping business, a sizable portion of your time will be spent not performing landscaping work but managing your accounts, maintaining your equipment, and soliciting new clients. You'll need to make a realistic assessment of how much of your time will be taken up by these nonbillable activities and how much time you'll spend providing actual services to clients to get an accurate picture of how much money will be flowing in.

Fixed vs. Variable Costs

A fundamental distinction that comes into play in all sorts of financial reports and analyses is the difference between fixed costs and variable costs. Here's the deal.

- **Fixed costs.** Commonly referred to as "overhead," these include all regular expenses not directly tied to the product or service you provide. Examples include rent, phone and utility bills, payments for outside help such as bookkeeping services, postage, marketing expenses, monthly hosting fees for your website, and most salaries (except in service businesses).
- **Variable costs.** These costs—sometimes also called product costs, costs of goods sold (COGS), or costs of sale—are directly related to the products or services you provide and include things like inventory, packaging, supplies, materials, payment processing fees for online sales, and sometimes labor used in providing your product or service. They're called "variable" precisely because they go up or down depending on the volume of products or services you produce or sell. In the case of services, one of the biggest variable expenses is almost always the wages or salary of the service provider.

As you can probably guess, there are some gray areas, such as labor expenses. Whether you'll categorize labor expenses as fixed or variable costs often depends on the type of workers you pay and the kinds of products or services you're selling. Salaries or wages of the managers and employees who are necessary to keep your business going (you or your bookkeeper, for example) are usually considered fixed costs. But salaries or wages for employees who create the products or provide the services you sell may be more appropriately treated as variable costs. For example, an ad agency that pays six freelance copywriters to service clients' accounts should treat their paychecks as variable costs.

To figure out whether a labor cost should be designated as fixed or variable, ask yourself: If I sell one, ten, or 100 more products or services this week, will my labor costs go up? If not, you're probably looking at a fixed cost. For instance, suppose you're trying to decide whether your administrative assistant's salary should be categorized as a variable cost or a fixed cost. If you produce and sell 1,000 more Baby Blankets, will your administrative costs go up? Probably not. So your admin's salary is a fixed cost. But if you have to hire five temporary employees to answer the phones at Christmas time and fill orders to handle the spiking demand for Baby Blankets, their wages should be classified as variable. (Hint: Money paid to workers who are temps or independent contractors is usually categorized as variable costs, because those payments are usually tied to providing a product or service.) Of course, if you sell more products or services regularly, you'll probably decide to expand your business and increase your overhead, because you'll have to hire more support staff, managers, and other necessary employees just to get along. At that point, you might revisit your allocation of fixed and variable costs.

TIP
Keep fixed costs as low as possible. If your business is slow to get started—and lots of businesses take months or even a year or more to become solidly profitable—high fixed costs can quickly eat up your funds. Rather than committing yourself to high overhead, it's usually better to keep expenses low, allowing increases only when your income justifies spending more.

Gross Profit and Net Profit

Another fundamental distinction you need to understand is the difference between gross and net profit. Gross profit refers to how much money you've earned from sales of your products or services over and above their variable costs. Net profit refers to the money that's left over after paying for variable costs *and* fixed costs. Net profit is sometimes called net income or pretax profit. Other than the various taxes you'll need to pay on net income (and you shouldn't underestimate how much this can be), this is your and any other business owners' money.

For example, if your business sells widgets for $10 each and each widget costs your business $6 to sell (including all variable costs, like buying the widget from your supplier and packaging or shipping costs), your gross profit on each widget will be $4. But the gross profit does not account for your fixed costs like rent, insurance, or salaries. You'll use the total gross profits earned by the business to pay for those fixed expenses. Assuming you have something left over after paying for fixed expenses, that's your net profit. (If you lost money, it's a net loss.)

For service businesses, gross profit is the difference between what rate is paid to the service provider versus what rate is charged to the client. For example, a human resources consulting firm could pay consultants $50 per hour, but charge clients $75 per hour. In this case, the variable cost for every hour of billable services would be $50, and revenues would be $75, resulting in a gross profit of $25.

One-person service businesses may find gross profit a tricky concept since they essentially pocket the entire amount charged. For a number of reasons—primarily so you're able to manage your financial data meaningfully—we recommend that freelancers take the step of valuing their labor separately from what they charge clients. Doing so will help you generate more meaningful financial reports which will help you grow the business. In addition, if you ever choose to expand by hiring employees or additional contract labor, you'll have a foundation from which you can build a more complicated fee structure beyond a one-person operation.

Gross Profit Percentage

Another financial measure that plays a big role in financial management and analysis is called a gross profit percentage, sometimes called a profit margin. The gross profit percentage is the portion of each sales dollar that exceeds the cost to your business of selling the product or service. As described above, when you sell a product, the amount of sales revenue that exceeds the cost of the item to you is the gross profit. Turning this into a percentage shows you overall how much of your overall sales revenues represents gross profit.

Gross profit percentage is calculated as follows:

Gross profit percentage = gross profit ÷ revenue.

For example, consider the above example of a business that sells widgets for $10 each, and those widgets cost $6 to buy, resulting in a gross profit of $4. When you divide the $4 profit by the $10 revenue, it results in a gross profit percentage of 40%. This means that of every dollar you bring in, 40% is gross profit; 60% is eaten up by the product or service itself. Using the human resources consulting business example above, the gross profit percentage would be calculated by dividing the gross profit ($25) by revenue ($75), for a gross profit percentage of 33.3%.

Using Spreadsheet Software for Financial Projections

The best way to do your financial projections is to use spreadsheet software such as Microsoft *Excel*. Many entrepreneurs wonder if it makes more sense to use the bookkeeping software they plan to use once their business is up and running, since most financial software includes various budgeting and planning features. In my opinion, while bookkeeping software is excellent at tracking actual financial data, spreadsheets offer more flexibility when crunching estimated numbers. I find it much easier to manually manipulate numbers with a spreadsheet customized with the appropriate formulas; bookkeeping software is usually much more complex and time-consuming to use just to run some sample numbers. (But again, it is indispensable for managing large amounts of actual data.)

If you have never used spreadsheet software, take heart: It is quite easy to learn. Ask a friend to show you how *Excel* or another program works or even tackle it yourself, with the assistance of the "Help" menu. Be sure to check out *Excel* tutorials on YouTube. If you need additional advice, find out whether there are any classes offered locally—libraries, universities, community colleges, and adult education programs often have training sessions. In a short time, you'll be able to start your number crunching in earnest. For more on spreadsheet software, see "Using Technology to Manage Money, Inventory, and Projects," in Chapter 10.

One major wrinkle in calculating an overall gross profit percentage for your business is in dealing with different categories of products or services. Many retailers, for example, sell lots of different products at different margins. A garden supply shop may have radically different profit margins for their plant sales than for outdoor furniture, seeds, irrigation equipment, or garden tools. To account for this, you should calculate gross profit percentages for each category of goods or services, and use those amounts to then calculate an average gross profit percentage for your business as a whole.

To accomplish this, you'll need to group your products or services into categories—groups of things that have roughly similar selling prices and variable costs—then, you'll calculate the gross profit percentage for each category. You'll also need to determine how much each category will contribute toward your total annual sales—in other words, what portion of your estimated overall sales will consist of sales from Categories A, B, C, and so on? With separate gross profit percentages and estimated income for each category, you can calculate the gross profit for each category, and calculate an average gross profit percentage for the business as follows:

Gross profit Category A
+ Gross profit Category B
+ Gross profit Category C
= Total gross profit (all categories)

Total gross profit (all categories) ÷ Total revenues (all categories) = Average gross profit percentage for business

The narrower the categories you create, the more realistic and accurate the average gross profit percentage will be. The downside is that calculating gross profit percentages for multiple categories is time-consuming.

Pricing

Pricing products and services is often confusing and stressful for new entrepreneurs because it can have such a major impact on the success or failure of your business. If you set prices too high, you'll have fewer customers willing to pay those prices. But if you set prices too low, you may not be able to cover your operating costs. Here's what we consider the most important general piece of advice regarding pricing: Make pricing decisions with your target market (your niche) in mind and adopt an overall pricing strategy. Keep in mind that the very same widget might be sold for $0.99 at your local 99 Cent store, $5 at a chain retailer, and $25 at a swank boutique. The price can vary so much because each of these stores has its own pricing strategy—and you should, too. Make sure you're clear about whether you're targeting a high-end, middle-end, or low-end market, and develop pricing that is consistent with the market you're trying to reach.

Finally, it's of course essential that the prices you ultimately choose work within your business plan. If your financial projections show consistent losses, something needs to be adjusted, and it may be your pricing.

Let's take a look at some pricing approaches for product-based and service businesses.

Pricing Products

When you're selling products, obviously you'll need to charge a price higher than what you paid for the goods or services you're selling, but by how much? Researching other businesses similar to yours—particularly those that target a similar market—is a great way to develop a sense of what pricing the market will bear. As a seasoned consumer, trust your instincts when analyzing other businesses. If a pricey boutique seems always to be empty, chances are that its pricing strategy isn't working. Letting market conditions guide your pricing can be especially helpful when pricing unique products like handcrafted jewelry or quilts, for which pricing may be very nonstandard.

Getting to know average or standard markup rates—in other words, how much other businesses charge for products or services above their costs—can also be a helpful guide in setting your prices. But if you only know what other businesses are charging, and not what they paid for their products or services, how can you figure out their markup rate? You'll need to dig a little deeper for this information. One easy source of markup guidance is simply the manufacturer's suggested retail price (MSRP, also called the suggested list price). If you buy a line of table lamps that cost you $30 per unit and the MSRP is $90, then you know the manufacturer is recommending a markup of 200% of cost. Besides using MSRPs, you should feel free to ask your manufacturers and suppliers for information they may have on average markup rates. Your suppliers can be a valuable source of this kind of information, above and beyond merely setting MSRPs for each product.

Trade associations and journals may be able to give you valuable data about industry standard markup rates. Directories and guidebooks are available on many industries—these books tend to be expensive (easily $100 and up) but are often treasure troves of valuable industry info.

Hoover's Inc. is a company that specializes in providing comprehensive market data—its website offers a wealth of information and publications for sale. Visit Hoover's Online at www.hoovers.com. Many of the titles offered at Hoover's are from Plunkett Research, another firm specializing in market data. Plunkett has its own website at www.plunkettresearch. com. Besides Hoover's and Plunkett, there are many more resources out there. Be sure to do your own research and look specifically for info pertaining to your type of business. Search online, visit the library of a local business school, ask local trade associations, and generally do some sleuthing to turn up the data you need.

Finding the right product price point

"To do anything in quantity, one thing I learned from having a smaller business that was all handcrafted in the U.S., made by two sewers of mine in Tucson, was it was very difficult to make a living. It wasn't even about making money at that point, it was just making a living or breaking even so I wasn't spending money on being a business. I realized early on that manufacturing was the way to go, and price point is key, and it's been a series of experiences and lessons about driving down my price point to expand my audience. So, it's been absolutely crucial to go to manufacturing."

— Nicola Freegard

Pricing Services

Those who work as freelancers or own service-based businesses often find it difficult to figure out what rates to use. Many people can't understand how to assign value to their time. Remember that your service rates are not just a measure of the value of your time—they also need to cover your overhead and yield your profits. Many service businesses use a fairly basic formula to calculate their hourly rate. To keep it simple, look at this formula as if you're a solo freelancer without any employees:

	Desired annual salary	This can be a regular salary or draws you take from the business; essentially your take-home pay.
+	Annual fixed costs	Also called overhead.
+	Desired annual profit	A typical profit goal is 20% above salary and overhead.
=	Total desired income	
	Total desired income	
÷	Annual billable hours	This is the number of hours you can charge clients for your time, and will probably be somewhere between 50% and 80% of the total hours you work.
=	Hourly rate	This is the amount you should charge in order to make your desired salary, cover your fixed costs, and make your desired profit—assuming you work the number of billable hours you estimated.

The gist of the formula is that it adds together all the money you want to bring in each year and divides that total by the number of hours you plan to work each year. The result is the hourly rate. This simple formula can be adjusted depending on the specifics of your business.

FORM ON NOLO.COM

Billable Rate Calculator. The Nolo website includes an interactive worksheet to help you calculate an hourly rate for your service business and step-by-step instructions for using it. See the appendix for a link to this and other worksheets in this book. For the automatic calculations in the worksheet to be active, you'll need to open the worksheet in a spreadsheet program such as Microsoft *Excel*.

Another way to set your hourly rate is to throw the formula out the window and simply set your rate for what the market will bear. Beware that this might not yield a profitable hourly rate, because you're not basing your rate on the actual numbers you'll need to achieve. On the other hand, it may be more likely to deliver a rate that customers will accept.

If you base your rates on the market, use any market information you can get to guide you—including what competitors charge, industry standards, and your own experience of using various rates. If you constantly fail to snag clients once you provide a quote, that's a sign your rates may be too high. On the flip side, if you get every job you bid on, you could probably get away with nudging, or even shoving, your rates upward.

It's not a bad idea to use a combination of the formula-based and market-based approaches. Using the formula will help ensure that you set a rate that is profitable, and using the market to adjust the rate up or down will help you stay competitive. For example, if the formula yielded an hourly rate of $45, but other similar businesses charge $65 to $75 per hour, you could feel comfortable increasing your rate to $55 per hour, making your business a bargain while still turning a profit.

Using pricing to define a niche

"Pricing can be really elusive. I did a comparative analysis of four or five spas in Albuquerque, and used that as my baseline. I decided to go near the top of that—maybe not be the highest, but up near the highest, because I knew that I always wanted to create the niche market as offering the best services, so I wasn't worried as much that it would be the cheapest pricing."

— **Elissa Breitbard**

Break-Even Analysis

Your break-even point is the point at which the income you'll bring in just covers your expenses—that is, the costs of providing your product or service (variable costs, since they change depending on how many products or services you provide), plus your overhead, like rent, salaries, and utility bills (fixed costs). If your business brings in income in excess of your break-even point, you'll make a profit. If your income is less than the break-even point, you're losing money. Because break-even analysis offers a snapshot of your profitability, it's a great tool for weeding out losing business ideas.

It's especially important for businesses that will have moderate to significant overhead to calculate their break-even point, because the higher these costs, the more you'll need to sell to cover them. As we describe in more detail below, overhead (also called fixed costs) represents costs to your business that you'll need to pay regardless of how high or low your sales are. Rent, insurance, and payroll are typical examples. If your break-even analysis shows that you'll need to achieve a highly optimistic (possibly even fantasy-level) sales number just to cover your rent and payroll, you will probably need to rethink your business model.

Here's a simple approach to doing a break-even analysis:

1. Calculate your **gross profit percentage** on the goods or services you'll sell. Remember, this is the percentage of each sales dollar that exceeds the cost to your business of selling the product or service; gross profit percentage = gross profit ÷ revenue. If your business will sell a wide range of different products or services with significantly different gross profit percentages, remember to calculate an average gross profit percentage for the business as a whole.

2. Tally your **fixed costs**, which are the costs your business must pay regardless of how much product or service you sell. As described above, fixed costs (or overhead) typically include rent, utilities, payroll, equipment rental, insurance, and—don't forget—a salary for you and any co-owners. You can total these costs either monthly or annually; the break-even point generated in the next step will apply to whichever time period you use in the formula.

3. Calculate your **break-even point** by dividing your fixed costs by your gross profit percentage. The result is the amount of sales revenues you'll need to earn in whatever time period you chose in the previous step (monthly or annually) just to break even. In other words, if you used your monthly fixed costs in the equation, that means that your break-even point represents how much monthly sales revenue you'll need to reap in order to cover your costs. If you used fixed costs for the whole year, your break-even point shows you how much sales income you'll need in that year to break even.

To summarize:

Break-even point = fixed costs ÷ gross profit percentage

FORM ON NOLO.COM

Break-Even Analysis Worksheet. The Nolo website includes an interactive worksheet to help you calculate your break-even point and step-by-step instructions for using it. See the appendix for a link to this and other worksheets in this book. For the automatic calculations in the worksheet to be active, you'll need to open the worksheet in a spreadsheet program, such as Microsoft *Excel*.

Conceptually, plenty of folks find it a little tricky to see how dividing your fixed costs by your gross profit percentage yields your break-even point. Think of it this way: However much money your business brings in, some of it will be eaten up by the cost of the product or service itself (your variable costs), leaving you a reduced amount left over to pay your bills. How much is left over is determined by your gross profit percentage—this number tells you just how much will be left over, on average, from each dollar, after paying for your product or service itself (your variable costs). When you divide your estimated annual fixed costs by your gross profit percentage, the resulting number (the break-even point) is the exact amount that's enough to cover your fixed costs.

If your break-even point isn't realistic, you'll have to evaluate whether you can make some sensible adjustments to your costs to generate a more achievable break-even point. For example, perhaps you could find a less expensive source of supplies, do without an employee, or save rent by working out of your home. After you've made these adjustments, rerun the calculation.

CAUTION

In business literature, break-even analysis can be described many different ways. For example, while we use a formula that includes gross profit percentage in the equation, others may use a formula using cost of goods as a variable. Some formulas yield the number of units you need to sell to break even; my analysis yields the total sales revenues you'll need to earn to break even. Also note that break-even analysis can get particularly complicated for businesses that sell many different types or categories of products. We offer a simple, streamlined approach intended to help you understand the basic formula and what the calculation represents.

Not Everyone Goes by the Book

As strongly as we recommend a business plan for every entrepreneur, we also know that some people suddenly find themselves in business without having tackled this step. Almost always, these are solo entrepreneurs who are starting without employees and without the need for significant start-up funds. For example, Kyle Zimmerman describes her experience of starting her photography studio as "backing into the business." She elaborates:

"Really, I kind of didn't think in terms of a business plan, or 'Wow, I'm going to start this business and I'm going to grow it, I'm going to end up having employees,' you know, I didn't have a plan. I just was one foot in front of the other. 'OK, I can't do it in my house, I'll have a space. Okay, I have a space, it costs a lot more money, I need to make more money. I need to get more work in the door. How do I do that? I'll add a person.' I just kind of organically grew it a step at a time, a day at a time, based on what I learned, because I didn't really know how to start a business. I just kind of did it."

Profit/Loss Forecast

If your break-even analysis shows that your business has a realistic chance of earning a profit, your next job is to create the profit/loss forecast (called a P & L forecast or an income statement) that estimates your profit or loss each month, based on revenue estimates, gross profit percentage, and fixed cost estimates. Every business plan should include a P & L forecast for a 12-month period; if you are seeking funding you may want to consider including additional forecasts, for Year Two or Three of the business.

While a break-even analysis calculates how much revenue you'll need to cover your fixed costs, a profit/loss forecast breaks down your income and expense estimates to calculate your profit (or loss) each month for a year or more. A P & L forecast will tell you whether your business operations are bringing in enough income to cover your expenses each month.

A profit/loss forecast is generated as follows:

1. Start by estimating your **monthly sales revenues.** In your research to come up with revenue estimates, you'll often find that trade journals, business newspapers, and other information sources use annual figures. If so, just break that figure down into estimates for each month, accounting for any seasonal sales fluctuations that you expect.

2. Next, figure your **gross profit for each month.** Do this by multiplying each month's sales revenue by the gross profit percentage for your business as a whole, which you calculated as part of your break-even analysis.

3. Determine your **monthly fixed expenses by category**, and add them together to get monthly totals.

4. Then, for each month, subtract your total fixed expenses from your gross profit and enter the result in the **net profit** row. If the result is a negative number, it means your expenses are more than your gross profit. Put parentheses around the result; in accounting symbols, a number in parentheses is a negative number.

FORM ON NOLO.COM

Profit/Loss Forecast Worksheet. The Nolo website includes an interactive worksheet to help you do a profit/loss forecast and step-by-step instructions for using it. See the appendix for a link to this and other worksheets in this book. For the automatic calculations in the worksheet to be active, you'll need to open the worksheet in a spreadsheet program such as Microsoft *Excel.*

CAUTION

Your P & L forecast isn't the whole picture. Other income and costs such as loans and start-up expenses aren't part of your P & L forecast, which reflects only money earned and spent as part of providing your products or services (sometimes called "operating income," as in, income generated from operations). For the full picture of all money that comes into and goes out from your business—including start-up costs, loans, taxes, and other money that isn't earned or spent as part of your core business operation—you'll need to do a cash flow analysis, discussed further below.

A completed P & L forecast will outline your business's profitability month by month. (Chapter 10 includes a sample P & L for an established business.) If your expenses are higher than revenues for a month or two, don't panic—most start-up businesses lose money for at least a few months—but you will need to figure out how to make it through these lean months (for example, by getting a start-up loan).

More important in the big picture is whether you can see a trend toward stable profitability over the long term. If you realize your plan needs revision to make the business realistic, resist the temptation to inflate your sales estimates. Instead, focus on lowering your costs, since costs are much easier to control than income.

Start-Up Cost Estimate

If your profit/loss forecast shows your projected income will be higher than expenses each month, you're on the right track. Next it's time to factor in your business start-up costs: the initial investment you'll have to make to get the business up and running. This basically includes everything you'll need to spend before you open your doors and start earning income.

Compared to the projections explained earlier, estimating your start-up costs is a breeze—just list them and add them up. Your list should include items like business registration fees and tax deposits you need to pay up front; prepaid rent and security deposits if you're renting outside space; costs of any initial inventory; computers and equipment; office supplies; insurance; employee salaries; fees for independent contractors and professionals (such as a Web developer to build your website, or a bookkeeper to set up your financial records); and anything else you'll have to cover before your business starts bringing in money.

If you don't have enough cash to pay all of your start-up costs out of pocket, you might be able to find a way to spread the costs over the first few months of business, when you'll have at least some cash flowing in. Your cash flow forecast, discussed next, is the tool to use in figuring out whether you can accomplish this. For instance, maybe you could lease, rather than buy, needed equipment, or purchase some items such as your computer and printer on credit. Or you may need to raise start-up money; see Chapter 3 for a detailed discussion of this task.

TIP
You may be able to deduct up to $5,000 of your start-up expenses, such as market research costs. See Chapter 11 for details.

Cash Flow Projection

A cash flow projection is an essential element in the financial portions of your business plan. Though your P & L forecast may show that your business will cover your estimated expenses, a cash flow projection analyzes whether the cash from those sales, as well as from other sources, such as loans or investments, will come in fast enough to pay your bills on time. Cash flow analysis accounts for the fact that there may be lag time between sales and the actual receipt of payment, which can dramatically affect your business's bottom line.

When your business is up and running, your cash flow projection will use actual income and expense data to help you project into the future and anticipate any cash shortages. (Chapter 10 includes a sample cash flow projection for an established business.) For this reason cash flow management is critical for any business—especially businesses with inventory, payroll, or other expenses that absolutely must be paid on time. Creating a projection showing a cash crunch well in advance will help you shift expenses, get a loan, or otherwise handle the situation before it's too late.

In your planning stages, a cash flow projection will help you survive the first few lean months of business, when income is likely to be slow and you may have start-up expenses to recoup. Seeing a projection of available cash may help you realize that you'll need to cut or delay some initial expenses, get a loan, or sell part of your business to investors.

Your cash flow projection will use many of the same figures you developed for your profit/loss forecast. The main difference is that you'll include all cash inflows and outflows, not just sales revenues and business expenses. Also, you'll record costs in the month that you expect to incur them, rather than simply spreading annual amounts equally over 12 months. Inflows and outflows of cash that belong in your cash flow analysis include loans, loan payments, and start-up costs. Once you're turning a profit, you'll also include income tax payments in your cash flow analysis, but, for now, assume that you'll be free from income taxes for your first year.

Here's the basic blueprint for a cash flow analysis:

1. For each month, start your projection with the actual amount of **existing cash** your business will have on hand.

2. Next, fill in your **projected cash-ins for the month**, which should include sales revenues, loans, transfers of personal money—basically, any money that goes into your business checking account. Add these together along with the cash you have at the beginning of the month to get your total cash-ins for the month.

3. Next, enter all your **projected cash-outs for the month**, such as your fixed expenses and any loan payments. Remember also to include costs of products and materials you use in your products or services—your variable costs. Add together all your cash-outs to obtain a total for the month.

4. Subtract total monthly cash-outs from total monthly cash-ins, and the result will be your **cash left at the end of the month**. That figure is also your beginning cash balance at the start of the next month; transfer it to the top of the next month's column, and do the whole process over again.

FORM ON NOLO.COM

Cash Flow Projection Worksheet. The Nolo website includes an interactive worksheet to help you do a cash flow forecast and step-by-step instructions for using it. See the appendix for a link to this and other worksheets in this book. For the automatic calculations in the worksheet to be active, you'll need to open the worksheet in a spreadsheet program such as Microsoft *Excel*.

Once you've completed a year's worth (or more, if you want) of a cash flow projection, you'll have a blueprint for your business's financial situation from month to month. If any months are projected to have a cash deficit, you'll need to tweak your plan to make sure you can cover all of your important expenses. As usual, this means you'll have to raise money, or juggle, reduce, or cut costs—not set unrealistic new sales targets.

Finalizing Your Business Plan

When you've finished drafting the narrative and financial sections of your business plan, it's time to think about how you want to package the plan, including how to format it and whether to tweak any of the sections to cater to specific audiences.

If you put the plan together for your own information, then you might want simply to review it, edit anything that needs fixing, print it out, and put it into a binder for your reference. As we've already explained, if you plan to present the information as part of a loan request or as a package for investors to review, you will want your plan to have a clean and professional layout. Unless you're a whiz with word processing or publishing software, you may find it difficult to format the text, and especially the financial tables, graphs, and other reports. A freelance graphic designer may be able to help you lay out the document professionally, which can go a long way in impressing your readers.

If you'll be presenting the business plan to outsiders, you may want to include additional information to help sell readers on your vision. To establish confidence in your team, consider including résumés for yourself, any co-owners, and any key managers. You could also include marketing materials such as brochures or screenshots from your website to show the brand image you've developed. It can also be helpful to include supplementary information, such as market data reports, articles from trade journals, or other external information that will support your plan and calculations. To make the report more readable, consider adding an executive summary at the beginning, highlighting the key points of the plan in no more than two or three pages.

You may find the need to include notes or explanations within your financial projections, particularly if you're providing the business plan to outside parties and need to explain any assumptions or details behind specific entries. Most spreadsheet software allows you to make annotations to individual entries to accomplish this. Another method is to include a concise narrative summary after each report, highlighting the result and adding any context that is necessary. Usually just a paragraph or two should do the trick.

Better late than never for a business plan

"I wrote my first business plan after being in business for ten years! It was part of the process of applying for a line of credit. We hadn't needed to borrow money to operate the business until our tenth year, hence, the business plan. I started Queen Bee on a small amount of money that I had saved from gifts over the years, and really by the seat of my pants. I didn't know anything about business, taxes, being an employer, etc. We enlisted the help of our business counselor to write a plan. It was a very good experience, just to be forced to think about the business, its mission, our goals, our obstacles. I find that writing things down often creates a structure for me to work with. What was hardest was just thinking about the business in such a seemingly dry way. I am a creative person and do not naturally gravitate toward such processes."

— **Rebecca Pearcy**

CHAPTER

5

Understanding and Choosing a Legal Structure

Choosing a legal structure for your business is one of the first steps in transforming your idea into an actual, legitimate business. For some, this is a particularly exciting moment. For others, uncertainty about the legal ins and outs of business structures turn this into a stalling point. But take heart: For the vast majority of small to medium-size start-ups, there's nothing terribly complicated about choosing and setting up the legal structure of the business.

In all states, the basic types of business entities are:

- sole proprietorships
- partnerships (general and limited)
- limited liability companies (LLCs), and
- corporations (including C and S types).

The differences among these types are fairly straightforward and easy to understand. In this chapter, I'll explain the characteristics, benefits, and drawbacks of each type of business structure, and help you figure out which one is best for your business.

TIP

You can change your business structure down the road, if your business grows or develops new needs. For example, if you start your tutoring business as a sole proprietor and later expand the business by taking on a partner, you can easily create a partnership, an LLC, or a corporation at that time. Or if you start your software firm as an LLC and later decide you want to issue shares, you can change the structure to a corporation.

RELATED TOPIC

Tax and bureaucratic details regarding each business type are covered in other chapters. Chapter 11 outlines the various taxes faced by different business types. Chapter 7 offers step-by-step instructions for tackling the bureaucratic hurdles involved in launching a business.

Overview of Business Types

Although I'm going to cover each business structure in detail in this chapter, it helps to have a general overview of how things work. The differences among the various business entities are most important in two areas: how taxes are paid, and who is liable for the business (for example, if you're sued because a defective product injures someone).

Here's a nutshell description of the distinctions among the basic business structures:

- **Businesses that operate as sole proprietorships or partnerships don't legally exist separately from their owners.** Taxwise, this means that the business itself doesn't pay taxes; the individual owners do. Any profits or losses "pass through" to the owners and are taxed as their personal income. In addition, the owners are personally liable for any business debts. This means that if your business fails and owes money to creditors, or someone wins a lawsuit against your company and its assets aren't enough to pay the judgment, you could find yourself paying with your house, car, or other personal assets. If you do not affirmatively choose a business structure, your business will by default be a sole proprietorship if you're the only owner, or a partnership, if you start the business with others.

- **Businesses that operate as LLCs or corporations are legally distinct from their owners;** they must be created by filing paperwork at the state level. The owners of LLCs and corporations are shielded from personal liability for business debts, which is one of the main reasons business owners choose these structures. In other words, creditors can come after business assets of an LLC or a corporation to satisfy a debt, but not the personal assets of the owners. LLCs and corporations differ from each other in how they are taxed: LLC income or losses are typically taxed as personal income or losses of the owners (like sole proprietorships or partners). However, corporations pay taxes themselves, separately from the owners.

Tax and Liability Treatment for Different Business Entities

Type of Entity	Personal Liability	Taxation
Sole proprietorships	Owners are personally liable for business debts	Profits/losses taxed on personal tax returns
Partnerships	Owners are personally liable for business debts	Profits/losses taxed on personal tax returns
Limited liability companies	Owners are shielded from personal liability for business debts	Profits/losses taxed on personal tax returns (unless the LLC chooses corporate tax treatment)
Corporations	Owners are shielded from personal liability for business debts	Corporation files its own tax return and is taxed as its own entity

CAUTION

Choose co-owners carefully. Owning and running a business with one or more people can be (and usually is) pretty intense. On a personal level, you'll want to make sure that you and any co-owners can work well together. Of course you won't agree 100% of the time, but if you constantly butt heads or aren't comfortable with each other's decisions, you'll have an awfully rocky road ahead of you. On a legal and financial level, it's critical that you trust your co-owners' good faith and good judgment. A co-owner's actions can have serious implications for the business and you personally, so use the utmost care when entering into a co-owner relationship. Working with co-owners is further discussed in Chapter 1.

Let's look at each business type in more detail.

Sole Proprietorships

SKIP AHEAD

Sole proprietorships are one-owner businesses. Any business with two or more owners cannot, by definition, be a sole proprietorship. If you know that there will be two or more owners of your business, you can skip this section.

Any one-person business that has not filed papers to become a corporation or an LLC is by default a sole proprietorship. It's that simple; there are no forms to file or other requirements to be a sole proprietorship. That's not to say there aren't other rules that may apply to your business—for instance, your city may require you to obtain a local tax registration certificate, license, or permit, or it may regulate what kinds of signs you may display at your place of business. But these bureaucratic hurdles shouldn't be viewed as part of any process of starting a sole proprietorship. In essence, there is no such process. A sole proprietorship is merely the default legal status for any solo person who engages in business. It's the most popular form of legal structure in the United States: About three-fourths of all businesses operate as sole proprietorships.

For instance, if you are a freelance photographer or writer, a craftsperson who takes jobs on a contract basis, or an independent consultant or contractor, and you haven't filed papers to create an LLC or a corporation, you are automatically a sole proprietor. This is true whether or not you've registered your business with your city or obtained any licenses or permits. And it makes no difference whether you also have a regular day job. This often comes as a surprise to folks who don't consider themselves "businesspeople" or what they do a "business," such as an artist who sells handpainted scarves at craft fairs every summer, or a musician who plays paid gigs every month or so. As long as you do for-profit work on your own (or sometimes with your spouse—see "Running a Business With Your Spouse," below), you are a sole proprietor.

Note that being a sole proprietor means that you are the only owner of the business—it doesn't mean that you're the only person working at the business. Sole proprietors can hire employees and independent contractors just like any other business type. More often than not, by the time a business is ready to hire staff, it will take on a more formal business structure, such as an LLC or corporation, if for no other reason than for protection from the liability risks that come with hiring staff (either employees or contractors).

> ⓘ CAUTION
>
> **Don't ignore local registration requirements and rules.** Most cities and many counties require businesses (even tiny home-based sole proprietorships) to register with them and pay at least a minimum tax. And if you do business under a name different from your own legal name, you usually must register that name—known as a fictitious business name—with your county. In practice, lots of small businesses ignore these requirements without consequence. But if you are caught, you may be subject to back taxes and other penalties. Skipping the formalities may also result in other snags such as not being able to open a business bank account. See Chapter 7 for an explanation of how to handle the necessary filings with the appropriate government offices and comply with requirements for permits and licenses.

Pass-Through Taxation

In the eyes of the law, a sole proprietorship is not legally separate from the person who owns it. This is one of the fundamental differences between a sole proprietorship and a corporation or an LLC, and it has two major effects: one related to taxation (explained in this section), and the other to personal liability (explained in the next).

At income tax time, a sole proprietor simply reports all business income or losses on her individual income tax return. The business itself is not taxed. The IRS calls this "pass-through" taxation, because business profits pass through the business to be taxed on the business owner's tax return.

Logistically, filing your taxes as a sole proprietor is very simple. You report income from a business just like wages from a job, except that, along with Form 1040, you'll need to include Schedule C (*Profit or Loss From Business*), on which you'll provide your business's profit and loss information. One helpful aspect of this arrangement is that if your business loses money—and, of course, many start-ups do in the first year or two as you get things off the ground—you can use the business losses to offset any taxable income you have earned from other sources.

EXAMPLE: Kate has a day job managing a neighborhood cafe, where she earns a modest salary. But Kate's real passion is for dance, and she decides to earn some extra income by teaching children's dance classes. Kate signs a lease for a studio space which costs $450 per month. She also buys some mirrors, mats, and other supplies which cost approximately $1,500 total, bringing her yearly costs to $6,900. She expects to earn approximately $600 per month in class fees, calculated at $15 per child, with a goal of ten children in the class and one class per week. This would result in an annual income of $7,200, and Kate thinks she can likely exceed that goal by having more than ten students in each class. Unfortunately, each month, Kate notices that the classes often have fewer than ten students. When Kate closes out her books at year-end, her income totals $4,320, leaving her in the red by $2,580. While Kate was disappointed that she didn't at least break even, the silver lining is that her loss of $2,580 can be counted against her income from her day job, reducing her taxes and translating into a nice refund check.

⚠ CAUTION

Your business can't lose money forever. Besides the obvious financial reality of needing to turn a profit at some point, there is also the issue that the IRS may deny a deduction for a losing business that it views as lacking a true profit motive. See the discussion of tax rules for money-losing businesses in Chapter 11.

RELATED TOPIC

Solid record keeping is essential, even for microbusinesses. If for no other reason than to file taxes properly and claim all the deductions you're entitled to, even tiny sole proprietorships need to treat financial management seriously. Make sure you have a separate business bank account and keep accurate records of all income and expenses. Bookkeeping and financial management are discussed in detail in Chapter 10.

Running a Business With Your Spouse

If your spouse will help with your business, there are some IRS rules to be aware of regarding what type of legal entity a husband/wife enterprise can be. These rules have tax implications which we describe below; small business taxes are described in more detail in Chapter 11.

Normally, two nonmarried people working at a business that's not an LLC or a corporation would be considered one of two things: (1) partners in a partnership, or (2) one would be considered a sole proprietor and the other an employee.

If the two are considered to be business partners, they will need to file a partnership tax return and each person would have to pay self-employment taxes on their share of business income. If one person is considered to be a sole proprietor, then she would owe self-employment taxes on her business income, and payroll taxes would apply to the employee's wages. Self-employment taxes and payroll taxes are essentially the same tax: They consist of Social Security and Medicare taxes. For details on this significant tax liability, see "Federal Income and Self-Employment Taxes" in Chapter 11.

With spouses, however, the IRS is more forgiving. The IRS typically allows a spouse to work without pay without being classified as an owner or as an employee of the other spouse's business. This situation is sometimes loosely called a "husband-wife sole proprietorship."

Having your spouse volunteer frees the business from paying payroll tax. That saves you money—and, if you have no other employees, also allows you to avoid the time-consuming record keeping involved in being an employer. Similarly, a spouse who is not classified as a partner won't have to pay self-employment taxes, and your business won't have to file a partnership tax return. On the downside, your spouse will not get Social Security or Medicare account credit.

If you and your spouse both want to be active managers of a co-owned business (as opposed to one spouse being the decision maker, and one being a worker) there's another IRS rule you should know about. Before

Running a Business With Your Spouse (continued)

2007, the IRS required married couples who co-owned a business, and who hadn't formed an LLC or a corporation, to file as a partnership—involving significantly more complicated tax returns than the relatively simple Schedule C form filed by sole proprietors. As of 2007, the IRS now allows husband-wife co-owners to file as "co-sole proprietors," which each filing their own Schedule C reporting his and her share of profits or losses. Each spouse will need to pay self-employment tax—but on the bright side, both spouses will receive Social Security and Medicare credits. Plus, the tax return will be considerably simpler. Note that this is only an option for married co-owners who haven't formed an LLC or a corporation. Owners of LLCs must file the more complicated partnership tax return, and corporations must file corporate tax returns for the business. See Chapter 11 for details on tax filing requirements.

If your spouse tries to squeak by as a volunteer when you're really working together as co-owners, you run the risk of being audited, having the IRS declare you're a partnership, and socking your spouse with back self-employment taxes.

For more information on the tax and entity implications of having your spouse participate in your business, see *Tax Savvy for Small Business*, by Frederick Daily and Jeffrey A. Quinn (Nolo).

Also consider that under marital property laws that vary from state to state, if a business is started or significantly changed when a couple is married, both spouses may have an ownership interest in the business regardless of whose name is on the ownership document.

If you are concerned about the possible consequences of divorce, read Nolo's *Business Buyout Agreements*, by attorneys Bethany Laurence and Anthony Mancuso, which discusses how divorce and other life events, such as retirement and death, can affect ownership of a business and explains how to plan in advance to accommodate the possibilities. You may also want to check with a lawyer who is experienced in handling marital property issues to see how your business could be affected in the event of a divorce in your particular state.

Personal Liability for Business Debts

Another crucial aspect of operating your business as a sole proprietor is that you, as the owner of the business, can be held personally liable for business-related obligations. This means that if your business doesn't pay a supplier, defaults on a debt, loses a lawsuit, or otherwise finds itself in financial hot water, you, personally, can be forced to pay up. This can be a sobering possibility, especially if you own (or soon hope to own) a house, a car, or other assets. Personal liability for business obligations stems from the fundamental legal attribute of being a sole proprietor: You and your business are legally one and the same.

As explained in more detail below, the law provides owners of LLCs and corporations "limited personal liability" for business obligations. This means that, unlike sole proprietors and general partners, owners of corporations and LLCs can normally keep their houses, investments, and other personal property even if their businesses fail.

Remember that insurance is an important tool that businesses of all types can use to protect themselves, and an active approach to minimizing your business's risks is also essential. (See "Analyzing Your Risks," below.) But insurance only goes so far. While insurance may protect you against a slip-and-fall lawsuit, it won't help you if your business simply fails to make a profit and ends up in deep debt. In that situation, a sole proprietor will be personally liable for satisfying those debts, which is a bad place to be.

In short, liability issues are the primary reason that business owners opt against sole proprietorships. If you're planning to start a tiny business that won't get into much debt and has an extremely low chance of facing any type of lawsuit, a sole proprietorship may be a fine choice. For example, a freelance writer or a knitting teacher might reasonably feel confident that operating as a sole proprietorship won't expose them to excessive liability. On the other hand, a dog boarding business (what if a dog was lost or hurt?) or a carpenter (what if you accidentally damage a structure?) would be well advised to consider a business type that provides limited personal liability, such as an LLC or a corporation. Ditto for any larger business that will be dealing with regular interactions with the public, significant amounts of money, high-dollar contracts, or other possible sources of lawsuits and liability.

Analyzing Your Risks: When an LLC or a Corporation Might Be Your Best Choice

Starting a business is always risky. In some businesses, however, the risks are particularly extreme. If you're planning to launch an investment firm or start a commercial building construction company, there is little doubt that you'll need all the protection you can get, including limited personal liability as well as adequate insurance. Other businesses are not so obviously risk laden, but still could land you in trouble if fate strikes you a blow. When analyzing your business, consider the following red flags for riskiness:

- using hazardous materials, such as dry cleaning solvents or photographic chemicals, or hazardous processes, such as welding or operating heavy machinery
- manufacturing or selling edible goods
- driving as part of the job
- building or repairing structures or vehicles
- caring for children or animals
- providing or allowing access to alcohol
- conducting or allowing activities that may result in injury, such as personal training or skateboarding, and
- repairing or working on items of value, such as cars or antiques.

If you've identified one or more serious risks your business is likely to face, figure out whether business insurance might give you enough protection. Some risk, such as from job-related driving, can be almost entirely managed by insurance. (Chapter 6 discusses insurance for both home-based businesses and those renting commercial space.) But if insurance can't cover all of the risks involved in your business, it may be time to form an LLC or a corporation.

Keep in mind that insurance will never insulate you from regular business debts. If you foresee your business's going into serious debt, an LLC or a corporation may be the best business structure for you.

CAUTION

Consider your funding needs in choosing a business entity. If you plan to seek equity financing, you'll need a business entity other than a sole proprietorship so you can provide an ownership share to the financer(s). If you plan to approach venture capital firms, you may want to structure as a corporation so you can issue stock.

Partnerships

Partnerships are quite similar to sole proprietorships, with the crucial difference being that the business is owned by two or more people. When two or more people engage in business activity and they have not filed papers with the state to become a corporation or an LLC (or another less common business form), by default the business is considered a partnership.

CAUTION

Partnerships and registration requirements. Though businesses with two or more owners are partnerships by default, they still must satisfy various governmental requirements for starting a business. See "Don't ignore local registration requirements and rules," under "Sole Proprietorships," above.

RELATED TOPIC

A certified "women-owned" business needs to be at least 51% owned by one or more women. Becoming certified as a women-owned business may help you obtain government contracts and be eligible for other programs. If you take on partners and want to become certified as women-owned, make sure to keep at least 51% of the ownership shares in the hands of women. Chapter 2 discusses the benefits of being a women-owned business and how to become certified.

General vs. Limited Partnerships

Usually, when you hear the term "partnership," it means *a general partnership*. As discussed in more detail below, general partners are personally liable for all business debts, including court judgments. In addition, each individual partner can be sued for the full amount of any business debt (though that partner can turn around and sue the other partners for their shares of the debt).

Another critical aspect of general partnerships is that any individual partner can bind the whole business to a contract or business deal—in other words, each partner has "agency authority" for the partnership. And remember, each of the partners is fully personally liable for a business deal gone sour, no matter which partner signed the contract. So choose your partners carefully.

There are also a few special kinds of partnerships, called limited partnerships and limited liability partnerships. They operate under very different rules and are relatively uncommon, so we'll look at them only briefly here.

A *limited partnership* requires at least one general partner and at least one limited partner. The general partner has the same role as in a general partnership: She controls the company's day-to-day operations and is personally liable for business debts. The limited partner contributes financially to the partnership but has minimal control over business decisions or operations, and normally cannot bind the partnership to business deals. In return for giving up management power, a limited partner gets the benefit of protection from personal liability. This means that a limited partner can't be forced to pay off business debts or claims with personal assets, but she can lose her investment in the business.

> EXAMPLE: A limited partner in an investment company contributes $100,000 to a real estate partnership. Within a year, the real estate market plummets and the partnership finds itself in debt for more than $1 million. The limited partner will lose the $100,000 she invested, but because she is a limited partner, her personal assets will not be vulnerable to pay off the rest of the business's debts. The partnership's general partners, on the other hand, will face personal liability for those debts.

Limited partners need to stay out of management activities in order to maintain their limited personal liability. If the limited partner participates in the control of the business, she can be liable to third parties who reasonably believed, based on the limited partner's conduct, that the limited partner was a general partner. For example, if a limited partner in a real estate limited partnership negotiated a deal with a home staging business and led the home stager to believe that she had authority as a general partner, she could be liable for the entire amount owed to the home staging business.

Another kind of partnership, called a *limited liability partnership (LLP)* or sometimes a *registered limited liability partnership (RLLP)*, provides all of its owners with limited personal liability. In some states, these partnerships are only available to professionals such as lawyers and accountants, and are particularly well suited to them. Most professionals aren't keen on general partnerships, because they don't want to be personally liable for another partner's problems—particularly those involving malpractice claims. Forming a corporation to protect personal assets may be too much trouble, and some states won't allow professionals such as lawyers to form an LLC. The solution is often a limited liability partnership. This business structure protects each partner from debts against the partnership arising from professional malpractice lawsuits against another partner. (A partner who loses a malpractice suit because of personal mistakes, however, doesn't escape liability.)

Pass-Through Taxation

Similar to a sole proprietorship, a partnership (general or limited) is not a separate tax entity from its owners; instead, it's what the IRS calls a "pass-through entity." This means the partnership itself does not pay any income taxes; rather, income passes through the business to each partner, who pay taxes on their share of profit (or deducts a share of losses) on their individual income tax returns—Form 1040, with Schedule E (*Supplemental Income and Loss*) attached. However, the partnership must also file what the IRS calls an "informational return"—Form 1065 (*U.S. Return of Partnership Income*)—to let the government know how much the business earned or lost that year. No tax is paid with this return—just think of it as the feds' way of letting you know they're watching.

Personal Liability for Business Debts

Since a partnership is legally inseparable from its owners, just like a sole proprietorship, general partners are personally liable for business-related obligations. What's more, in a general partnership, the business actions of any one partner bind the other partners, who can be held personally liable for those actions. So if your business partner takes out an ill-advised high-interest loan on behalf of the partnership, makes a terrible business deal, or gets in some other business mischief without your knowledge, you could be held personally responsible for any debts that result.

> EXAMPLE: Marie and Ivy are general partners in a profitable plant nursery specializing in native and drought-tolerant plants for sustainable landscapes. They've been in business for five years and have earned healthy profits, allowing them each to buy a house, newer cars, and even a few luxuries—including Marie's collection of garden sculptures and Ivy's roomful of vintage musical instruments. One day, Marie finds a website offering fertile hemp seeds that she knows would be a hit with their customers. She orders two cases of the seeds, without telling Ivy. But when the shipment arrives, so do agents of the federal drug enforcement agency, who confiscate the seeds which, as it turns out, violate U.S. drug laws. Soon thereafter, criminal charges are filed against Marie and Ivy. Though the partners are ultimately cleared, their attorney fees come to $50,000 and they lose several key accounts, putting the business into serious debt. As a general partner, Ivy is personally liable for these debts even though she had nothing to do with the ill-fated hemp seed purchase.

Before you get too worried about personal liability, keep in mind that many small businesses don't face much of a risk of racking up large debts. For instance, if you're engaged in a low-risk enterprise such as freelance editing, landscaping, or running a small band that plays weddings and other social events, your risk of facing massive debt or a huge lawsuit is pretty small. For these types of small, low-risk businesses, a good business insurance policy that covers most liability risks is almost always enough to protect owners from a catastrophe like a lawsuit or fire. Insurance won't cover regular business debts, however. If you have significant personal assets like fat bank accounts or real estate and plan to rack up some business debt, you may want to limit your personal liability with a different business structure, such as an LLC or a corporation.

Partnership Agreements

With a partnership agreement, you can structure your relationship with your partners pretty much however you want. You and your partners can establish the shares of profits (or losses) each partner will receive, what the management responsibilities of each partner will be, what should happen to the partnership if a partner leaves, and how a number of other issues will be handled. It is not legally necessary for a partnership to have a written agreement; the simple act of two or more people doing business together creates a partnership. But a clear written agreement is essential so that all partners will be on the same page regarding the important—and sometimes sensitive—details of their business arrangement.

In the absence of a partnership agreement, your state's version of the Uniform Partnership Act (UPA) or Revised Uniform Partnership Act (RUPA) kicks in as a standard, bottom-line guide to the rights and responsibilities of each partner. Most states have adopted the UPA or RUPA in some form. In California, for example, if you don't have a partnership agreement, then California's RUPA states that each partner has an equal share in the business's profits, losses, and management power. Similarly, unless you provide otherwise in a written agreement, a California partnership won't be able to add a new partner without the unanimous consent of all partners.

What's important to understand is that you can override many of the legal provisions contained in the UPA or RUPA if you and your partners have your own written agreement.

What a Partnership Agreement Can't Do

Although a general partnership agreement is an incredibly flexible tool for defining the ownership interests, work responsibilities, and other rights of partners, there are some things it can't do. These include:

- freeing the partners from personal liability for business debts
- restricting any partner's right to inspect the business books and records
- affecting the rights of third parties in relation to the partnership—for example, a partnership agreement that says a partner has no right to sign contracts won't affect the rights of an outsider who signs a contract with that partner, and
- eliminating or weakening the duty of trust (the fiduciary duty) each partner owes to the other partners.

There's nothing terribly complex about drafting partnership agreements. They're usually only a few pages long and cover basic issues that you've probably thought over to some degree already. Partnership agreements typically include at least the following information:

- name of partnership and partnership business
- date of partnership creation
- purpose of partnership
- contributions (cash, property, and work) of each partner to the partnership
- each partner's share of profits and losses
- provisions for taking profits out of the company (often called partners' draws)
- each partner's management power and duties, such as what departments they will manage and specific responsibilities such as hiring or budgeting
- how the partnership will handle departure of a partner, including buyout terms
- provisions for adding or expelling a partner, and
- dispute resolution procedures.

These and any other terms you include in a partnership agreement can be dealt with in more or less detail. Some partnership agreements cover each topic with a sentence or two; others spend up to a few pages on each provision. Of course, you need an agreement that's appropriate for the size and formality of your business, but it's not a good idea to skimp on your partnership agreement.

Take a look at the short sample partnership agreement below to see how a very basic partnership agreement can be put together. This sample is about as basic as it gets—the bare minimum—and you'll almost surely want to use something more detailed for your business.

FORM ON NOLO.COM

A Partnership Agreement Template is on Nolo's website. See the appendix for a link to this and other worksheets in this book. The partnership agreement template on the Nolo website includes a few more basics than the sample shown below.

RESOURCE

For more on partnerships. *Form a Partnership: The Complete Legal Guide*, by Denis Clifford and Ralph Warner (Nolo), is an excellent step-by-step guide to putting together a solid, comprehensive partnership agreement. Also, *Business Buyout Agreements: A Step-by-Step Guide for Co-Owners*, by Bethany Laurence and Anthony Mancuso (Nolo), explains how to draft terms that will enable you to deal with business ownership transitions.

Limited Liability Companies (LLCs)

The limited liability company (LLC) offers the simplicity and tax benefits of pass-through taxation (as with sole proprietorships and partnerships) without the exposure to personal liability. Traditionally, to obtain protection from personal liability, business owners would have had to form a corporation, which is a separate legal entity from its owners. (Corporations are discussed in detail in the next section.) LLCs

Sample Partnership Agreement

Krista Roybal, Sarah Wentzel, and Sage Harrington agree to the terms of the following agreement.

1. **Name of Partnership.** Krista, Sarah, and Sage are partners in the Spin-a-Yarn Partnership. They created the partnership on July 12, 20xx.

2. **Partnership Purpose.** The Spin-a-Yarn Partnership will operate a knitting studio in Chicago, Illinois, that will offer knitting and crocheting lessons, and a store with yarn and knitting/crocheting supplies.

3. **Contributions to the Partnership.** Krista, Sarah, and Sage will contribute the following to the partnership:

   Krista: $5,000 cash; one Macintosh computer (value $1,500); and one monitor (value $500).

   Sarah: $2,000 cash; one fax machine (value $400); one laser printer (value $1,200).

   Sage: $5,000 cash; various office equipment (value $500).

4. **Profits and Losses.** Krista, Sarah, and Sage shall share profits and losses as follows:

Krista	40%
Sarah	20%
Sage	40%

5. **Partnership Decisions.** Krista, Sarah, and Sage will have the following management authority:

Krista	2 votes
Sarah	1 vote
Sage	2 votes

6. **Additional Terms to Be Drafted.** Krista, Sarah, and Sage agree that in six months they will sign a formal partnership agreement which

covers the items in this agreement in more detail, and the additional following items:

- each partner's work contributions
- provisions for adding a partner
- provisions for the departure of a partner, and
- provisions for selling the business.

7. **Amendments.** This agreement may not be amended without the written consent of all partners.

Krista Roybal

Signature: _____ Date: _____

Social Security Number: _____

Sarah Wentzel

Signature: _____ Date: _____

Social Security Number: _____

Sage Harrington

Signature: _____ Date: _____

Social Security Number: _____

are less complex and costly to start and operate than corporations, and as a result have become increasingly popular in recent years.

> **CAUTION**
> **LLC laws and rules vary from state to state.** For example, California prohibits licensed professionals from organizing as an LLC (but not as a professional corporation or limited partnership). Some other states have extra LLC formalities for licensed professionals, which you can discover by asking your state licensing board.

Limited Personal Liability

Generally speaking, owners of an LLC are not personally liable for the LLC's debts. (There are some exceptions to this rule, discussed below.) This protects the owners from legal and financial liability in case their business fails or loses a lawsuit and can't pay its debts. In those situations, creditors can take all of the LLC's assets, but they generally can't get at the personal assets of the LLC's owners. Of course, no one wants to lose their business, but it's a lot better to lose only what you put into your business than to say goodbye to everything you own.

> **EXAMPLE:** Kayte and Debbie are starting a business offering in-home health care. They have worked as health care professionals for roughly 15 years apiece and have done well financially, with significant assets between them. They each contribute $15,000 to the business which in large part goes toward buying medical supplies, setting up a patient database that will facilitate insurance processing, purchasing computer equipment, and other start-up costs. Kayte and Debbie are willing to risk their investment to pursue their business, but they worry that if the business fails they'll be buried in debt. They decide to form an LLC so that, if the business should fail, they'll lose only their $30,000 investment; no one will be able to sue them personally for any additional business debts beyond that amount. Kayte and Debbie feel much less anxious with the knowledge that if their business fails, they won't be at risk of losing their homes or other assets.

Keep in mind that, like a general partner in a partnership, any member of a member-managed LLC can legally bind the entire LLC to a contract or business transaction. In other words, each member can act as an agent of the LLC. (Some LLCs are managed by managers, instead of by members. In manager-managed LLCs, any manager can bind the LLC to a business contract or deal.)

While LLC owners enjoy limited personal liability for many of their business debts, this protection is not absolute. There are several situations in which an LLC owner may become personally liable for business debts or claims. However, this drawback is not unique to LLCs—the limited liability protection given to LLC members is just as strong as (if not stronger than) that enjoyed by the corporate shareholders of small corporations. Here are the main situations where LLC owners can still be held personally liable for debts:

- **Personal guarantees.** If you give a personal guarantee on a loan to the LLC, then you are personally liable for repaying that loan. Because banks and other lenders often require personal guarantees, this is a good reason to be a conservative borrower. Of course, if no personal guarantee is made, then only the LLC—not the individual members—is liable for the debt.

- **Taxes.** The IRS or the state tax agency may go after the personal assets of LLC owners for overdue federal and state business tax debts, particularly overdue payroll taxes. This is most likely to happen to members of small LLCs who have an active hand in managing the business, rather than to passive members.

- **Negligent or intentional acts.** An LLC owner who intentionally or even carelessly hurts someone will usually face personal liability. For example, if an LLC owner takes a client to lunch, has a few martinis, and injures the client in a car accident on the way home, the LLC owner can be held personally liable for the client's injuries.

- **Breach of fiduciary duty.** LLC owners have a legal duty to act in the best interest of their company and its members. This legal obligation is known as a "fiduciary duty," or is sometimes simply called a "duty of care." An LLC owner who violates this duty can be held personally liable for any damages that result from the owner's actions (or inactions). Fortunately for LLC owners, they normally will not be held personally responsible for any honest mistakes or acts of poor judgment they commit in doing their jobs. Most often, breach of duty is found only for serious indiscretions such as fraud or other illegal behavior. For example, if an LLC member ignored repeated warnings and written reports that one of its manufacturers was using toxic ingredients in the pet products sold by the corporation, that member could be held personally liable for any damages that result from that breach of duty to the company.

- **Blurring the boundaries between the LLC and its owners.** When owners fail to respect the separate legal existence of their LLC, but instead treat it as an extension of their personal affairs, a court may ignore the existence of the LLC and rule that the owners are personally liable for business debts and liabilities. Generally, this is more likely to occur in one-member LLCs; in reality, it only happens in extreme cases. You can easily avoid it by opening a separate LLC checking account, getting a federal employer identification number, keeping separate accounting books for your LLC, and funding your LLC adequately enough to be able to meet foreseeable expenses.

Finally, bear in mind that while limited personal liability can prevent you from losing your home, car, bank account, and other assets, it won't protect you from losing your investment in your business. You can (and should) protect your business with insurance, which can prevent your business from getting wiped out if a customer, an employee, or a supplier wins a big lawsuit against it and the business has to be liquidated to cover the debt. But remember, insurance won't help if you simply can't pay your normal business debts. In that case, you may lose your business, but the LLC will protect your personal assets.

There's a new flavor of LLC on the scene: the low-profit limited liability company, or L3C. For details, see the section on emerging business structures at the end of this chapter.

LLC Taxation

Like a sole proprietorship or a partnership, an LLC is not a separate tax entity from its owners; instead, it's what the IRS calls a pass-through entity. This means the LLC itself does not pay any income taxes; instead, income passes through the business to each LLC owner, who pays taxes on the share of profit (or deducts the share of losses) on the owner's individual income tax return (for the feds, Form 1040 with Schedule E, *Supplemental Income and Loss*, attached). But a multi-owned LLC, like a partnership, does have to file Form 1065—an "informational return"—to let the government know how much the business earned or lost that year. No tax is paid with this return.

By filing a form with the IRS (Form 8832, *Entity Classification Election*), you can choose to have your LLC taxed like a corporation rather than as a pass-through entity. (In fact, partnerships have this option as well, but it is rarely exercised.) You may wonder why LLC owners would choose to be taxed as a corporation. After all, pass-through taxation is one of the most popular features of an LLC. The answer is that, because of the income-splitting strategy of corporations (discussed under "Corporate Taxation," below), LLC members can sometimes come out ahead by having their business taxed as a separate entity at corporate tax rates.

For example, if the owners of an LLC become successful enough to keep some profits in the business at the end of the year (or regularly need to keep significant profits in the business for upcoming expenses), paying tax at corporate tax rates can save them money. That's because federal income tax rates for corporations start at a lower rate than the rates for individuals. For this reason, many LLCs start out being taxed as partnerships, and when they make enough profit to justify keeping some in the business (rather than doling it out as salaries and bonuses), they opt for corporate-style taxation. (See Chapter 11 for more about taxes.)

LLCs vs. S Corporations

Before LLCs came along, the only way all owners of a business could get limited personal liability was to form a corporation. Problem was, many entrepreneurs didn't want the hassle and expense of incorporating, not to mention the headache of dealing with corporate taxation. One easier option was to form a special type of corporation known as an S corporation, which is like a normal corporation in most respects, except that business profits pass through to the owner (as in a sole proprietorship or partnership), rather than being taxed to the corporation at corporate tax rates. In other words, S corporations offered the limited liability of a corporation with the pass-through taxation of a sole proprietorship or partnership. For a long time, this was an okay compromise for small- to medium-sized businesses, though they still had to deal with requirements of running an S corporation (discussed in more detail below).

Now, however, LLCs offer a better option. LLCs are indeed similar to S corporations in that they combine limited personal liability with pass-through tax status. But a significant difference between these two types of businesses is that LLCs are not bound by the many regulations that govern S corporations.

Here's a quick rundown of the major areas of difference between S corporations and LLCs. (Keep in mind that corporations, including S corporations, are explained in more detail in the next section.)

- **Ownership restrictions.** An S corporation may not have more than 75 shareholders, all of whom must be U.S. citizens or residents. This means that some of the C corporation's main benefits—namely, the ability to set up stock option and bonus plans and to bring in public capital—are pretty much out of the question for S corporations. And even if an S corporation initially meets the U.S. citizen or resident requirement, its shareholders can't sell shares to another company (like a corporation or an LLC) or a foreign citizen, on pain of losing S corporation tax status. In an LLC, any type of person or entity can become a member—a U.S. citizen, a citizen of a foreign country, another LLC, a corporation, or a limited partnership.

LLCs vs. S Corporations (continued)

- **Allocation of profits and losses.** Shareholders of an S corporation must allocate profits according to the percentage of stock each owner has. For example, a shareholder who owns 25% of the S corp's stock has to receive 25% of the profits (or losses), even if the owners want a different division. Owners of an LLC, on the other hand, may distribute profits (and the tax burden that goes with them) however they see fit, without regard to each member's ownership share in the company. For instance, a member of an LLC who owns 25% of the business can receive 50% of the profits if the other members agree (subject to a few IRS rules).

- **Corporate meeting and record-keeping rules.** For S corporation shareholders to keep their limited liability protection, they have to follow the corporate rules: issuing stock, electing officers, holding regular board of directors' and shareholders' meetings, keeping corporate minutes of all meetings, and following the mandatory rules found in their state's corporation code. By contrast, LLC owners don't need to jump through most of these legal hoops—they just have to make sure their management team is in agreement on major decisions and go about their business.

- **Tax treatment of losses.** S corporation shareholders are at a disadvantage if their company goes into substantial debt—for instance, if it borrows money to open the business or buy real estate. That's because an S corporation's business debt cannot be passed along to its shareholders unless they have personally cosigned and guaranteed the debt. LLC owners, on the other hand, normally can reap the tax benefits of any business debt, cosigned or not. This can translate into a nice tax break for owners of LLCs that carry debt.

Forming an LLC

To form an LLC, you must file articles of organization (sometimes called certificate of organization or formation) with your secretary of state or another LLC filing office. The office will reject your LLC name if it's already being used by another LLC in the state database, so you'll need to make sure your name is unique before filing your paperwork. But don't make the mistake of believing your chosen name is clear to use just because it's not being used by another LLC in your state—you need to also make sure it doesn't pose a trademark conflict. (For more on LLC name and filing requirements, including a discussion of trademarks, see Chapter 7, which focuses on bureaucratic hurdles.)

RESOURCE

More on secretary of state offices. To find your secretary of state's website (many of which offer forms and instructions for creating an LLC), see the National Association of Secretaries of State at www.nass.org.

In addition to filing this paperwork with the state, you should also execute an operating agreement, which governs the internal workings of your LLC. Roughly analogous to partnership agreements, LLC operating agreements cover topics such as each owner's percentage of ownership in the LLC, each owner's share of profits (or losses), each owner's rights and responsibilities, and what will happen to the business if an owner leaves. Depending on your business and the number of people, the LLC operating agreement can be quite detailed; see the resource list below for several Nolo products to help you create a solid operating agreement.

Remember that additional bureaucratic requirements from the local to the federal level may apply to your business, independent of the LLC formation process. We cover these start-up hurdles in Chapter 7.

While starting an LLC is quite easy bureaucratically speaking, you should be aware that it might be more expensive to start than a partnership or sole proprietorship. A few states charge significant filing fees, plus annual dues (alternately called minimum taxes, annual fees, or renewal fees). These fees can push the costs of starting an LLC into the several-hundred-dollar range. Illinois, for instance, charges a $500 filing fee, and California requires that you pay a minimum annual LLC tax of $800 when you start your LLC—on top of its $70 filing fee. Many brand-new business owners aren't in a position to pay this kind of money right out of the starting gate, so they start out as partnerships until they bring in enough income to cover these costs. And if you're thinking of forming a corporation instead, keep in mind that most states charge at least as much in fees for corporations. This, plus the added expenses of running a corporation (legal and accounting fees, for example), will almost always make a corporation more expensive to run than an LLC.

CAUTION

Some LLCs must comply with securities laws. LLCs that have owners who do not actively participate in the business may have to register their membership interests as securities or, more likely, qualify for an exemption to the registration requirements. For information about exemptions to the federal securities laws, visit the U.S. Securities and Exchange Commission's website at www.sec.gov and click "Information For: Small Businesses."

RESOURCE

Recommended reading on LLCs. Nolo publishes several resources on forming an LLC, all by Anthony Mancuso and available at www.nolo.com. These include:

- *Form Your Own Limited Liability Company.* Provides detailed information on LLCs, including step-by-step instructions and forms to help you create articles of organization, operating agreements, meeting minutes, and more.
- *LLC or Corporation?* Explains the legal and tax differences between LLCs and corporations.

- *Your Limited Liability Company: An Operating Manual.* Covers how to prepare minutes of meetings, record important business, tax, and legal decisions, and more.
- *Nolo's Quick LLC: All You Need to Know About Limited Liability Companies.* Offers an overview of LLCs, as well as comparison to other business structures, but does not include any start-up forms.
- *Nolo's Guide to Single-Member LLCs,* by David M. Steingold. Provides an overview of how to form a single-member LLC, including unique tax and liability issues.
- If you want to create your LLC directly on the Internet, use Nolo's online LLC formation service.

Finally, the LLCs section of www.nolo.com includes detailed state-by-state advice on forming an LLC (along with dozens of articles related to business formation).

Corporations

For many, the term "corporation" conjures up the image of a massive industrial empire more akin to a nation-state than a small business. In fact, a corporation doesn't have to be huge, and most aren't. Stripped to its essentials, a corporation is simply a specific legal structure that imposes certain legal and tax rules on its owners (also called shareholders). A corporation can be as large as IBM or, in many cases, as small as one person.

One fundamental legal characteristic of a corporation is that it's a separate legal entity from its owners. If you've already read this chapter's sections on sole proprietorships and partnerships, you'll recognize that this is a major difference between those unincorporated business types and corporations. Another important corporate feature is that shareholders are normally protected from personal liability for business debts. Finally, the corporation itself—not just the shareholders—is subject to income tax.

SEE AN EXPERT

Running a publicly traded corporation is complex. This section discusses privately held corporations owned by a small group of people who are actively involved in running the business. These corporations are much easier to manage than public corporations, whose shares are sold to the public at large. Any corporation that sells its stock to the general public is heavily regulated by state and federal securities laws, while corporations that sell shares, without advertising, only to a select group of people who meet specific state requirements, are often exempt from many of these laws. If you plan to sell shares of a corporation to the general public, you should consult a lawyer.

Limited Personal Liability

Owners of a corporation are generally not personally liable for the corporation's debts. (There are some exceptions to this rule, discussed below.) Limited personal liability is a major reason why owners have traditionally chosen to incorporate their businesses: to protect themselves personally from legal and financial responsibility in case their business flounders or loses an expensive lawsuit and can't pay its debts. In those situations, creditors can take all of the corporation's assets (including the shareholders' investments), but they generally can't get at the personal assets of the shareholders.

> EXAMPLE: Carolyn and Stacey publish GreenScape, a glossy monthly magazine on landscape design. They decide to structure the business as a corporation in order to protect their personal assets, and to provide a way to raise start-up capital in the future by selling shares in the corporation to select investors. The magazine does well for several years, during which Carolyn and Stacey recoup their initial investments in the business. Just as they were considering selling some shares to raise funds for an expansion in distribution, their fortunes change. A recession causes a steep decline in advertising dollars. Subscriptions start to falter as well, and within a few months Carolyn and Stacey find it difficult to pay their printer and other critical bills. They finally decide to call it quits when a key advertiser fails to renew its contract. When they close their doors, GreenScape owes its creditors nearly $350,000 while its assets are valued at just $75,000. Carolyn and Stacey are deeply disappointed at the demise of their magazine, but are thankful that they won't be personally responsible for their debt since as owners of a corporation, they're shielded from personal liability.

Forming a corporation to shield yourself from personal liability for business obligations provides good, but not complete, protection for your personal assets. Corporation owners still face personal liability when it comes to personal guarantees, overdue taxes, negligent or intentional acts, and breach of fiduciary duty. For details on these liabilities (which are the same for LLCs and corporations), see "Limited Personal Liability" in the LLC section, above.

CAUTION
Keep your corporate veil intact. When corporate owners ignore corporate formalities and treat the corporation like an unincorporated business, a court may ignore the existence of the corporation (in legal slang, "pierce the corporate veil") and rule that the owners are personally liable for business debts and liabilities. To avoid this, it's important for corporate owners not to allow the legal boundary between the corporation and its owners to grow fuzzy. Owners need to scrupulously respect corporate formalities by holding shareholders' and directors' meetings, keeping attentive minutes, issuing stock certificates, and maintaining corporate accounts strictly separate from personal funds.

Remember that having limited personal liability won't protect you from losing your investment in your business. Insurance can be an important source of protection against catastrophes such as lawsuits, fires, or theft. But if you just can't pay your normal business debts, insurance won't help you. In that case, having a corporation will protect your personal assets, but not the business itself.

Corporate Taxation

Corporate taxes are more complicated than taxes for a pass-through entity (like a sole proprietorship, a partnership, or an LLC) for a number of reasons, including the fact that a corporation exists as a separate legal entity from its owners. To give you a general idea of how corporations are taxed we'll provide a brief overview. If you decide to incorporate, you'll likely want to consult an accountant or a small business lawyer who can fill you in on the fine print. (See Chapter 13 for information on finding and hiring a lawyer and an accountant.) Undoubtedly, you'll have a CPA or another tax professional actually prepare your returns.

First, you'll be treated differently for tax purposes depending on whether you operate as a regular corporation (also called a C corporation) or you elect S corporation status for tax purposes. An S corporation is the same as a C corporation in most respects, but when it comes to taxes, C and S corporations are very different animals. A regular, or C, corporation must pay taxes itself, while an S corporation is treated like a partnership for tax purposes and doesn't pay any income taxes separately from the owners. Like partnership profits, S corporation profits (and losses) pass through to the shareholders, who report them on their individual returns. (In this respect, S corporations are very similar to LLCs, which also offer limited liability along with partnership-style tax treatment.) These two types of corporations are explained in more detail just below.

Deductibility of Fringes and Perks

Like employee salaries, corporations can deduct many fringe benefits as business expenses. If a corporation pays for benefits such as health and disability insurance for its employees and owner/employees, the cost can usually be deducted from the corporate income, reducing a possible tax bill. (There's one main exception: Benefits given to an owner/employee of an S corporation who owns 2% or more of the stock can't be deducted as business expenses.)

As a general rule, owners of sole proprietorships, partnerships, and LLCs can deduct the cost of providing these benefits for employees, but not for themselves. (These owners can, however, deduct a portion of their medical insurance premiums, though it's technically a deduction for the individuals, not a business expense.)

The fact that fringe benefits for owners are deductible for corporations may make incorporating a wise choice. But it's less likely to be a winning strategy for a capital-poor start-up that can't afford to underwrite a benefits package.

C Corporations

As a separate tax entity, a regular corporation must file and pay income taxes on its own tax return, much like an individual does. After deductions for employee compensation, fringe benefits, and all other reasonable and necessary business expenses have been subtracted from its earnings, a corporation pays tax on whatever profit remains.

In small corporations in which all of the owners of the business are also employees, all of the corporation's profits are often paid out in tax-deductible salaries and fringe benefits—leaving no corporate profit and, thus, no corporate taxes due. (The owner/employees must, of course, pay income tax on their salaries on their individual returns.)

Marginal Tax Rates for Corporations

The following chart shows tax rates for corporations. For example, if a corporation's taxable income was $75,100, it would pay 15% of its first $50,000 of income, 25% of the next $25,000, and 34% on its remaining $100 in income. The corporation's marginal tax rate—the tax rate a corporation would pay on the last dollar of its income—would be 34%.

Taxable Income	Tax Rate
0 to $50,000	15%
$50,001 to $75,000	25%
$75,001 to $100,000	34%
$100,001 to $335,000	39%
$335,001 to $10,000,000	34%
$10,000,001 to $15,000,000	35%
$15,000,001 to $18,333,333	38%
Over $18,333,333	35%

Note: These corporate rates don't apply to professional corporations, which are subject to a flat tax of 35% on all corporate income.

Initial rates of corporate taxation are comparatively low (see "Marginal Tax Rates for Corporations," above). Corporations that keep some profits in the business from one year to the next—rather than paying out all profits as salaries and bonuses—can take advantage of 15% to 25% tax brackets. This practice, sometimes called income-splitting, basically involves strategically setting salaries at a level so that money left in the business is taxable only at the 15% or 25% corporate tax rate (which applies to profits up to $50,000 or $75,000). Since any amount of "reasonable" compensation to employees is deductible, corporate owners have lots of leeway in setting salaries to accomplish this.

> **EXAMPLE:** Chantal and Sophie are the owners of a successful software company. In one profitable year, they calculated their profit to be approximately $180,000. That year, they decided to give themselves each a $65,000 bonus out of the profit (on top of their $70,000 salaries). Because both salaries and bonuses are tax-deductible business expenses, this reduced their business's taxable income to $50,000, which was taxed at only 15%, the lowest corporate rate. If Chantal and Sophie had left all the profits in the business, the profits over $50,000 would have been taxed at 25%, profits over $75,000 at 34%, and profits over $100,000 at a whopping 39%. Of course, the bonuses Chantal and Sophie gave themselves increased their personal income, which was taxed on their individual returns. Still, their personal tax rates were lower than the high corporate rates of 34% and 39%, resulting in an overall tax savings.

This income-splitting strategy is available only to shareholders who also work for the corporation. If they're not at least part-time employees, then shareholders won't be in a position to earn salaries or bonuses and will be able to take money from the corporation only as dividends.

Double Taxation

This brings us to the vexing problem of double taxation, routinely faced by larger corporations with shareholders who aren't active employees. Unlike salaries and bonuses, dividends paid to shareholders cannot be deducted as business expenses from corporate earnings. Because they're not deducted, any amounts paid as dividends are included in the total corporate profit and taxed. And when the shareholder receives the dividend, it is taxed at the shareholder's individual tax rate as part of personal income. As you can see, any money paid out as a dividend gets taxed twice: once at the corporate level, and once at the individual level. You can avoid double taxation simply by not paying dividends. This is usually easy if all shareholders are employees, but probably more difficult if some shareholders are passive investors anxious for a reasonable return on their investments.

S Corporations

Unlike a regular corporation, an S corporation does not pay taxes itself. Any profits pass through to the owners, who pay taxes on income as if the business were a sole proprietorship, a partnership, or an LLC. Yet the business is still a corporation. This means, as we've discussed, that its owners are protected from personal liability for business debts, just as shareholders of C corporations and members (owners) of LLCs are. Until the relatively recent arrival of the LLC, the S corporation was the business form of choice for those who wanted limited liability protection without the two-tiered tax structure of a C corporation. Today, relatively few businesses are organized as S corporations, because S corporations are subject to many regulations that do not apply to LLCs. (See "LLCs vs. S Corporations," above, for more information.)

Forming and Running a Corporation

In addition to tax complexity, major drawbacks to forming a corporation —either a C or an S type—are time and expense. Unlike sole proprietorships and partnerships, you can't clap your hands twice and conjure up a corporation. To incorporate, you must file articles of incorporation with your secretary of state or other corporate filing office (find yours at www. nass.org), along with often hefty filing fees and minimum annual taxes.

And if you decide to sell shares of the corporation to the public—as opposed to keeping them in the hands of a relatively small number of owners—you'll have to comply with lots of complex federal and state securities laws. Finally, to protect your limited personal liability, you need to act like a corporation, which means adopting bylaws, issuing stock to shareholders, maintaining records of various meetings of directors and shareholders, and keeping records and transactions of the business separate from those of the owners.

RELATED TOPIC

Corporate name and other bureaucratic requirements. As with creating an LLC, you'll need to make sure your chosen corporate name meets all state requirements—in particular, that no other corporation in your state is using your corporate name. It's equally important that your chosen name doesn't pose a trademark conflict. We discuss corporate name and filing requirements, and also trademark rules, further in Chapter 7, which focuses on bureaucratic hurdles independent of the incorporation process.

CAUTION

Corporations must comply with securities laws. Corporations must either register their shares with the Securities and Exchange Commission or qualify for an exemption to securities registration requirements. For information about small business exemptions to the federal securities laws, visit the Securities and Exchange Commission's website at www.sec.gov.

To sum up, the protection afforded by incorporating comes at a price. Figure in the likelihood that you'll have to hire lawyers, accountants, and other professionals to keep your corporation in compliance, and it's easy to see how expensive running a corporation can be.

RESOURCE

Recommended reading on corporations. Nolo publishes two comprehensive resources on forming and running a corporation, both by Anthony Mancuso and available at www.nolo.com: *Incorporate Your Business: A Step-by-Step Guide to Forming a Corporation in Any State,* and *The Corporate Records Handbook: Meetings, Minutes & Resolutions.* Also, the Corporations section of www.nolo.com includes detailed state-by-state advice on forming a corporation (along with dozens of articles related to business formation).

Benefit Corporations, L3Cs, and Emerging Business Structures for Socially Conscious, Mission-Driven Businesses

Entrepreneurs who start businesses that want to emphasize sustainability or other goals in the public interest sometimes wonder if they should start a regular for-profit business versus structuring as a nonprofit. The nonprofit structure, however, is fundamentally different from a for-profit business and business owners may find it too constraining on important issues such as being able to make a profit and needing to manage the business with a board of directors.

RESOURCE

The basics of starting a nonprofit. *Starting & Building a Nonprofit*, by Peri Pakroo (Nolo), provides step-by-step advice on getting a nonprofit up and running, from obtaining federal tax-exempt status to recruiting and managing board members. Also, check out the Nonprofits section of Nolo.com for dozens of articles on the subject.

In recent years, businesses in many states have some new options that are somewhat like for-profit/nonprofit hybrids. Three new structures are benefit corporations, Certified B Corps, and LC3s.

Benefit Corporations

A benefit corporation is legally required to prioritize a positive social impact in addition to making profits for shareholders. Structuring as a benefit corporation may be appealing for businesses that want to incorporate a social mission into the core of their business.

Specifically, benefit corporations feature the following elements:

- The corporation has a **purpose** to create a material positive impact on society and the environment.
- The corporation is **accountable** through a fiduciary duty not only to corporate shareholders, but also to workers, community and the environment.

- The corporation is run **transparently**, and must publish public annual reports on overall social and environmental performance against an independent and transparent third-party standard.

As of late 2015, legislation has been passed allowing benefit corporations in the following states: Arizona, Arkansas, California, Colorado, Delaware, Florida, Hawaii, Idaho, Illinois, Indiana, Louisiana, Maryland, Massachusetts, Minnesota, Montana, Nebraska, Nevada, New Hampshire, New Jersey, New York, Oregon, Pennsylvania, Rhode Island, South Carolina, Tennessee, Utah, Vermont, Virginia, Washington DC, and West Virginia. Legislation has been introduced in several other states. For updated information, visit the Benefit Corp Information Center at www.benefitcorp.net.

Certified B Corps

Benefit corporations are virtually identical to another structure called a Certified B Corp, which is a business that has been assessed and certified to meet sustainability-related criteria by B Lab, a nonprofit. The difference between benefit corporations and Certified B Corps is just that benefit corporations are an actual corporate structure recognized by the state, while the Certified B Corp is a certification conferred by a nonprofit.

If you live in a state that does not recognize benefit corporations, you can still seek to be certified as a Certified B Corp. For more information, check out B Lab's website at www.bcorporation.net.

Low-Profit Limited Liability Companies (L3Cs)

Another hybrid-type business structure available in several states is the low-profit limited liability company, or L3C. An L3C is similar to a nonprofit in that its primary purpose must be to benefit the public. But an L3C is run like a regular profit-making business and is allowed to make a profit as a secondary goal. This type of business structure was born so that charitably oriented LLCs could receive seed money (specifically, "program-related investments," or PRIs) from large nonprofit foundations, taking advantage of IRS rules that allow foundations to invest in businesses principally formed to advance charitable purposes.

A small but growing number of states allow L3Cs, including Illinois, Kansas, Louisiana, Maine, Michigan, Rhode Island, Utah, Vermont, and Wyoming. It has also been adopted by the tribal governments of the Oglala Sioux Tribe and the Crow Indian Nation of Montana. However, because it's such a new business structure and definitive rulings on various aspects of L3Cs have not yet been issued by the IRS, plenty of questions remain. Keep an ear to the ground as the L3C develops.

For more information and the latest news on L3Cs and other emerging legal structures, check out the Nonprofit Law Blog (www.nonprofitlawblog.com). Also see Americans for Community Development (www.americansforcommunitydevelopment.org) which specifically focuses on L3C developments.

Choosing the Best Legal Structure for Your Business

When you boil down the differences among the various types of business organizations, most business owners choose operating structures based on one legal issue: the personal liability of owners for business debts. In particular, the LLC is more popular than ever because it offers that protection from personal liability along with the simplicity of pass-through taxation.

While protecting yourself from personal liability is never a bad idea, bear in mind that in some situations it may be perfectly acceptable to take the simple route and conduct business as a sole proprietorship or partnership. If your risks are so low as to be nonexistent, or if you simply don't have any personal assets worth protecting, you might be well advised to wait on forming an LLC or a corporation until your circumstances change.

On the other hand, any business that will engage in a high-risk activity, rack up large business debts, or have a significant number of investors should always insist on limited personal liability, either with an LLC or a corporation. This is even more true if the business can't find or afford appropriate insurance.

If you decide that limiting your personal liability is worth the extra cost and effort, you still need to decide whether to form a corporation or an LLC. With the LLC's arrival, many business owners who want limited liability protection realize that incorporation normally only makes sense if a business needs to take advantage of the corporate stock structure to attract key employees and investment capital. No question, corporations may have an easier time attracting capital investment by issuing stock privately or publicly. And some businesses may find it easier to attract and retain key employees by issuing employee stock options. But for a business that never intends to issue stock or go public, choosing to operate as an LLC rather than a corporation normally makes the most sense, if limited liability is the main concern. If the corporate stock structure isn't something you want or need for your business, the simplicity and flexibility of LLCs offer a clear advantage over corporations.

If you're still not sure what entity seems best for your circumstances, a consultation with a lawyer or an accountant might prove helpful. This is particularly advised if you have specific questions about whether you can minimize your taxes by structuring your business in a certain way.

SEE AN EXPERT

Location matters. Another important consideration in choosing your business structure may be related to the state you choose to locate it in, especially if you are going into business with people who do not live in your state. This is because states differ widely in how they tax different business entities and nonresident business owners. There can be big state tax complications when a business either operates in more than one state or has owners in more than one state. A tax attorney can tell you whether you can reduce your taxes and increase profits by choosing one state over the other as your headquarters.

Your Business Location: Working From Home or Renting Space

Finding and setting up a business space is an exciting milestone in starting any business. If you rent space, setting up shop can be exhilarating—from peering into the windows of a vacant office, retail space, or studio, to negotiating and signing the lease, to buying and installing the furniture and equipment—as your vision becomes reality. While setting up a home office might not be quite as thrilling, it is still a great feeling to create a base of operations that meets your business needs, allows for flexibility, and reflects your unique personality. For many entrepreneurs, the simple fact that the business is yours and that you can design it yourself is an incredibly liberating feeling—especially for those who suffered in beige cubicles for years!

When choosing a business space there are a few considerations to keep in mind. One is to make sure that the location actually makes sense for your type of business. If you're considering basing your business from home, you'll need to make a realistic assessment of whether it will work: Will it be a comfortable place to meet clients? If kids are in the picture, will they create havoc at your home business? While the flexibility of having a home-based business can be great, you should only go this route if the business is a good fit with your home life.

If it makes more sense to rent commercial space, you'll need to decide where to do so. Some businesses are highly dependent on their location while others aren't as sensitive. It's also critically important that the location you choose (whether your home or a commercial space) is legally acceptable—as in, zoned appropriately—for whatever you plan to do there.

This chapter will help you figure out how to find a suitable place that meets all your business, budget, and family needs and that complies with your local laws. I'll outline practical and legal considerations both for home businesses and commercial spaces, including zoning basics and insurance; home business tax deductions; and what to look for in commercial leases. I'll also offer tips for getting and staying organized in your workspace. For those of you who may not be sure if you're ready to rent a space outside your home, I'll also cover various options for sharing space, which is an increasingly popular and money-saving alternative to renting a space on your own.

> SKIP AHEAD
>
> **Planning to rent commercial space?** If you've already decided that you want to go this route, skip ahead to "Renting Your Own Office or Commercial Space," below. That section covers special issues such as finding the right commercial space and location, complying with zoning laws, and key terms in commercial leases.

Running Your Business From Home

For the last couple of decades, home-based businesses have been a transformative phenomenon in the world of small business. Sure, entrepreneurs have started businesses in living rooms and garages for generations, but what's different now is that the home isn't just an incubator: Businesses are staying put and even growing into highly profitable enterprises without ever leaving the nest, so to speak. Thanks to fast, affordable Internet connections and wireless networks, it's never been easier to exchange documents, do research, send emails, teleconference, and otherwise be connected to the world without setting foot outside your door. Many successful entrepreneurs have a major presence in the marketplace while occupying just a small footprint in their homes. According to www.business.gov (an official website of the U.S. government), over half of all U.S. businesses are based out of their owners' homes.

Working from home has many advantages:

- **Convenience.** Eliminating a commute saves valuable time each and every day. Compared to a half-hour commute each way, and estimating 250 work days of the year, working at home will save you 250 hours (that's six work weeks!) per year. This doesn't even include unforeseen hassles like getting caught in traffic or missing your bus or train to an office. Plus, for better or worse, small business owners tend to work long, irregular hours, so having your office at home makes it easier to work when you want to, or when you're inspired, even if you're in your pajamas.
- **Cost-savings.** An obvious benefit of a home business is that you save money that would otherwise be spent on renting space.

Plus, you won't have to shell out money for additional utilities, furniture, and equipment that you'd need to purchase for a commercial space. Commute costs—gas, car wear and tear, or public transportation fees—are also eliminated. (And you might even save money on work clothes, depending on your business.)

- **Flexibility.** Working from home allows you to deal with your nonbusiness life when necessary—for example, if a plumber is coming by, or if you need to care for kids who are sick and home from school. But don't fool yourself; you can't fully care for your kids or supervise a plumber's work and run your business at the same time (I can attest to this personally). But in a pinch, when you need to be home for whatever reasons, it can definitely help to have your business located at your house so you can squeeze in important work tasks when possible. Running back and forth between your home and an office in these situations is a big waste of your precious time. On the flip side, some businesses are not well suited to being run out of your home, and some homes just can't accommodate a business. It's also important to understand that home businesses aren't immune from the bureaucratic rules and laws, such as local zoning requirements, governing small businesses. Finally, there are several special tax rules for home businesses, as well as insurance issues, that you should understand.

Before we take a closer look at these issues, let us offer some big-picture advice. If you do run your business from your home, this absolutely doesn't mean you should run your business any less seriously. All of the factors that make a business successful are just as important for home businesses as for more traditional companies. You'll need to have a winning product or service that appeals to a profitable customer base, market it well, and manage the many aspects of your business—from your finances to your inventory to your staff—competently and efficiently.

The sections below explain the important rules you need to know before hanging out your shingle at home.

Working at home for the long term

"It's just the best way to do it that I can imagine, although it's not without its sacrifices of course. While I'm doing the work I love, I get little breaks where I can spend time with my toddler, and rather than having him far away from me where I don't know how he's being treated, I can rest assured that his wonderful nanny is keeping him happy, because my child care is happening just on the other side of the closed office door. And I get more time to take care of my home life—that is, cooking and keeping my husband comfortable. I can choose which hours or days to work and which to run errands or take care of family. In that way I 'have it all.' On the other hand, I can't spend as much time with my son as I wish I could—sometimes I can hear him giggling or crying in the other room and I wish I could go be with him. I'm pretty good at tuning out the distractions but I sometimes find by trying to do both things, I am doing neither one with the excellence and high standards that I wish for."

— **Isabel Walcott Draves**

Is Your Business a Good Fit for Your Home?

Basing your business from home can be a smart, frugal choice. But while some businesses are well suited for home offices, some are not. Working from home tends to work well for the following types of businesses:

- service-oriented businesses and freelancers, especially if they don't see too much client traffic; graphic designers, accountants, consultants, Web developers, writers, and similar small service firms for example.
- businesses in which most of the dirty work is routinely done offsite, such as plumbing, electrical, or building contractor firms
- Web-based and mail-order businesses that interact with customers solely online and sometimes by phone, and
- art and craft businesses that focus on handmade products, which by their very nature are not mass-produced and don't require manufacturing or industrial space.

On the other hand, some businesses just don't fit well into a home environment. When considering whether basing your business from home is a good idea, ask yourself the following questions. If you answer no to more than a few of the questions that apply to your business, you should seriously consider finding outside space:

- Will it be convenient to interact with customers and suppliers? Will they be able to easily park and pick up or unload material if necessary?
- Does your home have enough space for a regular co-owner or employee? How about meetings of more than a few people?
- Do you feel safe and comfortable seeing clients or customers in your home (for example, if you're a therapist or a designer)?
- Do you expect your neighbors to be okay with your home business? (In particularly quiet neighborhoods, neighbors might object even to light traffic from clients or coworkers.)
- Will your clients or customers take you and your company seriously if you work out of your house? Will a home office present a professional image?
- Will your home space be large enough for any services your business performs, such as furniture refinishing or bicycle repair?
- Does your home have adequate electrical circuits, including any high-capacity circuits necessary for tools or equipment?
- Will your home space provide enough ventilation for any potentially toxic activities? Will you be able to set it up to safely store or dispose of hazardous materials?
- Does your house have enough space for storing supplies or inventory?
- If you rent, will your landlord give your business the thumbs up?

CAUTION

Lacking the funds to rent an outside space isn't a good enough reason to base your business at home. Some of you may want to locate your business at home primarily to save money. But if your business isn't a good fit for a home business, don't make the mistake of ignoring the signs and working from home anyway. One option is to rework your business plan, minimizing or eliminating other expenses so that you can afford the space you need. Another alternative is to wait to launch your business until you have saved enough money to rent an appropriate space. Or, consider sharing business space with another business. We discuss that option in "Sharing Outside Office Space," below.

Balancing Family, Kids, and Home Businesses

Many women are drawn to self-employment in order to have more flexibility to spend time with their children and families. And, for this same reason, lots of women entrepreneurs want to work from home. If you're hoping a home business will allow you to spend more time with your kids, a reality check is in order. While it is possible that a home business can afford you more time with your loved ones, the balancing act is by no means an easy one. Every mom who has run a home business knows the sinking feeling of having her child screaming in the background during an important client phone call, or leaving peanut butter handprints on a project contract.

At a minimum, don't make the mistake of thinking that basing your business from home will enable you do full-time child care, particularly if your children are young. It may be possible to start a small, part-time freelance business while being your kids' primary caretaker, but you won't likely be able to work anything close to full time. (And if you do, plan on being incredibly stressed.) If you're starting a larger home business, you'll definitely need some child care help. Once your business is up and running you may be able to scale back your hours and spend more time with your kids (especially if you hire an assistant or employees), but the start-up days of even a small to medium-size business are very time intensive whether it's based in an office or at home.

If you have a spouse or partner and don't need a second income, he or she could help with child care instead of working at a job. Of course, many start-ups won't bring in enough income in the early days to support a family, so this may not be an option. Some couples manage to both work full or part time and care for the kids by splitting their work hours; say, dad starts work in the early morning while mom takes care of the kids; then at around noon mom starts work while dad handles child care until bedtime. This approach can be grueling, but it's an option to consider.

Another possibility is to hire a nanny or babysitter to take care of the kids while you're working. This way, you can be home with your kids but not have to be 100% engaged or on duty, allowing you to take care of business. A downside is cost. Another potential pitfall is that your kids may still insist on seeing you or being with you, even if a sitter or your spouse is there. Your proximity to the kids may be just too much for them to resist. Likewise, you may find it hard to concentrate with your children just a room or two away. To avoid this, be disciplined with your time, and be sure to set clear rules that everyone understands— including the kids and the child care provider, whether a paid sitter/ nanny or your spouse—about not disturbing mom except in truly urgent situations. Put a sign on your office door when you're in a phone meeting or working on an important deadline to make it clear you want no interruptions unless it's a truly urgent issue.

Finally, if having your kids home with you isn't a driving factor for choosing a home business, another option is to send them to a day care facility or preschool.

For more on child care and resources for arranging it, see "Child Care" in Chapter 3.

Preventing a Home Business From Taking Over Your Home

If you're not careful, every bit of available space in your home can quickly get eaten up by the business, including equipment like fax machines and printers, binders of financial records, file cabinets, marketing materials, and inventory. And if you're the disorganized type (you know who you are) the piles of paper, supplies, and other work-related materials can become a real eyesore and hamper your productivity. To prevent this, define a clearly demarcated space in your home (ideally, not your bedroom) for the business, and keep it organized. If you don't have a spare room that's big enough, or if you find the business keeps creeping throughout the house despite your best efforts, it may be a sign that you don't have enough (or the right kind of space) at your home and you should consider renting space.

Let's Get Organized

There are tons of books on getting organized, including some focused specifically on home offices. Spend a little time browsing your local or online bookstore to find one (or more) that meets your interests and needs. And, of course, there's no shortage of info online. One entertaining (and useful) website is www.workingnaked.net, run by Lisa Kanarek, the author of *Organize Your Home Office for Success* (Blakely Press). You'll also get lots of good ideas by looking at home office photos on www.houzz.com and www.pinterest.com.

If you're into organizing (hint: you subscribe to *Real Simple* magazine), you already know that Target, IKEA, and the Container Store have lots of organizing stuff. If you aren't naturally organized (especially if your workspace is small), it may be well worth your while to hire a professional organizer to help you—even a few hours can make a huge difference. Ask your friends and colleagues for recommendations, or check the National Association of Professional Organizers, www.napo.net for leads. Finally, if you need help with more than organizing your files, check out *Getting Things Done: The Art of Stress-Free Productivity*, by David Allen (Penguin).

Protecting Your Personal Life

When you live where you work, it's easy to find yourself working all the time. Similar to organizing the physical elements of your business, also organize your time and structure your day so that your business doesn't take over your life. Make a commitment not to work through dinner or at night unless it's absolutely necessary. Don't check work-related email or voicemail after hours—and make sure you have separate email and voicemail for personal use so you can stick to this rule.

In addition, make a point of getting out of the house regularly. Schedule coffee or lunch dates with your contacts (remember, networking is key for every business). Attend a conference or seminar relevant to your business, or go out on scouting missions and visit the competition. If you spend a lot of time on the computer, break up your day by taking your laptop to a coffee shop with WiFi. Do whatever it takes to avoid being isolated and burnt out, including taking personal time: See a matinee, take a yoga class, walk the dog, or have lunch with a friend away from home.

Zoning Restrictions for Home Businesses

As with leased commercial spaces, you need to make sure that the business activities you plan to carry on in your home do not violate any local zoning laws. As home businesses have exploded in popularity, more local governments have adopted specific zoning provisions to control them. Besides imposing various rules and restrictions, some areas may require you to apply for a special "home occupation permit" and possibly pay a modest fee before you begin operations. (Zoning laws typically refer to home businesses as "home occupations.")

In areas zoned for residential use only, the types of businesses allowed are typically pretty limited. A few areas actually forbid home businesses altogether. But most cities and counties allow home businesses that have little likelihood of causing noise or pollution, creating traffic, or otherwise disturbing the neighbors. Writers, photographers, artists, attorneys, accountants, architects, insurance brokers, piano teachers, tutors, and consultants are examples of businesspeople commonly allowed to work from home. Typically not allowed are retailers, automotive repair shops, cafés and bars, animal hospitals and breeders, or any type of adult-oriented businesses.

Some loft-type or urban apartments might be zoned for mixed use which allows a wider variety of activities. A common mixed-use setup is for the ground level to be used for commercial space and the upper level(s) for residential use. The allowed uses for the commercial space will depend on the specific zoning rules that apply to that building; common examples include a retail shop or an art studio.

Typical Restrictions on Home Businesses

Assuming that your local zoning laws do allow your type of home business, they are likely to impose some restrictions. On one hand, there's an awful lot of variation from city to city and county to county, so you absolutely need to find out the specific rules for your area and not assume there is a standard set of rules. On the other hand, some general types of restrictions (if not the actual details of the restrictions) are pretty common. These include:

- prohibiting any nonresidents of the home to be employed on-site, or restricting nonresident on-site employees to just one or two people
- requiring client or customer visits to the home office to be by appointment only
- restricting the business use of the home to a percentage of the floor space—say, no more than 25%
- prohibiting the use and/or parking of certain vehicles, such as trucks exceeding one ton
- restricting the number of customers that may come to your house—say, no more than two per day, and
- prohibiting signs outside of your house that advertise the business.

In addition to these general limitations, cities often impose restrictions on specific types of home businesses. For instance, a city might have a special rule for landscaping contractors that prohibits landscaping supplies from being kept at the home office.

Complying With Local Requirements

To find out the specific home occupation rules that apply to your business, contact the planning or zoning department for your city or county and ask for information on its rules for home businesses. Remember to ask whether any special rules exist for the specific type of business or activities you plan to conduct.

TIP

Local governments vary widely in the quality and clarity of zoning information offered to the public. Some areas have websites or pamphlets with clear, detailed information explaining home business restrictions and how to obtain any necessary permits. In other places, all that's available might be a grainy photocopy of the municipal code, which you'll have to decipher yourself. If there's no approval or permit process for home businesses in your area, it's generally up to you to comply with the local zoning codes. And those codes are subject to change; be sure to check with the local zoning offices for updates.

If you learn that your city does allow your type of home business in your area, you may have no further need to contact the zoning office. Many cities do not require any special permits, as long as a home business complies with all of the rules and restrictions contained in its planning code. Some cities, however, require all home business owners to get a "home occupation permit." Obtaining such a permit is usually a simple matter of filling out a form provided by the planning department and paying whatever fee may be required. If your business meets the restrictions your city imposes, your permit will be issued.

If you don't meet all of your city's rules for having a home occupation, or your area isn't zoned for your type of home business, you may be out of luck and simply not be allowed to run your business from home. In some locales, however, a home business that meets most but not all of the city's restrictions may be allowed to operate, but only if your business deviates from the rule in acceptable ways, and only after obtaining a home occupation permit.

EXAMPLE: Kira teaches guitar lessons at her home. She plans to offer individual lessons Monday through Friday, with approximately four classes per day. She also plans to offer one group lesson on Tuesday and Thursday with five students per class. Under her city's home occupation statute, no permit is necessary to run a home business unless the business sees more than two clients per day. In that case, a home occupation permit is required, and the limit of clients that may be seen at the home business is increased to ten. Kira obtains the home occupation permit and makes sure never to have more than ten clients at her house in any one day.

Finally, remember that you may also need to deal with other local permitting departments in addition to the zoning office. For example, depending on your business activities, you may need to get approvals from your county health or fire department. (See Chapter 7 for more on zoning and permits for your specific business.)

In the end, the most foolproof way to avoid trouble with zoning officials is to do your best to keep down your business's impact on the neighborhood. As long as you're not in flagrant violation of the zoning laws regarding home businesses and your neighbors are happy, you'll probably be fine.

Other Restrictions on Home Businesses: Condos and Rental Properties

Be aware that some condos, co-ops, and other buildings may have severely restrictive rules or outright prohibitions on home businesses. Private land use regulations may limit or prevent home businesses in condos, co-ops, planned subdivisions, or rental properties. Check the documents governing your home to see if you are bound by any such rules.

And if you rent, make sure your lease or rental agreement doesn't prohibit home businesses (or at least the kind you want to operate). Note that some states, including California and New York, limit landlords' ability to reject a tenant's child care business, based on strong public policies favoring home-based child care. If your lease specifies that the premises are "for residential purposes only," check with your landlord before you print business cards listing your home as your business address or start seeing clients at home. If you're working alone or your job primarily consists of making phone calls or using your computer, you should have no problem. Depending on the business, your landlord may require that you obtain certain types of liability insurance (discussed in "Risks and Insurance for Home Businesses," below).

Home Business Tax Deductions

When your business is located in your home, a pro rata share of your home expenses such as rent or depreciation, property taxes, utilities, and insurance may be deductible on your federal taxes. "Pro rata" simply means a share that's proportional to the percentage of home space that you use for your business. Alternatively, since tax year 2013, you can calculate your deduction using a simpler formula: the square footage of your home office multiplied by a rate specified by the IRS. We'll explain both of these methods of calculating your deduction below. Your business needs to satisfy some minimum criteria to qualify for the deduction; these are outlined below.

It's important to note that plenty of business expenses are fully deductible, even if your home office does not qualify for the federal deduction. For instance, you can always deduct office supplies, furniture, equipment that you use in your home office, and the cost of bringing a second telephone line into your home for business use, even if your business doesn't qualify for the home business deduction. If you do qualify, then additional expenses such as a portion of your rent, your utility bills and other indirect expenses can be deducted as well. As used in this chapter, "home business expenses" will refer to expenses that can only be claimed with the home business deduction.

This section explains which businesses may qualify for the home business tax deduction, offers general information about how the deduction is calculated, and points out other tax issues that apply. (For information on how businesses in general are taxed, see Chapter 11.)

IRS Requirements

First, some basics. The IRS definition of "home" is pretty broad, generally including any type of dwelling in which you can cook and sleep. This includes houses, condos, apartment units, mobile homes, boats, or wherever else you reside. Both renters and owners are eligible for taking the home business tax deduction.

Tax Concerns When Selling Your Home

Homeowners who operate (or are considering operating) businesses from home should be aware of a few tax rules that come into play when selling your home. These rules are too complicated to go into any real depth here, so be sure to talk to your accountant about any concerns you might have.

The good news: No tax on proportional gain. Before 2002, a home business owner who sold a home at a profit had to pay capital gains tax on the portion of the home used by the business. This was a widely cursed exception to the general IRS rule that exempted home sellers from capital gains taxes on gains up to $250,000 ($500,000 for married couples), as long as they owned and lived in the home for at least two of the last five years. As of 2002, this exception no longer exists. Now, when you sell your home at a gain, you do not need to allocate a portion of that gain to your home business. You can go ahead and claim all the home business tax deductions you're entitled to, without worrying that you'll be stuck with capital gains taxes for your home business portion. You'll only have to pay capital gains taxes if you exceeded the limits of $250,000 gain ($500,000 for married couples), which would apply whether or not you had a home business.

An important exception to the IRS's 2002 rule is that home businesses located in a separate structure will continue to be subject to capital gains taxes. So if you run your business from a separate, freestanding garage or shed, for example, you'll be stuck paying the gains taxes when you sell your home. To avoid this, stop claiming the home business tax deduction two years before you sell your home.

The bad news: Recaptured depreciation tax still in effect. The IRS's 2002 rule change does not change what's known as "depreciation recapture," however. As in the past, home business owners who sell their homes must still pay taxes on the depreciation deductions they've taken over the years. In other words, if you claim depreciation deductions for a home business, the total of those deductions will be taxed—"recaptured," if you will— when you sell your house.

The IRS has two requirements for any business owner who wants to deduct home business expenses (note that both criteria must be satisfied):

- You must regularly use part of your home exclusively for a trade or business.
- You must be able to show that you do one of the following things:
  - use your home as your principal place of business
  - meet patients, clients, or customers at home, or
  - use a separate structure on your property exclusively for business purposes.

Each of these criteria is examined a bit more closely below.

Exclusive and Regular Use of Home for Business

First, let's look at the "exclusive" part of the exclusive and regular requirement. Home business expenses may be deducted only for space in your home that is exclusively—as in, 100%—dedicated to business use. For example, a clothes designer who uses the dining room table to sketch out designs can't claim business deductions for using the dining room—assuming the dining room is also sometimes used for nonbusiness purposes such as eating and entertaining. A spare room, however, that's set up as an office space and used only for business would probably meet the exclusive use test. But if the room contains a bed for the occasional overnight guest or doubles as storage space for your kids' toys, then, technically, it wouldn't qualify.

The exclusive use rule has two exceptions if your business use is either (1) storing inventory or product samples, or (2) running a qualified day care center. In these two cases, you don't have to meet the exclusive use test. That is, the parts of the home you use for business—say, a closet for inventory storage or a living room for the day care center—may also be used for personal activities, and you will still qualify for the home business tax deduction. Note that the storage exception has a couple wrinkles (something the IRS has a special talent for): You must use a specific, identifiable space, such as a closet or garage, to store the items rather than having them scattered all over the house. And if you have a business location outside your home, you won't qualify for the deduction for storing inventory in a nonexclusive space.

> **EXAMPLE:** Erin runs a home business making and selling handmade blank books. She also sells instructional videos on how to do bookbinding, and regularly stores the inventory of DVDs in a large closet in her home. Because Erin has no other business location away from her home, she can claim a home business deduction for the closet space. This is true even though she also stores other things in that closet such as winter clothes and skis. However, if Erin ever opens an office or retail space outside her home, she will not be able to deduct the expenses of the DVD storage closet.

Compared to the twisty rules of the "exclusive use" test, the "regular use" test is a breeze. As long as you use your home business space for business on a frequent, continuing basis, rather than for a once-in-a-while trunk sale or another sporadic business activity, it will qualify for the tax deduction.

Principal Place of Business

Besides meeting the exclusive and regular use requirements, your home business space must also be the main place where you do business. Your home office will qualify as the principal place of business if you (1) use the office to conduct administrative or management activities, and (2) do not have an office or another business location outside your home set up to conduct these activities.

This rule is just as straightforward as it sounds. As long as you use your home office to keep track of your business files, do your book-keeping and accounting, maintain your client databases, or conduct whatever other type of administration is required—and you don't have a space away from home set up for these activities—your home office will be considered your principal place of business.

If your home business space doesn't satisfy the basic rule, there are two alternative ways that it can qualify as the principal place of business:

- **You regularly use the space to meet with clients or customers.** As long as you regularly use the home space to meet clients—say, once or twice a week—and don't use the space for nonbusiness purposes, you can claim the deduction for the space even if you have an office away from home.

- **The space is in a separate structure.** If your home office space is located in an external structure on your property—a detached garage, shed, or in-law unit, for example—and you regularly and exclusively use it for your business, it will qualify as your principal place of business even if you have another business space, such as a storefront or an office, and regardless of whether you meet clients or customers there.

Tips on Documenting Home Business Use

If you plan to claim home business tax deductions, you should make an effort to document your home office as a place of business. Here are some ways you can accomplish this.

- Take pictures of your home office and its features that show its business character: desks, computers, fax machines, calendars, filing systems, and the like.
- Draw a diagram showing the floor plan of your house with the home office clearly defined. Include room dimensions if possible.
- Keep a log of the times you work in the office.
- Keep a record of all client meetings at your office, including whom you met, when, and the subject of the meeting. Recording client visits to your home office is especially important if you also have an outside office.
- Get a separate phone line for the business.

Figuring Deductible Home Business Expenses

Once you've determined that you do in fact qualify for the home business tax deduction, the next question is exactly how much you can deduct. Obviously, you can't deduct all of your housing costs—only the expenses attributable to business purposes qualify.

Chances are that your accountant will do the nitty-gritty calculations involved in claiming the home business tax deduction. But having an overview of how this deduction works will help you understand which expenses you need to track, what measurements to make, and just generally help you manage the information that your accountant will need to make the deduction.

The old standard method, as defined by the IRS, is to determine a "business percentage" for your home—simply, the percentage of your home that is used for business. Then you'll need to categorize your home expenses and figure out to what extent they may be deducted.

Since tax year 2013, a new, simplified method has been an option to calculate your home office deduction: Multiply the square footage of your home office by a prescribed rate set by the IRS. We'll describe this below, after going through the old method which is still acceptable.

Calculating Business Percentage

You can calculate the percentage of your home used for business in one of two ways: the "square footage" method or the "number of rooms" method. Either approach is acceptable to the IRS.

- The **square footage method** simply divides the square footage of the business space by the square footage of the whole house. For instance, if you use 500 square feet for business, and your entire house takes up 2,000 square feet, then your business space uses 25% (500 ÷ 2,000) of your home.
- The **number-of-rooms method** is just as simple: If your house has five similarly sized rooms, and you use one of them for business, then the business uses 20% (1 ÷ 5) of your home.

Categorizing and Deducting Expenses

Once you have calculated a space percentage for your business, turn your attention to categorizing and listing the home office expenses you'll deduct. Home expenses fall into one of three categories—unrelated, direct, and indirect expenses—and each has different deductibility rules.

- **Unrelated expenses.** Expenses that are unrelated to your business space are not deductible at all. For example, you can't deduct the cost of repainting your bedroom or replacing your dining room window.
- **Direct expenses.** You can fully deduct expenses that directly affect your business space, such as the cost of installing new carpeting,

replacing a broken window, or repairing the heating vent in your office space. Note that direct expenses for a day care center may not be fully deductible.

- **Indirect expenses.** Expenses that affect the whole house—called indirect expenses—are deductible, but only partially so, based on the percentage of your home that is used for business. For instance, you can deduct a percentage of the cost of plumbing services, roof repairs, mortgage interest, real estate taxes, and utility bills. To calculate the portion of indirect expenses attributable to your business, you generally multiply the indirect expense by your business percentage. Rent, for example, is an easy expense to prorate. If your business uses 25% of your home, and your rent is $1,200 per month, then $300 per month is a deductible home business expense (25% x $1,200). The same simple approach generally works for calculating the deductible business portion of many other indirect expenses, such as homeowner's insurance, mortgage interest, home utilities, and repairs.

CAUTION

Repairs are generally deductible; permanent improvements are not. The IRS won't let you deduct the cost of major projects it considers "permanent improvements"—those that increase the value of property, add to its life, or give it a new or different use. The cost of repairs, on the other hand, may be deducted—either fully if a direct expense or partially if an indirect expense. The IRS defines "repairs" as those that "keep your home in good working order over its useful life."

If you own your home and you qualify for the home business tax deduction, an indirect expense that you may deduct is the depreciation of your home. Depreciation of your home is an allowance for the wear and tear inflicted upon it; the home business depreciation deduction is simply a deduction for the business portion of this. Calculating this deduction is more involved than the indirect expense deductions mentioned above so it's generally best to leave this for your accountant.

You'll need to provide your accountant information about the adjusted basis of your home and the fair market value of the home when you started using it for business, so be ready to dig up some of your real estate sales documents and appraisals.

Calculating Your Deduction With the Simplified Method

The simplified method for calculating your deduction does not change any rules regarding whether you're eligible for a home office deduction. It just offers a much simpler way to calculate your deduction.

Under the new rule, simply multiply the square footage of your home office by the IRS's prescribed rate. For tax year 2013, the rate is $5 per square foot, with a maximum footage allowed of 300 square feet. It's that simple.

Note that if you use the simplified method and you own your home, you cannot claim a depreciation deduction as described below. You still may claim deductions for mortgage interest and real estate taxes however, and you won't need to allocate these between your business and personal use.

For more information on the new simplified method, visit www.irs. gov (search "Simplified Option for Home Office Deduction").

RESOURCE

For more on IRS rules affecting home businesses. For more details on IRS requirements (such as "exclusive and regular use" rules and the deductibility of repairs versus permanent improvements and of direct vs. indirect expenses) download a copy of IRS Publication 587, *Business Use of Your Home*, from www. irs.gov. For detailed advice on tax deductions for home businesses, read *Home Business Tax Deductions: Keep What You Earn*, by Stephen Fishman (Nolo).

Risks and Insurance for Home Businesses

Remember my advice early in this chapter about being just as serious about running a home business as one on Main Street? The same goes for dealing with your home business's risk management and liability issues. Home businesses are often just as vulnerable to theft, fire, personal liability claims, and other risks as businesses based in storefronts or office buildings—sometimes even more vulnerable. It can be a real catastrophe if your computer system is stolen or destroyed, or if a client trips over your kid's skateboard on the way up your front walk and suffers an injury.

For starters, *do not* assume that business-related claims will be covered by a homeowners' or renter's policy. While many insurance companies will extend homeowners' coverage to a home business, they'll often require an endorsement—sometimes called a "floater" or "rider"—to a policy that specifically authorizes the coverage. You'll generally have to pay an extra premium for such an endorsement. Without one, the insurance company may deny claims related to a home business.

There may be other harsh consequences of running a business from home without informing your insurance company. In some cases, an insurance company may terminate your coverage altogether—even for nonbusiness claims—if it discovers that you've been running a business from your home without its authorization. In the event of a fire or a tree falling onto your house, the last thing you'll want to learn is that the insurance company denies your claim because it discovered you were running a business from the home. Ouch.

 TIP

Don't try to hide a home business from your insurance company. Apart from the fact that trying to deceive your insurance company is just a foolish idea, the insurance company would almost certainly take note of claims involving major business assets such as high-end computer systems, machine equipment, or inventories that seem excessive for home use. All it could take is a few questions or a visit from an insurance adjuster to expose your home business activity. When it comes to communicating with your insurer, the best advice is to be forthcoming.

Keep in mind that if your homeowners' policy does in fact cover home businesses—either with or without an endorsement—the coverage may be only for property loss, not for other claims such as liability or business interruption. If a client is injured on the stairs leading up to your front door, your business may have to pay for any damages awarded in a personal injury lawsuit, without any coverage from the homeowners' policy. And if your business records are destroyed in a fire, it's highly unlikely that your homeowners' policy would cover your financial losses because of your inability to collect accounts receivable or because you lost income from business downtime.

In short, don't find out about the limits of your homeowners' policy the hard way. If you have homeowners' or renters' insurance, contact the providing company and find out specifically how it deals with home businesses and what kinds of claims are covered. If an endorsement is required, the process is generally a simple matter of paying an extra premium and having documents drafted reflecting the home business coverage. Of course, you'll need to make sure that:

- the coverage limits are sufficient to cover the value of your business equipment, and
- liability or loss-of-income claims are covered (if not, and if these risks are a concern, you may need to purchase additional coverage).

Finally, make sure you obtain workers' compensation insurance and meet other requirements that apply if you have employees. You won't need workers' comp insurance if you hire independent contractors, just regular employees. See Chapter 12 for more about the legal requirements that apply to businesses that hire staff, either as independent contractors or employees.

 TIP
Home business coverage is becoming more widely available.
Insurance companies are increasingly willing to insure home businesses, no doubt due to the massive growth of this market. The good news is that costs are generally not prohibitive. An endorsement for a home business is typically no more than $1,000 a year—and sometimes much less. Another option is a "home business-type" policy that's becoming more common. These are distinct from homeowner's policies but aren't quite as robust as full commercial policies, and as a result are generally a good value. Larger businesses with significant assets or risks may need to look at full commercial policies, which may be more expensive. Ask your insurance broker for details.

If your current insurer doesn't offer the coverage you need, one possibility is to find a policy with a different company that meets your requirements. Another option, whether or not you have existing home coverage, is to look for a separate business policy. Business policies can get complicated and expensive, so it's a good idea to use a broker who can present you with options from a range of companies. As with choosing any professional, start by getting recommendations from colleagues and friends with similar insurance needs, and be sure to check references. Our advice in Chapter 13 on choosing and working with professionals such as accountants also applies to insurance brokers.

RESOURCE

Resource on buying insurance for your home business. *Insuring Your Business: Small Business Owners' Guide to Insurance,* a publication of the Insurance Information Institute website (www.iii.org) includes a special section on buying insurance for your home business.

Sharing Outside Office Space

If working from home isn't a good fit for your business, you don't necessarily need to lease a commercial space on your own. There are a number of options for sharing commercial space, including using a virtual office, joining a business incubator, subleasing from other businesses, or joining together with one or more other businesses to lease and share a space. Sharing an office through one of these arrangements helps to project a professional image (and has many other benefits, discussed below), at a fraction of the cost of renting your own commercial space.

Consider a sharing setup if renting is too expensive or just more than you need. Let's look at the various options.

Executive Suites and Virtual Offices

Executive suites and virtual offices are affordable, flexible options for small or home-based businesses that want to project a professional or corporate image, but don't have the budget or need for a full commercial space of their own. They both offer a variety of business support services, usually on an a la carte basis, allowing you to use and pay for only what you need.

With **executive suites** you'll typically rent a small office in a building with other small businesses or freelancers, and share amenities such as a receptionist and front desk area; business equipment like copiers and fax machines; conference rooms; kitchens; and even cafés. The offices are often furnished and include wireless Internet service. Conference rooms are generally professionally equipped with speakerphones, projectors, videoconferencing equipment, and more. Lease terms are generally much more flexible than regular commercial leases. You can often rent for as few as 12, six, or three months; some even offer month-to-month rentals.

Virtual offices are basically the same as executive suites, except that you may skip renting the office space altogether and just use all the other amenities such as receptionist services (including a front desk where clients could drop off or pick up packages and documents), other support services (such as data entry), and conference rooms. These amenities and services can give you the appearance of having a professional office even if you work from home. This includes having an address that may look more professional than using a P.O. box.

You'll find executive suites and virtual offices in most cities; Google "executive suites" or "virtual offices" and your city name to see what's available.

TIP

Executive suites and virtual offices can help you do business away from your base of operations. For example, if you need to have a client meeting in a different state, you could use a conference room provided by a virtual office. In addition, these flexible office space options can help a growing business establish itself in a new location in another city or state. Instead of committing yourself to a new commercial lease in the new location, you could use an executive suite to minimize your costs during the expansion.

While executive suites and virtual offices can be incredibly convenient and flexible, they may not be a good fit if you're looking to create an office space brimming with your own creative or edgy style. Executive suites and virtual offices tend to be pretty straitlaced and corporate, which is great for some businesses and not for others. If you envision an office with more personality, you'll probably want to lease collaboratively as discussed below.

Business Incubators

The term business incubator usually refers to a facility run by a nonprofit or quasi-governmental entity that aims to support small businesses and economic development. Business incubators are a lot like executive suites (which are usually for-profit ventures) in that they offer a range of shared amenities in addition to affordable commercial space. Receptionists and conference rooms are typical, and more amenities might be available depending on the incubator.

But business incubators tend to offer more than the standard business support services found with executive suites and virtual offices. These might include classes on business development topics like financial management or marketing; one-on-one consulting with experienced business mentors; networking opportunities; or financing services and loan programs. In a nutshell, business incubators are more invested in helping you succeed and, accordingly, offer more services and guidance. For this reason, if you can get into an incubator in your area it can be a great way to get your business off to a good start.

Also note that unlike executive suites that focus on offices, business incubators may offer other types of space, such as manufacturing or light industrial space.

To find a local business incubator, check with a Women's Business Center, Small Business Development Center (SBDC), or one of the other organizations listed in "Business Planning Resources" in Chapter 4.

Subleasing From Another Business

If your space needs are modest—for example, you just need a small office—one option is to find another business that has excess space and sublease from them. Particularly in a down economy, businesses will downsize or fail to grow as expected, leaving them with unused space. If they have a long-term lease, that extra space can be an expensive burden. Subleasing their excess space can be a win-win situation if the two businesses are a good fit.

If you need space on weeknights or weekends, you might find it easy to sublease space from another business. For example, a masseuse may rent space on weekend days from an acupuncturist whose office normally sits empty those days.

As for what makes a good fit, evaluate the available space, location, and details of the sharing arrangement, (and the price, of course), and whether they fit with your business needs. For example:

- Will the space present a professional enough image to your clients and other visitors? On the flip side, is the vibe too corporate or stiff for your funkier brand?
- Will the space provide enough privacy for your business and clients who may want to discuss confidential matters?
- Does the space to be subleased have a separate keyed entrance?
- Does the space provide enough room for your equipment and files, including any inventory you need to store?
- Will you and the primary tenant share a meeting space, and if so, will everyone's expected use pose conflicts?
- Does one business have heavy client or delivery traffic that might impact the other business?
- Will music or noise from one business be annoying to the other?

Besides the space considerations, also pay close attention to lease terms (the same as you would if you were signing a commercial lease, discussed below). If the primary tenant wants you to sublease until the end of their lease, make sure you're comfortable committing to that term (and be sure that the landlord has approved this arrangement). On the other hand, you'll also want assurance that you won't have to move in a few months if the primary tenant decides it wants or needs your space after all. If a minimum of a year or two years is important to you, make sure it's included in your sublease agreement. See "Finding the Right Setup" under "Renting Your Own Office or Commercial Space," below, for other considerations when renting outside space.

> **TIP**
>
> **Consider informal arrangements to share space.** Social media can be particularly effective in finding other folks whose space needs may dovetail with yours. For example, say a software consultant who works from home occasionally needs a conference room for meetings. By posting on her Facebook page and other social media, she might find a lawyer in solo practice who says his conference room is usually open, and on what days.

Collectively Leasing Space

Another affordable option is to go in on a commercial space collectively with one or more other businesses or freelancers. For example, if you're opening a photography studio and you know the owner of a graphic design business who's also looking for space, the two of you could find a space that meets both your needs. This can work well for businesses that don't need much space, since small commercial spaces can be hard to find. It will be much easier to find a 1,000-square-foot space that your two businesses will share, than for the two of you to find 500-square-foot spaces. This is even more true for smaller spaces—finding a 200-square-foot office for a freelancer is often next to impossible unless it's within a larger shared space.

For solo operators, one of the best aspects of leasing collectively is the interaction and networking it fosters. Even if you have a few people in your firm, shacking up with other complementary small businesses is a great way to fight isolation and generate productive cooperative energy. Businesses that share space can learn from each other, give support, keep each other motivated, and collaborate on projects. Creative businesses like graphic designers, photographers, writers, and digital media creators are great candidates for sharing arrangements; the same is true for professionals like attorneys, accountants, and consultants.

When sharing space with others, as corenters you should put the details of your arrangement in a legal agreement, separate from the lease with the landlord (by the way, you should all sign the lease). Your sharing agreement should cover issues such as each business's portion of the rent, how common spaces will be shared (such as scheduling procedures for the conference room), ownership and lease information for any equipment, who is responsible for cleaning and maintenance, and any other important issues.

Renting Your Own Office or Commercial Space

If you decide that renting your own commercial space is the way to go, you'll need to find the right space, in the right location, with the right zoning rules. We discuss how to go about this search below, and how to approach the process of negotiating a commercial lease.

A quick word of advice: An obvious and important factor in finding the right business space is determining in advance how much you can afford. As part of your business planning (discussed in detail in Chapter 4), determine how much rent you can afford each month, and stick to it. Don't be seduced by a swank office space in a trendy location if the rent doesn't fit in your budget. Unnecessary, inflated overhead costs can easily kill an otherwise promising business.

TIP
Square footage rates are generally given in cost per year. When talking to a potential landlord or commercial real estate broker, they will typically describe rent in "per square foot" terms, which is an annual figure. For example, a landlord might describe a space as 1,000 square feet at $14 per square foot. To determine the monthly rent, multiply the rate by the square footage of a space, then divide it by 12. So, for a 1,000-square-foot office space leasing for $14 per square foot, the monthly rent would be $1,166.67, as follows:

$14 x 1,000 = $14,000 ÷ 12 = $1,166.67.

Finding the Right Setup

When looking for a rental space, start by considering the physical features your business will need. Generally speaking, you'll be better off with a space that's at least roughly set up to do what you want to do, rather than a space that you'll totally have to transform. Many of you may simply want office space, which is usually pretty straightforward. But if you need specific features, say for manufacturing or cooking, you need to pay attention to many details.

It's highly unlikely you'll get a landlord to pay for major renovations (typically called build-outs; see "Negotiating Commercial Lease Terms" below) like adding a kitchen to your bar so you can serve meals with drinks, a loading dock to a building for your toy manufacturing plant, or more windows for your design business. So unless you have ample resources—or are a ninja negotiator—the best approach is to seek a space that has the major features installed. Chances are you'll have to make some modifications, but those will be significantly cheaper and easier to accomplish than starting from scratch.

When considering the physical features of potential spaces, it's important to keep in mind that your business (especially if it's food related or involves any hazards) may be subject to regulations regarding your facility. For this reason, it's important for you to do your homework about these types of regulations before you start your search for commercial space. For example, if you're starting a small food manufacturing business to produce baked snack crackers, your local regulations may dictate that your space needs a certain number of vents or a fire-resistant roof. A hair salon may have special waste disposal requirements, which may translate into a need for extra space for waste storage or equipment. Contact your city or county departments of planning, health, or fire, or another appropriate agency to find out. You should also check out state and federal laws that apply to your business. (See Chapter 7 for a discussion of licenses and permits.)

Besides major, obvious features that are needed for your type of business (such as a kitchen for a restaurant or hydraulic lifts for an auto repair shop), other physical features to consider include:

- electrical circuits, in terms of how many they are and the capacity of each one
- phone lines, including whether they are relatively new and whether you can use any provider
- broadband Internet access
- presence or absence of natural light
- ventilation, including openable windows and any fan/exhaust systems
- heating and cooling systems
- security, including sturdy locks for windows and doors and any security system, and
- anything else that's important to you, such as a shower, if you plan to bike to work.

When Buying Space for Your Business Might Make Sense

For the vast majority of start-ups seeking commercial space, renting the space is the most sensible way to go. In some cases, however, it might make sense to buy your building if it's financially feasible. Elissa Breitbard, owner of Betty's Bath and Day Spa, planned from the start to buy the building which turned out to be a great decision for the business. She explains: "We always knew we wanted to buy the building because we did such a big build-out. It's such a safety net to own your building, so I always think it's a great recommendation to take that route, to buy the building if you can. I think it is contrary to common wisdom; people think, 'Oh, it'll be cheaper to rent.' But if you have a big build-out, then the landlord's in control of what happens to the work you did. Our build-out was big and expensive so I knew we didn't want to rent. We did a lease to purchase."

If you are considering buying, rather than leasing, your business space, check with a real estate broker who specializes in commercial property. There are lots of books published on buying commercial property, but most focus on buying investment property. Even so, they might give you some ideas on things to consider when you buy commercial space.

> CAUTION
> **Parking is a major consideration for many businesses.** If there's not adequate parking for your anticipated car-based customer traffic, you might even face a zoning challenge from your local government. Even if this isn't the case, you'll want to avoid developing a reputation as a business with a nightmarish parking situation. If a significant percentage of your customers will come by car and there isn't enough parking at your chosen spot, it's probably best to look elsewhere.

Choosing a Location

When you have a good idea of what kind of physical features you'll need, the next consideration is location. Start by evaluating how important location actually is for your business. If you're an online clothing retailer, for example, you might be able to locate just about anywhere without impacting your business; if you own a brick-and-mortar clothing boutique, however, you might be heavily dependent on a good location for success.

If the success of your business won't depend much on the location, your prime consideration may be proximity to other places you frequent—your home, public transportation, your gym, your spouse's or partner's workplace, or your children's school, for example. If you conclude that location will have a significant impact on your business, it may be well worth it to snag the prime location and pay a higher rent, which ideally will be more than offset by higher sales.

To figure out how important location is—and if it's important, what makes a location good—you'll need to have a clear idea of how you expect to attract customers to your business. A big part of this is knowing who your target customers are and understanding their habits. (We discuss target customers and other important aspects of your market in Chapter 2.) With your target customers clearly in mind, you'll be able to anticipate where your store traffic will come from.

For example, a coffee shop targeting university students will obviously aim to attract foot traffic from the university area. A children's toy store might expect to get drop-in customers from neighboring toy stores, so it may want to choose a location close to competitors (rather than far from them, which may be a little counterintuitive). A wholesale computer parts shop might expect customers to find them via a yellow pages ad and might reasonably locate itself in an industrial area with low rent, even if it's a relatively low-visibility area that wouldn't draw drive-by traffic. An oil change business, on the other hand, might depend on drive-by drop-ins for its success, so it would want a high-visibility spot on a well-traveled street.

In short, the perfect location for any business is a very individual matter. Spend some time figuring out the habits of the customers you want to attract, then choose a location that fits. Some other location-related considerations include:

- **Is the neighborhood and building safe?** Starting a business usually involves long hours and late nights. If the building is located in a crime-ridden area, or if the entrance is in a dark alley and the building doesn't offer a security service, you may reasonably decide to keep looking.

- **Is the location convenient?** Being located near other businesses and services can help you save valuable time. For example, if the neighborhood offers a post office or overnight mail service and a copy shop with good hours, you may find yourself saving tons of time not having to drive across town to take care of copying and mailing tasks. Ditto for other types of businesses: having restaurants, grocery stores, dry cleaners, drugstores, and others nearby can make your day-to-day life easier.

- **Is there a local merchant's association?** In some neighborhoods, local businesses have banded together to promote themselves collectively. An active merchant association might buy collective ad space, hold "shop and stroll" events, and spearhead other marketing activities to help the area businesses. If there is a merchant association in the neighborhood you're considering, find out what fees may be due and any responsibilities of merchant members. Also ask neighboring businesses about their experiences with the association; if there is turmoil or contentious issues within the group—say, some businesses feel bullied into buying ad space they don't really want—you'll want to know before you join.

Evolving from working at home to a commercial space

"We started out at a pair of desks set up in Lauren's bedroom. Our first big upwardly mobile move was that when Lauren moved into a bigger apartment, we expanded our office space into the living room. A year or two into our business, though, Emira (who does all the sales work) found that she was spending way too much time traveling back and forth to meetings, so she started spending half her time downtown, in a small office in a beautiful (but cheap) old heritage building that she shared with a graphic designer. Eventually the temptation to work downtown, closer to our clients—and the itch to escape the isolation of the home office—drove us both downtown, but it was a very gradual process. We were probably at the four-year mark before we were totally 'home free.' Over time, as we hired staff—and as technology outpaced the ancient wiring in our beloved old building—we outgrew our funky little office and moved across the street into a newly renovated space in one of Vancouver's historic old buildings. It's as much a community as it is a building, because the environmentally conscious renovations and the location in an evolving area of town attracted forward-thinking, conscious businesses and nonprofits who are all trying to make the world a better place while making a living. We love it here and are hoping to stay put for a while."

— Lauren Bacon and Emira Mears

"Working from home was the starting point. We had a very college-y apartment in a very student neighborhood. Every time we had an appointment for somebody to come over, we would put these bridal portraits all over our walls and we'd take them off as soon as they left. It was very funny that our business grew like that. After one year of doing this very college-y type thing we actually made enough money to buy our first house. From there we set up an official room for brides that had permanent displays, very official; we had a real office and we turned our garage into a portrait studio. But we were still working from home. From there, we grew into the storefront studio that we have now. It's one mile away from the University of Florida, which is like the main center of everything in Gainesville. It's a very large, beautiful studio with a huge sign in the front."

— Sabrina Habib Williams

"In the beginning, I was working out of my house, and suddenly I was having too many people every day come to my house and my neighbors were wondering what I was doing. I was also attempting to do wedding photography, and when the wedding prospects would come into my house they would not trust me as much. They would say, 'The work is nice, but I don't know that you're really that professional. How can I know that you'll still be here?' So I knew then that I needed a space to validate the work, that the space was going to say a lot about stability. So that was kind of the impetus to get a space. And also to stop having people come to my house; it was too much."

— **Kyle Zimmerman**

> TIP
> **If possible, grow your business without moving.** If your business plan anticipates rapid growth, do your best to find a space that allows for the possibility of expansion. Being able to take over vacant space next door is obviously easier than relocating your business entirely. At the very least, if you plan to expand and the space might not accommodate your growth, make sure you sign a short-term lease so you have flexibility down the road.

Complying With Zoning Laws

Local zoning laws (often called "ordinances" or "land use regulations") prohibit certain activities from being conducted in particular areas or specific buildings. For example, zoning laws may allow commercial/ office use in a certain neighborhood but not light industrial use. Or conversely, the zoning may prohibit a retail business that's open to the public to operate in a neighborhood zoned for industrial use.

EXAMPLE: Amy is looking for space for her retail hardware business. She finds a great building in an industrial area near similar businesses, such as lumber yards and electric supply companies. Upon talking to the leasing agent, however, she learns that the area is zoned for wholesale and light industrial businesses, not retail businesses open to the public. She hadn't realized that the lumber yards and electric supply businesses were wholesale only. She continues her search in areas zoned for retail activities.

In addition to regulating the types of businesses allowed in certain areas, zoning laws also regulate specific activities. Depending on your area, you might be subject to laws regulating parking, signs, water and air quality, waste management, noise, and the visual appearance of the business (especially in historic districts). In addition to these regulations, some cities restrict the number of a particular type of business in a certain area, such as allowing only three bookstores or one pet shop in a certain neighborhood. Finally, some zoning laws specifically regulate home businesses. (Home businesses and zoning rules that apply to them are discussed separately above.)

Parking Spaces and Business Signs Are Commonly Subject to Zoning Rules

Local zoning laws commonly require a business to provide parking, and they also may regulate the size and type of business signs. Be prepared for your city or county to look into both these issues. If there's already a parking problem in your proposed area, you may have to come up with a plan for how to deal with the increased traffic your business will attract.

Many local laws limit the size of business signs (no signs over five feet by three feet, for instance), their appearance (such as whether they're illuminated, flashing, colorful, or made of neon), and their placement (flat against the building, hanging over the sidewalk, or mounted on a pole). There are even some regulations attempting to limit the use of foreign language on signs. Be sure to find out what your local regulations are before spending money on having signs made.

When considering a commercial space, make sure you are clear about the zoning rules for it and whether you'll be able legally to conduct your planned activities there *before* signing a lease. (Note that contingent leases will let you off the hook of the lease contract if you don't get zoning approval.)

What If You Hit Zoning Roadblocks?

It can be awfully disappointing for a zoning board to give your application for approval a thumbs-down, especially when you have your heart set on a space. If you get shot down, you have a few options, usually ranging from making appropriate changes to your business to giving up on that location and finding a new one.

If your desired activities are in the general ballpark of the zoning rules, a creative and assertive approach can often persuade zoning officials to work out an acceptable accommodation that will allow the business to use the desired location. If your business will be valuable to the community, present evidence of that fact, such as demographic data about the area, testimony from community leaders, or statements from other local businesspeople. (Here's where your network can really help!) Your goal is to show that the value of allowing your business in the area is greater than the minor zoning conflicts that may exist. If you can compromise in some other area, offer to do so.

If the zoning officials have already denied your application, it's often possible to appeal their decision, usually to a higher authority such as a board of appeals within the zoning agency or the city council. If you're successful, the zoning board may grant you a "variance," which is basically a one-time exception to the local zoning laws. Or the board may give you a "conditional use permit," which essentially gives you approval to operate your business as long as certain conditions are met, such as restricting the maximum occupancy to a certain number of people or providing additional parking spaces.

Also, never assume that you'll be allowed to do a certain activity simply because the previous tenants of the space did it. It's not uncommon for a new occupant to be prohibited from certain activities even if the previous business conducted those same activities for quite some time. One possible reason for this is that the previous tenant may have obtained a zoning variance (an exception to zoning laws) for her particular business—one that won't necessarily be extended to you.

Another possibility is that the previous business was operating when zoning laws changed, and the business was allowed to keep doing what it was doing, even if the activity violated the new zoning law—a system referred to as "grandfathering." When a tenant with a grandfathered exception leaves and new occupants come in, however, the new business usually has to abide by the new, more restrictive zoning law.

Your prospective landlord will usually provide basic information on how the building is zoned. If any of your planned activities fall into a gray area, don't rely on what the landlord says—do some additional homework to make sure you won't find yourself in violation of the zoning rules. Generally this involves talking with your local zoning officials; most zoning agencies are part of city or county planning departments. Look under "Planning" or "Zoning" in the government section of your phone book or check your city or county website. If your business will be located in a city, look for the city office; businesses in rural areas should contact the county zoning or planning offices.

Getting zoning approval typically begins with filling out a form issued by the city (or county) planning department in which you provide information about your proposed location and what you plan to do there. You may be required to submit detailed building plans to show exactly how you intend to use the space in question. Your application may be evaluated simply on the information you provide in the form, or the zoning department may send out an inspector to more closely examine the potential business space. Once the zoning department has all the information it requires to make a decision, it will either approve your application without limitations, approve it with certain conditions, or deny it altogether.

Negotiating Commercial Lease Terms

Since most start-ups aren't in the position to purchase commercial real estate—and since doing so isn't necessarily a good idea for a young business—let's assume you'll be renting, not buying, commercial space. If you're new to the world of commercial leases, bear in mind that there's generally a good amount of negotiation between the business and a commercial landlord. From the tenant's perspective, your goal is to make sure your lease covers important details that may affect your business, such as what kind of signs you're allowed to put up or how many electrical circuits are included in the space. Depending on economic conditions, landlords are often willing to accommodate your needs in order to keep up their occupancy rate. This is especially true in an economic downturn.

Besides the monthly rent amount, an important set of details relates to making any necessary improvements within the business space, collectively called "build-outs." In many cases a commercial space may be nothing but four walls. To make the space usable for your business, interior walls may need to be added, electrical systems may need to be upgraded, or plumbing may need to be reconfigured to accommodate a utility sink. The questions of who pays for the build-outs and who is responsible for getting them done are generally negotiated between the business and the landlord. As is often the case, your bargaining power will largely depend on general economic conditions and factors such as how long of a lease you'll sign, how large the space is, and how long it's been on the market.

Also keep in mind that the Americans with Disabilities Act (ADA) requires all businesses that are open to the public or that employ more than 15 people to have premises that are accessible to people with disabilities. Make sure that you and your landlord are in agreement about who will pay for any needed modifications, such as adding a ramp or widening doorways to accommodate wheelchairs.

Finally, make sure to pay careful attention to any other terms that may have a major impact on your business. For instance, if you plan to have nighttime hours for your hair salon, be sure that your lease does not prohibit lighted exterior signs. Or, if you are counting on being the only bookstore inside a new commercial complex, make sure your lease prevents the landlord from leasing space to a competitor.

The following checklist includes many items that are often addressed in commercial leases. Pay attention to terms regarding:

- rent, including allowable increases and method of computation

- whether the rent includes insurance, property taxes, and maintenance costs (called a gross lease), or whether you will be charged for these items separately (called a net lease)
- whether the rent includes heat, air conditioning, phone, parking, garbage collection, water, and other utilities (if not, what are other expenses you can expect to pay?)
- the security deposit and conditions for its return
- who is responsible for code compliance, security, and fire safety
- the length of the lease (also called the lease term) and when it begins
- whether there's an option to renew the lease or expand the space
- how the lease may be terminated, including notice requirements, and whether there are penalties for early termination
- exactly what space is being rented, including common areas such as hallways, rest rooms, and elevators, and how the space is measured (some measurement practices include the thickness of the walls)
- specifications for signs, including where they may be placed
- whether there will be improvements, modifications (called build-outs when new space is being finished to your specifications), or fixtures added to the space; who will pay for them; and who will own them after the lease ends (generally, the landlord)
- who will maintain the premises and provide janitorial services
- whether the lease may be assigned or subleased to another party, and
- whether disputes must be mediated or arbitrated as an alternative to court.

RESOURCE

For more on leasing office spaces. For detailed information on finding a space and negotiating a lease, see *Negotiate the Best Lease for Your Business,* by Janet Portman and Fred S. Steingold (Nolo).

Using an agent for a commercial lease

"For two years I searched for a commercial building to purchase. Nothing ever worked out, so we decided to pursue a commercial lease in a new space. Having an experienced and professional agent was key for us in navigating this realm; it would have been very difficult to do on our own. I would highly recommend to others that they work with an agent in this regard—it is impossible to know the ins and outs of real estate without being an agent and it can be easy to make naive mistakes."

— **Rebecca Pearcy**

Insurance for Commercial Spaces

Depending on your business, your lease or your lender may require you to purchase certain types of insurance. Regardless of any requirements posed by others, you'll want to be sure you have adequate insurance coverage for losses from theft, fire, personal liability claims (especially if you are not protected by the LLC or corporate structure), and other risks to your property and business, such as workers' compensation claims. An experienced business insurance broker can help you choose the appropriate coverage.

For more detailed information, see *Insuring Your Business: Small Business Owners' Guide to Insurance,* a publication of the Insurance Information Institute. It's free at the Institute's website (www.iii.org), or you can download a PDF or order a hard copy for a small fee. This useful guide covers all kinds of insurance—property, liability, business vehicle, and workers' comp and life insurance for employees, as well as insurance for specific types of businesses (home based, food service, retail, and so on).

Dealing With Start-Up Requirements and Bureaucratic Hurdles

D on't let the word "bureaucracy" glaze your eyes over. Most entrepreneurs are pleasantly surprised to learn that there's really not that much government or legal red tape involved in starting a business. For some reason, many people fear that small businesses are subject to an oppressive regime of bureaucratic rules and regulations, but in reality the start-up requirements are fairly minimal for the vast majority of businesses. The tricky part is figuring out what the requirements are and in what order you should tackle them. Some cities and states do a better job than others, with helpful websites offering clear, step-by-step start-up requirements—but they are the exception. Since business start-up tasks exist at various levels from your city to the federal government, it's often difficult to find a centralized resource summarizing what you need to do and when.

For example, your city tax office can tell you what forms you must file there but won't tell you how to obtain a permit in order to sell retail goods. And while your state sales tax agency may be able to tell you everything you need to know about getting a seller's permit, it won't explain how to obtain a federal employer identification number, which is required for most businesses.

That's where this chapter comes in. It offers a big-picture overview of the various bureaucratic tasks that most businesses must complete before opening their doors for business, and demystifies the regulatory structures governing small business. Most importantly, it provides specific information about how to complete the various start-up tasks. These steps are:

Step 1: File organizational documents with the secretary of state or similar filing office (not necessary for sole proprietors or general partnerships, just business entities with limited liability).

Step 2: Obtain a federal employer identification number (FEIN).

Step 3: Register your fictitious business name (FBN) with your county or state.

Step 4: Obtain a local tax registration certificate (also known as a business license).

Step 5: Obtain a permit to sell retail goods and collect state sales tax.

Step 6: Obtain specialized vocation-related licenses or environmental permits if necessary.

CAUTION

Don't blow off any of these steps. The bureaucratic hurdles described in this chapter are both basic and important—failing to complete them can have serious practical implications. For example, if you don't obtain a federal employer identification number, you won't be able to file taxes or to complete other important registration tasks. If you don't register your fictitious business name, you typically won't be able to open a business bank account. Generally speaking, and unless stated otherwise below, the rules below apply to all businesses, from huge corporations to tiny freelancers.

Step 1: File Organizational Documents With Your State (Corporations, LLCs, and Limited Partnerships Only)

SKIP AHEAD

Sole proprietors and partnerships can skip this step. Only corporations, LLCs, and limited partnerships need to file organizational documents with the state. (So do limited liability partnerships, which are fairly uncommon.) If you're starting a sole proprietorship or partnership, skip ahead to Step 2.

Recall from Chapter 5 that a fundamental difference among the various types of business structures is that some provide limited personal liability and some don't. The former—corporations, limited liability companies, and limited partnerships—exist separately from the owner(s) and need to be created at the state level. In a nutshell, this involves filing paperwork and paying a fee to your state, usually (but not always) via your state secretary of state office (you can find yours at the National Association of Secretaries of State, www.nass.org).

For corporations, the organizational document you file with the state is usually called articles of incorporation. For LLCs, it's generally called articles of organization (although some states call it a certificate of organization or formation). Limited partnerships also have to file a certificate of limited partnership or something similar. These forms are generally available from the state (often downloadable from the secretary of state's website) allowing you to simply fill in the blanks with information such as your business name, number of owners (called directors for corporations, members for LLCs, or partners for limited partnerships), and other information.

Besides filing the paperwork to create the business entity, you'll also need to draft documents outlining the rules governing your business. For corporations these are called bylaws; for LLCs they are called operating agreements; for limited partnerships they are generally called limited partnership agreements. Some states require you to file these with the same office where you filed the organizational documents; in other states you'll just keep your own copy. Even if you're not required to file them with the state, don't neglect creating these documents; it's important that you formalize the key details of your corporation, LLC, or limited partnership in writing.

RESOURCE

Resources on LLCs, partnerships, and corporations. Nolo (www.nolo. com) offers several books, online apps, software programs, and other resources with step-by-step instructions on drafting corporate bylaws, LLC operating agreements, or limited partnership agreements. See Chapter 5 for details.

Step 2: Obtain a Federal Employer Identification Number

A business's federal employer identification number (alternately called an FEIN, an EIN, or an employer ID) is roughly equivalent to a Social Security number for an individual. It's a number used by the government to identify your business, which you'll use over and over again on most of your important business documents, such as your business's local tax registration forms, your federal tax return, and any applications for business licenses.

For sole proprietorships and partnerships, getting an FEIN should be your first bureaucratic start-up task, mainly because you can get one before you've registered with any other agency or filled out any other forms. For corporations, LLCs, or limited partnerships, you need to create your business entity first, as described in the previous step. Without doing so, there won't be any business entity in existence to apply for the FEIN.

Who Needs an FEIN

Some of you are probably saying, "I don't plan to have employees, why do I need an employer ID number?" Blame the IRS for the confusing terminology. Although it's called an "employer" ID number, FEINs are required for most businesses, even those that don't have employees. The one exception is sole proprietors with no employees, who can use their own Social Security number instead of an FEIN. Partnerships, LLCs, and corporations need FEINs whether they have employees or not.

Applying for an FEIN

You can apply for your FEIN online, or by phone, fax, or mail. If you apply online, you'll get your FEIN the same day; the process takes approximately ten minutes. Go to www.irs.gov and search "EIN." Follow the prompts and enter the required information under "Apply for Employer Identification Number (EIN) Online."

Filing by phone also will get you your FEIN the same day. You'll need to fill out IRS Form SS-4 (*Application for Employer Identification Number*), then call the phone number listed on the SS-4 form. You will relay your information to the IRS representative, who will then give you your FEIN over the phone. Enter the FEIN in the upper right-hand corner of the SS-4, sign and date the form, and keep it for your records.

In the past, you were asked to mail the form to the IRS within 24 hours of the phone call; this is no longer required.

Most people apply online or by phone, but you may also apply by fax or by mail. To apply by fax or mail, fill out Form SS-4 then fax or mail it to the number or address listed for your state. For fax applicants, the IRS will fax you your FEIN within about four business days. If you apply by mail you'll receive your FEIN in about four weeks.

You can download Form SS-4 from the IRS website at www.irs.gov.

FORM ON NOLO.COM

IRS Form SS-4. For your convenience, a copy of IRS Form SS-4 and instructions for completing it are included on Nolo's website. See the appendix for a link to this and other worksheets in this book.

Step 3: Register Your Fictitious Business Name (FBN)

While some small businesses operate under the owners' names—for example, Wendy Lin Career Counseling or Judith Maleki Garden Designs—most operate under different names, such as CareerChoices Counseling or Everbloom Garden Designs. (Chapter 8 offers tips on choosing a marketable business name that supports the brand you want to build.) A business name that doesn't contain the legal names of the owners (for sole proprietorships or general partnerships) or that doesn't match the company's corporate, limited partnership, or LLC name on file with the state, is called a fictitious business name (FBN). As described further below, using a fictitious business name usually subjects you to an additional registration requirement.

Fictitious business names are sometimes called assumed names or "DBAs" for "doing business as"—as in, "Monica Armijo, doing business as Children's Educational Resources," or "Taggart Corporation, doing business as Mindshare Studios." Another term often used is "trade name," though this can be confusing because it doesn't indicate whether the name is the same as or different from the legal name. In this chapter and the rest of the book, the term fictitious business name will be used for any business name that doesn't contain the legal name of the business owner.

Most states require any business that uses a fictitious business name, regardless of the business entity, to register that name, usually with the county clerk in the county where its primary business site is located. Depending on your state, this requirement goes by different names: fictitious name certification, DBA filing, trade name registration, or something similar. FBN registrations are typically done at the county level, although, in some states, you register your FBN with the secretary of state or another state agency. The registration process is covered in more detail below.

States like to keep track of business names for a couple of reasons: One is to prevent the customer confusion that would result if two local businesses used the same name. Before a business can register its fictitious business name, many states either search their fictitious business name registries or require that the business do so to make sure the name isn't already being used. Note that FBN registries are totally separate from state databases of corporate or LLC names (discussed in Chapter 5). Fictitious business name requirements apply to all business types, so the FBN database will include any fictitious business names used by sole proprietorships, partnerships (limited and general), LLCs, and corporations.

Another reason behind FBN registration requirements is to give customers a quick way to find out who the owner of a company is without having to hire a private investigator. A state database of who is doing business under what names helps customers find out who the owners are of a particular business, allowing the customers to make a complaint or to take legal action against the owners. Requiring owners to register their business names makes it harder for fly-by-night businesses to operate anonymously and defraud customers.

The Importance of Filing an FBN Statement

Without proof of FBN registration, most banks will not open an account under your business name if it's not the same as your legal name. Also, if you don't register your name, it won't appear in any fictitious name databases in your state. This means that another business will be less likely to find out you're using it and may start using the name itself. Even though you have other legal avenues to stop another business from using a name that you used first, you don't want to create customer confusion between the two businesses and get into a name dispute with another business. If you lose a dispute over a name, at the very least you'll have to redo stationery, signs, and anything else that contains the name, such as T-shirts or maybe even your company logo.

Who Needs to Register

The rules for registering fictitious business names depend on which business structure you use and may vary by your location. Always check with your county clerk for specific rules that apply to your business.

Sole proprietorships. Generally speaking, a sole proprietor who includes her last name in the business name—such as Kapoor Healthcare Consulting—does not need to file an FBN statement. But it is not enough to include only initials, a nickname, or part of a name. For example, a business called NK Healthcare Consulting would have to file a fictitious name statement indicating that it is Neela Kapoor's business. In addition, in many states, if your business name falsely implies that more than one owner is involved, you must file a fictitious business name statement. If Marie Abaya were a sole proprietor, for example, and named her business Marie Abaya & Associates, she would probably have to file an FBN statement, even though she included her last name in her business name.

Partnerships. If a partnership includes the last names of all the partners—for example, Sophia Moreno and Ally Jones name their business "Moreno and Jones Physical Therapy"—they don't have to file a statement. Otherwise, an FBN statement will be required. For example, if Moreno and Jones did business under the name "Moreno Physical Therapy," they would have to file an FBN statement.

Corporations, LLCs, and limited partnerships. A corporation, an LLC, or a limited partnership does not need to file an FBN statement unless it operates under a name that's different from its official name as stated in its articles of incorporation, articles of organization, or certificate of limited partnership. For example, an LLC that registered with the secretary of state under the name "Fashion Recyclers, LLC" wouldn't have to file an FBN statement as long as it conducted business under that name. Any other trade name, "Recycled Fashion," for instance—or even "Fashion Recyclers" without the "LLC" tacked onto the end— may be considered to be "fictitious" and would have to be registered. The same is often true for corporations: If "Inc." is included in the corporation's name in the articles of incorporation, but not in the company's trade name, an FBN statement usually must be filed.

Filing With Your County

In a few states, FBN registration is accomplished through the secretary of state or another state agency; however, in most states, you'll register your FBN at the county level. This is generally true despite the fact that most laws governing fictitious business names are state laws. The result is that each county in your state may have different forms and fees for registering an FBN.

Contact your county clerk's office to find out its requirements and fees. Some counties offer a downloadable form and instructions online, but you'll often have to request a hard copy be mailed to you. Unless you live a good distance from the nearest county clerk, it may be easiest just to go to the office and complete the form in person.

Searching the County (or State) Database

In many areas, you'll be instructed to search the county or state database of registered fictitious business names before submitting your statement to make sure no one else has already registered the name you want to use. Typically, you can search a county's database (often an easy-to-search computerized system) for free if you go to the office in person. Sometimes you can pay a fee for a staff person to do the search for you. If you want the clerk's office to do the search, you must usually submit the request and fee by mail.

> (!) CAUTION
>
> **County databases won't tell you if a name is trademarked.** If you search your county database before registering your fictitious name to make sure it isn't already registered, remember that this is not the same thing as doing a trademark search. If the business name you want is not in your county fictitious business name database, that doesn't mean it's not being used by someone in another county or state, or that it hasn't been registered in the federal trademark database. Make sure you adequately research your business name before committing to it. See "Avoiding Trademark Troubles When Naming Your Business," below.

Completing and Submitting an FBN Statement

If the name you've chosen is available (both at the county level and with regard to trademark issues), simply fill out the FBN statement and submit it to your county clerk (or another agency, depending on your state) along with the appropriate fees. You typically can submit the form in person or by mail. Depending on the county, fees range from $10 to $50 for registering one business name and one business owner. Sometimes you may be charged an additional fee, around $5 to $15, to register additional business names to be used at the same business location or to register additional owners.

Publishing Notice of Your FBN Statement

Besides filing the paperwork and paying the necessary fees, in many states you'll need to publish your FBN statement in an approved newspaper in the county where you filed it. Contact your county clerk or state agency for details and a list of acceptable publications for posting your FBN statement (usually any newspaper of general circulation in the county will suffice). Publishing your statement is dead simple: Just take a copy of your completed statement to one of the acceptable publications, which will have a standard format to present the required information.

TIP

Obscure publications are cheapest. As long as a newspaper is on the approved list or doesn't otherwise violate your county's rules (for instance, some counties may not allow you to publish an FBN statement in a free newspaper), there's nothing wrong with picking the cheapest one.

The published notice must run for a certain frequency and duration, usually once a week for a month or so. After the FBN has been published for the required period, you'll usually need to submit an affidavit (sometimes called proof of publication) with the county clerk or state agency to show that publication has been completed. Many newspapers that provide publication services will automatically send in the affidavit for you after your ad has completed its run. Make sure to find out whether the publication you use will do this (and double-check afterward to make sure it has actually done it). If not, you'll have to get the affidavit from the publication yourself and submit it to the county clerk or state agency by the prescribed deadline. If the affidavit isn't filed in time, you may have to start the process all over again.

TIP

Save your ad receipt. For practical reasons, you may need to prove that you completed your fictitious business name filing requirements—including publication—before your ad has actually completed its publication run. Banks, for instance, tend to require proof that you have met fictitious name rules before they will allow you to open an account in that name. A receipt from the newspaper showing that you have paid for publication, along with a copy of the FBN statement certified by the county clerk or state agency, is generally sufficient to prove that you've met all the registration requirements, even if the ad hasn't yet run for the full term. So be sure to get a certified copy of your FBN statement from the county clerk or state agency when you submit it, as well as a receipt from the newspaper when you pay for publishing it.

After You File Your FBN

Your FBN registration will be good for a certain period of time, usually for five years or so, before it must be renewed. Keep track of your expiration date, as your county clerk or state agency may not notify you when your renewal date approaches. Also, if certain facts in your statement change, such as the number of owners or your business address, you may have to renew your FBN statement. Check with your county clerk or state agency to find out which types of changes trigger a renewal requirement. If you no longer want your FBN registered, you may file a form (often called a statement of abandonment) to cause the registration to expire.

Avoiding Trademark Troubles When Naming Your Business

When you're getting your business up and running, you'll need to be careful to choose a business name that won't land you in legal hot water. If you choose a name that's confusingly similar to another company's name, you could find yourself accused of violating (called "infringing") the other company's trademark, and you could be forced to change your business name and possibly pay money damages. The same is true for the names of your products and services: If they are confusingly similar to names of other businesses' products or services, you may be guilty of trademark infringement. For example, if you started a computer company and named it Macrosoft, you'd undoubtedly get a cease and desist letter from Microsoft. Even though the names aren't identical, Macrosoft would be confusingly similar enough to Microsoft to invite a lawsuit at the very least (a lawsuit that you'd likely lose).

The details of trademark law are beyond the scope of this book, but here's a quick overview of the basics. In a nutshell, a trademark is any word, phrase, logo, or other device used to identify products or services in the marketplace. Brand names (Ralph Lauren, Trader Joe's) serve as trademarks, as do slogans ("Just do it," for Nike, or "Got Milk?" for the California Milk Processor Board). The names of products or services themselves are trademarks (Big Mac, Windows XP), as are the names of the businesses that sell them (McDonald's, Microsoft). Using a name in public commerce to identify goods or services for sale is enough to make it a trademark; there is no registration requirement. However, registration with the U.S. Patent and Trademark Office will greatly strengthen your power to enforce your rights to the trademark.

If you are the first to use the trademark, then you will generally have the right to prevent others from using it in a way that would be likely to confuse customers. There are a number of criteria courts use to determine whether a trademark owner can prevent others from using the word or phrase, but the essence of the test is whether customers are likely to be confused by someone else using the trademark. If so—for instance, if restaurant goers would be likely to be confused by two separate businesses in the same city using the name "Sunshine Café"—then the first business to use the name has the legal right to stop the other business from using the name.

Also bear in mind that while trademark law is the main legal area governing business names, there are other laws and rules that can come into play here. Unfair competition laws may also prevent a business from using a name that's confusingly similar to a name being used by another business. And your state corporation or LLC office will prevent you from choosing a corporate name that's already being used by another corporation or LLC in the state.

The best way to avoid name conflicts is to do some research before settling on a name for your business or its products or services. Name searching can range from informal Googling to hiring a research firm to do a formal search. A good approach is to start with the following easy, free methods and continue in increasing depth depending on what you find and the scope of your business. Here are some tips:

- Check your local phone book, or other local directories like your city's chamber of commerce.
- Google your desired name to see if any other business is using it.
- Go to a domain name registrar and check whether a particular domain name you want for your website is available (see Chapter 9 for a discussion of domain names and registrars).

- If your name still appears to be available, check the federal trademark database at the U.S. Patent and Trademark Office to make sure no one has registered it. If you use a name that's registered with the federal database, you can be sued for "willful infringement." Go to www.uspto.gov/trademark and choose "Search Trademark Database." Alternatively, you can hire a search firm to do a formal, exhaustive search of the database, including finding names that aren't identical to the name you want, but look like, sound like, or have the same meaning as your desired name.

- Check state databases like the ones maintained by your state corporation and LLC filing office. States also maintain state trademark registries, which are separate from the federal trademark registry. Finally, counties maintain fictitious business name databases which are worth checking too.

If your search efforts don't find anyone else using the name, great. But if someone else is using the name, you'll need to determine whether your use would be confusingly similar to the other business's use. If you plan to open a local jewelry store in San Francisco called Fillmore Rocks, you probably don't have to worry about a jewelry store with the same name in Chicago. If your business sells online or serves a national audience, however, that may be a different story. The safest course is to choose another name, but if you or a lawyer determines your choice poses no threat of customer confusion, it might be okay to go ahead and use the name.

Trademark issues can be tricky; you may want to hire a lawyer. For the full treatment on trademark law and other legal issues affecting business and product names, see *Trademark: Legal Care for Your Business & Product Name,* by Stephen Elias and Richard Stim (Nolo).

Step 4: Obtain a Local Tax Registration Certificate

Most cities (or counties, if you live in a rural area) require all businesses (including home businesses) to register with the local tax collector, regardless of business type, structure, size, or name. Depending on your city or county, there may be different names for the process: tax registration, business tax application, business license application, or tax certification, for example.

I confess to having a pet peeve here: I am constantly annoyed by use of the term "business license" for this task, since it really has nothing to do with licensing per se. True licenses, which are discussed in Step 6, below, are typically administered at the state level. Certain businesses must obtain them if they engage in regulated activities, such as selling alcohol, installing electrical systems, or cutting people's hair. Getting such a license often involves taking a test or otherwise proving you're qualified to do a certain activity. Registering with your city or county, on the other hand, simply involves paying a tax or fee for the privilege of doing business in the city or county. For this reason I stick with the term "tax registration" for this task.

The reason you need to register with your local tax collector is that, just like the federal and state governments, your local government wants a cut of your business income. The tax registration requirement is basically your local government's way of keeping track of your business so that it will be able to collect any taxes due.

Cities and counties have been known to tax businesses with even more flair and creativity than the feds or the states. Localities tax businesses based on criteria such as net profit, gross income, number of employees, total payroll, number of vehicles, number of machines, and sometimes even seating capacity. Most cities categorize businesses and use different tax structures for each category. For instance, bakeries might be charged a 0.2% tax on gross receipts, landscapers a rate of 0.36%, and architects and other professionals a rate of 0.58%. Other types of businesses might be charged flat fees—for instance a winery might be charged $500 per year, and laundromats $150 per year. Finally, businesses might be subject to special taxes for particular activities. For example, businesses that sell fountain soft drinks may be charged a tax of 10% of the syrup price, or event venues may have to pay an amusement tax of 5% of the admission price. Categories, taxable activities, and rates vary wildly from one city to the next so you'll just have to check with your locality.

For the privilege of registering to pay local taxes, you'll usually have to pay an annual fee, which varies a lot from city to city, but is usually in the $25 to $100 range. Sometimes the annual fee depends partly on how much tax your business is expected to owe the following year, based on city (or county) tax rates. If the fee is based on estimated taxes, at least part of the registration fee may be a nonrefundable administrative fee. In that case, the other part of the fee will go toward paying your estimated taxes or will be returned to you if your taxes turn out to be lower than expected.

For your city's requirements, call your city tax collector. Look under "Tax Collector" in the city government section of your telephone book or check your city website. The tax collector's office will be able to provide you with the forms necessary to register in your city, as well as any breakdown of business categories and tax tables. If you're doing business outside city limits, call your county clerk, usually listed under "County Clerk" in the county government section of the phone book, or check your county government website.

Step 5: Obtain a State Seller's Permit

In most states, any business—whether it's a sole proprietorship, an LLC, a corporation, or any other type—must have a seller's permit if it sells any tangible goods to the public. Tangible goods are things you can touch, such as furniture, clothing, or food. Businesses that sell only services, such as a color consultant or tax preparer, are often exempt from the seller's permit requirement.

In a nutshell, a seller's permit will allow your business to collect sales taxes from customers to cover any sales tax that you'll owe to the state, which is generally calculated as a percentage of your taxable sales. You'll typically pay any taxes you owe at year end, semiannually, quarterly, or monthly. The general rule is that the higher your sales volume, the more often you'll owe your payment.

In the five states that do not impose general sales taxes (Alaska, Delaware, Montana, New Hampshire, and Oregon), you may not be required to get a permit for most sales transactions. However, cities and counties in those states may charge sales taxes (as in Alaska), and certain transactions in those states may be subject to something similar to a sales tax, though it may have a different name like a gross receipts tax. If you live in one of the nontaxing states, be sure to check with the sales tax agency to find out if your specific transactions will be subject to tax and whether you'll need a seller's permit. For information on how to find your state tax agency, see "Government Agencies With Business Start-Up Information" at the end of this chapter.

CAUTION

States are getting much more aggressive about taxing sales conducted online. If you plan to conduct sales online, make sure you understand whether those sales will be taxable. In a nutshell, online sales that used to be considered nontaxable because they were made to out-of-state buyers are the subject of a flurry of state legislation, as states are attempting to define many of these sales as taxable. See Chapter 11 for a more detailed discussion of sales taxes online.

Keep in mind that if you plan to sell tangible goods, you'll often need a seller's permit whether or not those sales will be taxable. For instance, most states exempt certain sales from state sales tax, such as sales of food or sales to out-of-state customers. But in most states, you'll need a seller's permit even to conduct these types of nontaxable sales. This means you need to get a sales permit before you begin to sell tangible goods; when the sales are made, you'll distinguish the taxable ones from the nontaxable ones. When it comes time to report and pay sales taxes to the state, you'll owe tax only on the taxable sales. (See Chapter 11 for a detailed discussion of reporting and paying sales taxes.)

Finally, note that if your business provides both services and products, you'll need a seller's permit. This is true even if the product sales are a small part of your business compared to your services; you need a seller's permit if you sell even a few tangible goods.

TIP

If your business both performs services and sells products, careful bookkeeping is essential. To assure proper tax reporting, you will need to keep your labor sales separate from sales of goods, since sales of services aren't taxed in most locales. (Chapter 10 explains simple bookkeeping and how to account for taxable sales separately from tax-exempt sales.)

To obtain a seller's permit, contact the agency in your state that governs sales taxes, which may or may not be the same agency that deals with income taxes. The process of obtaining a seller's permit typically consists of submitting a simple application form and, sometimes, paying a fee.

Expect the unexpected when starting your business

"Do lots of research, but accept that there will be things that pop up that you didn't expect. After running my ice cream company primarily at pop-up events, markets, and catering for a year, we opened our first retail space. We applied for every possible permit, purchased additional insurance, and worked with a plumber, electrician, and contractor. Then two weeks before our scheduled opening, I found out that we needed a separate sales tax certificate for the new location. The website said that it would take three to four weeks to process the application. It was then that I accepted that there would continue to be unexpected things that would pop up throughout the process. Accepting that helped me to handle other challenges as they came my way."

— **Catherine Oddenino**

Step 6: Obtain Specialized Licenses or Permits

Depending on the nature of your business, your bureaucratic tasks might be done after you complete the steps above. But you may not be ready for your grand opening just yet. You may be surprised to find out that even your simple little business is subject to an extra regulation or two. Some business activities are prohibited until you obtain a license or permit to engage in them, and some business locations require special approval from the local planning department. These extra requirements are especially likely to apply to businesses that have the potential for harming the environment or hurting the public, but they also apply in lots of seemingly risk-free situations.

Figuring out what additional permits or licenses you might need can be confusing as there are literally hundreds of independent agencies from the local to the federal level that regulate various businesses. Obviously, you don't want to waste your time calling each and every one of them to find out whether your business is subject to its rules. This section will help streamline the process by outlining the types of activities that are generally regulated and by whom. This should help you figure out when your business is likely to face a special regulation. We'll also look at some resources that help to make sense of the crazy quilt of local, state, and federal regulations that might apply to your business.

TIP

Who regulates what? Very generally speaking, local regulations tend to focus on the location of your business and whether it poses a nuisance or a threat to public safety. State and federal regulations typically focus more on the type of work you do and your qualifications to do it.

Zoning and Local Permits

Local business regulations usually deal with the physical location of the business and the safety of the premises and equipment. City zoning laws regulate which activities are allowed in particular locations. For example, your zoning board may not approve your business location if it's in an area zoned exclusively for residential use, there isn't enough parking to support your business, or there are too many similar businesses nearby. Even if your business activities are acceptable for the time being, you might not be allowed to put up the sign you want or put in additional seating once your business takes off.

If your business doesn't comply with zoning laws, you'll either need to get a permit known as a conditional use permit or be granted an exception to the law, sometimes called a variance. Your city or county planning department is generally in charge of zoning laws. Contact them to find out whether your business complies with local rules and, if not, how to request a conditional use permit or a zoning variance.

Assuming your business has met zoning requirements, it still might need to be approved by other city agencies, such as the fire or police departments, the building inspector, or the department of public health. To ensure compliance with local laws, such as health and fire codes, noise laws, and environmental regulations, you may need one or more permits from these agencies. When you register with your local tax collector (Step 4), you may receive information on these agencies and which types of businesses need to contact them. Your county clerk might also be able to direct you to information about regulatory agencies in your area.

RELATED TOPIC

More info on zoning laws. Chapter 6 includes details on zoning laws that affect commercial spaces—as well as zoning restrictions on home-based businesses.

State and Federal Regulations

State regulations often focus on how you conduct your business. For instance, your state wants to make sure that your cosmetologists are competent, your bartenders know when to cut someone off, and that your carpenters do safe work. Your state regulates these business activities through licensing. The business owner and certain employees (the ones performing the activity) often need to take a class, pass a test, and pay a fee to obtain the license.

Businesses are more likely to need a state license or permit if they are highly specialized or if they affect the public welfare. In other words, if there's a risk that poor handling of your business activities might harm the public, chances are good that a state license is required. Common examples of state-licensed businesses are bars, auto shops, health care services, and waste management companies.

Don't assume that your business is so simple or straightforward that you don't need a special license. You'd be amazed at how many activities states regulate. To name a few, locksmiths may need a license from the Bureau of Security and Investigative Services; people who train guide dogs may need one from the State Board of Guide Dogs; and furniture makers may be subject to licensing from the Bureau of Home Furnishings. To make sure you don't need a special license, take a look at a list of your state's regulatory agencies (find yours on your state's website), and contact any that seem relevant to your business.

The federal government doesn't regulate small businesses as heavily as local and state offices do, but you may need a federal permit or license to engage in certain activities, including:

- operating a common carrier for hire such as a trucking company (Surface Transportation Board of the U.S. Department of Transportation)
- constructing or operating a radio or television station (Federal Communications Commission)
- manufacturing drugs or meat products (Food and Drug Administration)
- manufacturing alcohol or tobacco products, or making or selling firearms (Bureau of Alcohol, Tobacco, Firearms and Explosives), and
- providing investment advice or counseling (Securities and Exchange Commission).

Federal and state laws cover many aspects of your business from hiring practices to shipping policies. We highlight the key laws in relevant chapters throughout this book.

Government Agencies With Business Start-Up Information

Here are some useful resources on business start-up tasks and issues.

State Agencies

Fortunately, many states have agencies or offices that act as clearinghouses for information on start-up tasks and issues; some of these offices have very helpful websites with comprehensive information for start-ups. If you aren't sure what regulations might apply to your business, see if your state has a small business assistance office or "one-stop-shop" for small business start-up information.

Start by checking the websites for your state's tax agency or secretary of state, both of which tend to offer this type of information. To find your state tax agency's website, either search the IRS website at www. irs.gov (under "State Government Websites") for its list of state tax sites, or Google your state name along with the words "tax department" or "tax agency." Secretaries of state are listed at the National Association of Secretaries of State's website at www.nass.org. For other state agencies, Google your state's name along with the name of the department you're looking for. Also try the state department of commerce or economic development, though these offices tend to focus more on incentives for luring big businesses to the state, not so much on small business start-up requirements. Eventually, you'll inevitably have to start making phone calls and asking questions. If an office doesn't have all the answers you need, make sure to ask if they can direct you to another agency that may be able to help.

CAUTION
Don't waste your precious time searching endlessly through a state website trying to find the information you need. If it's not readily available at the site, chances are it's either not there or is so hopelessly buried that it's not worth your time to ferret it out. In these situations, it may well be better to just get on the phone or even go to the state office in person.

Local Agencies

For local information on start-up requirements, check with the office that issues tax registration certificates to businesses, sometimes called a tax registration office, tax collector, or city treasurer. County clerks are another potentially good source of information. These offices are usually easy to find in your local phone book. Keep in mind that there are huge differences among cities, counties, and states in what small business information they have to offer. A county clerk's office in one county may prove to be an amazing resource, while the clerk of a different county may be clueless.

Also remember that while the Web is a potentially awesome resource for navigating the permit and start-up requirements in your area, many state and local governments are still lagging in posting this kind of practical information.

Other Useful Resources for Small Business Start-Ups

Don't forget to consult nongovernment resources such as Women's Business Centers, Small Business Development Centers (SBDCs), and any business incubators in your area. They often offer valuable and free assistance to small businesses on a range of issues, including permit and license questions, and they can be a huge help in navigating the unique twists and turns of your local small business bureaucracy. For details and contact info, see the resources we recommend in Chapter 4 ("Business Planning Resources").

Getting the Word Out: Cost-Effective Marketing

E ven the hottest products and services don't sell themselves. At the most basic level, customers need to know that your product or service exists and be convinced to buy what you're selling. The process of reaching out to potential customers and promoting your products or services to them is marketing.

Chances are you don't have the marketing budgets or resources that large corporations do, so you'll have to rely on more creative methods to get the word out about your products and services without breaking the bank. The good news is that for many small, local businesses, simple approaches like networking will cost you little (if anything) and can yield real results and profits. Other inexpensive marketing methods, such as sending out press releases and sponsoring special events, can generate far better exposure than spending a fortune on advertising.

TIP

Positive word of mouth is gold. As we discuss different marketing strategies, bear in mind that one of the most powerful ways to attract customers is to generate positive word of mouth. While the ultimate goal of marketing is to boost your sales, simply getting people talking about your business is a good start. When there's a buzz about your business, sales will almost always follow. Social media online present lots of new opportunities to generate word of mouth. See "Use Social Media to Enhance Customer Service," below.

In this chapter, we'll outline the most effective marketing methods for small businesses, focusing on strategies that will help get your marketing machine up and running with minimum effort or expense. We'll also cover tips and strategies for customer service, which is essential to retain the customers you worked so hard to attract in the first place. Even better, excellent customer service will inspire your customers to sing your praises to their friends and associates. With the solid foundation in marketing basics provided in this chapter, you'll be able to promote your newly launched business and expand your efforts as your business grows.

Common Marketing Terms

Marketing terminology is often used very loosely, making it difficult for beginners to understand the distinctions among specific types of marketing, such as publicity vs. public relations. Here are some quick definitions of the most common marketing terms used in this chapter.

- **Marketing** means just about any activity that promotes your business: advertising, special events, direct mail, online discounts and promotions, and the like. This chapter uses more specific terms to refer to individual types of marketing activities.

- **Advertising** means buying space or airtime to deliver a promotional message, usually through print media, television, radio, or the Internet. Of course, just about anything can carry an advertising message, including billboards, the sides of buses, walls in public bathrooms, and park benches, to name a few.

- **Listings or directories** include phone books, business directories, and other specialized publications, both online and print. Some are targeted at specific industries, such as a directory of local film production companies or neighborhood restaurants and merchants. Others may be broader, such as a listing of women-owned businesses which would encompass a broad range of business types, or the online yellow pages which is even broader. Often, you can be listed in a directory as a benefit of membership in an association such as the local chamber of commerce or other trade group. Directories often require payment for a listing, making them a type of advertising. But, unlike most ads, directories often serve as valuable resources that are used again and again, which means that they can be much more effective than typical display ads.

- **Public relations** means a coordinated, multifaceted effort to get exposure for your business. A public relations campaign for a software company's product launch might include hosting and promoting an event with free consulting and product demonstrations, running display ads for the software product in appropriate media outlets, booking speaking engagements for the company's president, and doing social media outreach—all coordinated to ensure clarity and consistency of message.

Common Marketing Terms (continued)

- **Media relations** refers to contacting the media and pitching story ideas in hopes of obtaining editorial coverage, such as a feature article or story on your business or its products or services. Most commonly, media relations involves sending press releases to editors and reporters at newspapers and print publications, television and radio producers, and the like to announce an event or provide information that could be the subject of a news or feature story.
- **Publicity** typically refers to marketing efforts that involve an event or a public appearance, such as holding a press conference, appearing on a talk show, hosting a fundraiser, or even staging some sort of prank that's sure to garner attention.
- **Viral marketing** is a method that focuses on getting people to pass on a marketing message, usually online, such as by forwarding a funny YouTube video. The goal is to get people to say, "You gotta see this!" and widely distribute your video or ad, creating a buzz.

TIP

The world we live in is a virtual marketing classroom. It's no secret that everyday life is saturated with marketing appeals. As annoying as it is to be courted daily by thousands of companies, there is a bright side for entrepreneurs: Whether you've "studied" marketing or not, you've unwittingly absorbed some basic marketing know-how (particularly those of you who are avid shoppers, subscribe to all kinds of magazines, watch a lot of TV, or spend any amount of time online). As an experienced marketing target, you probably know more about marketing than you think you do. Use your experience as a "marketee" to turn the tables and start thinking like a marketer.

RELATED TOPIC

This chapter focuses on traditional marketing programs, such as media relations and customer loyalty programs. Chapter 9 covers the topic of online marketing, through email promotions, e-newsletters, and other means. Also, Chapter 2 includes a special section on marketing your woman-owned businesses to government agencies.

Start by Knowing Your Market

In Chapter 2, we discussed the importance of developing your business idea with a target market in mind. At the most fundamental level, a business simply won't succeed if there isn't a solid customer base to support it. You'll need to identify that base as an initial step in developing and refining your business idea prior to launch.

Understanding your market—including potential customers (which may be individuals or other businesses), competition, and your industry—is also necessary to define a solid marketing strategy. What do your target customers want that the other guys don't offer? What industry trends can you leverage that your local competition isn't? Answering these and similar questions is essential to crafting a powerful marketing message that distinguishes your business from others in the field.

In addition, having a clear vision of your target customers is important so you can figure out where to target your marketing efforts. For example, what publications do your prospects read, where do they shop, what websites do they visit regularly, and what types of events do they attend? If your vision of your customer base is fuzzy or too broadly defined, you won't be able to answer these questions and your ability to actually reach your prospects will be seriously hampered.

Finally, it's important to know who your target customers are so that you can craft your marketing messages appropriately. For example, if your target customers are 18-to-25-year-old college students, your website and print materials will likely have a different tone, language, design, and overall vibe than if you were targeting 45-to-60-year-old health care professionals.

Chapter 2 covers the ins and outs of identifying and refining your target market, and doing market research in more detail. Be sure you have done this important work before starting any marketing campaign.

> ⚠ CAUTION
> **Make sure your business plan (Chapter 4) covers the costs of whatever marketing projects you want to pursue.** While this chapter focuses on relatively inexpensive marketing ideas, there are always costs involved, including fees for attending networking events, your time spent writing and pitching press releases, the costs of sponsoring an event or listing in a directory, and the like. Account for them in your business plan.

Your style helps define your brand

"I guess in the beginning when I first started shooting seriously, I wanted to be a fashion photographer. So I was in Europe and it became very clear to me that the photographers that I was looking up to were people with very strong styles. They knew exactly what their voice was with a camera. And I respected that. And I thought of that as branding in a way—they're just doing magazine editorials or advertising, they're not necessarily saying 'Buy Helmut Newton pictures!' But when you see that picture, you know who did it and where they come from."

— **Kyle Zimmerman**

Develop a Strong, Authentic Brand

Branding is the process of developing positive and specific associations with your business in your target customers' minds, above and beyond the basics of what products or services you provide. When a company has a well-developed brand, customers have an emotional tie to the company and a connection to the brand. For example, people associate Disney with being family friendly, cheerful, and fun; Volvo as providing safety and quality; and Levi Strauss & Co. as hip, yet timeless. Consumers these days tend to make buying choices largely by brand, not just by the features of the product.

Without getting into a lengthy history of branding, suffice it to say that the power and impact of branding has grown along with the presence and penetration of mass media. Television gave birth to the golden age of branding (think the TV show "Mad Men" and Don Draper), and these days the omnipresence of digital media has exploded the importance and scope of branding techniques.

What's important to understand is that the Internet hasn't just resulted in "more" branding, but has changed the rules altogether. Unlike the one-way street of TV communications, digital media is interactive, so a business's brand is enormously affected by the presence of the feedback loop from customers. To make the branding task even trickier, this feedback loop never stops, and it can be blindingly fast.

The Value of Authenticity and Transparency to Your Business Success

Specifically, two concepts have become critical elements of successful branding in the digital age: authenticity and transparency.

- **Authenticity** is crucial because today's customers are incredibly media savvy and can smell insincerity a mile away. Hollow marketing appeals just don't fly anymore. You can barely even get consumers to notice you at all in a world with way too much information floating around. Businesses that engender trust and loyalty have the best chance of breaking through in a very crowded marketplace.

- **Transparency** is essential because customers can so easily share and obtain information online. In today's connected world, you can't be inconsistent with pricing, or ignore customer complaints, or pretend a product flaw doesn't exist. Instant or near-instant access to data allows consumers to educate themselves—about price, about features, options, your business history, everything. Open businesses help build trust. Opaque businesses are quick to generate bad buzz in an increasingly social-media driven world.

So how can you build authenticity and transparency into your business? By building your business as a "whole business." Start with your core values, or the collective core values of your partners if you have them, and make sure these values inform every aspect and system of your business. Formalize your values by putting them in writing in your business plan, and regularly revisit them—especially if you have partners—to make sure everyone is on the same page.

For example, if you are starting a business making handbags, wallets, and similar accessories, and you and your partners strongly believe in building strong local economies, don't just assume that pushing the "buy local" message in your marketing and PR materials is enough. Start by clarifying with your partners what "buy local" means to you, and in what specific ways you'll reflect this value in your business. For example, establish targets for what portion of materials and supplies you'll buy locally, and what qualifies as "local": Within ten miles of your city? Statewide? What about materials that you can't source locally, like zippers or certain hardware? Will you hire a local Web developer for your website, or someone from out-of-state?

Most of your customers will understand that your business won't be able to be 100% local with its vendors and suppliers, but you need to think in advance about what buying practices you'll put in place and how you'll respond to any critics. What you want to avoid is putting yourself out there as a champion of local business, but without a ready answer when someone points out some aspect of your business that's at odds with your professed values. Putting careful thought into your values and defining them specifically for different aspects of your business operations will pay off with a business that operates with consistency and is perceived as authentic to your customers.

Use your well-defined values as a foundation as you develop all the various systems that make your business tick. All aspects of your business should be coordinated and cohesive—from the definition of your products/services, to your business operations, to your marketing messages, to your promotional activities, to how you hire and manage your employees, to your customer support practices. When all of these are developed in a holistic way, consistent with your values, the result is an authentic business that gains trust and loyalty in the marketplace.

The Importance of Consistency and Professionalism in Marketing and Branding Your Business

Besides developing a cohesive "whole" business from the ground up, be sure to be consistent with your marketing and branding outreach. Imagery and design are important ways for your business to convey your brand. This includes things like your business name and logo; website; business cards, brochure, and print material design; signage; and interior design of your business space. See Elissa Breitbard's comments, below, for tips on creating a marketable business name.

While it may not always be necessary to hire pricey consultants to develop and design these things, it is important that they convey a professional image. By "professional" we don't mean stodgy or uptight—your brand image is up to you, and it can be funky or straitlaced or anything in between. But regardless of your brand personality, you want to project an image of basic professionalism and competence. A dirty retail space, kludgy website, poorly painted sign, or illegible logo won't do anything for your reputation.

TIP

A logo is not always a start-up priority. Some small start-ups can do fine with just their business name. If you decide that you do need a logo, don't pay a fortune to a graphic designer to create it. We say this because far too many new entrepreneurs confuse the logo with the brand and think that paying top dollar for a professional looking logo will establish their brand as a professional company. This kind of thinking is backwards. It's your business practices, such as customer service, that will establish your brand, which will in turn "infuse" your logo with whatever reputation you've developed. In order to develop your brand well, focus on the business—not the logo—at the beginning.

A coordinated, consistent message is key to branding

"We've made it a real point to use the words 'blissful,' 'relaxation,' and 'wellness' as much as possible. These are words that Betty's evokes now, and that's because we've worked really hard at branding Betty's as such. One way we've done that is we don't do hair and nails. We're not a beauty salon; we're not a gym. You come here to relax. So I think part of the branding of Betty's is this relaxation, and that fits really well with our packaging and everything we retail supports that. So it's like everything we do supports that. Consistency of message—all the arrows point to the same thing. The other thing we've done is that we've created the 'Betty's scent'—and we use it in everything: our massage oil, our lotion, our gel. People then associate that smell with Betty's."

— **Elissa Breitbard**

"I knew that when I opened the studio here I was going to have to be very clear about my voice. And that I would do that with advertising since people didn't know me. But that I would make sure that the elements that I thought were important about my photography were always present consistently in the advertising. Lifestyle, natural, dynamic, something different in the crop—just always, every single time I would put something out, I would match it up to the criteria. If it doesn't fit, don't do it. I only did that a couple times where I went against my better judgment, and I was always wrong. I knew right away. The billboard would go up, and I'd just go 'Oooohh! Wrong!' Didn't follow the rules—my own rules."

— **Kyle Zimmerman**

Choosing Winning Names for Your Business, Products, and Services

Choosing names for your business and its products is an opportunity to use your creative juices to come up with a name that is both marketable and infused with your individual personality. There are a few helpful things to keep in mind when choosing your business names.

If possible, choose a business name that is also available as a domain name. Getting people to remember the name of your new business is challenging enough; ideally your customers won't need to remember a second name for your website. Chapter 9 includes a detailed discussion on choosing a domain name (part of the address people use to access your website, such as nolo.com).

Unless you have major branding resources, it's helpful for your business name to say what you do. This is especially important in the crucial early days before you've developed name recognition. For example, if you plan to open a payroll services firm, include "Payroll Services" in the name to ensure customers understand the nature of the business.

Before you finally commit to a name, get some feedback from potential customers, suppliers, and others in your support network. They may come up with a negative connotation to a potential name or suggest an improvement you haven't considered.

Think about whether it makes sense to include your personal name. When you include your personal name in your business name—particularly if you run a service-based business—customers may expect that you will handle their accounts personally. This can be an issue if you want to grow out of the hands-on work and act more as the business owner. It also can affect the value of the business if you ever want to sell it. That said, it's common for professionals such as architects, attorneys, accountants, or financial consultants to use their personal name, as in Suze Orman, Financial Consultant, or Jennifer Cantrell, CPA.

Be sure your business name will still be appropriate if and when your business grows, either in terms of location or business scope. For example, if you open Boston Bike Shop, what if you want to open a store in Cambridge? Or Los Angeles? Or online? Similarly, if you start an academic publishing company called Old School Press, what if you want to start producing digital media and software? It would be better to anticipate likely areas of expansion and name the business Old School Educational Media.

Be sure your name doesn't violate another company's trademark. See "Avoiding Trademark Troubles When Naming Your Business," in Chapter 7 for advice.

Should your business name include your personal name?

"I wish I hadn't used my name for the business. I'll never be able to sell this business. I don't feel like I could. Even if I were able to make it be the ultimate strong, powerful business that I want it to be, I could never with good conscience, with clean mind, turn it over and sell it. If this had instead been 'Life Is Art Portrait Studio,' owned by Kyle Zimmerman, I may have been able to take this a lot farther. Then there's the issue of people expecting me. So many times clients still come in, and if they're not getting Kyle, they're not feeling like they're being valued as clients, and that they're getting second best. Really, I can only shoot so many things. On a certain day, you know, I'm creative and I'm a good photographer, but I have really good photographers, who are on some days better than me, and I can see that. And I want that. I want my clients to know that I think they're doing really good to have my other photographer. But still, the staff answers the phone and it's a new client, and some friend of theirs has referred them, and that friend was photographed by me four years ago, and the pictures were amazing, and the friend was so happy, and they said, to the client, 'Ask for Kyle. Make sure you get Kyle.' And I'm like, I'll take it, I'll be grateful for the referral and I'm very happy, but ... it's one of the problems. "

— **Kyle Zimmerman**

Establish Excellent Customer Service Policies and Practices

Before you start any marketing efforts to bring new customers in the door, make sure you've thought about how you'll keep your customers once you get them. Excellent customer service is the key to achieving this. Customer service includes a broad set of activities and practices, from how your employees (if you have any) greet customers when they walk in the store, to policies for returns and exchanges.

TIP

It costs much less to retain your existing customers than it does to draw in new ones. Customer retention is an important strategy in getting the most out of your marketing budget. Think of your existing customer base like a leaking bucket; your goal is to keep as many customers "in the bucket" as possible so you don't have spend the resources necessary to replace them. Excellent customer service is perhaps the best way to keep customers from leaking away.

Pay attention to the following aspects of customer service and adopt practices and systems (preferably in writing, per my recommendations in Chapter 12) to inspire your customers to rave about your business.

- **Answer your phone promptly.** If you use an automated call system, keep it simple. Make sure one branch of your phone tree provides basic info like hours and location (and directions if it's at all tricky to find you).

- **Return phone calls and emails promptly.** It's unbelievable how many businesses are bad about doing this—and it's a surefire way to annoy (and lose) customers and clients.

- **If you have employees, train them in customer service.** While you may think treating people courteously and professionally is a no-brainer, it helps to be very specific with your employees about your customer service expectations. Put procedures and policies in writing—including how you want employees to answer the phones or deal with customers face-to-face. Train employees regularly, especially before holidays or other times when you are particularly busy.

- **Make sure your workforce is knowledgeable.** Customer service doesn't just mean treating people well. It also means knowing the answers to customers' and clients' questions about your products and services—whether it's curtains, cat toys, or car insurance—and about the competition. It's incredibly frustrating when store clerks don't know enough about the product offerings to answer basic questions. You need to create a reason for customers to shop with you, even if they could save a few dollars by going with the big box stores or buying online. Well-developed knowledge is a great way to achieve this.

- **Offer generous return and exchange policies.** Customers will feel much more comfortable making a purchase if they are confident your business will stand behind the product and give a full refund if they are not satisfied for any reason. If you've ever shopped at Zappos or REI, you'll know what I'm talking about. Of course, to protect yourself, you should set a reasonable time limit for returns or require a receipt. (Be sure you're don't run afoul of state and federal rules—see "Laws Affecting Customer Service Practices," below, for details.) But don't alienate customers by being too draconian—if someone wants to return an item one day or even a week after your 30-day limit, you'll generate much better customer goodwill if you cut them a little slack.

- **Take complaints seriously—and don't get defensive!** Make sincere efforts to make things right. For example, if your catering client complains about one of your dishes that you thought was delicious, resist the urge to argue. Instead, express how badly you feel that they weren't totally satisfied and ask what you can do to make it up to them. Of course you can't let yourself be taken advantage of, but more often than not you can find a win-win solution if you just look hard enough. Perhaps offer the client a half-off discount on the dish in question, and a 10% discount on the next event they want you to cater.

Customer service is key—and it's often less than best

"I think the biggest mistake I see over and over again has to be the customer service issue. Even freelancers who work for me when I'm running projects, the number of excuses that I get—they didn't do this, they didn't do that, they forgot the deadline—I mean, just be professional, be incredibly prompt, be incredibly responsive, and you're already like ten steps ahead of everybody else. The customer service issue is enormous. I think if people put half as much effort into that as they did into some other parts of their business, they would be ten times as successful as they are."

— **Emily Esterson**

Use Social Media to Enhance Customer Service

There are endless ways to market your business online, and using social media is one of the most powerful methods. When you engage with current and potential customers on Facebook or Twitter (to use just two examples), you are building relationships with your target audience which will go a long way in establishing your brand. As discussed in more detail in Chapter 9, it's essential to monitor your reputation online and take action when you find negative comments posted about your business. But beyond damage control, social media offers the opportunity to interact with your customers, answer questions about your products and services, give them tips and advice, and generally build a trusting relationship between your business and its patrons. Trust is key. When your business is accessible and responsive across multiple "channels"— in other words, not just via an 800 number, but also on Facebook or Twitter, for example—people will be more apt to trust you, which plays a big role in purchasing decisions.

- **Go out of your way to help existing and potential customers.** There's no better way to build trust and goodwill. For example, I took a ring that needed repair to a jeweler I had used only once (several years ago) to size a ring. This time he told me that there wasn't enough metal to reset the stone, meaning essentially the ring needed to be fully rebuilt which probably wasn't worth the cost. I was really disappointed as I wanted to wear the ring at a party in a few days. When the jeweler heard me say this he said, "Well, if you're really careful, I can use jeweler's cement to glue the stone in. But it won't stay in forever, don't wear it after the party!" He spent the next 20 minutes or so gluing in the stone—and refused to accept any payment. He's my jeweler hero, which I've told tons of my friends in town.

Besides having solid customer service, there are swarms of other details that can affect whether your business runs smoothly or more like a train wreck. Don't underestimate the importance of making sure that overall you're ready to handle the heightened attention your marketing will bring. For example, a restaurant should not start a big marketing campaign without already having a good chef and enough wait staff in place to handle a surge of diners. Otherwise, the unprepared restaurant's marketing efforts will likely result in unhappy diners and bad publicity. In short, make sure your house is in order before you worry about how to promote it.

> **RELATED TOPIC**
>
> **Technology can help improve customer service.** Customer relationship management (CRM) software can help you find and retain customers and reduce marketing costs. See Chapter 9 for details.

Laws Affecting Customer Service Practices

State and federal consumer protection laws cover a wide range of issues affecting businesses that sell products or services—from warranties you provide (whether explicit or not) to shipping practices to refund policies. For details, see the "Consumer Information" section of the Federal Trade Commission's website (www.ftc.gov). Also, the Small Business section of the Nolo website (www.nolo.com) has lots of useful articles on relevant subjects, such as deceptive pricing practices.

Plan Marketing in Advance

A problem that plagues many business owners is that they get so busy with running the business that marketing gets short shrift. For example, the harried owner of a retail store might realize in early November that she doesn't have a clue how she'll market the business for the holidays. At that late date she'll probably only be able to do a half-baked job.

To avoid letting this happen to you, draft a schedule of marketing outreach efforts for at least the next six months, ideally a year. Identify what the marketing opportunity is (for example, promoting your tax preparation services prior to tax time, or home organizing products at the beginning of the year), what methods you will use (as described below), and when you will take action (for example, setting deadlines for sending out a press release, postcard, or email announcement). With a schedule drafted well in advance, opportunities won't sneak up on you while you're busy paying attention to other aspects of the business.

There are endless ways to market your business—the key is to pick the methods that will give the most bang for the buck. Be creative and think broadly about how to leverage your relationships and networks. Consider the habits and inclinations of your target customers, and choose marketing methods that will resonate with them, and that make sense for the product or service you're promoting. The following sections outline some of the best and most cost-effective methods to choose from.

Networking

Networking is such an important part of establishing your business that we see it less as a task than an entrepreneurial way of life. In a nutshell, networking involves actively cultivating relationships with business owners, colleagues, community leaders—pretty much anyone who presents possible opportunities for your business. Friends and family are obviously part of your network, too.

Networking is not sales: Rather than aiming to make a sale to a potential customer, your goal is to get to know other businesswomen (and men) and influential people and share information about what you do in hopes that they will consider your business in the future and recommend it to their associates, friends, and family members, Networking is an excellent way to build your customer base, especially in the early days of your business. In addition, as mentioned in Chapter 2, networking in your pre-start-up days can help you refine your business idea and learn important information about your target market.

Building relationships through networking

"We've found over the years that word of mouth is unbeatable, so our marketing really focuses on building relationships with our existing clients and the networks they move in. Like many 'knowledge economy' businesses, we've found that the best way to attract clients and build a reputation is through education and outreach, both to our existing clients and to prospects. We do a lot of blogging, public speaking, workshops, and knowledge sharing that serve the dual purposes of both demystifying what we do and positioning our firm as experts. No advertising or paid marketing could achieve that effect so efficiently."

— Lauren Bacon and Emira Mears

"Because we're a local business, being in contact with other local businesses helps us get referrals. One thing we've done in the recession is branch out. For example doing weddings, we used to mainly keep in touch with florists, dress shops, whatever, but now we're branching out to local restaurants, having events there; reaching out to other local businesses that are not necessarily related to us but that share customers in common. Now [in the recession] we have to be a little more creative with the businesses that we keep in touch with and stretch our comfort zone, from the same old florists, the same old limo place, or whoever that we used to be in touch with."

— Sabrina Habib Williams

Finally, networking is also important because it helps establish other crucial business relationships. Often, a relationship with a vendor, a partner, an investor, or another business may turn out to be a key factor in your business's success. The best way to develop these contacts is through networking.

So how exactly do you go about networking? It's difficult to describe exactly how it works because it's so broad, but we like to think of it simply as socializing with an agenda, with the hope of advancing mutual business interests. You are "networking" every time you have lunch with another business owner, attend an event held by a local trade association or a national conference, write a letter to the editor, or participate in an online discussion group. Another way to find groups is to use www.meetup.com;

search for keywords like "business owners" or "coworking" or "women entrepreneurs" to see what groups have been established in your area. The trick to successful networking is to identify groups and communities that overlap with your target market (this could include target customers or the industry in which you operate), and to communicate a well-thought-out message effectively within those networks.

TIP

Develop a compelling "elevator pitch." This is a succinct description of your business that can easily be shared with people you meet. (The concept here is that your pitch should be short enough to deliver in an elevator ride—as if you found yourself in an elevator with a potential investor or other important person.) Your pitch should make it clear what your business does and what makes it appealing in a few short words. The most effective pitches focus on the business's specialty or niche instead of subjective qualities, which tend to be taken with a grain of salt. For example, instead of saying, "My restaurant serves really delicious food and has excellent customer service," a better pitch would be "My restaurant serves classic American cuisine with primarily organic ingredients and a large vegetarian selection." Someone hearing the second pitch would be more likely to remember and trust the concrete, specific details than the subjective (and predictable) claims of the first.

Once you start looking for networking opportunities, you'll see many business-related organizations host events specifically geared for networking. Trade associations, your local chamber of commerce, the local Rotary club, and professional organizations, among others, tend to host dinners, luncheons, seminars, conferences, and business-oriented "mixers" that include specific networking time for members to get to know each other. Most newspapers and industry publications have calendars of these types of business events. There may be fees to attend, so learn as much as you can about the focus of the event to figure out if you're likely to have mutual interests with other attendees.

Networking, traveling, and children

"I don't travel nearly as much as I used to, and I miss it. I really enjoy conferences, networking, and the intellectual camaraderie between like-minded professionals. I'm still able to travel for the more important business events, and I find local child care in the city I'm visiting, either through an online website for babysitters or through the hotel. It just means each out of town event has to be that much more compelling or lucrative, to make it worth spending extra on child care. Evening networking events are much more difficult too, unless you shell out for more child care or press unwilling family members into service.

"I've tried to take my kid with me to a couple of the more casual business events in my city, and it doesn't really work so well. You get the feeling that everyone is happy to meet your kid once, but you better not do it again if you want to keep your professional reputation. And god forbid your child doesn't behave!"

— Isabel Walcott Draves

"My business has been virtual since the beginning. I have gone 'ultra-virtual' since my daughter was born. Prior to having my daughter, my husband and I would attend several in-person sales, client, and association meetings both in and out of state. Now, we hold almost all of our meetings via telephone and online meeting. I save a lot of money on travel expenses, of course."

— Leila Johnson

Besides meeting contacts at organized networking events, introducing yourself to a potentially useful contact can be as simple as picking up the phone, writing a letter, or sending an email—as formal or informal as circumstances seem to merit. A letter of introduction on attractive letterhead might be best for an influential politician, for example, but an email might be fine to introduce yourself to a local business owner. In your letter, email, or phone call, explain who you are, what your business does, and why you think it might be mutually useful to get to know each other. Try to conclude by encouraging further communication in the future, such as inviting the contact to an event or asking if he or she would be interested in receiving email updates from your business.

Social Media Make Networking Easy

Using social media online is one of the best ways to network. We'll discuss that in Chapter 9 which focuses on how to market your business online, by using Twitter, LinkedIn, and other social media networks.

 TIP

If networking puts you outside your comfort zone, you're not alone. The best way to overcome any anxiety or shyness is to get out there and do it—take baby steps if necessary. If you tend to feel awkward when alone at events, take a friend with you. No matter how much you may dread it, make sure you introduce yourself and provide your business card to at least a few people if for no other reason than for practice. We won't lie, you will undoubtedly meet some annoying people along the way, even some jerks. But mostly you'll meet well-meaning folks like yourself who are looking for mutually rewarding opportunities. Your comfort level and networking skills will improve with each interaction, guaranteed.

A Website Is Key to Your Marketing Efforts

Every business should have at least a simple website with basic marketing information. These days, if customers Google your business and come up empty-handed, they might think your business isn't very professional, stable, or convenient; and might instead work with a competitor that does have a site. Beyond a basic website, there are lots of online marketing opportunities, such as emailing your target customers to let them know about upcoming promotions, events, and other business information and distributing substantive information and articles in e-newsletters. Chapter 9 focuses on promoting your business online, including creating a website, using search engine optimization (SEO) to drive traffic to your site, and engaging in social media. Refer to that chapter for more information specifically about online marketing.

Attend government contracting networking events

"It's a good idea to attend some of your local 'getting-to-know-you' conferences on government contracting, which almost give you a blueprint for getting noticed by government buyers."

— **Leila Johnson**

Engaging in Media Relations

One of the best types of exposure for any business is getting coverage via newspapers, magazines, radio, television, or the Internet. This type of coverage is called "editorial" coverage, meaning some mention of your business in news or feature stories, as opposed to paid advertising. Editorial coverage gives immediate credibility and will help enhance your business's image and reputation much more than advertisements or paid publicity. For example, a local newspaper article about your business being awarded a lucrative state contract will almost always generate a more favorable and lasting impression than an advertisement on the very same page.

You don't just have to hope for media coverage; there is a fairly standard process for obtaining it, and this process is what's known as media relations. The process is simple: You contact the media on behalf of your business and encourage an editor, producer, or reporter to write or produce a story about your particular business or industry. As with most marketing efforts, the more specific, targeted, and timely your message, the more impact it will have. Remember, the media is looking for a story or an angle. For this reason, you'll be much more likely to interest an editor in your business's recent expansion and opening of a new facility than of the very general fact that your business exists.

TIP

Don't forget blogs and bloggers when doing media relations.
When we talk about "the media" we also mean bloggers. A mention in an influential blog can bring a lot of exposure to your business and traffic to its website. To maximize your chances of such a mention, cultivate relationships with bloggers in your field. Share news tips with them and add meaningful (that is, not self-serving) comments on their posts. Relationships with bloggers are just as important as relationships with traditional journalists—maybe even more so if your business is heavily Internet driven. For more on blogs, including advice on starting your own, see Chapter 8.

Some people feel timid about contacting the media and asking them to cover a specific story. While you shouldn't be a pest, you also shouldn't feel shy about pushing your story idea. To do their jobs, journalists must come up with a constant stream of interesting new stories and topics. Local business journalists are often particularly challenged in finding newsworthy business stories. Just as you need their help, they need yours. Because you will often know more than reporters do about a particular story, you can offer valuable information that they can use. If you are honest and reliable, you will usually be treated with respect.

Conducting a Media Relations Campaign

When you're planning media relations efforts, remember to start your efforts way before you want to get coverage, especially if you're pitching monthly publications. While daily news outlets might respond to your pitch quickly, monthly magazines often have their content planned out months or even a year in advance. Plan your media relations efforts as early as possible so you won't miss opportunities.

The basic steps for conducting an effective media relations campaign are:

1. **Write a press release.** A press release is a key tool for pitching a story idea. Typically, a press release is a one-page announcement outlining the information you want the media to cover. You have two main goals in writing a press release: to capture the

journalist's attention, and to make it easy for the journalist to write the story you want published. Stylistically, press releases are usually written like news stories, offering journalists an example of the piece you want them to produce. (See "Writing a Strong Press Release," below, for more details on how to put together a winning pitch.)

2. **Make a list of target recipients.** For many small businesses, you'll target local media—the newspapers, business publications, and TV and radio news programs that serve your community. (As noted below, it's definitely more challenging to get national media to bite.) Check websites for lists of reporters and editors; sometimes it will be obvious who would be the most appropriate recipients of your release—for example, the food editor if you are publicizing the opening of your new café or homemade granola product. If you aren't sure whom to contact, call the news department or managing editor, briefly describe the nature of your press release, and ask who might be the best person to speak with. (For example: "Hi, I have a press release regarding a new line of skin care products my business is now producing and distributing. Can you tell me which reporter I should direct it to?") Sometimes, you'll be told simply to send it to the attention of the managing editor. If so, jump ahead to Step 4.

3. **Make initial contact with the journalist by phone.** If you are sending your release to a particular media person, it's a good idea to call first so your release doesn't get lost in the shuffle. When you call, introduce yourself and your business, briefly explain the nature of your news story, and tell the person you will be sending a press release. If you can't reach the journalist by phone (as is often the case), don't let it hold you up: Leave a message and send out your press release. While you could make this initial contact by email, a phone call usually makes a stronger impression. And creating lasting relationships with individual reporters is the best way to get positive coverage over the long term.

4. **Send the press release by email, fax, or both.** Years ago, press releases were sent by mail. Today, many media folks prefer you email press releases, so they can cut and paste when writing stories (both a PDF attachment and plain text in the body of the email work best). Faxes are also helpful because they don't get lost or buried as easily as email. While faxes are less tree-friendly, some old-school journalists prefer having a paper copy to review. To cover your bases, send your press releases in both forms, or, ask the reporter's preferred method(s).

5. **Follow up after you send the press release.** Within a day or so after sending your release, follow up with another phone call or email to make sure your press contact received the release and to answer any questions he or she may have.

If you don't get a response after an introductory phone call, a press release, and a follow-up call, let the particular story idea rest; this will help you preserve your reputation as a pleasant, professional person to deal with the next time you want to pitch a story. A journalist may not cover your story because he or she does not think it is newsworthy or because there are other stories that take precedence. A few months later, when you try again, you may be pleasantly surprised to find that you've pitched the right story on the right day.

In some cases, particularly if you are promoting a product, it may be appropriate to send a sample by mail along with your press release. For example, if you are promoting a line of exercise clothing made with innovative new organic fabric, you might want to include a fabric sample. If it's not cost prohibitive, you could even send an actual article of clothing. Journalists like freebies just like everyone else, so a nice sample will never hurt your pitch.

While you may be surprised at how simple it is to get coverage in local media, note that national (and major metropolitan area) media are a much harder nut to crack. In other words, don't count on getting covered in *The Wall Street Journal* or interviewed on a popular talk show without a professional publicist or great contacts (and a compelling and timely story, product, or service).

Of course, a lot depends on your business. If your company has an innovative organizing system, for example, *Real Simple* magazine might do a little piece on it. Or *AARP Magazine* might be interested in your new website for long-distance caregivers. The key is to think creatively of what publications, websites, and media outlets might be most interested in your product or service.

> **TIP**
>
> **When to hire a professional media relations consultant.** If national or major market coverage is important to your business, you may want to hire a media or PR consultant (either to run a full campaign or suggest specific ideas for you to pursue on your own). This can make a big difference in successfully obtaining coverage for your business. Make sure you hire someone with the kind of media relations experience and contacts you seek. Some PR people are much better at promoting local restaurants, while others specialize in publicizing high-tech companies and products.

Writing a Strong Press Release

Reporters, editors, and producers are chronically busy and squeezed by deadlines. The better your press release, the more likely a journalist will write about your business, giving you valuable exposure. Remember, journalists need good story ideas and clear information to get their jobs done. The easier you can make it for them to cover your story, the more likely they are to oblige. If you write a strong, clear press release, they may even use parts of your release verbatim. But because most media people are flooded with press releases and story pitches, you'll need to keep your press release as succinct as possible. Here are some tips on how to construct a compelling press release that is likely to generate media placements.

- **Create a news angle.** If it is appropriate, tie your release into a topic that's currently in the news. For example, if your press release is announcing your furniture manufacturing company starting a new line featuring environmentally friendly materials, you can reference the rapid growth of "green" businesses—a hot news topic.

Sample Press Release

FOR IMMEDIATE RELEASE

December 5, 2016

Krafty Squirrel Home Décor Hosts Holiday Craft Fair to Benefit Health Care for the Homeless

CHICAGO, Illinois—Krafty Squirrel Home Décor, a Chicago-based manufacturer of unique handmade home accessories, is hosting a Holiday Craft Fair on December 5, 2016, from 10 a.m. to 9 p.m., to benefit Health Care for the Homeless, a local 501(c)(3) nonprofit. The event will include a raffle of home décor items worth $500, and performances by local band Fuzzy Love.

Since the economic downturn, the number of homeless people in the Chicago area has increased by 25%, according to a survey by the Chicago Homeless Commission. At the same time, two of the city's homeless shelters have closed due to budget cuts, leaving a shortage of beds and meal services in the city.

The founders of Krafty Squirrel, Sophia Cheng and Michele Harrell, were inspired to help after hiring a formerly homeless artist to work at Krafty Squirrel. Monica M. had lost her job when a local restaurant closed, and within four months she had lost her apartment. Sophia knew Monica from local crafting circles, and when she learned Monica was homeless she offered her a job. "I learned from Monica—a talented and wonderful artist—how easily homelessness can happen to any of us," said Sophia. "We knew we wanted to help address this problem in the best way we could."

When they came up with the idea for a craft fair, Sophia and Michele contacted everyone in their crafting network and spread the word. Within two weeks they had 100 local artisans on board.

Shoppers will find a wide range of quality handcrafted items including photo frames, candle holders, framed art, jewelry, table linens, yard art,

Sample Press Release (continued)

scarves, and much more. Fifty percent of all profits will be donated to Health Care for the Homeless, which provides preventive and primary care for the local homeless population.

"We are so excited to have this fun event that brings together our love of décor and our desire to help our community," said Krafty Squirrel Director Sophia Cheng. "We're really passionate about fun design, but realize that design is a luxury not everyone can enjoy."

Besides Krafty Squirrel, event sponsors include the North Side Elks Lodge and Windy City Craft Supply.

Event Details
Holiday Craft Fair
December 5, 2016, 10 a.m. to 9 p.m.
North Side Elks Lodge #555, 1234 N. Lake Shore Drive, Chicago

Raffle: Winner announced at 7 p.m.

Live music: Fuzzy Love, at 3 p.m. and 7 p.m.

About Krafty Squirrel Home Décor
Sophia Cheng and Michele Harrell launched Krafty Squirrel Home Décor in 2002, to bring their unique handcrafted home décor items to lucky Chicagoans. Krafty Squirrel products include table linens, placemats, coasters, and picture frames, and emphasize recyclable and sustainable materials. Today, Krafty Squirrel Home Décor products are distributed by more than 50 retailers nationwide, and at the Krafty Squirrel website at www.kraftysquirrel.com.

Contact Information
Sophia Cheng, Director
Krafty Squirrel Home Décor
312-555-1212 ext. 123
sophia@kraftysquirrel.com

- **Start with a news hook.** Like a news story, your press release should have a strong first sentence, known as the story's "lead" (sometimes spelled "lede"). What is the most important point you want to get across? Write it in a clear, straightforward style and you will have your lead. Compare the following examples:
  - Weak lead: "Krafty Squirrel offers handmade home décor items with funk and flair."
  - Strong lead: "Krafty Squirrel Home Décor, a Chicago-based manufacturer of unique handmade home accessories, is hosting a Holiday Craft Fair on December 5, 2016, from 10 a.m. to 9 p.m., to benefit Health Care for the Homeless, a local 501(c)(3) nonprofit."
- **Date, time, and location information should be easy to find.** If your press release is promoting an event, don't bury important information deep within long paragraphs. Include important event details such as date, location, and registration deadlines in the first sentence or two, the last sentence (perhaps in bold text), or summarized in bullet points at the end of the press release.
- **Put the most important information first.** Like stories in the newspaper, your press release should include all important details up front, then work toward more general or background information in later paragraphs. You could even put background information at the end of the release, in a separate section.
- **Include quotes from yourself or other key people.** Reporters like to include quotes from real people in their stories, so include at least one or two catchy quotes in your press release. If you are writing the release and you are the best person to offer a quote, don't be shy about quoting yourself! Include your quote as if a reporter asked you a question, making it easy to incorporate into a news piece. It may feel strange but it's perfectly appropriate.
- **Provide a separate section with contact information.** The journalists who receive your release may have additional questions to ask you. Choose a point person who will be available to field any such questions and include her contact information clearly at the end of the release.

- **Include statistics or survey results.** Reporters love statistics that illustrate trends. For example, if you're promoting your line of handmade baby quilts, you could include recent statistics that the market for handmade items has grown 35% since the previous year, despite an overall downturn in the economy. You could also do your own survey using an online survey service such as Survey Monkey (see Chapter 2 for more information) and include key results in your press release. For example, you could state that 75% of people surveyed said they'd prefer to give a handmade gift rather than a similarly priced mass produced item.

- **Use tips.** Reporters and editors love to run stories that offer practical tips. They have a particular weakness for articles with a number in the title such as "10 Tips for Organizing Your Home Office" or "Five Yoga Poses to Change Your Life." When articles like these get picked up, your business may not be the focus of the article, but you will establish yourself as an expert and your business will be mentioned in your byline.

> **TIP**
>
> **Relationships with media people are the holy grail.** The most effective media relations come from relationships you build with reporters, editors, producers, and other media contacts. Because you are more likely to get news coverage from a reporter with whom you've worked before than from someone who's never heard of you, you should always treat your relationships with people in the media as the valuable resource they are.

Finally, keep in mind that having a story written about your business isn't the only way to get media coverage. Another great way to get exposure is to be interviewed and quoted for articles on subjects in which you have expertise, or to write an article yourself (as discussed below). Ideally, you'll develop relationships with editors and reporters who will know you're an expert in a certain area such as workplace wellness programs or adventure travel so that they call you for a quote when covering that topic. Similarly you might be invited to participate in a local TV show on a topic within your expertise. Foster this type of coverage by making sure your media contacts understand your area of expertise, and make it clear that you are willing to offer your opinions and information if they need it for a story.

Holding Special Events

Holding events such as a grand opening party, a product demonstration, an informational workshop, or a holiday gala will help you forge a closer bond with your customers, while simultaneously generating valuable publicity for your business. Special events tend to grab the attention of the media, making them a particularly effective marketing method. The icing on the cake is that events can (and should!) be fun, both for you and your customers. A local lingerie shop that offers a free bra fittings one evening per month with champagne will almost certainly get a few people (or more) in the door. Ditto for a tea shop that hosts regular tastings with pastries from a neighboring shop (we discuss collaborating with other businesses next).

One reason that special events are such effective publicity tools is that the media is generally more responsive to specific, time-sensitive activities or events than to businesses in the abstract. An event is an easy hook, particularly if there is any educational or public interest component to it. For example, if your financial management firm offers a half-day workshop on retirement accounts and minimizing taxes, a reporter might well be able to craft a story around the event and discuss the timely topic of saving money in a recession.

Even if your event isn't newsworthy enough to merit a whole story, most events can be listed in local business, entertainment, and other calendars, usually for free. For example, the business and entertainment sections of most daily papers have an events listings, and submitting your event is an easy way to get a dose of publicity.

Collaborating With Other Businesses

Joining forces with another business (or sometimes more than one) is a great way to gain exposure with each other's customer bases. This strategy obviously works best with businesses that share similar customer profiles but provide products or services that are different enough so that they are not competitors. Or your marketing collaborator could be a nonprofit rather than another for-profit business. The possibilities here are limited only by your creativity. Here are just a few ideas:

- An acupuncture clinic offers its clients 20% off if they show a recent receipt from a nearby yoga studio; the yoga studio mirrors the deal for its customers.
- An art cinema offers 50% off its ticket price if filmgoers show a receipt from the neighboring restaurant; the cinema and the restaurant have an agreement that the restaurant will reimburse the cinema for half the discount.
- A bookstore cohosts a local children's book fair with a literacy nonprofit, sharing the costs and revenues of the event.
- A clothing store and a nearby shoe store agree to display each other's marketing materials at the counter.

Listing Your Business in Directories

Getting your business listed in appropriate directories is a great way to boost your visibility with your target customers. Consumers who consult a particular directory have already determined that they are looking for a specific type of business. In addition to every city's phone books, most communities have other types of directories—for example, the local chamber of commerce membership directory, a community merchant's association, a directory of women-owned businesses, or the African American business league's directory. Some directories are still published in hard copy, although many are posted only online.

To find all the directories that may be appropriate for your business to be listed, you'll have to do some homework. Looking online is a good start, but you should also check with local resources, such as local government offices, chambers of commerce, economic development organizations, and trade associations. Local reference librarians can also be a big help.

With any kind of directory, the most important consideration is the audience it will reach. Once you've found some directories you think have potential, ask about how and where the directory will be distributed, how many copies are printed, and how often a new edition is published.

Most business directories (including membership directories, discussed below) charge fees. You'll have to evaluate whether the fees fit into your budget and whether the directory exposes your business to the right audience. While most directory fees are modest, some are prohibitively expensive; these may be worth considering if the audience you're trying to reach is extremely narrow and desirable, and the directory is highly targeted to and heavily relied on by that audience.

Joining a Professional or Trade Organization

Depending on your business and the groups you're eligible to join, it may make sense to join a professional association, such as women attorneys or an association of accountants, or a trade organization, such as women contractors or an electricians' organization. Business groups can offer valuable networking and marketing opportunities, but you'll need to evaluate whether the likely benefits are worth the membership fees, which typically are at least $200 and often quite a bit higher.

Some membership organizations, such as chambers of commerce, will list member businesses in their directories—print, online, or both. Some organizations, such as the Better Business Bureau or an association of green builders, may give you a sticker for your front window, a plaque you can post on the wall in your store, or a virtual certificate for your website.

In addition, the group may host networking opportunities such as luncheons or educational seminars. Some groups also offer cooperative advertising and marketing materials you can use with clients. Finally, professional and trade groups are also good sources for updated information on industry trends and laws affecting your business.

Ask other business owners in your area which groups they find valuable, and get details on all the benefits and fees before deciding which (if any) to join.

Sponsoring Events, Groups, and Public Media

Sponsoring an event, or a sports team, nonprofit organization, or public television or radio station is a great way to develop your brand and get recognition for your business. Sponsorships are a lot like advertising in that you pay money and your business is publicly recognized, usually with a display of your logo and sometimes a short marketing message. But unlike traditional advertising, a sponsorship does more than just communicate your marketing message: It also conveys a sense of connection to whatever cause or event you are sponsoring and can create a positive association in your potential customers' minds.

For example, if you sponsor a local golf tournament and have your logo prominently displayed on signs and event schedules, the golf-oriented attendees will see your business as an ally and begin to develop an emotional connection to your business. Similarly, a business that sponsors a gay and lesbian film festival will develop a connection to the gay and lesbian community. This emotional connection is at the heart of branding and is a powerful way to build a loyal customer base.

Sponsorship opportunities tend to fall in a few categories:

- **Events.** This includes sport tournaments, film festivals, trade shows, street fairs, concerts, and just about any other event open to the public. Event organizers often ask businesses to help fund events in exchange for recognition, usually on signs, in printed materials such as event programs, or in TV or radio ads. Many events have multiple sponsorship levels available that may start as low as $250 or so and go as high as $10,000 or more.

- **Facilities.** New building projects, such as sports arenas, court-houses, libraries, community centers, or university buildings—even park benches—sometimes receive corporate and business sponsors, who may be recognized on a plaque, a statue, or some other sign in the building. Being recognized this way shows your business is part of the community. Contributions may vary from very small to extremely large, with corresponding public recognition. While sponsoring the construction of a new theater is probably outside your abilities, it might be reasonable to sponsor a seat in the theater, with a plaque bearing your business's name.

- **Nonprofit organizations.** Nonprofits welcome donations from businesses and offer benefits for different levels of financial support. For example, an environmental organization might list your business in its marketing materials, annual report, or website, or add your name to a plaque recognizing donors in their lobby. This is an excellent way to build your reputation in the community served by and involved with the nonprofit. Besides donating money, you can sponsor a nonprofit event, such as providing wine for a fundraising dinner, or providing a product or service for a silent auction or raffle.

- **Public television and radio.** While public TV and radio sponsorships are beginning to blur into the more traditional commercials, there still is a distinct difference in the perception of sponsors of public media. You'll also typically reach a more affluent, educated demographic via public broadcasting than with commercial stations.

> **TIP**
>
> **Check out sponsoring a kids' sports team.** There are plenty of reasonably priced sponsorship opportunities, such as sponsoring a girls' softball team. This might primarily involve paying for the girls' jerseys (which include your company name) and the end-of-season pizza party. This is a great way to promote your business to all the families who attend dozens of softball games throughout the season.

Sending Postcards and Other Direct Mail

Besides sending out email promotions (discussed in Chapter 9), you can send out hard copy marketing materials by U.S. mail—a process that's called direct mail. People often perceive direct mail campaigns as complex and expensive, but they needn't be. If you keep the materials simple and develop your own mailing list instead of paying a firm for a list, you can engage in a direct mail campaign that's both thrifty and effective.

Choose a Message

To begin, decide what the goal and subject of your direct mail campaign will be. As with most types of marketing outreach, the more specific your message, the better. Instead of sending out a general brochure about your printing business, for example, send out a postcard offering a 50% discount off the first order for new customers. Special promotions, discounts, or giveaways are the best way to capture people's attention amid all the junk mail.

Generate a Mailing List

To develop your mailing lists, you may do anything from using the names and addresses of everyone you (or friends and colleagues) know personally to hiring a mailing list firm and paying a fee for a list to piggybacking on to a mailing sent by a complementary business. (For example, a pottery business might pay a fee to include its brochure in a garden nursery's mailing.) Whatever your approach, start with the people within your target customer profile and work outward. For example, if you want to target other businesses, scan other directories for contact information. Chapter 9 provides more advice about generating a mailing list.

Create Materials

Creating the printed materials for your mailing can be more affordable than you might expect. You don't need to produce a high-end direct mail package like the ones you get in your own mailbox, printed in full color on heavy paper with special die-cut shapes and other frills. Instead, focus on creating simple layouts of text and graphics on standard-sized pages or postcards. Ideally, you, a partner, or an employee can design your materials in-house, using relatively inexpensive software such as Adobe *InDesign*. Alternatively, a professional graphic designer can be immensely helpful, particularly if no one in your business has graphic design skills. To keep your costs down, look into hiring a graphic art student or even having them do the work as an intern for school credit.

Giving Out Free Samples

Everyone loves free stuff. If you have a product that lends itself to being sampled, consider setting up a table at a trade show or another venue and offering freebies to the public. While some people will take samples with no intention of buying your product, it's usually worth it to forge a connection with even a few potential buyers. Some examples of offering samples effectively include:

- a handmade soap maker who offers slices of her beautiful soaps at a table in a health food store
- a coffee shop that gives away small free cups of its house-roasted coffee at a street fair, or
- a massage studio that provides free five-minute massages at a local trade show.

When offering samples, prepare in advance to ensure that you make a powerful and positive first impression. Have your business name and logo prominently displayed. And remember to have business cards or brochures available so that the people sampling your product or service can find you later. If possible and appropriate, have your product immediately available for sale.

Establishing Customer Loyalty Programs

The phrase "customer loyalty program" sounds much more involved than it really is. What I'm talking about here is creating incentives for your current customers to come back for more. Here are a couple of ideas:

- **Offer punch cards for repeat customers.** After a number of purchases—measured either in units or dollar increments—the customer gets something free. For example, a yogurt shop might offer a customer a yogurt after purchasing ten cups or cones. Or a record shop might punch the card for every $10 spent, and at $100 give the customer $10 off the next purchase.
- **Offer financial rewards for referring customers to you.** A membership-based Pilates studio might offer a free month of membership to anyone who brings in a new annual member. Or an interior

design consultant might offer a $50 coupon to an existing client who refers another client. A spin on this is to provide existing customers a coupon that can only be used by new customers. My acupuncture clinic does this: Once I became a patient, they sent me a $30 coupon that could be redeemed by a new client. I gave it to a friend who then became a new patient.

- **Include freebies with each sale.** A shoe store, for example, could include a small tin of shoe polish with every order. A baby store could include a free rubber duckie or stickers with each sale, a bookstore could offer a bookmark, or a beauty supply store a free tube of moisturizer. It's amazing how much customer goodwill you can generate by including something of minimal financial value (but not junk that is likely to head straight for the landfill) in each sale.

Rewarding customers for steering business your way

"We do a lot of rewarding our customers for sending their friends to us. We send all these emails to our customers with coupons and rewards for sending their friends to us. And also because we run a very high-end studio, every time people came in to get their pictures made or to visit us or whatever, we gave them just for stopping by this beautiful little box with a high-value gift certificate inside to say hey, when you have special occasion coming up—like a baby shower, a bridal shower or somebody's birthday, you know, you don't have to buy a gift anymore. Just give them this. And it's beautiful, something that they're proud to give to somebody else."

— **Sabrina Habib Williams**

Preparing Print Materials

Brochures, catalogs, business cards, postcards, flyers, letterhead, shopping bags and boxes, and other printed materials can help you spread the word about your business. If you and any co-owners don't have graphic design skills, it might be worth hiring a professional graphic designer to create these materials. As mentioned earlier, for most small businesses it's not worth spending thousands of dollars for print design, but at a minimum you want your materials to convey a professional image. Also, make sure that your logo (if you have one) and any other graphic imagery remain consistent across all the media you produce, both in print and online.

When deciding what print materials to produce, keep in mind that many people prefer digital documents which are searchable and easier to store. For example, if you run an office supply mail-order company, many of your customers may prefer a digital catalog that they can search. Minimizing paper documents is also an eco-conscious choice that your customers may appreciate. You'll also need to account for printing costs in your marketing budget.

Publishing Articles and Newsletters

Publishing substantive information is a great way to establish your credibility and enhance your reputation, particularly for professional service businesses. Accountants and lawyers, for example, are perfect candidates for newsletters because the heart of their businesses is information. Newsletters—both print and email versions—are powerful marketing vehicles, helping to strengthen the relationship with existing clients and to broaden the customer base when existing customers pass on the newsletter to others.

On the flip side, newsletters do require a fairly sizable time commitment, and possible expenses if you need to hire someone to help. Writing and editing are time-consuming tasks (even for professional writers), and you might need to hire a designer for the layout work. Also, you'll have to commit to a publication schedule—typically weekly, monthly, or quarterly—and stick to it, so as not to jeopardize your reputation. (Chapter 9 covers the topic of e-newsletters in more detail.)

If you really want to publish but can't commit to a newsletter, consider publishing occasional articles on relevant topics. For example, if you produce children's audiobooks, you could write a piece on kids' audio for a librarians' or parents' magazine. Or consider writing an op-ed piece (or even letter to the editor) on a news topic that relates to your business. Putting out regular flyers, brochures, or emails highlighting your products or services and any special events at your store is much easier than a substantive newsletter, and might be all you need.

Advertising Your Business

While advertising is seriously overemphasized as a marketing method, it can be effective when used judiciously and in conjunction with other types of marketing outreach. It can quickly get expensive, so plan any advertising campaigns carefully to make sure you're getting the most for your money.

Ad Costs and Frequency

When choosing where to advertise, the basic approach is to find the widest exposure for the least money. (And you'll need to choose the right exposure—not just the widest—which we discuss in the next section.) A standard measurement to help you compare advertising costs from one media outlet to another is "cost per thousand" or CPM (thousand expressed as "mille"), which shows how much it costs to show an ad to 1,000 viewers. CPM is calculated by dividing the total cost of the ad by the estimated audience for the ad, then multiplying by 1,000. For example:

Ad cost	$ 1,000
Estimated viewers	25,000
CPM ($1,000 ÷ 25,000) x 1,000	$ 40

Advertising costs can be sliced and diced in many different ways, but this basic calculation is an easy way to compare costs among media outlets. Generally speaking, highly targeted media outlets aimed at the most affluent readers will have the highest CPMs. For example, a trade magazine for health insurance executives will likely have a high CPM— say, $145—while the CPM for a more general consumer magazine on healthy living would be much lower—say, $35. If your company sells a health-insurance-related software application, it may well be worth the big bucks to advertise in the magazine for health insurance executives to get your ad in front of the right eyes.

To find out what a publication costs, contact its advertising department and ask for its rate sheet, which may be part of a larger press or media kit. You may be able to find one at its website for download; otherwise an ad representative will mail one to you. Media kits generally include information about the demographic profile of the media outlet's readers, circulation numbers, and ad rates. For websites, the kit will generally include detailed traffic information including the number of unique visitors per month. Media kits for magazines typically include schedules of upcoming issues and the topics that will be covered; this can be really helpful information for you in deciding when and where to advertise.

You'll notice that ad rates are graduated, with the cost per ad going down the more you commit to buy. For example, a monthly magazine may charge $1,000 for a display ad if you buy the ad just once; $925 for the same ad if you commit to buying it three times; $895 if you commit to a six-month run; and $855 if you commit to a year-long run.

While you may be skeptical of an ad rep's claims that you'll get more results with more advertising, in this case they're telling you the truth. Advertising isn't usually effective unless it's done for at least a short duration, not just once. Most people won't even notice your ad until it has run a few times, and you may not see any results for even longer.

Very generally speaking, you'll want to advertise a minimum of a month in a weekly publication or four months in a monthly publication. Some consultants say six months is necessary to get results. Don't waste your money buying just one or two ads; this won't generate the name recognition and trust required to get people in your door.

CAUTION
Be sure you comply with laws against deceptive or misleading advertising. Search "Marketing and Advertising" on Nolo's website (www.nolo. com) for useful articles on keeping your advertising accurate and legal, and related topics, such as deceptive pricing or credit policies.

Where to Advertise

Besides doing the math to figure out which publications offer the most affordable CPM, you should focus on publications that you expect your target market to read. For the most part, you'll be looking at advertising in local media outlets. Advertising in national media is incredibly expensive, easily costing tens or hundreds of thousands of dollars even for a modest campaign. Local media will be considerably more affordable. Online publications vary a great deal in what they charge for banner and other ads, but as with traditional advertising the more traffic they have, the more they'll charge.

Some cities have targeted publications, such as a magazine aimed at women, a kid-oriented tabloid aimed at parents of young children, or a newspaper covering outdoors activities and local conservation efforts. If your business caters to similar audiences, these types of targeted publications might be a good option. A bonus is that many targeted local publications (unlike national niche publications) are less expensive than other general-interest media since their readership is smaller. Just make sure that people actually read the publications you're considering. There's no point buying even cheap advertising in a local magazine that no one picks up.

Another typically affordable local option is a free weekly that's published in your city. Arts and entertainment weeklies tend to be widely read so you'll reach a large audience. In addition, readers tend to use them as practical guides for the week's movies and entertainment listings, so they may refer to them over and over during the week, possibly giving your ad more exposure. If your business has any arts or entertainment events—say, your wine bar has free music four nights a week—it may be a must that you have an ad in your city's weekly, since readers often use the advertisements in the entertainment section to learn about what's happening around town.

Besides the traditional types of print media, there are all sorts of publications that sell affordable ad space. Consider the following:

- **School or parent association newsletters.** This is a particularly good option if your kids are in the school and you already know many of the parents and teachers.
- **Local nonprofit newsletters.** As with sponsorships, described above, running your ad in a nonprofit newsletter may demonstrate your involvement in your community and your support for certain issues.
- **Performing arts events programs.** Many theater and music organizations sell ad space in their event programs, and showing your company's support for these groups by buying an ad can reflect favorably on your business.

If you have a slightly higher budget, you might consider advertising on radio or TV. Part of the reason radio and TV ads are expensive is that they reach large audiences. If you are targeting a narrow niche, going this route probably isn't worth the expense. On the other hand, if you are targeting a broad customer base and have the budget for it, radio and TV can get you lots of exposure. Billboards are similar: They reach wide audiences but are expensive.

Of course there are plenty of other ways to advertise, including the sides of buses, floors of grocery stores, park benches, kiosks in public places—the list goes on and on. Always consider who the audience is, how big it is, and the cost of the ad when deciding where to put your ad dollars.

 TIP

Don't neglect to track the effectiveness of your marketing efforts. It's important to know which efforts are working and which aren't so you can kill ineffective campaigns and redirect those resources toward the ones that are getting results. Tracking can be as simple as asking customers how they heard about your business, or offering a discount if a customer provides a coupon or discount code. For online marketing, you or a consultant can analyze the traffic coming to your site to see what keywords they have searched for and what sites they came from.

Marketing through community outreach

"We do a lot of what I consider guerrilla marketing. We focus more on press and we do a lot of silent auctions. It just keeps us in the community's mind. We really pick and choose what we're going to be involved with. We did big air time on KUNM's (Albuquerque's public radio station) fund drive. It's like this fine line between community outreach and marketing, and the two play into one another. We now have a reputation as being a community-minded business."

— **Elissa Breitbard**

Help With Preparing a Marketing Plan

There are lots of organizations that can help you prepare a marketing plan and marketing materials, including Women's Business Centers, SCORE, and Small Business Development Centers—many of the same groups that can help with your business plan. (See Chapter 4 for a complete list and contact info.)

As usual, there are tons of resources online, including the websites of business magazines such as *Inc.* (www.inc.com) and *Entrepreneur* (www.entrepreneur.com) and blogs such as John Jantsch's popular blog Duct Tape Marketing (www.ducttapemarketing.com/blog).

In addition, there are lots of books on marketing covering everything from branding to customer service to designing a publicity campaign. Marketing guru Seth Godin, author of *Purple Cow*, has a dozen or so marketing books that are hugely popular. Since marketing plans and projects vary widely by business, search around and find something that fits your needs and interests.

E-Business: Conducting and Marketing Your Business Online

A few short years ago, e-business basically meant having a website. Thanks to major developments in new technologies, business models, and marketing strategies, there are endless new ways for you to profit online and connect with your potential customers. Social media sites, such as Facebook, LinkedIn, and Twitter, are part of a major shift toward online communities that offer endless new ways to interact with existing and potential customers. Open source content management systems (CMS) and plug-ins allow businesses to have more robust, professional websites on considerably smaller budgets. (Don't worry if you don't know what CMSs or plug-ins are. You will by the end of this chapter!) Search engine optimization (SEO) has gone from a peripheral concern not even a decade ago to a highly evolved, complex process supported by a whole industry of consultants and firms. With these and countless other advances in e-business, it can seem overwhelming to get your business online, to stay current with what's happening in e-business, and to separate what's truly effective from over-hyped technologies.

The good news is that marketing and/or conducting your business online doesn't have to be complicated, time-consuming, or super expensive—and it shouldn't be unless your strategy and budget supports such an approach. Really, it's not that different from traditional marketing: If you were starting a small chocolate shop, you wouldn't be worried about paying for pricey demographic studies, hiring a national advertising firm, and starting a branding campaign the likes of Hershey's, would you? Same goes for doing business online. Instead of stressing out about the endless options for establishing and expanding your online presence, focus on the ones you can handle both in terms of time and money. As your business develops, you can expand your efforts if circumstances warrant.

Whether you want to send out simple marketing emails for your interior design business or you need a robust e-commerce operation for your Web-only pet products company, this chapter will help you develop a realistic online strategy that truly serves your business.

We'll provide a bird's eye view of the e-business landscape, including:

- how to assess your overall business strategy and ensure your online operations are compatible
- the best methods and tools to promote your business online, including email marketing, blogs, and social media
- how to drive traffic to your site, through search engine optimization (SEO) and other means
- details involved with e-commerce (online sales), including merchant accounts, payment gateways, and shopping carts
- the process of planning and developing a website, including how to find, hire, and work most effectively with a Web developer
- how to evaluate alternatives, such as template-based website builder services or opening an affiliate store with e-commerce sites like Amazon, eBay, or Etsy
- the basics of registering your domain name and setting up a hosting service, and
- legal rules governing ownership of and copyright to your site's content.

E-Business Is More Than Just Having a Website

Though a website is generally the centerpiece of a business's online presence—a "base camp" of sorts—other online methods of communicating with potential customers, such as blogs, social media, and promotional emails are becoming an ever-bigger part of how online business is done. The truth is, things change fast when it comes to online communications methods. Chances are that by the time this book hits bookstore shelves, there will be a "next big thing" online. So do your best to get up to speed before devising your e-business strategy. I'm not saying you need to become an expert in every aspect of current Web technologies—that would be virtually impossible, even for many tech folks—but take some time to familiarize yourself with current technologies and tools as an early step in your e-business efforts.

Web Jargon Defined

To help stay clear about what's what online, here are definitions of some of the most common Web terms.

Blog (short for "weblog"), a website using a format of short posts, ordered in reverse chronological order (as in, the most recent post at the top of the page), which often include links to other sites. Blogs are regularly updated—sometimes several times daily—with new information by one or more contributors, called bloggers. Blogs started out as largely personal communication vehicles, but the blog format is now widely used by reputable businesses and online publications.

Content management system, or CMS, refers to software that allows anyone, including nonprogrammers, to update and manage the content at a website. The user logs into the CMS using a regular Web browser and can add, edit, or remove content without special technical skills, such as knowing HTML (hypertext markup language, which is the language used to create Web content).

Crowdfunding is a method of raising money online directly from your social media network and other supporters. Crowdfunding websites (also called "platforms") like Kickstarter or Indiegogo make it easy for users to create fundraising campaigns that can be promoted among social media networks, such as Facebook or Twitter. See "Crowdfunding and Social Media" in Chapter 3 for more on the subject.

E-business is a very general term referring to the full range of ways a business can operate in the online world, from having a simple marketing website to sending out marketing emails to operating complex e-commerce sites, and everything in between. A website is generally—but not always—the focal point of e-business. For example, a retail store may rely heavily on its email promotions to generate walk-in business, and rarely update its website which basically just provides hours and contact information.

E-commerce refers to an online sales operation, generally via a website that is set up to allow online orders and process credit card or other types of payments.

Web Jargon Defined (continued)

Email lists are compilations of email addresses of people who have expressed interest in receiving emails from a business about special promotions or events. If the content of the email is substantive in nature, the email usually is called an **e-newsletter**.

Listservs are essentially email discussion groups about specific topics that allow people who have signed up to them to share information with each other. Any subscriber can send an email to a listserv, and that email will automatically be sent to all other listserv subscribers. This differentiates a listserv from an email list, in which communications are typically only one-way from the site administrator to the list.

Online presence refers to the broad collection of ways a business is represented in the electronic world. For instance, in addition to having a website, you could maintain a blog; manage Facebook, Pinterest, and Twitter pages; be listed in numerous online directories; be a regular commentator on other blogs and online forums; have a monthly email newsletter; supply informative articles to other websites; or moderate a listserv. The sum of all these activities is often called your online presence.

Plug-ins are small pieces of software that add to another application's functionality. You'll typically install a plug-in to expand your existing software's capability. For example, you can install various plug-ins that help your Web browser track various blogs and social media sites; with the plug-in installed, the browser will offer new buttons and functions. Or, you can install a calendar plug-in to your Web content management system to enable adding and editing events into a searchable calendar at your site.

RSS, which stands for "really simple syndication," is a technology that allows users to subscribe to frequently updated sources of information and read all the headlines (and sometimes a line or two of text) on one page. The RSS feed (the information you're tracking) will appear in an RSS reader, which is software that aggregates all your feeds onto one page. Many RSS readers/aggregators are browser based; you simply log into a certain Web page to read your RSS feeds.

Web Jargon Defined (continued)

Social media includes sites like Facebook, Twitter, and Pinterest that focus on content that is submitted by users. These sites are "social" in that users typically identify friends within the system and create groups and communities within which they share links, photos, and other posts.

Spam is unsolicited marketing email, and is frowned upon by savvy businesspeople and their recipients alike.

Web 2.0 refers to the transition of the Web toward social media and user-generated content. Previously, websites tended to feature content created and maintained by the site owner; now, sites tend to feature content submitted by users such as blog posts, comments (such as product evaluations for shoes on Zappos or customer reviews of restaurants and other service providers on Yelp), videos, and photo albums.

Web developers (also known as Web builders) specialize in all aspects of creating websites, including organizing the information, graphic design, and programming. We use the term "Web developer" as opposed to "Web designer" because graphic design is only one aspect of creating a website.

Question: Do You Really Need a Website? Answer: Yes

This chapter presumes that you will have a website. Period. Businesses without websites run the risk of being perceived as unprofessional or even untrustworthy, so you'll want at least a minimal site that describes your business and provides contact information. Most businesses are well advised to do something beyond the basics, but exactly how extensive will depend on the specifics of your business strategy and budget considerations.

Start With Your Business Strategy

Way before you start thinking about the cool features or content you want to include at your website, put careful thought into your broad strategy for e-business and how it fits into your overall business and marketing strategy as defined in your business plan (the topic of Chapter 4). In particular, make sure that your website serves your business strategy and not the other way around. For example, don't let a Web developer talk you into an online store, a blog, or other interactive features if they don't directly serve your business needs, target your market, or fit within your resources.

If your business plan doesn't address your e-business strategy, you should take the time to fill this gap in your planning. In particular, clarify whether your e-business activities will mainly promote your offline business, or whether a good portion of your sales will actually be made online. These fundamental strategies and goals will be reflected in all sorts of different choices, from budgets for building your website, to hiring ongoing technology consultants to help with search engine optimization, and other costs related to running and marketing the site.

For example, if your business plan for a plant nursery envisions a mostly local clientele—say, you're targeting a large and growing luxury resort industry in your area—a simple marketing website that promotes the brick-and-mortar business may be perfectly adequate. The site could include the nursery's location, hours, and contact information, along with some photos and copy about the products you carry. If your budget allows, you could add some inexpensive features like a monthly e-newsletter with planting tips and promotions designed to draw people into the store.

On the other hand, if your business plan for your scuba gear company estimates you will do 75% of your sales online, you'll definitely need to adopt a more extensive e-business strategy. You'll want to devote a significant portion of your expenses to website development, main- tenance, and traffic building. While search engine optimization services may be overkill for the plant nursery, they would be essential for the scuba gear business since traffic is essential for online sales. Of course, this is even more true for any business that will operate entirely online.

Queen Bee Creations: A Social Media Butterfly

With a wide presence across the Web, Queen Bee Creations and Chickpea Baby (www.queenbee-creations.com) is a great example of how to use social media to develop your brand and build a loyal following online. Besides having a beautiful and functional website, Queen Bee has a Facebook page where it interacts with its enthusiastic customers. It posts notices of sales and promotions, announces new products, and lists events such as craft fairs where customers will find Queen Bee. "We actively post on Facebook and keep it updated," said Queen Bee's founder and president Rebecca Pearcy. Queen Bee also uses Instagram and Pinterest to share photos of its products and cool stuff from its backroom operations, like the dies use for bag construction.

All of this activity online has spurred other online coverage, such as reviews on Yelp (all glowing), media interviews, and mentions in other blogs like BikeCommuters.com which posted about Queen Bee's bike panniers, generating several user comments and helping to build buzz about the company. Queen Bee's social media strategy shows the power of developing community among its customers and building word of mouth online.

If you don't expect the Web to generate a significant portion of your sales (either via sales online or from drawing Web visitors into your physical store), be careful not to be seduced by the latest interactive features and other Web-based applications. Keep it simple. You don't want to lose focus of your core business operations.

For most businesses, there's plenty of middle ground to explore, including many simple ways of promoting your business and interacting with your customer base online that don't cost a fortune. This chapter outlines the best online marketing options—most of which cost little money—such as email outreach, blogging, and networking with social media. Consider these along with your offline marketing efforts (discussed in Chapter 8), such as special events, directory listings, and customer loyalty programs, in order to develop a comprehensive strategy that will guide your website planning. Let's take a look at some of the most effective ways to develop your business online; then we'll look at a methodical process for building your site which may include many of these components.

> ⓘ **CAUTION**
>
> **E-commerce isn't for everyone.** Some business owners have the mistaken impression that it's easy and cheap to sell products or services online. However, there are many complexities and costs involved, as discussed in "E-Commerce," below. Selling even a few products online requires you to manage, at a minimum, payment processing, shipping, online customer service, and returns. If these activities weren't included in your original business plan, you might quickly find yourself overwhelmed and unable to keep customers (or yourself) happy—a bad situation for any business. With careful strategic thinking before launching a website or other e-business activities, you can plan for the resources you'll need and avoid this mistake.

Promotional Emails

Sending well-planned emails (whether regular or occasional) to a list of willing recipients is a great way for your business to promote its products or services. If you use email, you've undoubtedly received at least a few marketing emails; it's a heavily used strategy by REI, Sur la Table, Macy's, and countless other retailers, big and small. Marketing information sent by email might be called an email announcement, email promotion, or marketing email. (Just don't call it an e-newsletter unless it truly offers substantive information, as discussed in the next section.)

You can collect email addresses by having a sign-up form at your website (often in a sidebar or header throughout your site, as well as a checkbox within any shopping cart pages if you offer e-commerce), as well as a mailing list sign-up sheet in your physical business—say, at the checkout counter. Make sure people know what they're signing up for, whether it's notices of sales, discounts, new inventory, or other specials. Don't include anyone on your list unless they specifically ask to receive your marketing emails; just because they were a previous customer or provided their email address for some other reason doesn't mean they want to receive your promotions. (For more details on managing your list and avoiding being a spammer, see "Ethical and Effective E-Marketing" below.)

To get the best response, send out a promotional email only when you truly have something to promote. Sales and discounts are always good fodder. Even better, structure the promotion so that members of the email list get something extra—like an early-bird notice, "email list only" sale, or an additional discount—which can really help get customers in your door. Everyone loves to feel they're part of an exclusive group with special access or deals. Some simple examples include:

- A clothing store sends a promotional email a week or so prior to any big sales. Twice a year it has an "email list-only" 50% off sale on a Sunday (when it is usually closed) for members of the email list. Later, when the store increases its staff, it starts a quarterly e-newsletter covering fashion trends. (More on e-newsletters in the next section.)

- A local comedy club sends a monthly promotional email highlighting the upcoming month's comedy acts at the club. Weekly dinner specials are also included. The email contains an "Email Exclusive Coupon" for half off a dinner with the purchase of another dinner.

- A spa sends an occasional promotional email with package deals, such as a Valentine's Day couple's massage special; a Mother's Day massage and facial package; or special discounts to celebrate the spa's fifth year in business.

- An imports store sends out an email a few days before the arrival of a new container, alerting recipients to the new inventory.

E-Newsletters

In addition to marketing announcements or promotions, you can send out more substantive information to your audience in the form of e-newsletters. These are excellent vehicles for creating a bond with your audience because when done right, e-newsletters offer helpful, informative content that readers truly value. Professionals such as lawyers, accountants, and consultants of various stripes often are in a good position to do e-newsletters since the heart of their businesses is understanding and analyzing information.

Most e-newsletters are free, though some publishers may charge for certain types of email reports, such as comprehensive statistical studies on a particular industry; these follow a different business model than what we're talking about here. For the purposes of marketing your business, it's generally best to offer your e-newsletter for free.

With a little out-of-the-box thinking, just about any business can come up with a winning focus for an e-newsletter. Here are a few examples:

- A restaurant does a monthly e-newsletter on cooking with seasonal ingredients, including recipes.
- A photographer's e-newsletter includes practical photography tips, such as how to photograph children, use props, or shoot in low light.
- An independent cinema sends a monthly e-newsletter with schedules and descriptions of upcoming screenings. The cinema writes its own descriptions of and commentary about the films, so it feels justified in calling these e-newsletters.
- A landscaping service sends a monthly e-newsletter with gardening tips for the upcoming month, such as when to prepare the soil, what seeds to plant, and how much to water.

In deciding whether to publish an e-newsletter, keep in mind that everyone has overloaded email boxes these days, so if your content is not truly helpful, practical, or otherwise compelling, your efforts may well end up being deleted within seconds of receipt. If you can't come up with subject matter of real interest to your customers (as opposed to a thinly veiled marketing outreach), you might be better off simply sending promotional emails to your list—for example, announcing an upcoming trunk sale at your gift shop.

It's crucial to recognize that e-newsletters (and print ones too) require a considerable commitment. Don't underestimate the hours it will take you to write, edit, proofread, and send them. Quality is also important:

Your text should be well written and free from errors and typos. Last but definitely not least, when you commit to publishing a newsletter, it means that you commit to putting one out regularly, usually once a month or at least once a quarter. Make a realistic evaluation of whether you or a staffer has the writing skills and the time to be able to reliably create a quality newsletter and manage a mailing list. If not, then it's best to put off your newsletter plans until you have the resources in place.

Resources on Social Media, Blogging, and E-Business

There are loads of resources on the many different aspects of online marketing—but watch out for those that advocate a sleazy approach. Sites and books that offer truly helpful and thoughtful advice are few and far between; way too many focus on questionable practices bordering on spam. Here are some of the best of the best.

- ReadWrite (www.readwrite.com). A blog that offers intelligent analysis of Web-based products and trends, and is an excellent source of general Web-oriented information.
- Mashable (www.mashable.com). A quality website which focuses on social media, offering news, resources, and guides.
- *Groundswell: Winning in a World Transformed by Social Technologies*, by Charlene Li and Josh Bernoff (Harvard Business Review Press). A must-read on social media, this book is based on hard-core customer data and analysis.
- *Likeable Social Media: How to Delight Your Customers, Create an Irresistible Brand, and Be Amazing on Facebook, Twitter, LinkedIn, Instagram, Pinterest, and More*, by Dave Kerpen (McGraw-Hill). An excellent guide to social media.
- Blog software sites, such as wordpress.org and squarespace.com. Great sources of information, with user guides, and detailed advice and practical information on blogging basics.

Ethical and Effective E-Marketing

When sending emails to your customers, keep in mind the following:

- **Make sure people want your emails.** Don't automatically add someone to your email list just because they bought something from your online store.
- **Don't promise an "e-newsletter" if your emails are more promotional in nature.** Many folks get peeved when they receive purely marketing information when they originally signed up for a "newsletter" which implies more substantive topic-based articles. Marketing-oriented emails are totally fine, as long as you tell people that the emails will be promotional in nature.
- **Manage your email list scrupulously.** Managing hundreds or thousands of email addresses—including dealing with address change and unsubscribe requests—is not easy. We highly recommend you use an email marketing service, such as MailChimp (www.mailchimp.com) or ConstantContact (www.constantcontact.com), to help avoid mistakes that can cost you customer goodwill.
- **Keep email outreach on the up-and-up with "double opt-in" systems.** Services like MailChimp use a double opt-in system, which helps ensure that the recipients of your emails actually want them and won't think you're a spammer. A customer opts in the first time by providing an email address to receive your email communications—perhaps she signed up on your website or at a trade show. Then, an email is sent asking the requestor to confirm that she indeed wants to be included on your list. It's yet another reason to use an email service company like MailChimp which automates this process.
- **Make it easy for people to unsubscribe.** Services like ConstantContact always include clear links or buttons in every email allowing recipients to remove themselves from the list. If you don't use an email outreach service, make sure your emails include easy unsubscribe instructions.
- **Keep email addresses private.** If you don't use an email service like MailChimp (and you really should), at the least put all the addresses in your email list in the blind copy, or Bcc field. Failing to do this risks irritating your customers and makes your business appear unprofessional.

What Is a Listserv?

A listserv is similar to an email list, in that people who have signed up for the listserv receive emails. However, with a listserv, the emails can be sent by anyone who is part of the listserv, not just by its manager. For example, someone who reads a listserv email could respond to the whole group by sending an email to the listserv, which would be distributed to all recipients of the listserv. In contrast, email lists are one-directional, from the business to the list.

Listservs are most common in nonprofit organizations and schools, but some businesses also have customers who want to engage in an ongoing email discussion group. Business listservs tend to be appropriate only when a business's customer base has a compelling desire to interact, such as software companies whose customers like to share user tips with each other.

Blogging

"To blog or not to blog?" is a question many business owners grapple with. Blogs have been around for several years but really became popular as marketing vehicles in the 2000s. Note that we're not talking about using the big social media sites like Facebook; we discuss that option below. For now, let's consider a blog that you might start on your own.

A blog is basically just a website composed of chronologically ordered posts with the most recent entries at the top, much like an online journal. Photos or images are often included with individual posts. Posts tend to be short and almost always include one or more links to related information at other websites. In addition, many blogs allow readers to post comments. Inexpensive and free blog software (*WordPress* being the primary one these days, and Tumblr another popular choice) makes it easy to add new posts—much easier than it typically is to add content to traditional websites.

TIP

WordPress **isn't just for bloggers anymore.** Originally, *WordPress* was developed as a CMS specifically for blogging. It offered clean templates and an exceptionally easy to use back-end interface making it incredibly popular off the bat. Over the years, as more and more features have been added to the *WordPress* platform and it can be more easily customized, small businesses are increasingly turning to *WordPress* as the platform for their websites. People have discovered how easy it is to use the *WordPress* CMS to create a robust site that doesn't look anything like a blog, but like a "regular" small business site. Just as early bloggers flocked to *WordPress* for its easy-to-use interface, small business owners love *WordPress* for the very same reason. It's incredibly easy to maintain and update a *WordPress* site on your own—most folks find it considerably easier than *Joomla* or *Drupal* sites.

Early blogs tended to be more like personal journals, but now blogs have been embraced by businesses, media outlets, and issue-oriented websites seeking new ways to connect with audiences. A number of characteristics have made blogs attractive to the masses:

- Blogs are easy to update.
- Blogs allow an informal, friendly voice and more flexible coverage of topics.
- When reader comments are allowed, blogs help forge a connection between the blogger (that is, your business) and its readership (that is, your potential customers).
- Quality blogs attract traffic and can help boost a site's search engine rankings. (Search engine optimization is discussed in its own section below.)

The trick to a successful business blog is to offer information that's interesting to your potential customers and that favorably inclines them toward your business and products or services, without being too self-serving or marketing heavy. For example, if all your business blog posts are about how great your business is—and even worse, if it's all in marketing-speak—you'll quickly turn off readers. But if you present interesting topics to your readers in a sincerely helpful, information-sharing way, you'll be more likely to attract regular readers who develop a favorable impression of your business. This may even mean occasionally linking to competitors, if appropriate.

Also, blogs that allow users to post comments tend to develop a more loyal readership. Keep in mind, however, that allowing reader posts means you will have to monitor those comments for offensive, libelous, off-topic, or otherwise unacceptable material. It's up to you what line to draw, but inevitably you won't please everyone. If you leave offensive posts untouched, visitors will likely be turned off; while if you edit posts, people are sure to complain that you're censoring them. Still, allowing user posts is a great way to connect with your audience. Just strive to be fair in your policies in editing the posts.

A few examples of business blogging that could be done successfully include:

- a business consultant's blog about branding and marketing strategies, with links to other articles about trends in online business

- a bakery's blog offering baking techniques and tips, allowing comments from readers and encouraging people to submit photos of their own culinary creations

- a yoga studio's blog about the health benefits of yoga and tips for doing various poses correctly, as well as links to stores selling yoga clothes, external articles, and studies about yoga's role in healthful living, and

- a contractor's blog, sharing her experiences and projects, with photos of kitchens as they are being remodeled, and links to sites with helpful information and/or quality products (such as countertops or flooring materials).

Besides drawing traffic (and potentially boosting your search engine rankings), a quality blog will help develop your brand as a reputable company that's in the know regarding industry developments. Keep this in mind when evaluating your expected results from a planned business blog.

Even more important are some fundamental realities to look at when considering a business blog. At a minimum, don't overlook the following:

- **The blog needs to be regularly updated, ideally a couple of times per week or more, in order to able to generate regular traffic.** Don't start a blog unless you're sure you or someone at your business has the time to keep it updated.

- **The blogger needs to be well-informed on the topic, and Web-savvy—enough to create posts that are interesting and helpful to others seeking information on that topic.** You don't have to be the world's top authority on your topic, but you do need to be able to ferret out useful information online and provide links to that info.
- **The blogger needs to have some basic writing skills.** An informal, lively writing style is best on blogs. Personality and a unique voice is great, as long as you keep it professional; remember, you're promoting a business. On the flip side, avoid dry, academic writing or copy that sounds like a sales pitch.

Tips for Developing a Realistic Social Media Strategy

As the founder of SmartGirl.org in 1996, Isabel Walcott Draves started building and working with online communities and user-generated content more than a decade before anyone had even heard of "social media." These days, she works as an Internet start-up consultant helping large and small businesses develop and implement social media strategies. Here's her advice on how to effectively use social media without being overwhelmed.

"There's really no such thing as a free lunch. Lots of companies think that they can use social media to make up for not having a marketing budget. But blog posts and tweets don't write themselves, and people don't join your Facebook group just because you created it. Social media takes time, and it takes a skill set that not everybody has. So if you're not willing to learn how to do it and take the time to do it right, you have to hire someone who's good at it to handle it for you, and that means money.

That being said, if you have an interesting company or cause and a charismatic personality, you can recruit high school and college interns and harness their energy for your social media presence. The right way to manage the process is to develop a team where everyone puts in just a little time so it's not all on one person. Start by listening, then responding, before you go out tooting your own horn. Another thing to remember is not all social media is for everybody. I've advised companies not to have a Facebook or Twitter presence, not to start a blog. For B2B companies, it can be much more important to have an open helpdesk Q&A forum online, for example—which also qualifies as social media."

Social Media: Facebook, Twitter, and More

If you spend any time online, you undoubtedly have at least heard of the terms "social media" or "Web 2.0," which refer to networks featuring user-generated content, such as Facebook, Instagram, Tumblr, Pinterest, Yelp, YouTube, LinkedIn, Flickr, or Twitter, to name just a few. In the broadest strokes, social media sites differ from traditional, old-school websites in that they consist almost entirely of content contributed by site users like you and me. After creating a user account, you can post all sorts of content, including text, photos, videos, and other multimedia. These sites are "social" in that users typically create networks of friends or followers, and in this way build online communities within which they share information.

While some social media sites like LinkedIn are geared specifically toward professional and business networking, many others such as Facebook and YouTube began as vehicles for largely personal interaction among friends (Facebook started as an online network for Harvard students). But just about every sort of social media site has now been infiltrated (for better or worse) by businesses that have developed ways to use these sites to promote themselves and their brands. As you can imagine, some do it more effectively than others.

Very generally speaking, a business engages in social media by creating an account in the name of the business, then networking in whatever ways are appropriate within that community. There are endless ways to do this! Any detailed discussion of how to best use the many various social media communities is way beyond the scope of this chapter, but here are a few tips, ideas, and examples to get you on the right track.

- **Implement a comprehensive social media strategy.** As with any type of marketing, using social media to promote your business is best done with a well-thought-out plan and a clear idea of where you'll focus your efforts. Figure out which social media sites will work best for your business and what your communication goals are before jumping in. Keeping your strategy firmly in focus (and your audience) will also help you avoid being swayed by overhyped technologies that may not be a good fit.

- **Know your audience, and use social media that your audience uses, in the way that audience uses them.** For example, a funky vintage clothing store or an edgy hair salon could probably do well connecting with customers on Facebook where large audiences tend to congregate and interact in an informal atmosphere, often sharing info on their favorite places to shop or eat. On the other hand, a software publisher might find more success using Twitter, which tends to attract a more tech-oriented audience. Similarly, a health care consulting firm targeting hospital executives might want to focus on LinkedIn, where audiences and topics tend to be more professional and more serious in tone.

- **Pay particular attention to industry-specific sites, including review sites.** In most industries, there are at least a few websites that serve as valuable sources of information and consequently get a lot of traffic. In some cases, these sites have the potential to be an important factor in your success. If you run a B&B or a hotel, for example, you absolutely should keep an eye on TripAdvisor.com where users rate their stays at hotels, motels, B&Bs, and vacation rentals worldwide. The content there is generated by users, not the hotels themselves, offering a window into what people are saying online about you and your competitors. (And, as discussed in "Monitoring Your Reputation Online" below, it's critical that you respond to any serious problems posted there by disgruntled guests.) If your head is in the sand and you never visit TripAdvisor you'd be at a serious disadvantage. Similarly, if you're a freelance photographer, you should consider having an Instagram or a Flickr account. Because photographers tend to congregate at these sites, knowledgeable clients (say, wedding planners or PR agencies) often go there to find good photographers and check out their work. If you don't have an account with photos showing your best work, you'll be missing some potential opportunities.

- **Consider using online coupon services, such as Groupon or LivingSocial.** Since 2010 or so, online coupons (sometimes called "daily deal" sites) have exploded in popularity. The general deal is that users sign up for a free account, then they get an email every day with that day's offer, which tends to be something like half-off at a local restaurant, spa, or photography studio, for example. If the user wants to buy that coupon they usually have 24 or 48 hours to do so, or they can ignore the offer. Because the discounts are often steep, businesses that participate usually see quite a boost in sales after running one of these promotions. But beware: The popularity has also burned many businesses, who have found themselves deluged with coupon-wielding customers and having to honor so many discounted transactions that they suffer financially. If you participate in an online coupon, make sure to pay close attention to the contract details, such as the revenue split (Groupon usually takes half of the discounted amount) and any additional fees.

- **Keep an eye on the horizon and pay attention to shifting trends.** A social media hub that's red hot with millions of users can quickly become deserted when the next big thing comes around. One example is MySpace, which was the top social media site for a few years, only to become something of a ghost town. Many musicians and bands still have MySpace pages, but by 2010 or so, the rest of the world of social media users largely jumped ship to Facebook. In 2011, Google+ entered the scene and ramped up quickly with sizable number of enthusiastic users, with some predicting it would be a "Facebook killer." As of late 2015, this doesn't seem to be coming to pass after all. The point is to keep an ear to the ground so that your investments in social media don't languish. Only you can decide if and when it's time to expand to a new site and/or abandon efforts at sites where you're already established. But you won't be able to make those decisions if you don't stay current with trends, at least at a minimal level.

- **Understand the ins and outs of any online community you're thinking about joining.** Create a user account for yourself personally to learn how the community operates. Learning the conventions and customs that others use will help you avoid making any faux pas— more than just embarrassing, these kinds of missteps can damage your business's reputation and cost you customer goodwill.

Monitoring Your Reputation Online

One of the downsides of social media is that people can complain about your business online—and when they do so, it's often done loudly and bitterly. Both online and off, people tend to voice complaints much more loudly than praises; it's just human nature. But online complaints are particularly problematic for businesses because they reach so many more people than just someone kvetching to their friends and social circles. Unfortunately this means every business—whether they have much of an online presence or not—needs to be proactive about damage control, and at least periodically check out what (if anything) is being said about them online.

If there are particular sites where your customers are likely to post reviews of your business (for example, TripAdvisor for hotels, or Yelp for restaurants), be sure to review those sites at least every month or so. Also, set up a Google Alert for your business name (and any other relevant terms, such as names of your main products, or your personal name); that way you'll get an email notification any time your business (or its products, services, employees, and so on) is mentioned online. Go to www.google.com/alerts to sign up for this free service.

If you do find instances of customer complaints about your business, respond carefully and thoughtfully. You don't need to respond to every minor complaint that you might read (overreacting can make your business look desperate and petty). This is especially true if you have mostly positive reviews, with just a sprinkling of mildly negative comments. Potential customers are savvy enough to know that there will always be complainers, so if most online reviews are positive they'll likely believe the majority's opinion.

If, however, there are serious complaints, or a large number of them, you'd likely benefit with a response. Don't just give an empty apology; look into the problem before you respond and take whatever action is appropriate. Then respond with a brief apology and explanation of how you remedied the situation. In particularly egregious circumstances, you might even want to offer that user some sort of a refund, either in the public forum or in a private email. The bottom line is to take your customer relations seriously and respond in a way that the customer—and the rest of the world reading that thread—understands you truly want to make the situation right.

- **Be creative!** From creating a hilarious or insanely clever YouTube video that goes viral to finding novel ways to use Twitter for customer service, there's no limit to the ways you can use social media for your business. For example, Blendtec, a company that makes high-end blenders, got tons of exposure with its "Will it Blend?" series of videos. The videos showed the results of "blending" things like iPhones, glowing light sticks, golf balls, and a digital video camera (with the warning not to try it at home!). The videos were distributed at YouTube and at the Blendtec website.

Local Search Listings

An easy and important way to market a bricks-and-mortar business online is to make sure it is listed accurately with local search services such as Google My Business and Yahoo! Local. Doing this makes your business appear on maps when people search for your kind of business in your city, including some that appear on mobile devices. If you don't have a listing or it's not accurate, your business may not show up—or it may appear in the wrong location, resulting in irritated customers who are driving, biking, or walking all over trying to find you.

If, on the other hand, you have a clear, accurate, and compelling listing, you have a solid chance of attracting searchers into your business. With Google, your listings can contain your address, phone number, website, hours of operation, and more information including photos and videos. You can even create coupons—for free—that will appear next to your listing that customers can print and use. There are lots of additional free and pay-based services, but it's important (at a minimum) to claim your listing and make sure it's correct.

Note that accuracy is an issue because Google has created millions of listings using public data sources such as phone directories and other websites. These listings are initially "unverified" until the business owner "claims" the listing, at which point the business owner can edit the information and make sure it's correct. (Yahoo! seems to have less of an issue with inaccurate, unverified listings, but it's still important to actually go and create your Yahoo! Local.) The vast majority of Google listings are unverified, which at a minimum means that those business owners aren't taking advantage of a powerful and free resource. It's worse if the unverified listing has the wrong address or other errors. Worse still is the possibility that your unverified listing can be hijacked by spammers and sleazy competitors. Google is tightening its rules and security, but many businesses have fallen victim to this—which could have been prevented if they had claimed their listings.

Since Google has by far the biggest market share of search traffic, your priority should be to claim and manage your Google listing. Go to Google My Business at www.google.com/business to claim and edit your listing. It's free, but you'll need to create a Google account if you don't already have one. To create or edit a Yahoo! Local, go to https://aabacosmallbusiness.com (formerly Yahoo! Small Business).

Using different types of social media

"I use Facebook, Twitter, and LinkedIn to market our business. Each one plays a different role and has proven to be effective. Facebook is great for me to stay in touch with clients by building a minicommunity. With Twitter I'm able to find and 'meet' people who are writing about something I'm interested in or who might be seeking my services. (I can gladly say that I found a new client via Twitter.) And I love LinkedIn's Groups because they help me to stay on top of industry trends."

— Leila Johnson

E-Commerce

Many small business start-ups are online-only operations; others sell products or services online as adjuncts to bricks-and-mortar stores. In either case, keep in mind that selling products or services online adds complexity and costs to your business and your site. (And don't forget the related offline logistical details, such as shipping and customer service.) From a technical standpoint, your site will need to install *shopping cart* software that handles, at a minimum, the functions of the shopper's selecting products and proceeding to checkout. Some shopping cart software does much more, such as allowing you to provide discount codes, create custom categories of products, manage inventory, and more.

Besides shopping cart software, an e-commerce operation generally requires that your business have a *merchant account*, which is essentially a business bank account specifically set up to accept credit and debit card payments. It's the same thing that a brick-and-mortar business needs to have in order to accept credit cards. In addition, an e-commerce site needs something called a *payment gateway,* which is the service that securely processes the transfer of money from the buyer's payment instrument to the seller's merchant account. Think of the payment gateway as analogous to the credit card swipe machine that's used in brick-and-mortar businesses.

Each of these services charges its own set of fees. These can include an application fee, annual and/or monthly fees, and per-transaction fees, which may be a set amount or a percentage of the transaction total. With the hundreds of shopping carts, merchant accounts, and payment gateway services available and the complicated mix of fees they charge, picking the best suite of services for your e-commerce can be confusing, to say the least.

The good news is that a few standout e-commerce services have become well established. Services like PayPal and Google Wallet are particularly popular as they offer bundled services, including shopping carts, merchant accounts, and payment gateways. Both of these services offers a variety of options, but they simplify the process for customers by offering a streamlined, integrated suite of components rather than forcing you to research and choose them on your own.

If you don't use a bundled service, you'll need to choose shopping cart software (popular carts include WooCommerce, Shopify, and X-Cart, but there are many, many others), set up a merchant account (it's not a bad idea to start by inquiring with your existing business bank), and choose a payment gateway (Authorize.Net is a well-established and popular choice). They'll need to be compatible with each other and with any other technology used at your website, such as a content management system (like *WordPress* or *Joomla*). The Web developer who will be setting up your e-commerce operations should provide recommendations for shopping cart software, merchant accounts, and payment gateways. Also, ask other business owners you know for their experiences with various service providers.

RESOURCE

Lots of legal rules apply to online sales—from advertising to shipping practices. Search "Sales & Marketing" at www.nolo.com for a variety of useful articles.

Be careful when hiring Internet consultants

"One of the biggest mistakes I see companies with money making is hiring major ad agencies, PR, or marketing firms who claim to have social media expertise but are really just applying their existing perspectives to the new tools. In December 2009, a blogger did a search of Twitter profiles and determined there were 15,740 'social media experts' there—three times as many as there had been seven months before. The biggest single piece of advice I could give would be to engage a person or company who has long-term experience with user-generated content, without the relentlessly promotional mentality of an ad agency."

— Isabel Walcott Draves

Traffic Building and SEO

There are a number of ways to market your site and drive traffic to it. The extent of your website marketing activities will depend on how your website fits into your overall marketing strategy for your business. If you're planning an e-commerce site that will be the sole source of sales and income for your business, then marketing your site will be critical. If, on the other hand, your website is a basic marketing site that isn't a significant source of referrals and doesn't play a major role in marketing your business, don't break the bank to promote it. That said, all businesses should do simple things, such as including their website URL on their business cards, any ads they run, flyers, and other materials they produce. This section covers the basics of search engine optimization and other ways to drive traffic to your site.

Search Engine Optimization (SEO)

Wouldn't you be thrilled if your website turned up at the top of Google results when someone searched for your type of business? Well, so would the rest of the world. In an increasingly crowded online marketplace, e-commerce has grown more dependent on search engine results, giving rise to a major industry: search engine optimization, or SEO.

In a nutshell, SEO is the practice of customizing a number of internal and external aspects of your site so that it appears high in search engine results. In other words, a well-optimized online toy store might rank #5 in Google results pages for the search "children's toys" whereas a poorly optimized site might rank #537. The goal of SEO, of course, is to drive traffic to your site. There are many other traffic-building methods (the best of which we discuss below), but SEO is worth mentioning here since it gets loads of attention on one hand, while on the other hand the vast majority of small business owners say they really don't understand how it works.

Well, the question of "how it works" is really a good one since no one but the programmers at Google and Yahoo (and the few other search engines that anyone uses) truly know how the search engines do their magic. Search engine algorithms are closely guarded secrets and they change without notice, so SEO specialists are constantly trying to aim for a shifting and unseen target. That said, SEO practices have evolved, and there are definitely some effective ways to boost your website's search engine results.

There are currently two major SEO strategies:

- **Develop as many quality inbound links as possible**—that is, links from *other* sites *to* your site (not the other way around). The engineers at Google and others have figured out a way to measure this in their algorithms, so all other things being equal, a site that has 5,000 other sites linking to it will rank higher than a site with ten sites linking to it. It's a pretty smart concept, when you think about it: In a sense, the search engine companies are letting the market decide which sites are better and more worthy of being ranked highly. If lots of other quality sites link to a site, the thinking goes, that site must have some quality content or other valuable resources that are attracting the links. In this way, the search engines have built a quality criterion into their algorithms, which is undoubtedly useful for searchers—who wants to be directed to a lame site? (By the way, a huge focus of the social media networking we discussed above is on creating links and driving traffic to a business's website.)

• **Make sure your site's content—particularly titles and body text— includes keywords and phrases that your target customers are likely to search for.** For example, if you operate an online store selling handmade jewelry with semiprecious stones, you'd want to include important keywords and phrases in your content such as "jewelry," "handmade," "semiprecious," "amethyst," "sterling silver," "custom jewelry," and any other phrases that your potential customers might use in a Google or Yahoo search.

The subject of SEO is a huge and ever-changing one, so this is just a bare-bones introduction. Doing full-scale SEO for a site can definitely get complicated, involving in-depth keyword research, traffic analysis, pay-per-click advertising, and more. Businesses for which SEO is critical (for example, businesses whose sole or major source of income comes from website sales) often hire consultants who specialize in this constantly evolving field to handle the optimization process. (Note that optimizing your site is generally not included in a basic website development contract; you'll need to pay more for these services.) Thankfully, plenty of businesses aren't that dependent on Web traffic for revenues, making SEO less mission critical. For these businesses, a more moderate approach can be effective.

SEO Resources

Search engine optimization is a constantly evolving topic. Here are some of the best resources to keep you up to date.

- **Search Engine Watch** (www.searchenginewatch.com) is a comprehensive site with the latest news on SEO strategies and techniques, and a huge archive of articles on search engine-related topics.
- **SEOBook** offers a number of different tools for keyword research and analysis, including a keyword selection tool and a browser plug-in toolbar. Many of the tools and services are free, but you must register. See http://tools.seobook.com.
- **Keyword Discovery** (www.keyworddiscovery.com) and **Wordtracker** (www.wordtracker.com) are well-regarded subscription-based keyword research tools that offer sophisticated tools for choosing keywords and analyzing site traffic.
- *Search Engine Optimization: An Hour a Day*, by Jennifer Grappone and Gradiva Couzin (Sybex), is a detailed and practical book that's aimed at busy business owners who are short on time but who need to take search engine optimization seriously. The authors maintain a blog at www.yourseoplan.com to offer the latest breaking information.

And here's another tip that should make you feel better if you find this SEO stuff overwhelming: The trend with search engines is to favor sites that have quality, helpful content. What a simple concept! But it hasn't always been this way. Just a few years ago, shady SEO firms used a host of deceptive practices like stuffing sites with invisible keywords or setting up bogus "link farms" meant to trick the search engines into boosting the site's rankings (and charging the sites hefty fees for such "services"). Those days are over. Google and Yahoo! wised up and revised their algorithms to reward sites with legitimate, quality content—and to punish sites that use the bogus tactics.

The net result is that simple, quality content will help improve your search engine results by attracting links from other quality sites. This concept is not hard or complicated for nonspecialists to understand or achieve. Yes, it can be time-consuming to create actual substantive content, as opposed to fluffy marketing copy, but it's not rocket science. See "Other Ways to Drive Traffic to Your Site," below, for some simple ways to approach the traffic-building task.

TIP

Add Google Analytics to your site. Google Analytics is free software that will track and analyze traffic to your site. You'll be able to see where your site visitors came from, what they searched for to find your site, which pages they visited and for how long, and more. Installing the code is a simple matter of cutting and pasting into your site; either your Web developer can do it or you may very well be able to manage doing it on your own. Google Analytics is free, but you'll need a Google account. Go to www.google.com/analytics to sign up.

Other Ways to Drive Traffic to Your Site

Earlier, we mentioned that having inbound links to your site will help it rank better with search engines. Well, a much more obvious benefit of having lots of inbound links is the natural traffic that will result from them. Following are some simple methods for getting other sites to link to yours.

Create content at your site that other sites will want to link to. This can (and often does) include writing a blog and participating in social media networks. If your blog is compelling and you promote it well within other blogs and social media, other sites will link to it. Or, instead of a blog, simply write short articles with useful information that is likely to be shared online. Nolo, this book's publisher, uses this strategy and publishes an enormous amount of free information at its site to draw traffic. Taking this a step further, you can share your site's content by licensing it to other sites with a requirement that the other site provide a link back to your site.

Use social media channels to broaden your reach. Social media channels like Facebook, Twitter, Instagram, and YouTube are teeming with users. The trick is to get involved in the channels that are frequented by your customers and potential customers, and to engage with them via entertaining or helpful content. Remember, being too self-promotional on social media can backfire, so make sure you proceed cautiously to ensure your substance and tone are appropriate. Facebook is an important channel for many businesses and offers some great opportunities to connect with your audience and steer them to your site. There are also frustrating aspects, such as Facebook's trend toward requiring payment to boost the visibility of your page and its posts. Users are largely at the mercy of Facebook as to these and other rules or algorithms that often change without notice. But, if you hold your nose and dive in, you may find that Facebook can really help your site's traffic.

Include sharing and syndication buttons at your site. As discussed above, the Web has evolved toward sites that allow users to interact with others who share the same interests, and sites that customize the information users receive. For example, users of sites such as Facebook and Twitter can easily share their favorite articles with other Facebook and Twitter members. Other sites, like StumbleUpon or reddit, sometimes called "social bookmarking" sites, allow users to rate articles in a public forum. RSS technology and sites like Google allow users to "subscribe" to blogs and other information sources, aggregating headlines from selected sites onto one page. The list goes on and on. One way to take advantage of this trend is to include buttons at your site that allow users to share your content or receive it in an RSS feed. For example, if your site features a how-to article on home repair, you could include a Facebook button, allowing a user to click on it and quickly share the article with their Facebook contacts. Or if you write a blog on the latest digital audio technology, you could include an RSS button allowing users to receive updated headlines from your blog on their personalized page where they track dozens of blogs.

Write for other sites. If you have expertise in a certain area, whether bird-watching or golf gear, find online publications that are looking for writers—you'd be surprised how many there are. You may not get paid for your writing but you can usually get a link to your site. Remember that it's best to be brief when writing for websites, so you usually won't need to write much more than 500 words, often less.

Submit press releases to online newswires. As discussed in Chapter 8, sending press releases to local reporters and editors is a great way to get exposure for your business. On the Web, you can submit press releases to distribution services such as PRWeb (www.prweb.com) or SourceWire (www.sourcewire.com) which, for a fee, can get your release picked up by Google News and Yahoo! News as well as hundreds of other news outlets. When your press release includes one or more links back to your website, this can result in quality inbound links.

List your business in online directories. There are loads of directories online, grouped by industry type, location, or other criteria, such as women-owned businesses. As long as the directories are fairly reputable and not "link farms" (meaningless collections of hundreds or thousands of links, created by shady SEO scams), this can be a great way to develop inbound links. Some directories charge fees, so do some research before deciding where to list. Pick the ones that look like they get the most traffic and that fit into your budget. For example, if you run a bed and breakfast, there may be several travel-related directories online, such as one maintained by your state's board of tourism, another by a bed and breakfast trade group, and another by your city's chamber of commerce. To choose which one(s) to list in, find out the fee and the number of visitors the directory gets every month. Based on this information you may determine that one directory is a much better deal since it gets double the traffic for roughly the same fee as the others.

Join membership organizations that provide an online directory listing. Related to the above, keep in mind that some organizations such as the National Association of Women Business Owners (www.nawbo.org), your local chamber of commerce, or a relevant professional or trade organization will list your business in their online and print directories as a benefit of membership. Again, evaluate the membership fees and estimated distribution of the directories before deciding on which ones to join.

Planning a Website Project

There are several considerations you should wrangle with before launching your website project, even before you contact a Web developer. From defining who in your company will be involved with the project to scoping out a rough budget, doing a diligent amount of preparation will help you set business priorities for your website, get the most out of your meetings with potential Web developers, and set the stage for an efficient workflow once you get the project underway. While our advice assumes you will hire a Web developer, a lot of this is relevant for those pursuing do-it-yourself options such as Homestead (formerly Intuit Websites) or Weebly (discussed below).

TIP

Think of planning a website project like planning a new kitchen. If you've ever remodeled your kitchen or done an addition to your house, you know the importance of preparation and staying on top of the details. Asking for design changes midstream, or realizing late in the game that your appliances won't fit in the spaces you've planned for them, is a quick way to blow your budget. Planning a website is very similar.

Identify Participants

Define early on which people in your company will be involved in the website project—in particular, who will have the authority to make decisions about the site. With small start-ups, this is usually pretty straightforward: The business owners typically are involved, meaning they help to set goals, review the site in various stages of development, and have approval authority. However, if there are several business owners and one or more are not involved from the beginning, the possibility exists that the noninvolved owners may raise objections down the line, after significant time and resources have already been spent on the site. To avoid this, make sure all business owners agree from the beginning who will have decision-making authority and what approval process will be followed. Also, any key employees who will be heavily involved in the online part of your business should definitely be included in the process.

Research Other Sites

One of the best ways to educate yourself about the world of possibilities online and to generate specific ideas for features, designs, content, and other elements to include at your site is to browse the Web. Check websites of businesses similar to yours for practical ideas on what type of information and features might be effective for your type of business. The more you get to know how other sites approach e-business, the better you'll develop an understanding of e-business strategies and methods. Review sites with a critical eye, and do your best to break down what works and doesn't work at these sites. Even if a site is very different from how you envision yours, there may be elements that could work for your site—for example, a useful interactive feature or a particular color scheme or composition. Most Web developers will ask you for such examples (especially for design elements, which are often easier to demonstrate with examples rather than abstract descriptions), so it's a good idea to do this research before meeting with a developer.

Sketch an Outline of Site Content

What information do you plan to include at the site? Well before the project gets underway, you'll want to take a stab at the overall scope of the information you plan to offer. This isn't the same as starting to write the actual text or take photos yet—it's way too early for that. But you should draft at least a rough outline of your planned content (a blog or a reservation calendar, for example) as a starting point for designing the overall structure of the site.

Remember that your site content should be closely related to your site strategy and goals. It generally makes sense for you to take the first stab at outlining content because you know best what kind of content exists or can easily be created for your business. Your Web developer can—and likely will—help you refine a content outline, but you are in the best position to make the first draft.

Learn About Technology Options

Assuming you use a professional Web developer, at some point they will recommend what kind of technology—generally called a development platform—they will use to build the site. To help you understand what your developer is talking about, here's a quick overview. We're over-simplifying here, but a development platform is, in a sense, a "prefab" website kit. Instead of writing code from the ground up, the developer applies a customized design and configures various elements within the development platform to meet your specific needs and the design specifications that have been agreed upon.

Development platforms can be either proprietary (requiring annual licensing fees to be paid to the platform owner) or open-source platforms (free). The clear trend these days is to use open-source platforms, which not only are free to use, but, in the case of popular platforms, are supported by an extensive community of developers who constantly test and make enhancements to the platform. The most popular open-source platforms include *WordPress, Joomla,* and *Drupal;* in the world of proprietary platforms, *ExpressionEngine* is fairly popular.

One important budget-related consideration is that development platforms continually release upgraded versions, and you'll need to upgrade yours at least occasionally. Your developer can tell you which upgrades are essential and which might be okay to skip. For example, if you built your site using *WordPress* and six months later *WordPress* released a new version of the platform, your developer might tell you that upgrading is a low priority since the new version contains few changes from the previous version. Six months later, however, there might be yet another new version that your developer tells you is essential to implement as it addresses important bugs and site security issues. In that case, it might cost you a few hundred dollars to hire the developer to upgrade your *WordPress* installation to prevent your site from succumbing to errors or hackers.

Another technical issue to be aware of is that if you want to update the site content regularly on your own, without having to hire a developer, confirm with your developer that your site will have a solid content management system (CMS). I'm generalizing again, but basically with a CMS, you can use whatever browser you normally use (Firefox, Safari, Internet Explorer, Chrome), log in with a username and password, and be able to edit the pages of content at your site. Having a site with a CMS—also known as a "content-managed site"—frees you from having to hire a developer for every little change, thus saving you money. The more you anticipate making updates or changes to your content, the more you stand to save with a content-managed site.

WordPress has by far the most user-friendly CMS, but all of the development platforms mentioned above have relatively easy to use CMSs. Talk with your developer about which ones will best meet your needs, and ask for a demo of how they work before finalizing your decision about which development platform to use.

> **TIP**
>
> **Does my e-business need an app?** For many businesses, developing their own app is an unnecessary expense and a distraction from the main business operation. Developing apps can be quite expensive, plus you'll need to manage all the customer service aspects of offering that app including tech support, releasing updates, and more. Instead, make sure your site is built with responsive Web design so it displays well on mobile devices. That said, if mobile users are a core element of your business strategy, the expenses and resources necessary to develop an app may be well worth it.

Set a Realistic Budget

When attempting to set a realistic budget for creating and maintaining your site, keep a few parameters in mind. Very generally speaking, the cost to build a content-managed website that you can update yourself will usually start at around $3,000. (For info on do-it-yourself options, see "DIY Websites: Do or Don't?" below.) To build any additional features— e-commerce, a photo gallery, a graphical calendar, an online registration system, a blog, and the like—the price will go up. Remember also that there are often third-party fees beyond what a Web developer charges, such as payment processing and security certificate fees for e-commerce sites. Don't forget domain name registration (roughly $10 per year) and hosting fees (which start at $10 or so per month.)

In addition, it's essential to factor in the cost of maintaining your site after it has been created. Assuming you create a site with a content management system, you should be able to handle a significant portion of updating on your own. But don't underestimate the time commitment required—you'll need to define an updating schedule, establish who will be doing the updating work, and make realistic estimates for the time it will take to get the updates done. The following maintenance tasks are typical:

- writing new content
- adding, removing, or editing products and descriptions in an online store
- taking new photographs—particularly for e-commerce operations when new products are added
- responding to emails from site visitors
- if you sell products online, generating and analyzing sales reports and dealing with customer service issues, and
- promoting and marketing the website.

Even with a CMS, you may occasionally need to hire a Web developer to make deeper technical changes—say to add a calendar function or change the layout of an HTML template. As mentioned earlier, you'll also need to update the underlying software of whatever development platform and plug-ins you're using, usually every year or so. And if your site is a major source of your income, you may need to hire an SEO specialist to keep the site optimized and to analyze traffic reports. With Web developer fees ranging from $50 to $150 an hour, maintenance can get expensive. Do your best to anticipate your needs and develop realistic budget estimates for these ongoing tasks.

Establish a Schedule

For some business owners, the timing of the launch of their website is crucial—say, you absolutely need to go live before an important trade show, or before your store's grand opening. For others, it may not matter very much at all. The point is to consider whether the timing of your website project is an important issue, and if so, schedule accordingly.

It typically takes *at least* a few months from the start of a website project until the site's launch, and usually longer—for complex sites, considerably longer. If holiday online sales are a big part of your business strategy, get the ball rolling in time to get your site up and running by mid-October; this means at a bare minimum getting a contract signed with a developer by August, which means starting your search for a developer and other preparations in early summer. Of course, even this is cutting it close, considering the time it takes to market a site and gain exposure for it. The essential thing is to start the process well before you need your site to be launched.

Also, consider your own busy schedule when planning a Web project. Web developers typically need a fair amount of input from you during the development process, which may require several meetings. For example, you'll likely need to review and approve several demos and provide guidance on site content. Don't assume that once you start the project, the Web developer will just run with it and finish it off; account for the time you'll need to spend reviewing progress and providing information to the developer.

Finally, your cash flow can be an issue in timing your Web project. Make sure you'll have the necessary cash or credit for any advance deposits and other payments.

Choosing and Working With a Web Developer

Finding a quality developer to build your site can be frustratingly difficult. Ironically, lots of Web developers are poor communicators and tend to drown potential clients in tech-speak, making it hard to discern whether they understand what you want or what they're offering. Obviously, you want a developer who is easy to communicate with and clearly understands your vision, as well as does quality, professional work.

This section offers advice on how to find a Web developer—and gives tips on what to consider when choosing one. Remember, it's best to do the planning tasks outlined above before starting your search so that you can find someone that fits your needs.

Starting Your Search

Just as when you are looking for any professional, the best way to find a Web developer is to ask other business owners for recommendations. In addition, look for examples of good local websites and find out who built them. Sometimes a website will include a credit saying who built it; other times you may have to ask the business owner.

Keep in mind that in the last few years, Web developers have multiplied like little tech-savvy rabbits. Lots of talented developers—and plenty not so talented—operate under the radar, often with no yellow pages listing or other advertising presence. Because of this, traditional approaches such as searching the phone book are likely to miss a significant number of prospects. Searching online for developers in your area is a better bet, but you'll still want to get references before signing a contract with anyone. Make sure you talk with plenty of other business owners to get the word on the street about who does great work, at a reasonable price and on schedule.

What to Look for in a Web Developer

Even simple Web development projects involve a number of elements that require different skills. You'll need more than a good programmer; you'll typically need a team and a project manager that follows a methodical process. Include the following considerations in your evaluation process.

Team of specialists. Generally speaking, you'll usually get a better result from a firm that assigns a team to each project, rather than one person who does it all. A solid team usually includes a graphic designer, a programmer, an editor/writer, and ideally a project manager who coordinates everyone's efforts (including yours). Sure, sometimes a talented graphic designer might also be a top-notch programmer, or the programmer might be an excellent editor—but this is not usually the case. The best approach is for each major task to be handled by a specialist.

Project manager approach. An important but often overlooked issue is how well a Web developer—specifically, the project manager, assuming the firm you're considering will include a project manager on the team— manages and coordinates all the various aspects of the project. The project manager should be able to articulate a clear process for the various tasks involved, such as defining the information organization, doing the graphic design, creating the content, and programming the site.

Approvals-based process. It's particularly important that the process be approvals based, meaning that you, the business owner, will be asked to approve the Web developer's progress at specific points in the project. For example, if a Web developer does not follow a methodical process, and does not obtain your approval of early stages of site development, you may find yourself presented with a nearly finished site that has no resemblance to what you envisioned. If this happens, the developer may virtually have to start all over again—a situation that could have been averted if approvals had been requested along the way.

Ability to work collaboratively. If you plan to handle certain aspects of Web development in-house or through other contractors with whom you have a relationship, you'll want to look for a Web developer who can work collaboratively with you and your team. For example, if you want to maintain absolute control over the design elements of your site (as may be the case if you have a solid relationship with a graphic designer), but want the developer to handle other technical issues, make this fact clear to the prospective developer and evaluate whether you will be a good fit working together.

Relevant experience. Of course, be sure to visit other sites that the developer has created. Web developers' own websites will usually have online portfolios showing websites they've done. Visit those sites and poke around to make sure they work well. Ideally, the developer will have experience with sites and features that are similar to what you want. Even better, the developer has experience working with businesses similar to yours. Since strategic considerations are critical in website projects, the more your developer understands your business and the strategies driving it, the better,

Use of technologies. Some Web developers use specialized development platforms and other technologies that are proprietary or difficult for others to use. So, if you end up parting ways with your developer, you might get stuck with a website that is difficult or nearly impossible for others to maintain and update. Ask your prospects what technologies they use, whether they are widely supported, and what difficulties might arise for other developers in maintaining the site. You may feel uncomfortable asking this, but it's a perfectly legitimate question that the developer should answer clearly.

Proposals, Quotes, References, and Contracts

After you have met with a few potential developers and have narrowed your list down to a few prospects, ask each of them to give you a proposal and quote in writing. Generally speaking, it's best to get at least two or three proposals or quotes to compare. Some developers might give a bare-bones quote focused on numbers; others will give more of a proposal that outlines their planned approach. Though an exhaustive, novel-length proposal isn't necessary, a proposal is better than a strictly numbers-oriented quote, because it will demonstrate whether the developer understands your particular needs and has come up with the right solution for you. At the very least, a proposal should show what specific services will be offered; ideally the cost will be broken down into an itemized list, showing separate line items for information architecture, design, programming, content development, and training.

Once you choose a developer, it's essential that you write and sign a contract clearly outlining the project. At a minimum, that contract should include:

- **An overview of the scope of services.** Make sure that you and the Web developer are on the same page regarding who will be responsible for creating and finalizing content. Web developers typically will work with your text and photographs, but will not write content from scratch or take photographs without charging extra.

- **A list of deliverables**—in other words, anything the developer will deliver to you (both as the project progresses and at the end of the project), such as a site map, a color mock-up, and an HTML template.
- **A clear schedule** giving deadlines for various aspects of the project, often tied to deliverables.
- **Intellectual property provisions,** detailing who will own the materials developed in the project—including graphic designs, templates, written content, photographs, software programming, and any other material subject to intellectual property protection.
- **Compensation and payment terms**—including specifics on how fees will be calculated if work goes beyond the scope originally anticipated. If there will be any financial penalties for delays, or bonuses for early completion, mention those in your contract.
- **Termination provisions,** detailing what will happen if the working relationship falls apart or either party wants to end the project.

CAUTION

Get it in writing. This advice cannot be overstated: Do not work with a Web developer without a contract. If the developer is reluctant to sign a written contract, it's a clear sign that he or she lacks the professional standards that you want. Even worse, without a contract the Web developer may own copyright to the code, content, or other aspects of your site that the developer creates. Avoid this at all costs by insisting on a contract that addresses intellectual property ownership. For more on this crucial issue, see "Intellectual Property: Who Owns Your Website?" later in this chapter.

Creating Your Website

An efficient, methodical process will go a long way toward making your website project a success. This section outlines a simple, generalized approach that will help ensure an efficient workflow between you and your Web developer, including all the participants you've included.

Keep in mind these steps aren't written in stone; there's always a certain amount of fluidity in Web development projects.

In the real world, it's not uncommon for Web projects to get a bit circular at times, forcing you to revisit earlier steps to make modifications. For example, you may need to refine your site's information architecture after you create content if some of that content does not fit into your original design. This is normal, as long as it's not chronic and extensive. The reality is that following a methodical process will improve efficiency. Even if you're planning a small, simple site on your own, following a process similar to the one described here will help increase your chances of success.

Clarify Strategy and Goals

All website projects should start by clearly identifying strategy and goals, priorities, budget, and schedule. (See "Start With Your Business Strategy" and "Planning a Website Project," above.) It's crucial in this early stage that you and your Web developer have open and clear communication about these issues.

Workshop-type meetings in which your business's Web project participants and possibly other staffers or associates contribute ideas are often helpful. And it's often useful to solicit comments from a wide range of people in the early stage, even those who won't be involved in the project as it progresses. Soliciting feedback from people who will be affected by the website—such as your marketing team, trusted colleagues, and potential customers—helps ensure that you will include a wide range of perspectives and avoid tunnel vision.

Define Information Architecture

The term "information architecture" may sound like tech-speak, but it's actually an accurate description of an important, fundamental aspect of all websites: how the information is organized. This is also sometimes called information design or content mapping. In all websites, defining the information architecture is the first step in actually starting to build the site.

A basic tool in defining information architecture is called a site map. Closely related to a simple content outline (as in, a basic text outline), a site map is a visual representation of content modules and how they are related to one other. Another fundamental tool is called a user interface diagram, or UI diagram, which is a mock layout of how content and other elements such as links and images will be organized on the site pages—basically another way of saying how the pages will look to users. A UI diagram is analogous to an architectural blueprint for a building. To help understand the difference between a site map and a UI diagram, bear in mind that a site map shows what content will be at a site, and a UI diagram shows how and where it will be displayed to site users.

Web developers vary a lot in how they use site maps and UI diagrams. Some Web developers simply use content outlines instead of graphical site maps. Others like to diagram everything out graphically. Diagramming can be time intensive, so your developer might just do a few to give you an idea of the organization before building your site. If every last button and detail isn't included on the diagrams presented to you, don't approve the diagrams without clarifying with your developer that those little details will be taken care of without extra charge. Asking for things to be done that weren't on the approved diagram may be considered a change order, and subject to additional fees. Ideally, every element that you envision for your site will be on the architecture diagrams that you'll approve before the project moves to the design stage.

Define the Website's Look and Feel

Once a site map and UI diagrams are approved, the developer will usually start working on the graphic design and other visual elements of the website, which as a whole are generally called the site's look and feel. Color palettes and typefaces are major elements to consider, as well as images and composition.

Web developers will typically ask you for some initial direction, such as whether you want your site to appear traditional, modern, funky, high tech, or whimsical and what colors you envision at the site; it's common also for the developer to ask for URLs of other sites you'd like to mimic.

Your input at this stage is important so that the site conveys the right message and strikes the right tone for your business. Based on your guidance, the developer will usually make mock Web pages, sometimes called color comprehensives, for you to review and approve.

> ⓘ CAUTION
> **Don't overdo your design.** In particular, avoid the temptation to go overboard with motion graphics, animation, or other multimedia. At a minimum, these features can be distracting; at worst, they can prevent visitors from being able to access your site if they don't load correctly or are incompatible with the visitor's browser setup. If you do use these technologies, make sure your developer knows how to implement them without creating errors or search engine issues that prevent people from accessing your site. Whenever possible, give visitors a choice of whether or not to view an animation or video; don't have it load automatically. And overall, use animated features when they make sense—to demo how your baby sling should be worn, or how to assemble your furniture product—not just to add meaningless bells and whistles to your site.

A good website can be expensive

"We hired a designer and programmers to completely redesign our website about two years ago. It was a very expensive undertaking, but it paid off quickly. The website is a balance of content that we are able to edit ourselves, and content that we pay our programmer to update or change."
— **Rebecca Pearcy**

Create Content

With information architecture and visual elements approved, you or the developer (depending on your contract) can get started on creating the content that will populate the website's pages. If your developer will be creating the content, they'll probably ask for source materials to get them started.

Regardless of who is creating the content, here are some key tips.

Start with what you have. Your business may have brochures, flyers, or other written information already developed. The existing content will need to be reworked somewhat to make it shorter and more concise for the Web, but it's still much easier to adapt something that's already written than to start from scratch. If you don't have any written materials or graphics, someone will need to prepare them. The good news is that people prefer brevity online, so stick with short paragraphs, lists, bullet points, and little blurbs.

Create content that will help draw traffic and attract inbound links, which has the added benefit of boosting your search engine results. The most effective websites include content that is useful, entertaining, or otherwise interesting to your target audience. How-to articles are always popular, as are lists such as "Top 10 Ways to Make Your Home Greener," or "Five Tips to Socialize Your Dog."

Include keywords in your site content that potential customers would use when searching online for a business like yours. Include them so they read naturally; don't create awkward text that is crammed with keywords. Site visitors can usually see through this tactic or at the very least will be turned off by your poorly written copy.

Don't forget that content includes images, such as photos, illustrations, and graphic art. If you're starting with very little visual content, remember it's almost always cheaper and easier to take some digital photos or buy stock photos than to commission illustrations or other graphics.

⚠ CAUTION

Banish bad clip art from your site. Aren't we all tired of seeing hideous websites? Though a discussion of design aesthetics is beyond the scope of this chapter, one thing to watch out for is the bad clip art—that's the small illustrations and graphics, that are sometimes animated—widely available online, often for free. Some clip art is of high quality, but the vast majority tends to be very amateurish looking and will make your site look amateurish as well. Don't pepper your site with angels, teddy bears, or animated floaty balloons because you think they look cute. An unprofessional-looking website is simply bad business.

Build the Website

Often, while the content is being written and photographed, the programmer is busy building the site based on the approved site architecture diagrams and design mock-ups. When the build is complete, it will be ready for the content (both text and images) to be entered into the CMS. Depending on your contract, either the Web developer or you will do the content entry. If you do it, you'll likely need some guidance as to how to use the CMS first, which may be a minitraining in addition to the full training done at the conclusion of the project (see "Train the Site Managers," below).

Though your Web developer may build the site on a test server, she may prefer to build the site on the Web server where it will ultimately have its home. If so, you'll need to tackle domain name registration and Web hosting before the developer starts the build. (See "Domain Names and Hosting," below.)

Test the Website

When your site is complete, it should be thoroughly and methodically tested in multiple browsers to make sure links and features work, images load, and text displays correctly. This is called "QA" or quality assurance. Any glitches or bugs will then be fixed. It's normal and not a bad reflection on the Web developer if the site contains some bugs. What's important is to find them and fix them before launching your site to the public. Professional Web developers should include a testing phase. Once it is completed and all bugs reported and corrected, the site is ready to be launched.

Train the Site Managers

When the site is finished, the Web developer will generally offer a one- to three-hour training to whoever at your company will be in charge of maintaining the site (the site managers or administrators). If you'll be outsourcing maintenance to the Web developer or an experienced outside contractor, the training may not be necessary.

DIY Websites: Do or Don't?

A common question for small business owners embarking on their e-business plans is whether, instead of hiring a Web developer (discussed above), they could use one of the do-it-yourself options such as template-based website builder services or hosted solutions. Considering that many of these services can be quite inexpensive or even free, compared to a typical minimum $3,000 for a basic site built by a developer, it's certainly understandable that they are appealing to cash-strapped start-ups.

There are a few different types of services here, so let's talk about them separately. First we'll look at template-driven sites created with "website builder" software. Then we'll consider options such as Etsy, Amazon, and eBay, which similarly allow you to do business online without having to hire a developer.

Using Website Builder Services

Services such as Homestead (formerly Intuit Websites), Weebly, or WebStarts allow customers to build a site using a simple browser-based interface that does not require any technical knowledge or skills. The user will generally choose a prebuilt design template and customize it with menu headers, images, and text. Homestead charges a monthly fee of $5.99 that includes a five-page site, hosting, and phone support five days a week. Similar services (often called "website builder services" or "hosted solutions" since the website is hosted on their servers) are often offered by website hosting companies. Fees can be as low as $5 per month or even free, but these lowest-end fees don't usually offer much in the way of features or support. Business sites can usually expect to pay $25 per month and up.

Generally speaking, these template-driven services might be appropriate only for the smallest of businesses that are truly pressed to get a minimal presence online. The biggest drawback is that these types of sites are seriously limited both in terms of design and functionality. While it's true that Homestead offers hundreds of design templates, customizing the template often results in shoddy-looking sites, with poorly formatted text and clunky menus. Function-wise, it is often difficult or impossible to add features that you want such as calendars, blogs, e-commerce, or interactive features. If it is possible to add these features at all, it will usually be only with whatever plug-in that service provider has created for its template site, which may be primitive at best.

Another downside of using do-it-yourself template sites is that they usually take more time, effort, and skill than you think they will. These services claim that even the least computer-savvy user can easily build a site, but that's usually not the case. At the very least, inexperienced users will typically find they'll need to spend a fair amount of time learning the site-building system, often through trial and error, before being able to get a site up and running. When considering a Web builder service, be sure to look for user comments (often at websites separate from the builder service) to get a sense of how easy or difficult they found the service to use.

Even if you are able to figure out the builder software fairly easily, another issue to consider is that a lack of experience in designing a website will often result in a poorly organized site. Deciding what content to include and how to break up and organize that content at the site can be more complicated than you think. An experienced Web professional can make a huge difference in developing carefully considered content and organization—resulting in a site that's more tightly aligned with your strategic goals.

With all those downsides in mind, let's consider the positives: cost and convenience. Website builder services with prebuilt design templates will significantly reduce the up-front cost of creating a site and minimize the complicated decisions and maintenance that are required when building your own site. These services generally include hosting and will usually handle software upgrades for free. Not having to deal with these issues can be a true relief for new business owners who are swamped by the many other details of getting their businesses off the ground.

A final note: This field of template-driven, do-it-yourself sites is growing rapidly, and features are definitely improving. Expect to see more and better options in coming years.

TIP

Look into website builder services for specific industries. For example, there are several quality builder services specifically for professional photographers: livebooks, PhotoShelter, and SmugMug, to name a few. Industry-specific website builder services can be valuable since they typically offer features and functions important to that industry—for example, the photo-oriented services mentioned above all have much more sophisticated portfolio options than would a garden variety service like WebStarts. Fees are often higher, but can be well worth it if the service offers the right features and options to promote and run your business well.

Etsy, Amazon, eBay, and Affiliate Stores in E-Commerce Sites

Another alternative (or addition) to hiring a Web developer to build your site is to open a store within an existing e-commerce site such as Amazon, Etsy, or eBay. Creating a store within one of these mega e-commerce portals is definitely a quicker, easier, and less expensive way to get started selling your products online. Typically the registration and setup processes are easy to complete; as long as you have good photos of and copy about your products, you can be up and running in a day or two. (Again, remember this doesn't include the very important tasks of doing solid business planning to ensure your venture will be a success.)

There are downsides, however, to having just a store at Amazon or eBay and not your own website. In particular, branding your business and its website is a lot harder to do from within the vast "shopping mall" of the big e-commerce sites. Instead of developing name recognition for your business and its domain name, customers will have to find you amongst the thousands and thousands of other Amazon, Etsy, or eBay sellers. Anyone who has shopped at Amazon and similar e-commerce sites can testify that finding a store or product can be like finding a needle in a haystack. Even if you give your store a specific name, shoppers within sites like Amazon are much less likely to remember your store name than if you had a custom-built store with its own domain name and the ability to use the site design and content to develop your brand more strongly.

Another aspect to consider is that having a store within a big e-commerce operation restricts the content and functions you can offer. With your own site built by a developer, you can develop creative, strategic content to draw traffic—say, with a blog, an interactive customer service area, or other unique content. While stores within Amazon, Etsy, eBay, and others do allow you to offer some customized content, you'll be much more limited.

RESOURCE

Looking for how-to advice on selling on Etsy, Amazon, or eBay? All have detailed guides to setting up shop on their websites. Start there and see if it makes sense for your business.

Establishing a craft business at Etsy

"The Etsy store is clearly an awesome choice for many craft businesses these days   I would have had one in my early days if it had existed. It seems like a great starting point to get you to the next level of having your own website and establishing brand identity. The downside of Etsy seems to be how big it has become; there are so many shops on there now, it is overwhelming to the consumer."

— **Rebecca Pearcy**

Domain Names and Hosting

Before your site can go live, you must register a domain name and sign up with a Web hosting company. Your domain name is part of the address visitors will use to access your site, such as nolo.com or amazon.com. Your Web host is the company that keeps your site pages on computer servers that are connected to the Internet 24 hours a day, so the pages are always available for visitors to view.

Choosing and Registering a Domain Name

Your first task is to choose an available domain name—that is, a name that is not currently registered to, or being used by, another group (or one that poses a trademark conflict because it's confusingly similar to another company's trademark). Ideally, when you chose your business name you made sure the same domain name was available. If you're already committed to a business name and the domain name isn't available, come up with an available variant that will be easy for your customers to remember. (Adding a geographical reference can be a good solution; for example if coffeebuzz.com isn't available, you could use coffeebuzzsanfran.com if you're located in San Francisco.)

CAUTION

Domain names can pose trademark conflicts. Even if a domain name is available to use, you need to make sure it is not confusingly similar to the name of another business or its products or services. Your domain name is at risk if it legally conflicts with (is the same as or very similar to) any one of the millions of commercial trademarks that already exist. For more in-depth information about domain names and trademarks, see "Avoiding Trademark Troubles When Naming Your Business," in Chapter 7.

Once you select an available name, you should register it online at a domain name registrar. One popular and inexpensive registrar is Namecheap at www.namecheap.com, but there are hundreds of options out there. If you'd like to do some comparison shopping, you can find a list of approved registrars at www.internic.net.

While there can be big differences in cost from one registrar to another, all are relatively cheap. Namecheap charges about $10 per name per year; I've seen others charge $35 or more. With domain name registration, more expensive does not mean better. In fact there's hardly any difference in the services and benefits provided from one registrar to the other—but you do want one that has decent customer service. In particular, avoid registrars that don't offer any phone support.

Although registering a domain name is pretty simple, there are a few potential pitfalls. In particular, make sure that your business is listed as the domain name registrant, which is essentially the owner of the name. Also make sure your business is listed as the administrative contact. If someone else handles domain name registration for you—say your Web developer or the hosting service—make sure that they don't list their company as either the registrant or the administrative contact. If your Web developer or some other technology consultant will be helping you maintain the site, it's okay for them to be listed as technical contact.

Why the caution? Well, consider what might happen if your Web developer handles the domain name registration process for your business and lists herself as the registrant of the domain name you've chosen. Say six months later you decide to hire a different developer due to conflicts with the original developer. If the original developer is listed as the domain name registrant, she could hold your site hostage, preventing you from changing Web hosts or other critical tasks. Sadly this is more than hypothetical; more than a few businesses have been down this sorry road, so make sure your business doesn't make the same mistake.

Choosing a Web Host

A Web host is a company that maintains servers, which are simply high-performance computers that are connected to the Internet continuously, serving the Web pages stored on it to the world. When your Web pages are on the host's server and your Web host has configured your domain name correctly, your website will be live and all the information it offers will be available to visitors around the globe, 24 hours a day, 365 days a year.

Your Web developer will probably recommend a host that the developer regularly uses. If you want more options, get recommendations from other business owners. Also, check out www.comparewebhosts.com. Ultimately you'll want to find a Web host that supports the services your site will offer (such as e-commerce), has reliable servers, and provides good customer service. Make sure there are reasonable customer service hours during which you can talk to an actual human. More than a few host companies offer no live-person customer service, which can be infuriating if you're experiencing any problems.

Web hosts may charge by the month or by the year. Fees are based on how much data you need the server to store—that is, the size of your website in disk space—or how much data you transfer to and from your website each month. A host that I use regularly, BlueHost (www. bluehost.com), starts at about $7 per month for small, basic sites.

Intellectual Property: Who Owns Your Website?

Intellectual property laws establish ownership rights and other rules for various types of works such as text and artwork protected by copyright, marks used in business protected by trademark, and inventions protected by patents. Copyright is of particular importance in Web development projects, as many of the components of websites are protected by copyright. As mentioned earlier, it's crucial that your contract with a Web developer includes clear, detailed terms on ownership and permissions for any materials developed for the website protected by copyright. Other intellectual property laws, such as trademark or patent, also may come into play, though not as often.

Copyrightable materials include text, photos, artwork, and designs, as well as technology developed for your site, such as databases and programming. As you can imagine, serious troubles can arise if ownership of any aspect of your website is in dispute. The way to avoid this is by including clear copyright terms in your contract with the Web developer. This section gives a quick overview of copyright basics and the specific issues that arise in Web development projects, to help you head off any copyright conflict.

RESOURCE

Resources on copyright and intellectual property issues. The "Patent, Copyright & Trademark" section of Nolo's Legal Encyclopedia at www. nolo.com has many articles on these issues, including how to get permission to use copyrighted materials. If your website, brochure, product (a T-shirt, tote bag, magnet, or CD cover, for example), or something else uses someone else's copyrighted photos, art, or text, make sure you have permission to do so. For the full treatment on copyright and the permissions process, see *Getting Permission: How to License & Clear Copyrighted Materials Online & Off*, by Richard Stim (Nolo).

Copyright Basics

When someone owns copyright to certain works, such as an article, poem, photo, drawing, or song (to name just a few), it means that others may not reproduce, modify, distribute, or sell the works without the copyright owner's permission. In legal terms, permission to use someone else's copyrighted content is known as a license. When you license content, you do not own it; you simply obtain the right to use it in specific circumstances. In contrast, buying the copyrights to a creative work, known in legal terms as an assignment, gives you all the rights to the work as if you were the original copyright owner.

The general rule is that the person who creates content owns the copyright. However, if the work qualifies as a "work for hire," then the hiring party, not the creator, legally owns the copyright to it. The rules regarding what constitutes a work for hire vary depending on whether the work is created by an employee or an independent contractor.

RELATED TOPIC

The issue of whether a worker is an employee or an independent contractor is not always straightforward. See Chapter 12 for a complete discussion of distinguishing between these types of workers.

Rules for Employees

When an employee creates any work in the course of employment, the work is considered a work for hire, so that the employer—not the employee—owns the copyright to that work. Having your website created by employees, not contractors, is the simplest and most straight-forward way for your business to make sure that it owns copyright in all aspects of the site.

Unfortunately, this isn't an option for many start-up businesses that aren't ready to hire full-fledged employees. But fortunately, there are other ways to make the work a work for hire, even if it is created by an independent contractor, not an employee.

Rules for Independent Contractors

When an independent contractor creates certain types of content, the hiring party owns the copyright in the work if the contractor and hiring party have made a written agreement stating that the work is a work for hire. A written work-for-hire agreement is essential whenever a nonemployee creates the work. Without a written agreement, the nonemployee Web developer owns copyright to the materials he or she develops for the website.

But there's an important wrinkle: You cannot turn every kind of creative work into a work for hire using a written agreement. According to copyright law, a work-for-hire agreement will give copyright to the hiring party only if the content is:

- part of a larger literary work, such as an article in a magazine or a poem or story in an anthology
- part of a motion picture or another audiovisual work, such as a screenplay
- a translation
- a supplementary work, such as an afterword, introduction, editorial note, appendix, or index, or a chart or bibliography
- a compilation
- an instructional text
- a test or answer material for a test, or
- an atlas.

Without trying to puzzle through how on earth lawyers came up with these categories, it's important to understand that depending on whom you ask, the categories may not include the components of websites. This naturally raises the question: If website materials cannot be the subject of work-for-hire agreements, how can you obtain ownership from a Web development contractor? The answer is that you'll need to have a written and signed copyright assignment—an outright sale of all copyright from the contractor to your business. Though it's possible that website materials might legally fall into one of the work-for-hire categories, the safest route is to assume they do not, and to handle ownership transfer with a copyright assignment.

RESOURCE

For more on intellectual property contracts for Web development projects, see Nolo's Website Development Agreement available on www.nolo.com.

Protecting Your Interests

It's obviously in your interest to own all aspects of your website so that you have the legal right to do anything you want with the site. For example, if you fail to obtain a copyright to the site's text content from the Web developer, the developer could potentially prevent you from making any changes to the text on the site. The same is true for images, graphic designs, and technologies created by the Web developer for the website. This may sound far-fetched to you now, but consider what might happen if you and the developer ever got into a conflict and decided to part ways. A developer with a bone to pick who owns any rights to your site could deal a serious blow to your online business.

Be aware that sometimes a Web developer will not want to assign copyright ownership to your company for certain aspects of the site. As discussed below, this may be perfectly legitimate. What's crucial in this situation is for you to get permission—legally, a license—from the Web developer to use his or her copyrighted work as necessary for you to get the full benefits of your website. Without such permission, you'll be at the mercy of your Web developer when you want to edit content or make changes to technology owned by the developer—a situation you definitely want to avoid.

There are a number of situations in which it might make sense for a Web developer to retain ownership—for example, if the developer has created a proprietary content management system, shopping cart, or other functions. Developing Web applications and using them for multiple clients is the lifeblood of some Web firms, so they naturally are not willing to transfer ownership of that programming code to your company. Instead, they'll give your business permission, or a license, to use the technology in specified ways. This is perfectly legitimate, but you'll need to be careful about a couple of things:

You need to protect your company's ability to make changes to the site down the road. You should always think about—and ask prospective developers about—what will happen if you end your relationship with the developer in the future. If the developer creates the site with proprietary technology, you may find it difficult or impossible to make changes without using the original developer. More than a few businesses have learned this lesson the hard way and have had to create new websites from scratch after ending their relationships with previous developers who refused to grant permission to the businesses to make changes to the code the developers owned.

If you are hiring the developer to create functions or other programming code that will give your business a competitive edge online, then you won't want the developer to hold on to any rights—instead, you'll want to obtain full ownership of that code so that it can't be used for other businesses. This isn't usually the case with small, basic websites that simply want to establish an online presence. But if you are paying a developer to create an innovative shopping cart or search function that will help distinguish you from your online competition, it's essential that you own that code when it's complete so that it can't be used by anyone else without your permission (and possible licensing fees paid to you). Unsurprisingly, you'll likely have to pay a premium for this type of full transfer of rights.

In deciding what ownership or licensing arrangements will work for your business, keep in mind the following rule: The more important content or technology is to your site, the more crucial it is that you either get ownership or a broad license to use and possibly modify those materials. This is true whether or not the Web developer has a valid reason to retain ownership. If it's essential that you own copyright ownership in a database or another technology, don't enter into an agreement that won't confer the rights you need.

RESOURCE

For more help with Web issues. *Don't Fear the Internet* is a clean, user-friendly resource for non-Web designers. It is aimed at artists, photographers, and other creatives who want a decent website but don't have the technical skills. See www.dontfeartheinternet.com.

Keeping Your Books and Managing Your Finances

f you've run a business before, managed budgets at a previous job, or just are great at handling your own money, you may find it easy to track your business's finances and keep the books in order. But, if this is all new to you, and you are particularly math-phobic, you might worry that tracking and managing your business's income and expenses are dreadfully difficult tasks. Thankfully, this is an overblown (but very common) fear. Business bookkeeping and financial management can be pretty simple and straightforward, even for those of us who aren't true "money" people.

As with so many aspects of running a business, the trick is to establish a system early on to help you stay organized. With a system in place—and by "system" we mean a simple process for organizing your receipts and files, as well as having bookkeeping software set up and configured—you'll definitely be able to handle most or all of your bookkeeping tasks, even if you've never done it before. While experience with managing money certainly won't hurt, the basics are not hard to master, even for the inexperienced.

If you're itching to launch your venture and still worried that you have too much to learn in a short time, stop fretting. You don't need to turn into a financial whiz overnight. In practice, we advise every small business owner to consult at least once or twice during their start-up days with an experienced bookkeeper or accountant (or possibly both) to help the business get started on the right foot. For those of you who feel like total novices when it comes to the money stuff, consulting with a professional will help you get over the hump of your financial learning curve.

This chapter provides an overview of what's involved in basic bookkeeping and financial management for small businesses. We'll cover money-related concepts and practical tasks business owners need to understand, including:

- what receipts and records your business should keep and simple ways to organize them
- how typical bookkeeping software works, including setting it up and entering your income and expense data, and

- the fun part: generating reports showing how well your business is doing financially (or how poorly it's doing, which is undeniably less fun to discover). Generating reports from your income and expense data will also help you manage the cash that flows through your business so that you can pay your important bills on time.

We discussed a few financial concepts and tools in Chapter 4 on developing your business plan, with a focus on generating projections using sales and expense estimates to see if your business is likely to turn a profit. We'll revisit some of these financial management tools here—profit/loss analysis and cash flow projection, in particular—but instead of using them to make projections, we'll focus on tracking and managing actual, current income and expense figures.

As we look at various financial calculations and reports in this chapter, keep in mind that bookkeeping software will do these calculations and generate these reports for you in the click of a button. But I've made sure to describe what is going on "behind the scenes" of the software, so to speak, so you understand the real meaning behind the numbers, and how to use them to answer your specific financial questions. As you'll see, none of it is rocket science. That said, the ease of using bookkeeping software to automate these reports is undeniably a blessing for today's entrepreneurs. Considering how affordable financial management software is (generally under $400, and often far less or even free), it really doesn't make sense to track your finances by hand, which is not only much more time-consuming but more prone to errors. Bookkeeping software and other technologies discussed below are ideal for managing the money-related aspects of your business.

CAUTION

Do not neglect to open a business bank account! I have met far too many new business owners who sheepishly admit they do not have a separate business bank account, and have been running their whole operation out of their personal bank account. This is a huge mistake for a number of reasons.

One is that if you hoped to protect your personal assets by creating an LLC or a corporation, you'll basically throw any such protection out the window by commingling personal and business funds. On a more important day-to-day level, mixing your business transactions with personal transactions will make it impossible to do the types of simple financial management tasks described in this chapter. Run, do not walk, to your local community bank and open a business bank account as soon as you're ready to launch.

Bookkeepers and Accountants: Which Do You Need?

There's typically a big cost difference between accountants and bookkeepers—accountants usually charge significantly more—so when hiring these professionals you'll want to hire the right one for the right tasks.

 RELATED TOPIC

See Chapter 13 for advice on choosing a bookkeeper and an accountant. It includes information on different types of accountants, such as certified public accountants (CPAs) and professionals who specialize in tax preparation. Tax basics are covered in Chapter 11.

Bookkeepers

Bookkeepers specialize in the day-to-day tasks of tracking a business's income and expenses, often being in charge of doing data entry and generating reports such as monthly profit/loss statements (explained later in this chapter). In addition, bookkeepers are often hired to prepare payroll for businesses with employees (including determining how much tax to withhold from paychecks, issuing the checks, and managing payroll tax deposits), file statements for property or unemployment taxes, and related bureaucratic tasks.

Businesses like retail stores with lots of transactions every day may want to have a bookkeeper on staff, either full- or part-time, to handle all the data entry. Microbusinesses like consultants and freelancers might simply do the data entry themselves, or have a bookkeeper do data entry once per month.

In your start-up days, a session or two with an experienced bookkeeper can be immensely helpful in setting up your system, including clarifying what records you should keep, choosing and setting up your bookkeeping software, and understanding how to use it.

Accountants

Accountants specialize in making sense of your financial data and handling tasks such as filing tax returns and managing tax savings strategies. Accountants can analyze your financial data and give advice on questions such as whether it's a good time to expand your business or how to set up employee benefits to maximize tax savings. Since accountants typically have deeper knowledge of tax rules than bookkeepers, they are usually in the best position to answer any squirrelly, gray-area tax questions, such as whether certain types of transactions are subject to state sales tax.

It's generally advised for all small businesses to hire an accountant at least once a year to prepare your business's tax return. For smaller, day-to-day tasks and routine filings, you'll save money by hiring a bookkeeper.

> ### Having professionals clean up your records can be costly
>
> *"Remember, it is much more expensive to have the professional clean up your financial records than to have them maintained well in the first place. And we hate doing that work, so your fees may reflect that. Bookkeeping is not a place to cut corners."*
>
> **— Jennifer Cantrell, CPA**

Accounting Glossary

Learning some financial lingo goes a long way toward becoming savvy with the money side of your business. This will give you a better sense of basic written reports and help you communicate with others about important financial information.

Accounting. The process of using your business's income and expense data to perform various calculations and formulas to answer specific questions about your business's financial and tax status.

Bookkeeping. The task of recording the amount, date, and source of all business income and expenses. Accurate bookkeeping is necessary for meaningful accounting.

Invoice. A written record of a transaction, generally submitted to a customer or client when requesting payment. Invoices are sometimes called *bills*.

Statement. A written summary of an account. Unlike an invoice, a statement is not generally used as a request for payment, but is used to outline the details of an account.

Ledger. A collection of related financial information, such as revenues, expenditures, accounts receivable, and accounts payable. Ledgers used to be kept in hardbound books (which explains why a business's financial information is often referred to as the "books"), but are now commonly kept electronically using various software programs.

Account. A collection of financial information grouped according to customer or purpose. For example, if you have a regular supplier, the information regarding your purchases from, payments to, and debts to that supplier would be called your "account." A written record of an account is called a *statement*.

Receipt. A written record of a transaction. A buyer receives a receipt to show that he or she paid for an item. The seller keeps a copy of the receipt to show that he or she received payment for the item.

Accounts payable. Amounts that your business owes, such as unpaid utility bills and purchases your business makes on credit.

Accounts receivable. Amounts owed to your business that you expect to receive, including sales your business makes on credit.

Working with bookkeepers and accountants

"With advice and guidance as to system setup, a lot of small businesses can at least initially maintain their own records in a format that is acceptable for tax preparation. As you grow and the business has additional needs for capital, etc., the bookkeeping needs will expand. Most bookkeeping firms who work with small businesses provide either monthly, quarterly, or annual services to coordinate with tax preparers. We have some clients who have full-time accounting departments who consult with us throughout the year and we prepare the tax returns."

— **Jennifer Cantrell, CPA**

"Bookkeeping, financial management, and taxes—these are the scary things for most crafters and creative people! I used to handle all of these things myself. It took me too long to realize that I should really leave them to a professional. Currently we use QuickBooks for our internal financial management and work with a tax accountant who handles all of our taxes. We have our own bookkeeper on staff that works part time—I can't tell you how much I love signing checks but not having to actually track all the bills and manage the businesses finances! It is fabulous."

— **Rebecca Pearcy**

"This is where you should spend some money, on your books. More than anything else. If you have a desire, and as you start to feel comfortable with the money, then you'll start to learn about the books. I've learned a lot, but I still know that it's not what gives me my juice. I don't want to spend every day doing the numbers. I am much more useful in inspiring people and taking pictures, and interacting with clients, and that's where every single ounce of my energy should go."

— **Kyle Zimmerman**

Financial Management: The Big Picture

The ins and outs of managing a business's finances aren't fundamentally complicated, but entrepreneurs who are new to these tasks often find themselves intimidated or overwhelmed by this world of numbers. To help clarify the overall process, let's take a look at the big picture of what's really involved in this critical aspect of running a business.

Why Track Your Business's Finances?

At the risk of stating the obvious, it's helpful to consider the end goals of managing your business finances. Carefully tracking income and expenses helps you in crucial ways:

- **You'll improve your chances of making a profit.** Having a clear understanding of income sources and patterns will help you see which areas of your business are the most profitable. You'll be able to price goods and services more competitively, pace growth more effectively, and trim costs strategically—for example, cutting back on travel expenses or outsourced services that aren't sufficiently helping generate income.

- **You'll have well-organized financial information that is necessary to file your various tax returns.** There's no worse nightmare than facing a tax deadline and having months' worth of unorganized receipts that haven't been entered into your record-keeping system (or worse yet, not having a record-keeping system in place at all). Being organized will help you avoid penalties from late or incorrect tax returns. You'll also be in a position to reduce taxes by timing your purchases strategically and claiming all your deductible expenses—things that often escape businesses with disorganized records.

- **You'll be able to manage your business's cash flow, ensuring you can pay important bills on time.** Cash flow management is a critical element in every business. When it's done poorly or not at all, you may find yourself short of cash when it's time to pay taxes, payroll, or other crucial expenses. This is exactly the type of scenario that forces businesses to close up shop for good.

- **You'll be able to demonstrate that you have professional business practices to potential funders.** For example, if you want to raise funds for an expansion, lenders or investors will undoubtedly want to see your financials. If your books are in bad shape, it will be difficult or impossible to generate reports that are impressive or even meaningful. If your books are in great shape, on the other hand, you'll be able to inspire confidence and improve your chances of getting the funds you need.

For any of you intimidated or overwhelmed by the money-related aspects of running a business, just keep these fundamentals in mind.

You'll need well-maintained books to pursue funding

"Having a professional maintain your books or at least advise and review them regularly may seem like an unnecessary expense—until you need a loan or line of credit! Bankers are experienced enough to look at a set of financial statements and know they are wrong. I sit on the WESST (a Women's Business Center in New Mexico) loan review committee and I can tell you that just a few weeks ago we denied a small business loan because we felt the financial statements were inaccurate and the answers they gave did not satisfy us enough to give them the loan."

— Jennifer Cantrell, CPA

What's Involved in Financial Management?

At the most basic level, you can break down the process of financial management into three broad steps. We'll explain these in more detail later in the chapter; for now let's just look at an overview.

Step 1. **Keeping and organizing records of expenses and income.** The process starts with keeping records (basic receipts, usually) of all the money the business spends (expenses) and all the money it earns (income). This means carefully keeping and organizing your expense records (such as bills from the office supply store, invoices for your Web hosting charges, and receipts of payments to your employees and freelancers) and your income receipts (such as a cash register tape of your café's income, check stubs from your client's payment checks, or your invoices to clients marked "Paid").

Step 2. **Entering this information into bookkeeping software.** On some periodic basis—say monthly for a small consulting business, or daily for a busy café or retail store—you'll enter the information from the income and expense receipts into a bookkeeping system. More often than not this will be some sort of financial management software such as *QuickBooks* (for details, see "Using Technology to Manage Money, Inventory, and Projects," below).

Step 3. **Generating financial reports.** Finally, with up-to-date information entered into your bookkeeping system, you'll generate reports such as a profit/loss or accounts receivable report to reveal how your business is doing. These reports summarize the data in your bookkeeping system to show you different aspects of your business's financial situation. For example, a profit/loss report shows whether you made a profit in a given time period (usually monthly), while an accounts receivable report shows how much your clients owe you at any given time. Generating reports should be done on some periodic basis, with some reports following different schedules than others. Most businesses should generate a profit/loss report each month, as well as quarterly and annually.

TIP

There are no legal or bureaucratic requirements that your records be kept in any specific organizational system or official format. As long as your records accurately reflect your business's income and expenses, the IRS will find them acceptable. Legalities and tax rules aside, your financial records should be organized well so you can easily find the information you need. Besides helping to keep day-to-day chaos to a minimum, a well-organized system with accessible, reasonably neat files will be a godsend in the event of an audit. (While there is no legal rule that you keep your financial records in a specific organizational system or format, there is a requirement that some businesses use a certain method of crediting their accounts; see "Cash vs. Accrual Accounting," below.)

What bad record keeping can cost you

"Many years ago, I had a client who purchased a small business. The seller admitted that his records were not very accurate and that he could not really prove up his sales figures or his expenses. We were able to negotiate a really low purchase price for my client, because the seller just couldn't prove his information was accurate. My client paid $30,000 for the business, kept accurate records, ran it for seven years, and sold it for $1,000,000! There is no better example as to why keeping accurate records is important."

— **Jennifer Cantrell, CPA**

Cash vs. Accrual Accounting: Which Method's Right for You?

Before diving into the practical steps involved in bookkeeping and accounting, there's one fundamental distinction that needs to be addressed: the difference between cash and accrual accounting. These are the two principal methods of keeping track of a business's income and expenses; they're sometimes called cash method and accrual method, or cash basis and accrual basis accounting. In a nutshell, the difference between these methods has to do with the timing of when transactions are credited to or debited from your accounts. In short:

- Under the *cash* method, income is counted when cash (or a check) is actually received, not necessarily when the sale occurs; expenses are counted when they are actually paid, not necessarily when you made the purchase.
- Under the *accrual* method, transactions are counted when they happen—for example, when you complete a sale, or make a purchase—regardless of when the money is actually received or paid.

For example, say your handbag business buys a new sewing machine in May. Per your agreement with the supplier you pay in full for the sewing machine 45 days later, in July. Using cash method accounting, you would record the expense in the month of July, the month when the money was actually paid. But under the accrual method, the payment would be recorded in May, when you got the sewing machine and became obligated to pay for it.

In the real world, it can sometimes be tricky to figure out how to record transactions under the accrual method. For example, what if you have an agreement with a supplier that you'll pay for inventory after 90 days, minus unsold inventory that you return to the supplier? Or what if a customer prepays for an item that is backordered? In general, under accrual accounting, the job completion date is the key factor: Don't count the transaction until you deliver all of the goods, finish all parts of a service, or otherwise meet all terms of a contract. In situations like these, the help of an experienced bookkeeper is a godsend.

Your choice (cash or accrual method) will depend on several factors.

IRS Rules on Accounting Methods

IRS rules may dictate your choice between using the cash or accrual method. The general rule is that businesses with inventories (retail businesses, for example) must use the accrual method, but there are exceptions. Businesses that have sales of less than $1 million per year are generally free to adopt either accounting method even if inventories are involved—but note that other rules may apply regarding tracking inventories in your books. For businesses with gross sales of more than $1 million but less than $10 million annually, there are more rules and exceptions that may allow a business to use the cash method. IRS Publication 538 (*Accounting Periods and Methods*, available at www.irs. gov) explains IRS rules and the tax implications of your choice. At the end of the day, it's best to ask an accountant or a bookkeeper for advice.

Control Over Your Business Finances

Perhaps even more important than the IRS rules is to consider which method will give you the most control over your business's finances.

In general, the cash method is simpler and may be the best route for freelancers and small firms because it simply involves tracking actual cash in and out of the business, without having to make adjustments for income that's owed to the business or expenses that are due to be paid. However the cash method does not give as accurate a picture of your operational profitability as does the accrual method. Under the cash method, for instance, your books may show a three-month period to be spectacularly profitable because a lot of credit customers paid their bills in that period, when actually sales have been slow. Again, ask an accountant or bookkeeper for guidance.

Choosing cash vs. accrual method

"We really discourage our small business clients from selecting an accrual method unless we are forced otherwise. The accrual method makes you pay income taxes on money you haven't received. Why would you want to do that?"
— Jennifer Cantrell, CPA

Tax Implications

Taxwise, the use of cash versus accrual method affects the tax year in which income and expense items will be counted. For instance, if you use the cash method, and you incur expenses in the 2015 tax year but don't pay them until the 2016 tax year, you won't be able to claim them on your 2015 tax return. But you would be able to claim the 2015 expenses in the 2015 tax year if you use the accrual method, since that system records transactions when they occur, not when money actually changes hands.

For example, if your baby blanket business used accrual method accounting, fabric purchases made in December 2015 and paid for in January 2016 could be included as deductions for the 2015 tax year. But if you used cash method, the fabric expense could not be claimed until the 2016 tax year.

TIP

Establish a financial management system and *use it*. Bookkeeping and related tasks often fall by the wayside because small business owners become consumed with the many other day-to-day details of running their businesses. But blowing off your books is a terrible idea—you'll seriously regret it when you face a tax deadline and have months of receipts in scary piles. Set aside a regular time to do data entry (ideally, when you're refreshed and energetic, not late at night after you put the kids to bed). And assign yourself days to focus on generating financial reports and analyzing them. Most small businesses generate profit/loss and cash flow statements monthly, quarterly, and annually.

Step 1: Keeping and Organizing Income and Expense Records

It goes without saying that the data in your bookkeeping system need to accurately reflect reality. So the first step in bookkeeping and accounting is keeping careful track of each payment to and expenditure from your business. As boring and obvious as it sounds, the key to doing this is to conscientiously keep and organize all income and expense receipts. The best way to stay organized is to have a system in place—in other words, a set of files (including hard copies and digital documents), folders, cash registers, or whatever else that you use consistently over time so that you always know where to find the information you need.

Freelancers and small service businesses may be able to get by with a shoe box or an accordion folder with receipts organized by month. Larger, busier businesses will likely use some sort of cash register-based system, which may include point-of-sale (POS) software, which typically goes beyond tracking transactions to managing categories and subcategories, inventory, and more.

Whether your needs are simple or complex, the important thing is to make sure that you and any staff know the system and use it consistently. If your records aren't accurate, the financial statements you make from them won't be, either.

Let's look at some typical ways that businesses keep their income and expense receipts organized.

RESOURCE

IRS Publication 583, *Starting a Business and Keeping Records*, offers detailed guidance on establishing a record-keeping system. It provides practical tips as well as tax rules, such as how long records must be kept, which businesses must use the accrual method, what tax year to use, and more. Go to www.irs.gov to download the publication.

Income Receipts

Every time your business brings in money—generally through sales of your products or services—you need a record of it. Businesses such as grocery stores, high-volume restaurants, or busy retailers that make hundreds or even thousands of sales a day will likely need a cash register to record each sale. Other businesses with lower sales volumes—say, a landscaping company or custom furniture shop—might be able to get by simply writing out a receipt for each sale from a receipt book. Freelancers and consultants generally use their invoices marked "Paid" as income receipts.

No matter how it's generated, an income receipt should include the date, a brief description (or code) of the goods or services sold, an indication of how payment was made, whether the sale was subject to sales tax, and if so, the amount of sales tax separate from the total.

You should also document any income your business receives from sources other than sales and keep these receipts separate from your sales receipts. For example, if you get a loan or contribute your own personal money to the business, record this fact with some sort of receipt or promissory note. Be sure your written records adequately describe the source of income so you'll know whether to count it as taxable income or not. Most sales income, for example, will be taxed at the end of the year, while income that you personally contribute to the business will not.

Distinguishing Taxable From Nontaxable Sales

As discussed in more detail under "Sales Taxes" in Chapter 11, many sales of goods are subject to sales tax, which retailers must pay to the state. But other large categories of sales are often exempt from sales tax, such as sales of services, sales to out-of-state residents, or sales to resellers. So some sales income is taxable, and some is not. Your income records must reflect whether a sale is taxable, and if so, the amount of sales tax. This distinction will be essential when you compute and file your state sales taxes.

If you use a cash register, taxable sales will generally be marked as such by the push of a button at the time of each sale, and tax amounts will be shown separately. If you write out a receipt of each sale by hand, be sure to show any sales tax separately, not just as part of a total. If the sale is nontaxable, make that clear by writing "no tax," "nontaxable," or the like.

Note that whether a sale is taxable for *sales tax* purposes is a different issue from whether income is taxable or not for *income tax* purposes. Generally, taxable income—that is, money you take in that is subject to income taxes at the end of the year—includes any money earned by your business, minus certain deductions. As discussed in Chapter 11, all of this income must be reported on your year-end income tax return, whether or not it is subject to state sales tax.

Expenditure Receipts

Just as you keep a record of each individual sale, you need to keep a record each time you spend money for your business. Business expenditures include paychecks to employees, money spent on supplies, office rent, telephone bills, payments on loans, and all other costs associated with your business. For legal and practical reasons, each and every one of these expenses must be recorded.

Most of us keep receipts for things we buy, especially big-ticket items like computers and appliances. When running a business, this habit needs to be consistently practiced—and not just for the pricey items. Each expenditure receipt should include the date, the amount, the method of payment, who was paid and—most important—a description of what type of expense it was, such as rent, supplies, or utilities. The description is important because later, when you enter your expenses into your bookkeeping software, you'll need to assign one or more categories to each expense. These categories—such as rent, advertising, supplies, utilities, meals, travel, and taxes—are important for tax purposes, because different types of expenses have different rules for deductibility. If any important information isn't included on the receipt, write it in. You'll want this later, when entering receipts into your bookkeeping system.

Bear in mind that you'll often have a number of receipts for just one purchase: a credit card slip, a register receipt, and an itemized statement, for example. If you throw all three receipts into your files to be posted later, you run the risk of counting all three separately. Ditto if you have a checkbook register entry plus a register receipt. To avoid counting transactions more than once, either discard multiple copies of receipts immediately after the transaction or staple them all together. It's also a great idea to write the check number on the cash register receipt so you can easily cross-check when entering receipts into your software.

Step 2: Entering Receipts Into Bookkeeping Software

In the old days, businesses kept track of their finances by entering their income and expenses by hand into a hardbound book called a ledger. While some people still do this, we highly recommend you use some kind of financial management software. (See "Using Technology to Manage Money, Inventory, and Projects" for advice on the topic.) Once you enter your income and expenses into the software, you can easily generate sophisticated financial reports that would have taken many hours and considerable skill to create a decade ago. This is a much easier way to keep track of your finances and much less prone to errors.

On some regular basis—every day, once a week, or once a month at a minimum—you should transfer ("post") the amounts from your income and expenditure receipts into your bookkeeping software. (Entering income and expense receipts could also be described as entering transactions.) Later, you'll use the data you've entered to answer specific financial questions about your business, such as whether you're making a profit and, if so, how much.

Generally speaking, the more sales you make, the more often you should enter your receipts. A busy retail operation that does hundreds of sales every day should post daily, while smaller, slower businesses with just a few large transactions per month would probably be fine posting weekly or even monthly. With a high sales volume, it's particularly important to see what's happening every day and not to fall behind with the paperwork. For this reason, most busy, high-volume businesses will have a modern cash register that's programmed to automatically "dump" the day's information into the bookkeeping software at the end of each day.

When entering information into your bookkeeping system, remember the adage "garbage in, garbage out." If the information you enter isn't accurate or the bookkeeping software isn't set up correctly in the first place, you won't be able to generate the meaningful financial reports that are so crucial to any business. Take the time early on to learn (with the help of a bookkeeper, if necessary) how your software works, configure it correctly, and enter data carefully to minimize errors.

Let's take a look at some of the details involved in setting up your bookkeeping software and entering transactions. Remember, once the transactions are entered, accounting software makes preparing monthly and yearly financial reports incredibly easy.

TIP

Learn the concepts behind the numbers. Even though bookkeeping software allows you to generate sophisticated financial reports with a few mouse clicks, you should still take the time to understand how the numbers fit together and what they mean. The more you know about your numbers and the relationships between various figures, the better able you'll be to make positive and profitable business decisions.

Creating Accounts

When setting up your bookkeeping software, one of the first things to do is set up accounts to mirror the business accounts you have in real life: a checking account and a credit card account, for instance. It's critical to post transactions to the appropriate accounts, so that you can reconcile your bookkeeping records against the bank or credit card statements. Reconciling each month is an important way to make sure your records are complete and accurate; I'll describe the reconciling process in a bit more detail below.

 TIP

Create a "catch-all" account for business expenses paid for with personal accounts. Inevitably, business owners occasionally spend money from their personal accounts (either using cash or a debit or credit card) on business expenses. While you should strive to avoid this, it just happens from time to time—for example, your husband bought a toner cartridge for you and paid with his debit card; or you bought paper for your office printer, along with school supplies for your kids, and paid for everything with your personal checking account. One good way to account for these is to create a "general register" account in your bookkeeping software as a catch-all account that will include any transactions (usually expenditures, not income) that for whatever reason weren't made from an official business checking or credit account.

Depending on your circumstances and how your accountant or bookkeeper advises you, there are other accounts you can create to track your business's finances. Common examples include separate accounts for receivables (amounts owed to you) and payables (amounts you owe to others), or accounts to track depreciable assets such as computers or vehicles. Again, a bookkeeper can be quite helpful in helping you figure out which accounts to set up.

Creating Income and Expense Categories

Besides creating accounts, an important part of setting up your book-keeping software is creating categories for income and expenses. As mentioned above, different types of income and expenses are treated differently for tax purposes, so it's crucial that they are tracked separately in your bookkeeping system. As we discuss in more detail in Chapter 11, some expenditures can be deducted right away in full, others may be deducted only over several years (referred to as "depreciating expenses"), while other costs may not be deductible at all.

Income will typically include "taxable sales," "sales tax," and "nontaxable sales" categories and possibly others—say, "travel reimbursement," "loan," or "interest income." Businesses typically have many different categories for expenses such as rent, utilities, computer equipment, employee wages, legal fees, postage, or travel, to name a few.

RESOURCE

The IRS has oceans of rules. For more information on different types of business expenses and their deductibility, read *Deduct It! Lower Your Small Business Taxes*, by Stephen Fishman (Nolo). Reading the rules issued by the IRS isn't a bad idea, either. IRS Publication 334, *Tax Guide for Small Business*, is a good place to start. It's available at www.irs.gov.

Besides categorizing income and expenses to account for different tax treatment, there's another essential reason to categorize expenses: Careful, strategic categorization will allow you to generate financial reports that reveal which aspects of your business contribute the most (or least) to your bottom line, which in turn will allow you to make adjustments to maximize profits. We'll discuss the details of financial reports in the next section, but the point here is that the categorization is essential. Without tracking income and expenses by category, you won't be able to generate meaningful financial reports later on.

EXAMPLE: Adriana is launching a spa that will offer hot tubs, massages, and facials. When setting up the bookkeeping system (with the help of a trusted bookkeeper), Adriana makes sure to include separate categories for income from these three separate services. This way, she will be able to generate reports showing which services bring in the most gross income. In addition, Adriana makes sure to categorize expenses associated with each service so that she will be able to generate reports showing which services are the most profitable. After six months in business, the financial reports show that the massages consistently generate the most gross income. The profitability picture is different, however. When expenses associated with each service are factored in, Adriana sees that hot tubs are actually the most profitable service, because there are much lower costs associated with them than with the massages or facials. Adriana decides to put some effort into lowering the costs associated with massages in order to make them more profitable. If Adriana had not created separate income and expense categories for hot tubs, massages, and facials, the financial records would not have revealed the revenue and profit trends, and Adriana would have missed out on the opportunity to tweak her marketing and pricing in order to boost profits.

When deciding what expense categories to create and track, keep in mind the distinction between fixed costs and variable costs. Variable costs, you may remember from Chapter 4, are tied to your products or services, while fixed costs (overhead) more or less stay the same regardless of your production and sales volume. Without keeping careful track of variable costs, you won't know how profitable your individual products or services are, or whether your pricing is too high, too low, or just right. Fixed costs are also crucial to track, in large part because they can be such a drain when business is slow.

There's something of an art to defining the expense categories that are relevant for your business. You want them to be tightly defined—but not so narrow that you end up with dozens of tiny groups. For example, a repairperson would likely use categories such as lumber, paint/sealants, hardware, and equipment rentals, but wouldn't go so far as to have a separate category for nails versus screws. A hair stylist might use categories like booth rental, cutting tools, and hair products; depending on her circumstances, she might want to further subcategorize the hair products into shampoos, conditioners, and styling products. An experienced bookkeeper familiar with your field can be extremely helpful in setting up your categories and subcategories in a way that will help you generate the most meaningful reports for your business.

As for actually setting up the categories in your bookkeeping software, all programs make this really easy. Generally speaking, you'll create the categories when you set up the software; later, when you enter your transactions, you'll choose from the list of categories you've created. Undoubtedly, over time, you'll refine your bookkeeping system and your categories, and all bookkeeping software allows you to add, edit, and delete your categories whenever you want.

Define income and expense categories to help you make decisions

"For all record keeping, what is really important (besides accuracy) is that the categories are designed to provide the owner with the information they need to run the business profitably. If you care about the sales by each type of item you sell, define your financial statements that way. If you don't care whether postage is separately reported from office expenses, don't set up the account. Bookkeeping is as much about giving the owner the information she needs to make good decisions as it is about tax preparation. The financial statements are the best tool you have for making decisions."
— **Jennifer Cantrell, CPA**

Entering Transactions

When it comes time to enter the information from your receipts (in other words, entering your transactions), you'll find that most bookkeeping software has an interface similar to a checkbook: Each transaction, whether an income or expense, is entered into a "register" where you'll include information including date, check number, payee, description, amount, category(ies), and any notes. With income transactions, remember to enter any sales tax amounts separately from the total income. How to do this will vary depending on the bookkeeping software you use, but it will typically record the transaction as a "split" transaction, showing a pretax subtotal separately from the sales tax amount.

> **TIP**
> **Some states require nontaxable sales to be broken down into certain categories,** such as wholesale sales, services, sales to out-of-state customers, or freight charges. As discussed in Chapter 11, check with your state sales tax agency to find out which, if any, nontaxable subcategories you must use in your record keeping. As mentioned above, creating custom categories and subcategories in your bookkeeping software is incredibly easy.

When you have entered a receipt, mark the receipt as entered. Use whatever system works for you; you could handwrite an "E" on the receipt, use a stamp that says "Posted," or something similar. Then file the receipt away, ideally in a well-organized file system that will allow you easily to find a receipt should any questions arise later.

Finally, keep your bookkeeping records safe and regularly back them up. They will be essential to create financial reports revealing your business's financial health (explained in "Generating Financial Reports," below), and to complete your local, state, and federal tax returns. Losing your financial records can be an expensive disaster—dealing with an IRS audit without them is just one nightmare scenario—so be sure to treat them as the important business documents that they are.

> **TIP**
> **Treat credit card purchases like cash.** Even though the cash method of accounting records expenditures when they are paid, not when incurred, you should record purchases made with a credit card as if they were paid with cash. The IRS considers credit card purchases paid on the date of purchase, not when payment is made on the credit card.

Step 3: Generating Financial Reports

When up-to-date and correctly categorized data are entered into your bookkeeping software, you're all set to do the important (and actually quite fun) part of financial management: generating reports showing you the financial health (or illness) of your business. Really, all the griping you hear from business owners about the pain of bookkeeping has to do with the previous steps of organizing your income and expense information and regularly entering it into the system. Once the info is entered into the software, generating the reports is a piece of cake.

Financial reports pull together various income and expense data to answer specific questions about your business's financial situation. For example, a profit and loss report compares monthly income to monthly expenses to show whether your business is selling enough products or services to cover costs each month. A cash flow projection shows similar information, but includes other sources of income such as capital contributions from owners or loans (that is, not just revenues from sales), and organizes the information slightly differently to show you whether the timing of your income is adequate to pay your bills on time.

In short, financial reports bring together your income and expense data and sculpt it so that you can see the big picture of your business.

We'll discuss three basic financial reports in this section: a profit and loss report, a cash flow projection, and a balance sheet. There are many other ways to slice and dice a business's financial information, but these three represent the basic reports that every businessperson should understand and regularly use.

Understanding your books will help you profit

"The most important thing is understanding your financial statements. Seeing where you're losing money. Seeing where you're spending too much money. Seeing where you're wasting the money. Because business is all about making a profit. Not about making a loss. And I spent many years making a loss, doing the things I love, and now I'm making a living doing the things I love."
— **Nicola Freegard**

Profit and Loss Report

A profit and loss statement (also called a P & L, or an income statement) shows you pretty much what the name implies: how much profit or loss your business is making in a given period of time. You'll typically generate a profit and loss statement each month, as well as quarterly and annual summaries. We'll use a monthly period when describing the process of creating a P & L below.

RELATED TOPIC

Creating a profit and loss statement with projected numbers is part of your business planning process (as covered in Chapter 4). There is a spreadsheet to create your estimated P & L on Nolo's website. See the appendix for a link to this and other worksheets in this book. We explain how to do a P & L after you've opened your doors and have actual numbers to work with.

In the most basic terms, a P & L is made by totaling your monthly revenues and then subtracting your monthly expenses from that total. If you use accounting software, it will generate a P & L at the click of a button based on the income and expense data you've already entered. For each month, you'll be able to see whether your revenues are higher or lower than your expenses and by how much. The monthly results are totaled to obtain your annual profit or loss.

An important detail involved in profit/loss calculations is that fixed costs need to be considered separately from variable costs. Fixed costs (also called overhead) are the costs associated with running your business in general, not with individual products or services themselves. Examples include rent, utilities, and insurance. Variable costs (also sometimes called costs of goods sold, or COGS) are the expenses that are directly tied to the product or service that you're selling. Examples include the costs of materials, packaging, shipping, and labor costs directly tied to producing the product or service (but note that labor costs can be tricky; see the tip below.)

For example, say your business produces and sells organic cotton bedding. Your variable costs would include the costs of the fabric, thread, and trims; fees paid to the sewing facility that makes the bedding; costs for labels and packaging of each product; and costs for boxes and any other packaging required to ship the bedding products to retailers. As the name implies, these costs will vary depending on the amount and type of product you make and sell or service you perform. For example, if you produce more or less of a particular sheet set or if you use heavier-weight fabric, your variable expenses will go up or down accordingly.

TIP

Labor costs: sometimes variable, sometimes fixed. If you ask a group of accountants whether the labor costs associated with making a product are fixed or variable, you're likely to get conflicting answers. Some argue that, as long as the workers are paid regardless of whether they're working on that product, their salaries should be considered fixed, like rent or utilities. Others say that, to have accurate financial records, you need to reflect the cost of the labor that goes into a product. You or your accountant can decide how your business will categorize labor costs for making a product. Labor costs for providing services, on the other hand, are almost always treated as variable costs.

In contrast, fixed costs do not go up or down depending on the products you make or the services you perform. These costs, such as rent, office utility bills, and insurance for company vehicles, will be more or less the same, regardless of the amount or type of bedding products you make. This is precisely why age-old business wisdom says to keep your overhead costs as low as you can. In times of slow sales, you want to be saddled with as few fixed costs as possible.

Now that you know the distinction between variable and fixed costs, you need to understand how they're each subtracted from your revenue on a typical profit and loss statement.

- A profit and loss statement starts with your total sales revenues, then subtracts your variable costs. The result is called your *gross profit*—how much money you've earned from sales of your products or services over and above their cost to you.
- Next you subtract your fixed costs from your gross profit. Any money you're left with is usually called *net profit,* but is sometimes called net income or pretax profit. Other than the various taxes you'll need to pay on this income (and you shouldn't underestimate how much this can be), this is your and any other business owners' money.

To sum up, the formula used in a profit and loss statement is basically as follows:

Sales revenue

– Variable costs (costs of goods sold)

= Gross profit

Gross profit

– Fixed costs

= Net profit

A typical P & L is shown below.

The power in a P & L is in its ability to help you identify which aspects of your business need adjusting in order to boost profits. Being able to see the totals of each of your various expense categories over the course of several months can help you pinpoint areas in which you're spending too much money. And tracking income totals month by month will help you quickly spot trends such as a downturn in revenues, which will prompt you to take action to boost sales.

Sample Profit/Loss Statement

Profit/Loss Statement

	Jan	Feb	Mar	April	May
Sales Revenues	$ 47,550	$ 43,250	$ 52,500	$ 50,250	$ 58,900
COGS					
Inventory	22,050	20,200	24,750	24,050	28,300
Packaging	2,400	1,900	2,550	2,200	2,100
Shipping	1,703	1,688	1,575	1,388	1,995
Total COGS	26,153	23,788	28,875	27,638	32,395
Gross Profit	21,397	19,462	23,625	22,612	26,505
Fixed Expenses					
Office rent	3,500	3,500	3,500	3,500	3,500
Salaries	12,500	12,500	12,500	12,500	12,500
Utilities	550	550	550	550	550
Telephone service	200	200	200	200	200
Office supplies	150	150	150	150	150
Postage	50	50	50	50	50
Website hosting/maintenance	500	500	500	500	500
Insurance	450	450	450	450	450
Professional services (accountant, etc.)	200	200	200	200	200
Miscellaneous	250	250	250	250	250
Total Fixed Expenses	18,350	18,350	18,350	18,350	18,350
Net Profit (Loss)	$ 3,047	$ 1,112	$ 5,275	$ 4,262	$ 8,155

Sample Profit/Loss Statement (continued)

	June	July	Aug	Sept	Oct	Nov	Dec	Year Total
	$ 54,750	$ 52,350	$ 62,450	$ 55,600	$ 49,800	$ 52,100	$ 54,500	$634,000
	26,800	24,500	30,600	27,250	24,000	23,900	25,500	301,900
	1,550	2,890	1,870	1,600	1,580	2,750	2,375	25,765
	1,763	1,403	1,878	1,730	1,810	2,005	2,100	21,038
	30,113	28,793	34,348	30,580	27,390	28,655	29,975	348,703
	24,637	23,557	28,102	25,020	22,410	23,445	24,525	285,297
	3,500	3,500	3,500	3,500	3,500	3,500	3,500	42,000
	12,500	12,500	12,500	12,500	12,500	12,500	12,500	150,000
	550	550	550	550	550	550	550	6,600
	200	200	200	200	200	200	200	2,400
	150	150	150	150	150	150	150	1,800
	50	50	50	50	50	50	50	600
	500	500	500	500	500	500	500	6,000
	450	450	450	450	450	450	450	5,400
	200	200	200	200	200	200	200	2,400
	250	250	250	250	250	250	250	3,000
	18,350	18,350	18,350	18,350	18,350	18,350	18,350	220,200
	$ 6,287	$ 5,207	$ 9,752	$ 6,670	$ 4,060	$ 5,095	$ 6,175	$ 65,097

Cash Flow Projection

A cash flow projection is a crucial tool to use in your ongoing business, even if your profit and loss reports show that your sales revenues exceed expenses. Why? Only a cash flow projection will show you whether your business will have enough cash available at any given time to pay your operating costs. Having thriving sales isn't enough, especially if you sell on credit. If your customers pay you in 90 days, but you must pay your expenses in 30 days or even immediately, you may face a situation where, even though your P & L says you are making a profit, you can't pay your rent, insurance, payroll, taxes, or other key bills. If you see the cash crunch well in advance, you'll usually be able to juggle expenses or take other measures such as taking out a loan or a line of credit to get through the squeeze. But if the cash crisis sneaks up on you without warning, you may not have enough time to react, possibly even forcing you to close up shop.

RELATED TOPIC

Creating a cash flow projection with estimated income and expense figures is part of your business planning process (as we explained in Chapter 4). A cash flow projection spreadsheet is included on the Nolo website. See the appendix for a link to this spreadsheet and other forms in this book. Below we explain how to do it after you've opened your doors and have actual numbers to work with.

A cash flow projection focuses on the actual cash payments made to and by your business. These payments are called cash-ins and cash-outs (or inflows and outflows) to differentiate them from sales and expenses, which may not be paid right away. You'll use actual income and expense data as the basis for estimating cash-ins and cash-outs for upcoming months, helping you predict when you might run short. This will allow you to take action early, such as by tightening up on your credit terms, raising more capital, getting a loan or line of credit, or putting more effort into collecting accounts receivable.

A cash flow projection uses most of the same numbers as a profit and loss report, plus a few additional ones. The main difference is that a cash flow projection includes all sources of income (not just sales income) and only income that's paid in cash (not credit). In other words, while a profit and loss report reflects how much revenue your business is earning through business operations (that is, sales of your products or services), a cash flow projection shows how much cash your business will have on hand from all sources, including paid sales, loans, investments, interest, lottery winnings, whatever. Similarly, a cash flow projection includes all money paid out of the business, whether for supplies, taxes (including any estimated taxes owed; see Chapter 11), loan repayments, or any other expenditures.

The basic formula for cash flow analysis is:

Cash in bank at beginning of month

+ Cash receipts for the month

– Cash disbursements for the month

= Cash in bank at end of month

A cash flow projection starts each month with the amount of money in the bank. (Generally, this is the same amount that's left over from the previous month.) Next, add any cash that came in during the month in all relevant categories, such as sales income, loans, cash contributions, revenues from sales of stock, and interest earned—the total cash-ins for the month. Next, subtract the money spent during the month: the cash-outs. The result is the cash left at the end of the month. Enter that figure into the beginning of the next month's column, and do the same process for the next month. If you use accounting software, a cash flow spreadsheet can be generated automatically once you've entered figures for income and expenses.

So far, so good: You've tracked actual cash-ins and cash-outs. Now comes the powerful part of making projections. Remember, the real power of a cash flow projection is not in tracking actual cash-ins and cash-outs, but in predicting future cash flows. Periodically, say once a month or every couple of months, you should use your actual figures as a basis for making estimates for upcoming months, and complete a cash flow projection for the future, generally up to one year.

If you're fortunate to see that you will have enough cash to cover your expenses each month, great. If not, don't panic. First, congratulate yourself for doing a cash flow analysis and figuring out ahead of time that you won't be able to cover all your expenses. Then come up with a plan. This might include:

- putting off some expenses that can wait
- being more aggressive about collecting accounts receivable
- getting a short-term loan or line of credit, or
- implementing a cost-effective quick promotion to sell more product or services.

An example of a cash flow projection is shown below. This sample shows that cash is expected to be a little tight each and every month (look at the last row, "Cash at End of Month"), so the business owner might consider ways to cut costs or to tighten credit terms.

Of more pressing importance is the projected cash shortfall starting in April in this sample. The good news is that the forecast points out this shortfall to the business months in advance, giving the business owner a chance to figure out what to do while there's still time to take action. She could contribute some personal money to the business, use a line of credit to fill the cash gaps, or could try to cut some nonessential expenses, at least until later in the year when there will be a bit more cash available.

TIP

Credit lines provide cash flow flexibility. A very helpful resource for any small business is a revolving line of credit from the bank. A line of credit works on the same principle as a credit card, but generally offers better cash terms than credit card cash advance terms. Your business can borrow funds up to the credit line limit on an as-needed basis and has to pay interest only on the outstanding balance (not the entire credit line). You can choose to pay funds back and reborrow them as necessary during the time the credit line is open. Credit lines can be open for a specified period, such as five or ten years, or can be open-ended (like a credit card).

How do you track finances and inventory?

"I devote two days a month to accounting. I do my own bookkeeping and billing, making sure my clients have paid me, and entering my invoices and so forth, and then I print out a P&L statement and I look at the P&L every month just like a regular business. I'm learning all the ins and outs of QuickBooks. I'm sort of a basic user but I'm trying to become more of a power user."

— **Emily Esterson**

"One big way that we have managed growth is to be able to track information (Which colors sell best? Which bag is the most popular? What is our profit margin on various products? Why does that item take twice as long to make as this other one?) and be able to pull it up easily so that we can make informed decisions into the future. We use QuickBooks and Excel spreadsheets to organize and recall most of this information. I personally do not use those tools very much (or very well), but I have hired people who can answer these questions for me by using those programs."

— **Rebecca Pearcy**

"I had my challenges in creating systems, but I went to QuickBooks very early and brought in some very good advisors to help me. I had been fortunate that I had worked in film, so I knew how to run a budget—one of the things that had been taught to me was how to use an Excel spreadsheet. QuickBooks offers a wonderful program for manufacturers and it's worth the investment. It really helps manage your figures so you can look at your profit and loss statement at the end of every month and understand how your month is going and where your weaknesses are."

— **Nicola Freegard**

Cash Flow Projection

	Jan	Feb	Mar	April
Cash at Beginning of Month	$ 3,350	$ 1,700	$ 1,600	$ 3,300
Cash Ins				
Sales paid	11,500	8,500	10,050	7,250
Loans & transfers	10,000			
Total Cash Ins	24,850	10,200	11,650	10,550
Cash Outs				
Start-up costs	8,500			
Inventory	4,500	3,250	3,000	2,250
Office rent	1,200	1,200	1,200	1,200
Salaries	3,000	3,000	3,000	3,000
Utilities	250	250	250	250
Telephone service	150	150	150	150
Office supplies	100	100	100	100
Postage	50	50	50	50
Website hosting/maintenance	100	100	100	100
Insurance	1,000			
Loan payment	500	500	500	500
Professional services (accountant, etc.)				500
Sales taxes to state	600			
Estimated taxes to fed	2,600			2,600
Estimated taxes to state	600			600
Miscellaneous				
Total Cash Outs	23,150	8,600	8,350	11,300
Cash at End of Month	$ 1,700	$ 1,600	$ 3,300	$ (750)

Cash Flow Projection (continued)

May	June	July	Aug	Sept	Oct	Nov	Dec
$ (750)	$ 1,200	$ (200)	$ 3,350	$ 4,250	$ 1,900	$ 1,350	$ 900
9,800	9,900	12,500	10,500	9,950	8,800	10,400	14,500
9,050	11,100	12,300	13,850	14,200	10,700	11,750	15,400
2,500	2,750	2,000	4,250	3,750	4,000	5,500	5,500
1,200	1,200	1,200	1,200	1,200	1,200	1,200	1,200
3,000	3,000	3,000	3,000	3,000	3,000	3,000	3,000
250	250	250	250	250	250	250	250
150	150	150	150	150	150	150	150
100	100	100	100	100	100	100	100
50	50	50	50	50	50	50	50
100	100	100	100	100	100	100	100
		1,000					
500	500	500	500	500	500	500	500
		600					
	2,600			2,600			
	600			600			
7,850	11,300	8,950	9,600	12,300	9,350	10,850	10,850
$ 1,200	$ (200)	$ 3,350	$ 4,250	$ 1,900	$ 1,350	$ 900	$ 4,550

Watch cash flow with government contracts

"Once you land a contract, you'll find that payment terms are often set by the government agency—net 30 or net 60 (meaning, payable in 30 or 60 days) is not uncommon. Cash flow is important to every business, but lack of it can kill a new business quickly. So, make sure that you have planned for these payment terms as you look at revenue coming from your government work."
— **Leila Johnson**

Balance Sheet

A balance sheet is a financial report showing the net worth of your business at a particular point in time. Businesses typically generate balance sheets monthly, quarterly, and annually. In a nutshell, a balance sheet shows a complete picture of a business's financial situation by summarizing its assets, liabilities, and owner equity (sometimes called net worth) in the business. The general formula is:

Assets – Liabilities = Equity

The value of a balance sheet is that it provides a view into the business's financial position. It will reveal whether a business is, on one hand, overleveraged with too much debt, or perhaps on the other hand in a good position for expansion. In short, it offers a snapshot of the financial health of a company.

While balance sheets aren't quite as intuitive to read for the uninitiated, the elements that are included and how they relate to each other aren't that complicated. As with the other financial reports described in this section, a balance sheet can easily be generated from your bookkeeping software, assuming all transactions have been entered and categorized correctly. But it's worth going through each element of a balance sheet so that you truly understand what it means and how to decipher a balance sheet, rather than just relying on your software to spit one out for you without grasping the full meaning of the information it summarizes.

As mentioned above, a balance sheet reflects a business's assets, liabilities, and equity. In other words, when you subtract a business's liabilities from its assets, the result is the net equity the business owner(s) have in the business. This report is called a balance sheet because it reflects the balance between assets and liabilities, on one side of the equation, and equity on the other side. When the data in your bookkeeping software are accurate, the assets will equal (or "balance") liabilities plus equity.

Let's look at each of these elements in a bit more detail.

Assets

Assets include anything of monetary value that your business owns. The standard balance sheet format lists assets in decreasing order of liquidity—in other words, how easy it is to convert the asset to cash. The following categories are typically used to reflect this breakdown:

- **Current assets** are those that can be converted to cash within one year. These include cash (of course), checking accounts, money market accounts, accounts receivable, and inventory.
- **Noncurrent assets** (sometimes called capital, long-term, or fixed assets) are defined as things with a useful business life of more than one year. These include land, buildings, vehicles, business equipment, and furniture. With the exception of land, tangible noncurrent assets depreciate, which means they lose value each year; this is reflected as a "depreciation expense" in the balance sheet. Other assets that would be considered noncurrent include intellectual property, such as patents, trade secrets, copyrights, trademarks, customer lists, or even company goodwill. Valuing these intangibles can be difficult, and they are typically heavily discounted on a balance sheet if included at all.

Liabilities

Liabilities are things that your business owes to others. Like assets, liabilities are typically divided into current and noncurrent.

- **Current liabilities** include debts your company owes within the next year. Examples include accounts payable, payroll owed to employees but not yet paid, and accrued but unpaid taxes.
- **Noncurrent liabilities** include debts payable over a term longer than one year. This includes mortgages or other debts due more than one year from the date the balance sheet is prepared.

Equity

Equity is what's left over when you subtract liabilities from assets. This is the net worth of the business, which is essentially the amount that would be paid out to the owner(s) if the business liquidated. Equity includes:

- any **capital contributions** to the business, including money contributed by the owners and any stock sold to the public, and
- any **retained earnings**, which is the total of all annual profits since the beginning of the business (including the current year) that haven't been paid out to the owner(s).

An example of how a balance sheet typically presents this information is shown below.

Balance Sheet

	Current 4/1/2017	Previous Year 4/1/2016	$ Change	% Change
Assets				
Current Assets				
Cash in bank	$ 15,700	$ 14,050	$ 1,650	11.74%
Accounts receivable	2,350	1,800	550	30.56
Inventory	5,500	3,900	1,600	41.03
Other current assets	0	0	0	0.00
Total Current Assets	$ 23,550	$ 19,750	$ 3,800	19.24%
Fixed Assets				
Machinery & equipment	$ 13,500	$ 11,075	$ 2,425	21.90%
Furniture & fixtures	2,500	2,000	500	25.00
Land & buildings	0	0	0	0.00
Other fixed assets	0	0	0	0.00
(Accumulated depreciation on all fixed assets)	(7,350)	(7,155)	(195)	0.00
Total Fixed Assets (net of depreciation)	$ 8,650	$ 5,920	$ 2,730	46.11%
Other Assets				
Intangibles	0	0	0	0.00%
Goodwill	0	0	0	0.00
Other	0	0	0	0.00
Total Other Assets	0	0	0	0.00%
Total Assets	$ 32,200	$ 25,670	$ 6,530	25.44%

Balance Sheet (continued)

	Current 4/1/2017	Previous Year 4/1/2016	$ Change	% Change
Liabilities and Equity				
Current Liabilities				
Accounts payable	$ 4,250	$ 2,985	$ 1,265	42.38%
Payroll unpaid	0	0	0	0.00
Taxes payable	1,700	985	715	72.59
Short-term debt (due within 12 months)	0	0	0	0.00
Credit card debt	0	0	0	0.00
Other current liabilities	0	0	0	0.00
Total Current Liabilities	$ 5,950	$ 3,970	$ 1,980	49.87%
Long-Term Debt				
Bank loans payable	$ 0	0	$ 0	0.00%
Other long-term debt	0	0	0	0.00
Total Long-Term Debt	$ 0	0	$ 0	0.00%
Total Liabilities	$ 5,950	$ 3,970	$ 1,980	49.87%
Owners' Equity				
Invested capital	$ 15,000	15,000	$ 0	0.00%
Retained earnings	11,250	6,700	4,550	67.91
Total Owners' Equity	$ 26,250	$ 21,700	$ 4,550	20.97%
Total Liabilities & Equity	$ 32,200	$ 25,670	$ 6,530	25.44%

Where to Learn More About Small Business Financial Management

If you struggle with the money management side of running a business, you are far from alone. When asked what areas they feel weakest in, small business owners almost always put financial management at or near top of the list. Check out the following resources to get schooled in the basics.

- *Small Time Operator,* by Bernard Kamoroff (Taylor Trade Publishing). Devoted to the ins and outs of small business accounting and money-related issues, this book is a great place to start if you want a crash course on the basics.

- *The Accounting Game: Basic Accounting Fresh from the Lemonade Stand,* by Darrell Mullis and Judith Orloff (Sourcebooks, Inc.). This is a perennially popular title for its ability to break down the complexities of accounting into simple terms.

- *Entrepreneur* **magazine's website (www.entrepreneur.com).** Offers an archive of practical articles in its Finance section, covering profit/ loss statements, cash flow projections, and much more.

- *Inc.* **magazine's website (www.inc.com).** Includes lots of articles useful for start-ups, including financial basics.

- **Classes offered at local technical colleges or nonprofits such as Women's Business Centers or microlenders.** In most communities you should be able to find classes in financial management as well as using bookkeeping and accounting software. Many of the same resources that offer help with preparing a business plan, such as Small Business Development Centers and SCORE, can help with financial management tasks. See "Business Planning Resources" in Chapter 4 for details.

Using Technology to Manage Money, Inventory, and Projects

As we've mentioned throughout this chapter, bookkeeping and accounting software makes the job of managing your business's finances easier and enables you to do much more sophisticated reports than you'd normally be able to do manually. In addition, other software and hardware products help business owners manage the money side of a business. These include spreadsheets, point of sales (POS) systems, project management software, and customer relationship management (CRM) software. This section reviews bookkeeping software and other applications and databases that will help you manage your business. Bear in mind that many business management applications are essentially databases that are precustomized for specific purposes, such as project management. They may be called "off-the-shelf" solutions to differentiate them from more general database applications, such as *FileMaker Pro* or Microsoft *Access*, that need to be customized (likely with the help of a database specialist) to fit your needs—for example, if you have complex tracking needs. We also discuss customized databases below.

Bookkeeping Software

As discussed throughout this chapter, bookkeeping software is so powerful because it automates the process of generating financial reports, such as cash flow projections and balance sheets. If you take care to enter and categorize your income and expense records regularly, you can easily crunch that data and answer important questions about your business such as how much profit (or loss) you're making, how much you're spending on certain expenses, or how much money your customers owe you.

QuickBooks is by far the most popular bookkeeping software; it offers different products for different sizes and types of businesses, including an online version that stores all your information on their servers. *Sage 50* (formerly *Peachtree*) is another reputable product but not used as widely. Another option for businesses at the small end of the spectrum is *Quicken*, which focuses more on personal finances but offers a *Home & Business* version with plenty of features for small operators.

Cloud Apps Can Streamline Your Systems

While many of the technology products we discuss in this section are huge productivity assets for small businesses, they also can create headaches—for example, you'll need to keep your software up to date and you may face the nightmare of "technology difficulties" when things go wrong.

Enter cloud applications which you use online for monthly fees, instead of installing software on your own computer. With cloud apps, you'll typically use a browser to log into your account and access your data. Most cloud apps allow you to export data which you can then store on your own computers or hard drives. There are cloud apps—sometimes called "hosted solutions"—for bookkeeping, project management, and many more business needs.

One of the most compelling benefits of using cloud apps is that you won't need to deal with installation or updates on your company computers or network. This can be a serious and stressful time drain for small companies, which is one reason cloud apps are so popular.

Another big plus is that you can access your data anywhere you have Internet access. Related to this, remote teams can easily collaborate with each other, even if they're on opposite sides of the globe. If you've ever dealt with the headaches of emailing files among multiple team members, you'll appreciate the value of real-time editing documents in the cloud. Many apps are geared for mobile devices, allowing your team to keep projects moving forward even if they're on the go.

Choose a product that offers the features you need, keeping in mind what information you need to track and what reports you need to generate. For instance, if you need to manage multiple categories of inventory, and regularly must deal with returns from retailers, make sure the software and the version you choose makes it easy to enter and categorize inventory, and to generate reports such as a yearly summary of returns by category or by a particular retailer. *QuickBooks* offers dozens of add-on products, including many industry-specific applications to help you manage certain kinds of businesses, such as restaurants, retail, or manufacturing.

Finally, make sure your bookkeeper and accountant can work with whatever software you choose. Virtually all financial management professionals work with the various *QuickBooks* products.

Integrating Applications and Databases With Bookkeeping Software

If a feature isn't built in to your bookkeeping software, and there's not an add-on product that achieves what you need, it's possible that your business will need an external application or database to manage that information. For example, if you need to carefully track the hours and expenses of your consulting projects, you may want to use project management software (discussed below) in addition to your bookkeeping software. We discuss different types of management applications below.

With many types of business applications and databases, it makes sense to integrate them with your bookkeeping software, which allows them to share information, rather than having to enter information into both systems. For example, if your project management software is integrated with your bookkeeping software, when you create a client invoice within the project management software and mark it "paid," it will automatically enter a payment into your bookkeeping system. This saves time and avoids the potential for errors and inconsistencies when entering the same data into two different systems.

There are many more details than we can cover here, but be aware that integrating applications with your bookkeeping software is a common issue for entrepreneurs. It's typically a matter of balancing the improved and streamlined operations that integration offers, versus the cost. Integrating applications and databases with bookkeeping software typically requires the help of an experienced consultant and may be relatively expensive, often in the thousands of dollars. For larger or growing businesses, the benefits of streamlining your operations may be well worth this expense.

If you'll be using multiple applications that you want to integrate with each other, you'll need to make sure they're all technically compatible. The vast majority of external applications and databases have *QuickBooks* compatibility.

Spreadsheet Software

A spreadsheet is a document that allows you to store information in rows and columns, making it easy to sort the information in different ways. For example, a spreadsheet containing information about your clients could have column headers of "First Name," "Last Name," "Business Name," "Business Address," "Business Phone Number," and so on, with each row containing that information about one of your clients. If you had 50 clients, you'd have 50 rows of data, and you'd be able to sort the list by first name, last name, business name, or any other of the columns.

Beyond sorting, the real power of spreadsheets is in their ability to do mathematical formulas. (See the spreadsheets, such as the break-even analysis worksheet discussed in Chapter 4, and included on the Nolo website. See the appendix for a link to the spreadsheets and forms in this book.) Spreadsheets are particularly useful for doing budgets, project estimates, and projections, in which you'd use estimates instead of actual financial data. (To track actual data you'll probably use bookkeeping software as described above.)

For example, you could use a spreadsheet to cost out a landscaping project, entering individual expenses in separate lines: Dirt; Gravel; Weed Barrier; Plants; and so on. You could define one cell to display the sum total of all the individual expenses, so when you tweak individual line items the total will be automatically updated. Using a spreadsheet in this way makes the budgeting process much easier and faster than if you had to manually add together the expenses each time you made a change.

In essence, a spreadsheet is like a minidatabase, which is software specifically for managing lots of pieces of information. (We describe databases separately below.) Like databases, spreadsheets allow you to do mathematical formulas and functions, as well as sorting and filtering of text data. But to do sophisticated or complex formulas, sorting, or filtering, you'll probably want to go with a true database which will typically have more robust reporting functions already built in and require much less customization. For example, you could easily customize a client and project database to create a report showing clients that you acquired in a specific year, with a list of projects you completed for each of those clients, sorted by the total amount of project fees. You could track similar information with a spreadsheet and create a similar report, but it would take considerably more work to do so. In addition, if you have lots and lots of data, using a database is preferable to scrolling through hundreds of lines of a spreadsheet.

If you don't use databases for whatever reason—perhaps your needs are simple, or you can't afford to buy and customize a database at the moment—spreadsheets are a great alternative. They're cheap, easy to use, and quite powerful for a wide variety of applications. Besides budgeting and job costing, they can be great for tracking project hours or maintaining client or vendor lists.

The most common spreadsheet software is Microsoft *Excel*, which you may already own as part of a Microsoft *Office* package. Another very cool option these days is to use Google spreadsheets, which are Web-based and allow multiple users. For example, a small sales team could use a Google spreadsheet to manage their list of prospects. Whenever a sales person contacted a prospect, she could enter the encounter information into the Google spreadsheet which would automatically be visible to all other members of the team, who could also edit the spreadsheet.

Point of Sales (POS) Systems

Generally speaking, a point of sales (POS) system is a system for tracking and managing retail sales and inventory. While a handwritten receipt book could in theory be called a POS system, what is usually meant by this term is a computerized cash register system that handles each sales transaction as it is made; calculates the sales total and any sales tax; tracks inventory by SKU (stock-keeping unit) and automatically updates inventory databases; and generates detailed sales and inventory reports.

POS systems vary widely in what hardware and software they use; hardware often includes a computer and terminal or an electronic cash register, a bar code scanner, and a credit card swiping machine. The software varies in the complexity of the information it can track and report. You'll typically integrate the POS software with your book-keeping software so that sales are automatically recorded into your books.

While *QuickBooks* and other bookkeeping software generally offer some inventory management functions, POS systems generally allow for more advanced management and reporting. More complex POS systems can manage inventory across multiple stores. Many POS systems are tailored for specific industries such as hair salons, medical offices, grocery stores, or restaurants.

To find the right POS system for your operation, start with some online research. There is no shortage of discussions online among business owners sharing the good and bad of their experiences with various POS systems. Offline, ask other business owners for their experiences.

TIP

Don't be shy about asking other businesses what technologies they use. While you might find it difficult or awkward to approach other businesses who may be your competitors, you'd be surprised how easy it is to stop into a store similar to yours and strike up a conversation with the clerk or business owner (whoever is there) about your similar businesses. A direct question, "What kind of POS system do you guys use?" is likely to get a direct response, and possibly a conversation about their experiences. This information can be incredibly valuable. Of course this approach may be ill-advised if competition is fierce between you and another business. Use your judgment.

Project Management Software

Service firms, consultants, and freelancers can often benefit from using project management software. Applications such as *Basecamp*, Microsoft *Project*, and *Studiometry* help with a variety of details involved in managing projects, including coordinating project team members, tracking billable hours, managing different billable rates, tracking project expenses, and invoicing clients. Freelancers often find the time tracking and invoicing features particularly useful in preparing professional-looking invoices automatically, based on hours and billable rates entered into the system.

Each project management application may have a particular focus or strength in certain features and be less strong in others. Choose an application that handles the aspects of projects that will be important to you. As mentioned above, find out from other business owners (either directly or by reading comments online) what they like and don't like about the software. Features may include:

- scheduling, including shared calendars
- budgeting and estimating projects and components
- time tracking
- billing and invoicing
- establishing different rates for different types of work
- file sharing and document distribution, and
- messaging and chat.

Project management software may be integrated with your bookkeeping software if the two applications are compatible. If you plan to integrate these applications, make sure to confirm compatibility before purchasing.

Most project management software is pretty affordable. How you pay will depend on whether you purchase and install software, or use an online version. Overall, yearly costs start at around $100 for small businesses with just one user. Larger businesses and multiple users might end up paying a few thousand dollars a year.

Customer Relationship Management (CRM) Software

Customer relationship management, or CRM, software helps a business manage potential and existing customers with the general goals of finding and retaining customers and reducing marketing costs. It started out as a tool to help salespeople—often a sales department—manage prospects, accounts, and territories, including tracking what types of outreach and communications had been made to individual contacts. Today, CRM has grown into a more comprehensive strategy for managing customer service and marketing efforts.

CRM software is essentially a database that contains key information about current and prospective customers. From a sales point of view, the CRM application should identify the best prospects and provide key information about their needs in order to help the sales team turn them into paying customers. The CRM database can also support customer service operations by including all information that may help a representative effectively assist a customer, such as what products or services were purchased, details of previous service calls, warranty expiration dates, and log-in information for the customer's online accounts, for example. Data in a CRM system can also be helpful to marketing departments in identifying trends and evaluating the popularity of the company's products and services. This, in turn, can help the marketing team develop marketing campaigns and messages.

As with other types of business management software, CRM software can be integrated with your bookkeeping application, depending on compatibility. Make sure your choices are compatible before purchasing.

A popular CRM application is *Salesforce*, which can be integrated with *QuickBooks*. Other reputable products include *SAP CRM* and *SugarCRM*. Most of these applications have different versions, some installed and some online, with a wide variation in cost. Very generally speaking, a basic version for a small or one-person company might cost a few hundred dollars per year; a large company might spend tens of thousands of dollars a year for robust data functions and multiple users.

Customized Databases

Boil them down, and much of the technology we've been talking about above are essentially databases. A database is simply software that helps you manage information—about clients, vendors, products, parts, employees, and more. Bookkeeping software is really nothing more than a database that's precustomized to handle financial information; CRM software is essentially a database that's tailored for customer data.

When your business has complex tracking or reporting needs that can't be handled by an off-the-shelf solution, you may need to create a customized database from the ground up. With database software like *Filemaker Pro* or Microsoft *Access*, you can customize a management solution to handle your data and generate reports to suit your unique business needs.

Of course, customization from scratch comes with costs. While purchasing database software isn't terribly expensive in itself, hiring a consultant to customize it for you can easily run into the tens of thousands of dollars. You'll also need to maintain the database, including making changes as needed and dealing with bugs and problems, so you'll need a maintenance budget of probably at least a couple of thousand dollars a year, maybe considerably more. Make sure there's not an off-the-shelf product that could meet your needs—likely at a significantly lower cost—before committing to the expense of a customized database.

How do you use technology to manage your business?

"One of the greatest things that I did was to sign up for Basecamp, *a project management service. It's like $24/month for the lowest level, which is all that I really need, and it allows me and clients to log into our project file and swap files back and forth.* Basecamp *is a very convenient system and I like it a whole lot. So now I've just set down the rule that when you work with me we use this particular system and I give everyone a password, and we manage the projects that way. It's worked out excellently. It's one of the best things I ever did. You can look at everything without downloading it, so it doesn't clutter up your machine, which is really nice."*

— Emily Esterson

"We use software for just about everything we do at Betty's—it's how we run our accounting, it's how we do our point of sales, it's how we do our online instant gift certificates which has a huge big database. The technology for the online gift certificates accounts for probably a fifth of our revenue. It's huge. A big exception is that we don't use software for scheduling. We made this conscious decision, one of those business owner decisions that you just have to tweak and figure out what's right for you. We spent $30,000 three years ago on a software program, and then returned it because we realized we wanted the intimacy and flexibility that our paper and pencil system allowed us—even though it is completely laborious. But it really, truly functions and works. We have a complex seniority system with eight rooms and 35 therapists, and none of the software systems were detail-oriented enough for our liking. So that's been really interesting, figuring out when technology works for you, and when it doesn't."

— Elissa Breitbard

TIP

Ask your bookkeeper and other business owners what software they recommend. Talk to people within your network who might know of industry-specific applications with features customized for your type of business. A bookkeeper can also help you set up the software and show you how to use it. You can usually test-drive these applications at their websites or with a trial version of the software. If there's not an industry-specific application for your type of business, *QuickBooks* offers several different versions to meet the needs of all sizes and types of businesses.

Federal, State, and Local Tax Basics

Grumble all you want, but dealing with and paying taxes are unavoidable realities when working for yourself. Whether you're a freelancer or an owner of a larger business, taxes will affect you in many ways that aren't an issue for women who work 9-to-5 jobs:

- Your own personal income taxes will be higher than taxes for those who aren't self-employed, because you'll be fully responsible for paying self-employment taxes (when you're an employee, your employer covers half of this tax).
- Your business will have to pay other types of taxes such as state sales taxes and a variety of local taxes and fees such as county property taxes or city tax registration fees.
- Besides the actual tax money you'll be shelling out, your business will have to handle all kinds of filing and reporting requirements.

It's little wonder that businesspeople tend to consider taxes Enemy Number One.

The good news is that if you have a well-organized bookkeeping system as discussed in Chapter 10, you'll be in an excellent position to meet all your tax requirements with a minimum of hassle. A solid bookkeeping system will also facilitate careful tracking of your expenses, which translates into deductions and a lower tax bill. If you follow the advice repeatedly offered in this book and hire an accountant to help prepare your federal and state income tax returns, you'll simply provide her with financial reports generated from your bookkeeping software showing your categorized income and expenses. This will make it easy for your accountant to prepare your returns for you. (An accountant or bookkeeper can also prepare other tax returns such as for sales or property taxes—but many of these are easy enough for you to handle on your own, again assuming your books are in order.)

CAUTION

You may owe taxes even before you turn a profit. Lots of new businesspeople believe that if there is no profit, there is no tax. Sadly, this is not the case. As discussed in this chapter, state and/or local taxes on gross receipts and on sales of retail goods (sales taxes) are but two examples of taxes that may need to be paid regardless of whether your business is turning a profit. Similarly, county property taxes or local registration fees (arguably, taxes under a different name) are generally assessed without regard to whether your business is profitable or not.

This chapter provides a broad overview of the taxes faced by small businesses and their owners, including income taxes (and making estimated tax payments), sales taxes, property taxes, and local taxes, as well as explains how to minimize taxes through deductions.

SEE AN EXPERT

Having an accountant handle your federal and state taxes is almost always well worth the expense. Income tax rules and filing procedures can get complicated quickly, even for a relatively simple business. While it's wise to learn the basics as outlined in this chapter, it's almost always a good idea to turn over the task of preparing federal and state income tax returns to a professional accountant. If you have well-organized records, annual tax prep for a small-to-medium-sized business will probably cost less than $1,000. For really small operations it might be even less than $500. (Plus, accountant fees are tax-deductible business expenses.) Considering the importance of competent tax preparation, you should accept early on that this is an unavoidable cost of running any business. Chapter 13 provides advice on hiring an accountant.

Taxes are taxing

"We pay taxes we didn't know existed. Like, tangible items taxes—what? I pay taxes when I buy a camera, and then I pay taxes because I own a camera! Every year! Where did this math come from? You have to have a ful stash to be able to afford your IRS and state and city surprises. Jeff (my husband and business partner) and I were doing the math, and 48% of every dollar that comes in goes out in taxes for us. So we work half the year for the government and the other half for us."

— **Sabrina Habib Williams**

Tax Basics

Small business owners quickly learn that taxes lurk everywhere. Depending on the type of business and its location, you might have to pay taxes based on your business's gross income, net profit, or gross retail sales; how many employees you have and how much you pay them; how much property your business owns or leases; its seating capacity; or how many vehicles your business owns—and the list goes on and on. To complicate matters further, the many different taxes are administered by different government agencies, each with its own rules, forms, and filing procedures.

In getting your brain wrapped around the wild world of taxes, we find it helpful to break it down according to who is doing the taxing: generally, the federal government, state governments, and local governments (cities and counties, typically). Let's consider each.

- **Federal taxes.** The United States Internal Revenue Service (IRS) collects the following from small businesses and their owners: taxes on individual or corporate income, self-employment taxes (which go to the Social Security and Medicare systems), and payroll taxes.
- **State taxes.** States typically collect the following from businesses and their owners: taxes on individual or corporate income, taxes on sales of retail goods or sometimes services (usually called "sales taxes" but sometimes "gross receipts taxes"), and payroll taxes. States also often collect special taxes (called "excise taxes") on certain types of business activities such as distributing alcohol, cigarettes, or gasoline. In addition, many states impose taxes on corporations, LLCs, and limited partnerships.
- **County and city taxes.** Cities, counties, or sometimes both may impose taxes on businesses based on several factors. Most cities assign businesses to categories (for example, retail businesses, wholesalers, and services) and then tax each category based on certain criteria, such as gross receipts, gross payroll, or number of employees. In addition, counties often assess and collect property taxes on real and personal property owned by businesses within

the county. Cities and counties also may impose a sales tax. This tax may be collected by the state along with the state sales tax.

In addition to the taxes listed above, your business may have to pay additional fees for creating a corporation or an LLC, registering your business with your city, or obtaining a business license. Most states, for example, charge fees for filing articles of incorporation (the form that's used to create a corporation) or articles of organization (the form to create an LLC). Many cities and counties require all businesses in the area to register with the local tax collector and pay a registration fee. And, if your business requires a special license, such as a permit to handle food or a cosmetology license, you'll usually have to pay for it. While these fees arguably could be called taxes, this chapter does not deal with them as such. The various registration, permit, and license requirements—including their associated fees—are covered in Chapter 7.

Tax laws can be complicated

"I don't do brain surgery for a reason: I'm not qualified. There is a misguided belief, promoted by software companies such as QuickBooks, that with the correct software, anyone can be an accountant. The tax law changes so fast that even as professionals we struggle to keep up. Sometimes, new tax legislation can impact tax returns that have already been filed."

— **Jennifer Cantrell, CPA**

Minimizing Taxes Through Deductions

Every business aims to maximize profits while minimizing taxes. But how do you accomplish this if taxes are tied to profits? The main strategy is to claim every legitimate business deduction possible. "Claiming a deduction" essentially means to subtract ("deduct") an expense from your taxable income—which means you'll have less income that will be taxed. Of course, you can't deduct just any expense you want. To stay out of trouble with the IRS and your state tax agency, you need to understand which deductions are allowed and which are not. (Note that deductions are often irrelevant for local and sales taxes, which tend to be based on gross income—also called "gross receipts"—without taking any deductions into account.) You'll also need to have accurate paperwork to back up your deductions (a major reason why you need an organized bookkeeping system).

The Internal Revenue Code (IRC) states that any "ordinary and necessary" business expenses can be subtracted from your business income for federal tax purposes. (IRC Section 162.) The costs of raw materials that go into your product, office rent, equipment, office supplies, your business computer system, office utility bills, business insurance, interest on business loans, salaries, and payroll taxes are just a few examples of costs that easily count as deductible expenses. As long as an expenditure is in fact made for business—not personal—purposes, the general rule is that you can deduct it from your business's gross income. Of course there are exceptions (for example, clothing isn't deductible unless it's a uniform—and no, a business suit doesn't count). If in doubt, ask your accountant or bookkeeper.

When you file your state income tax return, you'll generally fill out a form that uses the information from your federal return, with a few adjustments to reflect your state's rules on deducting business expenses.

RELATED TOPIC
Info on home business tax deductions. See Chapter 6 for details on the tax deductibility of a home office and related business expenses.

Start-Up Expenses

Start-up expenses—those incurred before you actually launched your business—are subject to special tax rules. The general rule is that businesses may write off up to $5,000 of their start-up costs (such as fees paid to accountants, market research costs, and licenses and fees) in the first year of business. (Note that inventory costs differ from start-up expenses, and may be deducted as the inventory is sold.) If you spend more than $5,000 in start-up costs, you'll have to deduct that excess amount in equal amounts—a process called amortization (discussed in the following section)—over the next 15 years.

For more details on tax treatment of start-up expenses, see IRS Publication 535, *Business Expenses*.

Current vs. Capital Expenses

In the eyes of the IRS, not all expenses are alike. As discussed in Chapter 10 on bookkeeping and accounting, the IRS has different rules for different types of expenses, which is why it's important to track your business expenses by category. For example, you may generally deduct only half of your meals and entertainment expenses, while office supplies are 100% deductible.

Perhaps the most fundamental distinction of concern to the IRS is between current and capital expenses. Current expenses can best be described as your everyday costs of doing business, such as rent, supplies, utility bills, and the like. These expenses are fully deductible in the year they occur. Capital expenses, on the other hand, are not fully deductible in the year you incur them. You incur a capital expense when you purchase an item with a useful life of at least one year—called a "business asset." Business assets include items such as vehicles, furniture, heavy equipment (for example, line production machinery or a printing press), and real estate.

Rather than fully deducting a capital expense in the year it was made, you must spread out the deduction over a number of years. (A major exception to this, the 179 deduction, is discussed below.) This process is variously called "depreciation," "amortization," or "capitalization." Different types of assets have different depreciation rules, and the number of years over which the cost of an item must be depreciated varies. Depreciation rules are explained in IRS Publication 946, *How to Depreciate Property* (available at www.irs.gov), as well as in other IRS publications that cover specific types of assets.

Side Businesses and Hobby Businesses

If you run a tiny side business doing something you love—say, photography, playing music, or making furniture—can you deduct expenses just like a "regular" business? Generally yes, as long as your business meets the IRS criteria of being a real business rather than just a hobby. In a nutshell, the IRS rule is that if your motivation in conducting the activity is to make a profit, it counts as a "real" business allowing you to deduct business losses—expenses that exceed income produced by the activity—against other income, say from a full-time job or another business. In other words, if your side photography business earned $1,000 but had $5,000 in expenses, you'd be able to claim the full $4,000 loss against your taxable income including wages from your day job. If, on the other hand, you fail to demonstrate a profit motive, the activity would be considered a hobby and subject to more restrictive tax rules that don't allow you to deduct expenses from the activity beyond any income it makes.

In the case of an audit, the IRS uses a number of different criteria to decide whether your business truly has a profit motive. Broadly speaking, it looks to see whether you run the activity in a businesslike manner. If you keep your books up to date, regularly prepare financial reports, have a separate bank account, satisfy license and permit requirements, consult with accountants and lawyers, and actively market the business, these practices will help to persuade an IRS auditor that your activity really is a business. In addition, there's a rule called the "3-of-5" test. If your business makes a profit (even a tiny one) in three out of five consecutive years, it is legally presumed to have a profit motive. If you don't make a profit in three out of five years, you still may be able to prove that your business is motivated by profit using the criteria described above.

The Section 179 Deduction

The IRS allows every business to treat a certain amount of capital expenditures as current expenses and fully deduct them in the year they were made. This major exception is known as a "179 deduction," because it's established in Internal Revenue Code Section 179. Tax law changes since 2003 have dramatically increased the limit from $25,000 in 2003 to $250,000 in 2009—and federal stimulus legislation doubled the limit to $500,000 for tax years 2010 through 2013. This allowed businesses to write off up to $500,000 in expenditures that normally would have qualified as capital expenditures. The limit went back down to $25,000 in 2014—but in mid-December 2014, Congress extended the $500,000 limit, effective for calendar year 2014. Once again, the limit went back down to $25,000 as of January 1, 2015, but in mid-December 2015 Congress permanently set the Section 179 annual limit at $500,000, retroactive to January 1, 2015. The result is that businesses may now write off up to $500,000 of expenditures and not have to worry about figuring depreciation.

Whether and to what extent you should take advantage of a 179 deduction depends on your circumstances. Generally, you should take a 179 deduction only when your taxable income is high enough that you'll get a decent tax benefit right away. Businesses with low incomes might want to depreciate assets instead (take their deductions slowly) so that they'll have more deductions available in future years when their income might be higher. That said, bear in mind that Section 179 limits can change yearly without notice, so when the 179 deduction is particularly generous you may want to take advantage of it before it goes away.

 RESOURCE

Learn more about business taxes and deductible business expenses. This chapter only begins to scratch the surface of a huge and complex body of information. Start by checking the IRS website at www.irs. gov/Businesses/SmallBusinesses-&-Self-Employed. You'll find an organized list of forms and publications for small businesses, including Publications 334, *Tax Guide for Small Business*; 535, *Business Expenses*; 946, *How to Depreciate Property*; and 463, *Travel, Entertainment, Gift, and Car Expenses*. The IRS website also has all the necessary tax forms and instructions available for download, plus lots of useful links, such as to state tax agencies, online tools, and webinars. If you'd prefer to have IRS forms mailed to you, call the IRS at 800-829-3676.

For plain-English guides to business tax law, check out these Nolo publications (all available at www.nolo.com):

- *Tax Savvy for Small Business*, by Frederick W. Daily and Jeffrey A. Quinn. An excellent guide through the tax maze.
- *Deduct It! Lower Your Small Business Taxes* and *Home Business Tax Deductions*, both by Stephen Fishman. A wealth of details about deductibility rules for specific types of business expenses, including how to write off your start-up costs.

Child Care Expenses: Deductible?

If you have young children and own a business, child care may certainly seem like an ordinary and necessary expense for you to be able to run your business, right? Unfortunately, the IRS doesn't see it that way. Costs of day care for your little ones are not considered "ordinary and necessary" expenses of running a business and are thus not deductible business expenses.

The good news is that there are other ways to get favorable tax treatment for any amounts you spend on child care. One is to claim the federal child care tax credit on your personal return. Another is to set up a child care center at your business that qualifies for a tax deduction. Let's look closer at both of these.

Child Care Tax Credit

Expenses for child care may be deductible on your personal income taxes. If you qualify, you may claim a federal tax credit of 20% to 35% of your annual child care costs. You can claim up to $3,000 of expenses for one dependent, and $6,000 for two or more dependents. Your credit is then calculated by multiplying your claimed expenses (up to the limits mentioned above) by the percentage that applies to you; the percentage is determined by your income level. (You'll find the rate schedule in IRS Publication 503, *Child and Dependent Care Expenses*.)

For example, if you and your husband paid a nanny $10,000 per year to care for your three children after school, you'd be allowed to claim $6,000 of those expenses (the maximum you could claim for two or more children). If you jointly earned $75,000 that year, you could write off 20% of that amount, based on the IRS's rate schedule. This translates into a credit of $1,200 ($6,000 x 20%).

To qualify:

- Your child(ren) must be under 13 years old and live with you. There are more detailed rules for divorced parents who share custody; see IRS Publication 503, *Child and Dependent Care Expenses.*
- You (and your spouse, if you are married) must work, look for work, or be a full-time student. Single parents qualify if they are working or attending school full time, even if the child's other parent is not.
- You (and your spouse, if you are married) must have earned income for the year.
- Your child care provider must be someone whom you can't claim as a dependent, such as an older sibling. This may include a licensed day care provider, preschool, grandparent (if the grandparent is not your dependent), or an on-the-books nanny— but can't include anyone you pay under the table.

For more details, see IRS Publication 503, *Child and Dependent Care Expenses.*

Employer-Provided Child Care

While your own child care costs aren't considered an ordinary and necessary business expense, the costs of creating and operating a child care facility for children of your employees (and your own too) does qualify for a business tax deduction. Employers are entitled to a 25% federal tax credit for the cost of qualified child care expenses, which include the costs of constructing and operating a child care center for your employees, and any amounts paid under a contract with an outside facility to provide child care services. There's also a 10% credit for your expenses in finding child care facilities and referring your employees to them. This credit maxes out at $150,000 per year.

There are a number of requirements for your facility to qualify for the credit: The primary use of the facility must be for child care; it must meet the requirements of all applicable laws and regulations of the state or local government in which it is located, including the licensing of the facility as a child care facility; the facility must be open to employees of the business; use of the facility may not discriminate in favor of highly compensated employees, and if child care is the principal business, at least 30% of the enrollees must be dependents of employees of your business.

Of course, most small businesses don't have the resources to create and operate child care centers—but if you do, this can be a powerful draw for employees. Businesses that provide on-site child care are also likely to have high morale and a loyal workforce. Plus, you'll have on-site care for your own children. If you're considering creating a child care facility for your employees, talk with an accountant about more detailed tax implications.

Avoiding audit trouble with money-losing businesses

"We will not take deductions for expenses in years where there is no income reported; it really raises a red flag. If you want to prove you are in business to make a profit—do! Don't try to take your kid's allowance or the gas you put in the jet ski. Use legitimate deductions, advertise, get a license, and track your efforts on a time basis as well, and document, document, document, document. Put everything you have into it and you will never have to face this. Realistically, in 24 years of practice, I have only had one audit on this issue and the return was accepted with no change."

— **Jennifer Cantrell, CPA**

Federal Income and Self-Employment Taxes

Let's start at the top with a look at federal taxes. The subsections below discuss the basic taxes faced by sole proprietors, partnerships, and LLCs, as well as the filing requirements that apply to each. Just review the subsection discussing your type of business structure to learn about the federal tax requirements that will apply to your business.

TIP

Any one-year period other than the calendar year (ending on December 31) that a business uses for tax purposes is called a "fiscal year," a "tax year," or an "accounting period." The IRS allows sole proprietorships, partnerships, LLCs, and S corporations to use a fiscal year only if there is a valid business reason for it, such as significant seasonal fluctuations in business. Fiscal years must begin on the first day of a month and end on the last day of the previous month one year later. An unincorporated business that wants to use a fiscal year must submit Form 8716, *Election To Have a Tax Year Other Than a Required Tax Year*, to the IRS and have it approved.

Sole Proprietors

If you are familiar with the process of filing IRS Form 1040, based on income you earned at a job, you'll already be familiar with much of the process of filing federal taxes as a sole proprietor. That's because income from your business will be treated as personal income and reported on Form 1040, the same form used to report wages or returns on investments. What's different is that as a sole proprietor, you'll also file two additional supplementary forms: Schedule C to report your business profit, and Schedule SE to calculate and report self-employment taxes. The business itself does not file federal tax returns or pay federal income taxes, just the sole proprietor.

Remember, a sole proprietorship is one and the same as its owner (the sole proprietor) for most legal and tax purposes. As a result, all business profits are considered taxable income to the sole proprietor, even if they remain in the business bank account and aren't paid out to the sole proprietor.

Income Tax

Sole proprietors report business profits or losses on Schedule C, *Profit or Loss From Business*, which you'll submit once a year with your 1040 return, usually by April 15. A sole proprietor who owns more than one business must file a separate Schedule C for each business.

Schedule C, Lite: Schedule C-EZ

Super-small sole proprietorships may be able to use a simplified schedule to report their income, Schedule C-EZ, *Net Profit From Business*. (This schedule may only be used by sole proprietors.) To use this simplified form, you must have:

- less than $5,000 in business expenses
- no inventory during the year
- no employees during the year
- used the cash method of accounting (see Chapter 10 for an explanation of the difference between the cash and accrual methods of accounting)
- owned and operated only one sole proprietorship during the year
- not deducted expenses for business use of your home, and
- not reported a net business loss.

In addition, you can't use Schedule C-EZ if you depreciate assets or want to claim passive activity losses from previous years. See the IRS instructions for additional details on who may use Schedule C-EZ.

While Schedule C-EZ is marginally easier to fill out than Schedule C, it's not worth using it unless you truly meet all the requirements. Don't, for example, neglect to claim more than $5,000 in business expenses or to claim depreciation expenses just so you qualify to use the schedule.

You're not required to file Schedule C if your sole proprietorship doesn't make at least $400 profit in the business year, though it's a good idea to file one anyway. If your business loses money in any year, filing Schedule C allows the loss to be deducted from any other income you make for that year, reducing your total taxable income. Or, you can carry over the loss into a future profitable year to offset those profits and reduce your taxes. Another reason to report losses or profits under $400 on Schedule C is that doing so triggers the beginning of the time window during which the IRS can audit you. Otherwise, the IRS can audit you anytime, virtually forever.

In addition to filing an annual return and paying any taxes due, sole proprietors must usually estimate their federal taxes and pay them in quarterly installments. We discuss this process below, under "Estimating and Paying Your Federal Taxes Quarterly."

Self-Employment Taxes

Besides paying income taxes, sole proprietors also must pay what are called "self-employment taxes," which are the sole proprietor's contributions to the Social Security and Medicare systems. When you're an employee, you contribute to these two programs through deductions from your paychecks. And employees' contributions are matched by their employers, so that employees have to pay only half as much into these programs as the self-employed do. If you're a sole proprietor, you must pay the entire amount yourself.

The self-employment tax rate is 15.3%, of which 12.4% goes toward Social Security and 2.9% goes toward Medicare. While the Medicare portion is calculated based upon a sole proprietor's total profits, the Social Security portion is capped at a certain amount that changes each year ($118,500 for 2015). Note also there is a Medicare surtax of 0.9% on income above $200,000 for individuals and $250,000 for couples filing jointly.

Now for the good news: Half of your total self-employment tax can be deducted from your taxable income at year-end. And if your sole proprietorship makes less than $400 profit in the business year, you don't have to pay self-employment taxes.

Self-employment taxes are reported on Schedule SE, *Self-Employment Tax*, which, like Schedule C, is submitted with your 1040 income tax return each year. Remember, also, that most sole proprietors must estimate their taxes and pay them in quarterly installments. (See "Estimating and Paying Your Federal Taxes Quarterly," below, for details.)

TIP
Having to report income is not the same as owing tax on that income. Sometimes, a tax agency like the IRS or your state tax office requires

you to submit a tax return even if you don't owe any taxes. Generally, a "filing" or "reporting" requirement means simply that you need to provide income and expense information, which may or may not add up to an actual tax obligation.

Partnerships

Like sole proprietorships, partnerships are pass-through tax entities, meaning that partnership profits are taxed on the individual returns of the business owners (as in, the partners of the business). Partners have to pay taxes on all business profits, whether or not they take any money out of the business. Besides income taxes, partners must also file and pay self-employment taxes.

This section explains what partnerships and their owners need to do to comply with the IRS rules.

Income Tax

Even though the partnership itself does not pay taxes on profits, it must report profits and losses on an informational return, Form 1065, *U.S. Return of Partnership Income*, which is generally due by April 15. Along with Form 1065, the partnership must also submit a Schedule K-1, *Partner's Share of Income, Deductions Credits, etc.* (Form 1065), for each partner, reporting each partner's share of profits or losses. A copy of the completed K-1 must also be given to each partner on or before the date that the partnership return is due to the IRS.

Any partnership profits are taxed as personal income of the individual partners; profits and losses are reported along with their personal returns (Form 1040). Each partner reports her share of business income or losses using Schedule E, *Supplemental Income and Loss*. Schedule E repeats the income information reported on Schedule K-1 (which each partner should have received from the partnership). Since the partnership already filed Schedule K-1 with the IRS, partners do not need to submit this schedule with their individual tax returns.

In addition to the above requirements, partners must usually estimate their taxes and make quarterly estimated tax payments. The process of making estimated tax payments is described in its own section below.

Self-Employment Taxes

Partners and other self-employed individuals who earn more than $400 profit during the business year must contribute to Social Security and Medicare through federal self-employment taxes. The self-employment tax rate is 15.3%, of which 12.4% goes toward Social Security and 2.9% goes toward Medicare. While the Medicare portion is calculated based upon the partner's total share of profits, the Social Security portion is capped at a certain amount that changes each year ($118,500 for 2015). Note also there is a Medicare surtax of 0.9% on income above $200,000 for individuals and $250,000 for couples filing jointly.

On a brighter note, a partner can deduct half of the total self-employment tax from her taxable income at year-end. And if the partner earns less than $400 in profit, no self-employment taxes need be filed or paid.

Self-employment taxes are reported on Schedule SE, which, like Schedule E (*Supplemental Income and Loss*), is submitted yearly with a partner's 1040 return.

And don't forget about estimating and paying taxes quarterly—partners of profitable businesses must usually do so, or face the IRS's penalties. (See "Estimating and Paying Your Federal Taxes Quarterly," below, for more on quarterly taxes.)

TIP
A husband and wife who co-own a business must each report their share of the business profits as net earnings on separate Schedule SEs, even if they file a joint 1040 return. The IRS now allows business-owner spouses to file as "co-sole proprietors" and skip the partnership paperwork (unless they have formed an LLC). But they need to report their shares of business income on separate Schedule Cs and pay any self-employment taxes due on that income. For more on this subject, see "Running a Business With Your Spouse," in Chapter 5.

> **TIP**
> **Partnerships and LLCs can be taxed like corporations if the business owners so choose.** Most partnerships and LLCs won't make this choice, but in some circumstances, doing so might reduce the overall tax burden of the company. Generally speaking, going this route is not advised unless a trusted accountant gives you a solid reason to do so. This chapter assumes your partnership or LLC will stick with pass-through tax status.

LLCs

As discussed in more detail in Chapter 5, a limited liability company (or LLC) is a hybrid of a partnership and a corporation. LLCs give their owners (usually called "members") protection from personal liability much like a corporation, yet are taxed like partnerships, with profits taxed to the members as individuals. In addition to regular income taxes, LLC members are subject to self-employment taxes, which are also based on business income.

Although the LLC itself is not taxed, it must report its income and losses to the IRS each year if it has two or more members. Single-owner LLCs are treated like sole proprietorships, meaning that the owner reports profits on her individual return and the LLC does not have to file a return.

The subsections below offer details on meeting the federal tax requirements for LLCs.

Income Tax

LLCs with only one member are treated as sole proprietorships for tax purposes, so that business profits and losses are reported on Schedule C (*Profit or Loss From Business*), to be submitted with the member's regular individual income tax return. A single-member LLC is considered a "disregarded entity" and does not have to file its own return.

LLCs with two or more members must file an annual informational return with the IRS, similar to the requirement faced by partnerships. The IRS doesn't have tax forms specifically for LLCs, so LLC profits and losses are reported on Form 1065, *U.S. Return of Partnership Income.* No tax is paid with this return, which is generally due by April 15.

Along with Form 1065, an LLC must also submit a Schedule K-1 (again, the same schedule used by partnerships) to the IRS for each member, reporting each member's share of profits or losses. A copy of the completed K-1 must also be given to each member on or before the date that the LLC return is due to the IRS.

Profits earned by an LLC are taxed as personal income of the individual members. Members use the information from Schedule K-1 to report their share of business income or losses on their individual federal income tax returns (Form 1040) using Schedule E (*Supplemental Income and Loss*). Since the LLC already filed Schedule K-1s with the IRS, members do not need to submit this form with their returns.

Like sole proprietors and partners, LLC members will typically have to estimate their taxes for the year and pay them in quarterly installments.

Self-Employment Taxes

LLC members who earn more than $400 profit during the business year must contribute to Social Security and Medicare through federal self-employment taxes. The self-employment tax rate is 15.3%, of which 12.4% goes toward Social Security and 2.9% goes toward Medicare. While the Medicare portion is calculated based upon the member's total share of profits, the Social Security portion is capped at a certain amount that changes each year ($118,500 for 2015). Note also there is a Medicare surtax of 0.9% on income above $200,000 for individuals and $250,000 for couples filing jointly.

CAUTION

There are some gray areas in the rules on self-employment taxes for LLC members. Since LLCs are partnership-like in some respects, corporate-like in others, the rules on whether LLC members are subject to self-employment tax can get a little twisty. Generally speaking, an LLC member who is actively involved in the business must pay self-employment taxes, while an LLC member who is inactive and merely invests in the company may be exempt from the self-employment tax obligation. If you're not sure whether this tax would apply to you, it may be wise to consult an accountant to get a definitive answer for your situation. (Chapter 13 gives information on finding professionals to advise you.)

Fortunately, if self-employment taxes are due, you can deduct half of the total self-employment taxes you pay from your taxable income at year-end. And if an LLC member earns less than $400 profit in the business year, she'll be exempt from having to pay self-employment taxes.

Self-employment taxes are reported on Schedule SE, which, like Schedule E is submitted yearly with an LLC member's 1040 return.

Also remember that LLC members must usually make quarterly estimated tax payments. The process of estimating and making these payments is discussed in a separate section below.

RESOURCE

This chapter does not discuss tax rules for corporations. If you're considering incorporating your business, bear in mind that corporations are subject to more complicated tax rules than other business types. See the "Corporations" section in Chapter 5 for an overview of the potential tax advantages and disadvantages of corporations. If you need more detailed information, take a look at these Nolo publications: *Tax Savvy for Small Business*, by Frederick W. Daily and Jeffrey A. Quinn, or *Incorporate Your Business: A Step-by-Step Guide to Forming a Corporation in Any State*, by Anthony Mancuso.

Estimating and Paying Your Federal Taxes Quarterly

In a nutshell, business owners have to pay federal estimated taxes each quarter if they expect to owe at least $1,000 in federal taxes for any particular year (including income taxes and self-employment taxes). At year-end, if you've paid more than what you owe, you'll get a refund. On the other hand, if you didn't pay enough in your quarterly installments, you will owe more.

Now for the detailed version of the IRS rule. You'll have to pay estimated federal taxes if both of the following are true:

- You expect to owe a total of at least $1,000 in federal taxes for the current year, including income taxes and self-employment taxes.
- You expect any withheld taxes (as in, taxes withheld from a day job's wages) to be less than the smaller of:
  - 100% of your total tax owed for the previous year, or
  - 90% of your total tax obligation for the current year.

Let's try to put this rule into plain English. First, it requires you to make estimated payments only if you expect to owe at least $1,000 to the IRS at year-end, above and beyond any taxes withheld from wages. This translates to about $3,000 to $6,000 in adjusted gross income from your business, depending on your tax bracket. If your business is barely breaking even (not uncommon in a business's early days), you probably won't have to make estimated payments.

Second, even if you do expect to owe at least $1,000, you can escape the requirement to pay estimated taxes if enough taxes are withheld from a paycheck—if in fact you receive one. If the business is your only source of income, then you'll be stuck paying estimated taxes. But if you do have a day job, there are two ways you can avoid the estimated tax requirement: If the taxes withheld in the current year will add up to at least what your entire tax bill was for the previous year, you're free of the estimated tax requirement. Or, if the taxes that are withheld in the current year will add up to more than 90% of what you'll owe in taxes for the current year, you won't have to pay estimated taxes.

Most businesspeople, of course, anticipate becoming profitable eventually—preferably sooner than later—so at some point you'll need to start paying estimated taxes. In the real world, what usually happens is that once you become profitable and owe income taxes for the first time, your accountant will calculate the next year's estimated tax payments based upon what you owed the previous year. The accountant will likely even prepare the vouchers for you, so all you have to do is send in the payment with the voucher stub by the applicable deadline.

> **TIP**
> **Hiring an accountant to do your tax preparation lets you focus on running your business.** Simplifying the estimated tax payment process is yet another reason it's highly recommended you use an accountant for tax preparation each year. While it's important for business owners to have a clear understanding of the big picture of taxes as described in this chapter, it makes the most sense to let an accountant handle tax details while you focus on guiding your business to success.

Each quarterly payment must be filed a half-month after the end of the quarter. For federal estimated taxes, the quarterly due dates are as follows:

Due Dates for Estimated Taxes	
Income made during:	**Tax installment due:**
Jan. 1 through Mar. 31	April 15
Apr. 1 through May 31	June 15
June 1 through Aug. 31	September 15
Sept. 1 through Dec. 31	January 15 of the next year

If your business uses a fiscal rather than a calendar year, your payments will be due on the 15th day of the fourth, sixth, and ninth months of your fiscal year and the first month of the following fiscal year.

> **TIP**
> **Note that the second estimated tax payment is due two—not three—months after the first!** You might expect quarterly payments to be evenly spaced out every three months, but you'd be wrong. Your first estimated tax payment is due on April 15 (along with your year-end payment for the previous year), and your second estimated payment will be due just *two* months later, on June 15. The third payment will be due three months later on September 15, and then there will be a four-month gap until the fourth estimated payment, due on January 15. Leave it to the IRS to throw a curveball into the otherwise straightforward concept of "quarterly payments."

State Income Taxes

Besides the IRS, most states have income tax requirements that apply to small business owners (and sometimes to the businesses themselves). The subsections below discuss typical state requirements, again divided by business type. Read the section that discusses your type of business to learn the rules that will apply to you. Since specific tax rules vary considerably from state to state, it's important that you check with your state tax agency for its exact requirements.

Sole Proprietors

You must report and pay state income taxes in much the same way as federal income tax. Any profit generated by a sole proprietorship is generally treated as personal income of the sole proprietor and reported on an individual state tax return. In most states, the sole proprietor will need to attach a separate schedule, similar to the federal Schedule C, to report business income. Unlike the federal rule, some states require this schedule to be filed even if your business loses money or makes less than $400 profit. In these states, you won't owe any taxes unless you've made a profit, but you must file the form in any case.

Like federal taxes, many states require businesses to estimate and pay their income taxes in quarterly installments.

Partnerships

Like the federal government, most states require partnerships to file informational returns reporting business income and losses. Many of these state forms are almost identical to the federal Form 1065. Partnerships may also be required to file a schedule analogous to the federal Schedule K-1 for each partner, indicating the partner's share of the business profit or loss. The partnership must give each partner a copy. Typically, the state schedules are similar to the federal version but account for differences between state and federal tax laws. Generally, no tax is due with the partnership return or schedules.

Any partnership profit is taxed as personal income of the partners, who report their shares on their individual state income tax return. Partnership income is usually recorded on a schedule similar to the federal Schedule E and included with the state tax form. Keep in mind that some states require partners to file this schedule even if the partnership loses money and no taxes are due.

Finally, like federal taxes, state income taxes must often be paid in quarterly installments.

LLCs

Though the federal government treats LLCs with pass-through tax status almost exactly like partnerships, the tax treatment LLCs receive in their states of formation may vary somewhat. Most states follow the IRS's lead and treat LLCs as pass-through entities unless the members have elected corporate tax treatment for the LLC. Some states, however, also impose special taxes on LLCs themselves, despite treating them as pass-through tax entities in most other respects.

Most states collect income tax from LLC members on their share of business profits, following the IRS classification scheme that treats LLCs as either partnerships or sole proprietorships. An LLC with a single owner is usually treated as a sole proprietorship, and business profits will be taxed on the sole member's individual state income tax return. LLCs with two or more owners are typically treated as partnerships and must file the same tax returns as owners of partnerships in that state.

Unlike the IRS, which imposes no taxes on LLCs themselves, several states levy taxes on LLCs in addition to taxing LLC members on their share of LLC income. These taxes are alternately called "franchise taxes," "annual fees," "surcharge taxes," or other similar names. Depending on the state, these additional costs can range from $10 to thousands of dollars, so be sure to understand your state's rules well in advance of tax time.

Like federal taxes, state income taxes for members must often be paid in quarterly installments.

City and County Taxes

Local governments often impose some sort of tax on all businesses within the city or county limits. As an initial step, you may be required to go through a tax registration process before you start your business. (We discuss typical registration processes in Chapter 7.) Once you've registered, you'll obtain what's often called a "tax registration certificate" which in essence authorizes you to conduct business. Registration gives notice to your local tax authorities that your business exists and allows them to tax it, based on whatever method your locality has adopted for your type of business.

TIP

A tax registration certificate is not the same thing as a business license, though some areas may call it a "business license." As discussed in Chapter 7, true business licenses are generally issued after you've proven your competence at a certain activity, typically after taking a class and/or taking a test. Examples include going through a testing process to obtain a cosmetology license, a contractor's license, or a locksmith's license. Simply paying a fee to your local government in order to register your business is quite a different thing; nevertheless, some areas mistakenly use the term "license" to describe your basic business registration.

The taxing schemes used in various cities and counties are usually based on certain attributes of your business. Most localities divide businesses into a number of different categories or types, such as retail sales, wholesale sales, hotels/apartments, and service businesses. Each category uses a certain criterion to calculate taxes, usually called a tax base. A common tax base, for example, is "gross receipts" (total income, before expenses). Each category has a certain tax rate for each tax base.

For example, a city might use gross receipts as its tax base for both retail sales businesses and entertainment businesses. However, the city may tax retail sales businesses at $1.50 per $1,000 of gross receipts, while it taxes entertainment businesses at $5.50 per $1,000. Other criteria used as tax bases include total payroll, number of employees, or number of company vehicles. Certain professionals, such as accountants, attorneys, and podiatrists, may pay taxes based on the number of years they have been licensed in the state. The bottom line is that local tax systems have just about as many ways of taxing your business as there are types of businesses.

Because rules vary widely from city to city and county to county, you'll need to check with your local tax agency to find out how it will tax your business. When searching for the appropriate tax agency, look online or in the government section of your telephone book under City Government (or County Government if you live in an unincorporated area) for names such as "Tax Collector," "Business Licenses and Permits," or "Business Tax Division." And, since local taxation of businesses is usually closely tied to start-up registration requirements, most businesses will automatically receive tax-filing information either when they register or soon after by mail.

In addition to the taxes described above, many localities impose taxes on certain kinds of business property, such as real estate, business equipment, furniture, and vehicles. Property tax reporting procedures vary considerably from area to area, but a common requirement is for businesses to provide their local tax authority with an itemized list of business property subject to tax. Check local rules to determine whether any property taxes apply to your business and how to go about paying them.

RESOURCE

Where to get tax forms and schedules. Tax forms become easy to find in early spring at public libraries, government offices, and of course IRS branches. At any time during the year, you can obtain the most current forms, schedules, and publications by ordering them over the phone or downloading them from the Web.

- **Federal.** Order federal tax forms and other publications from the IRS by calling 800-829-3676. Or download them from the IRS's website at www.irs.gov.
- **State.** For state tax forms, contact your state tax agency. Also, most states have tax forms and information available online. To find your state tax agency, search "State Government Websites" on the IRS website (www.irs.gov).

- **Local.** Local tax forms and instructions are often automatically sent to your business once you've registered with your city or county (a topic discussed in Chapter 6). Otherwise, contact the agency in charge of business taxes in your city or county (depending on where your business is located) for more information on how to obtain local tax forms. To find your local tax agency, look in the city and county government sections of your telephone book (or the appropriate website) under "Tax Collector," "Business Tax Division," or "City Clerk" ("County Clerk" if you're doing business outside of city limits).

Sales Taxes

In most states, businesses that engage in retail sales are subject to state, county, and local sales taxes. One state agency often manages collection of these taxes, and then distributes the collected taxes to the counties and districts across the state. For this reason you'll often hear the term "state sales taxes" even though the tax may ultimately be divided among state, county, and local governments.

Keeping track of your taxable sales and meeting the filing and paying requirements is usually a big task for any small business. The rules can be complicated and they're usually fraught with exceptions and gray areas. If you think you'll be subject to sales tax (or the sales tax's cousin, the gross receipts tax), you should get the advice of a bookkeeper or an accountant to make sure you stay in compliance with your state and local rules.

The subsections below will help you understand the big picture of sales taxes, including which businesses and which transactions may be subject to sales taxes, and what requirements states typically impose upon businesses engaged in taxable sales.

 CAUTION
Sales tax rules are closely related to seller's permit requirements.
Most businesses that engage in retail sales must apply for a seller's permit. This can be true even if the business ultimately makes no taxable sales—for instance, if all sales fall into a tax-exempt category, like groceries. (See Chapter 6 for more information on seller's permit requirements.)

Sales taxes can be especially tricky

"Sales tax obligations can be even more difficult to deal with than the IRS! Every state is completely different. Some states do not have sales tax. Sales made on the Internet are usually only taxed in the resident state. This is an increasing area of audit for almost all states—additional revenue! Again, seek professional help."

— **Jennifer Cantrell, CPA**

Taxable vs. Nontaxable Sales

In most states that impose sales taxes, the general rule (exceptions are covered below) for whether a transaction is taxable is:

- the transaction must involve the sale of a tangible item, and
- the sale must be made to the final user of the item.

Tangible items are things you can touch: cookware, handbags, computers, books, furniture, and the like. Nontangible items might include services (say, graphic design or electrical contracting), downloadable books, software, or intellectual property, such as patents or copyrights.

A final user is a consumer (generally, an individual or a business that will actually use the product) rather than a reseller (a wholesaler or distributor that would sell the product to another party). Sales that are made directly to end users, rather than resellers, are taxable retail sales, while sales to resellers are nontaxable wholesale sales.

Sounds simple—until you factor in the myriad variations, exceptions, and gray areas from state to state. For starters, states have wide variation in their definitions of the fundamental terms "tangible item" and "final user." A few states (including Hawaii, New Mexico, and South Dakota) don't limit their sales taxes to tangible items, and impose sales taxes on services. Still other states charge sales taxes on some (but not all) services, and others tax services only when they're performed along with a taxable sale of a tangible item—for example, charges for delivering a taxable item, such as furniture.

Resale Certificates

As mentioned above, states generally impose sales taxes only when the sale is made to a final user. But what if a customer claims to be a reseller so that they won't be charged sales tax—how would you know whether they're telling the truth? The answer is that they need to present you with what's called a "resale certificate." A resale certificate is an official form, issued by the state sales tax office and filled out by the buyer, which states that the buyer is purchasing your product(s) for resale. Depending on your state's law, the certificate must usually contain certain information, including:

- the purchaser's name and address
- the number of the purchaser's seller's permit
- a description of the property to be purchased
- a statement that the property is being used for resale, in terms such as "will be resold" or "for resale" (language such as "nontaxable" or "exempt" is not enough)
- the date of the sale, and
- the signature of the purchaser or an authorized agent.

If someone claims to be a reseller, but does not give you the appropriate certificate proving their status, you should assume the customer is the final user and treat the sale as taxable. If you sell to the same customer repeatedly, you'll usually need to collect only one resale certificate, which you should keep on file at your office. From then on, whenever you sell items to that company, you shouldn't have to collect another resale certificate.

Just as your customers can escape paying you sales taxes by presenting a resale certificate, you can use one to purchase goods and supplies free of sales tax, as long as the goods and supplies are for legitimate resale. This applies whether you'll resell purchased goods as is, or whether you'll incorporate purchased materials into your products. If you buy regularly from the same supplier, you should only have to present your resale certificate once.

Besides variations in definitions and basic rules, every state's rules are clouded by swarms of exceptions and exemptions. Here are several examples of common exemptions from sales tax:

- most groceries (but not restaurant or take-out food)
- sales to out-of-state customers
- sales to the U.S. government, and
- some sales related to the entertainment industry.

With the complexity and variations involved in sales taxes, it's essential that you check with your state tax agency or with a trusted professional such as an accountant or lawyer to make sure you understand the details that apply to your business.

 TIP

An example of a sales tax gray area involved graphic artists in California. In the late 1990s, California's sales tax agency audited some graphic artists and charged them with massive back taxes and penalties for unpaid sales taxes. The graphic artists involved (as well as concerned graphic artists across the state) were stunned to learn that the state did not consider their transactions to be services which are not taxable in California, but instead to be taxable sales of tangible items, merely because the artists' work was given to the client on a physical piece of paper. The sales tax regulations were amended in 2002, resulting in more fair treatment of graphic artists' work. The moral here is not to rely on common definitions, but to find out specifically how your state tax agency interprets sales tax terminology.

The Nexus Requirement and Sales to Out-of-State Customers

Ready for another exception to the general sales tax rule stated above? Here is what's known as the "nexus" requirement: Your business is required to collect sales taxes only on sales conducted within states in which your business is physically located. In other words, sales to out-of-state customers (such as by mail order) are not subject to sales tax. In legal terms, having a physical presence is known as having a "nexus." This rule was established by the U.S. Supreme Court in *Quill v. North Dakota*, 504 U.S. 298 (1992).

So, if your business has a store in New York and warehouses in Illinois and California, then your business would have a nexus in all three states and would need to collect sales taxes from customers there. On the other hand, mail orders shipped to customers in Wisconsin, where your business has no physical presence, would not be taxed. This explains why mail order forms often contain language such as "New York residents add 8.5% sales tax." When you see such language, you know that the business is located in New York and must collect sales tax from customers in the state, but not from residents of other states.

Your business is likely to be deemed to have a nexus in a state if any of the following applies:

- You operate a retail store in the state.
- Your company's salespeople conduct business within the state.
- You own or lease a warehouse or an office in the state, even if it's not open to the public.
- You have sales affiliates, subsidiaries, or affiliated companies in a state that has passed legislation extending the definition of "nexus" to these types of entities. (See the next section, "Sales Taxes Online," for more details.)

Once a nexus exists in a given state, your business will be subject to all of that state's sales tax laws, including any seller's permit and sales tax collecting and reporting requirements. For this reason, many businesses limit their physical presence to one or two states and conduct nationwide business by mail order or e-commerce.

If some of you find yourself wondering, "Are e-commerce operations really exempt from sales tax requirements?" you've hit upon a major issue in the world of sales taxes. Let's take a quick look at this complicated and evolving issue.

Sales Taxes Online

Do a Google search for "online sales taxes" and you'll quickly see there's a lot of sound and fury regarding this topic. Before going into any details, simply keep in mind that online sales tax rules are still emerging and highly controversial. Expect a good deal of development and change over the next few years.

Currently, the rules that apply to most small businesses that sell products online are no different from those for non-Web retailers. Businesses that sell products online are subject to the sales tax laws in the states in which the business has a physical presence. Even for online businesses, only a traditional physical presence counts with regard to sales taxes; the fact that customers can access your website from a particular state currently isn't enough to create a nexus in that state. Online retailers don't need to pay sales taxes on transactions in every state where the website appears (which, of course, is everywhere). E-tailers need only to pay sales taxes on sales in states in which the business has an office, salespeople, or another type of physical presence. Of course, if the business has a nexus in a state that doesn't charge sales taxes, then transactions there are tax free.

However, there has been significant legislative activity in many states aimed at trying to force large online retailers, such as Amazon.com, Overstock.com, and others, to pay sales taxes even if these e-tailers don't have a physical presence in a particular state. The most popular strategy in recent years has been to enact laws broadening the definition of "nexus" beyond just having a physical presence, to include having sales affiliates, subsidiaries, or affiliated companies. For example, in 2011, California enacted legislation commonly referred to as the "Amazon tax" law requiring online retailers to collect and remit state sales taxes if they generate at least $500,000 in annual revenue from California customers through in-state sales affiliates (websites that get commissions by having links to the larger online retailer). Similar laws have been passed, are pending, or have been proposed in many states, including New York, Illinois, and several others.

It's tough to say what the future holds. Amazon and other e-tailers have challenged some of the laws requiring them to pay sales taxes, but they appear to be waging a losing battle. While the legal and legislative skirmishes aren't over, courts seem to be leaning toward upholding the state efforts to collect sales taxes based upon expanded nexus definitions. There is also a push for federal legislation on Internet sales tax collection that would supersede state laws, simplifying and streamlining sales taxes nationwide.

The bottom line is that if your business will be conducting sales online, you'll definitely need to monitor this issue. A good online resource is the Institute for Local Self-Reliance, which offers detailed, current information about state sales tax legislation. Go to www.ilsr.org and search for "online sales taxes."

Use Taxes

Above, we discussed a number of types of transactions in which you would not owe sales tax, including when you purchase equipment from out of state. Now for the bad news: Many of these transactions are actually subject to a related tax called a use tax. In keeping with its name, a use tax is due when you use a tangible good on which you didn't pay sales tax. For instance, if you order 20 computers, 20 chairs, and 20 desks for your office from an out-of-state mail order catalog, you probably didn't pay sales taxes on those items, because most states don't require businesses to collect sales tax from out-of-state purchasers. But under use tax laws in many states, your state can collect use taxes from you, the buyer, to make up for the revenue it would have gotten if you had bought the equipment within the state. Use taxes typically are not due if you purchase goods for resale and have a resale certificate.

To pay use taxes, you typically fill out a use tax return, which is often the same as or related to the one that your business will use for paying sales taxes to the state. Essentially, you'll enter information on the form about the purchases you made that are subject to use tax, and follow the form's instructions for calculating your tax. There's not much more to it than sending it off to the state sales tax office, along with a check (assuming you owe money).

Note that while many states have traditionally been lax in enforcing and collecting use taxes, many are now stepping up their efforts to collect them. With state tax coffers low due to the economic downturn, collecting use taxes has moved to the front burner in many states.

Tracking, Filing, and Paying Sales Taxes

When you obtain a seller's permit in most states, you obligate yourself to file a sales (and use) tax return. This means that you'll need to keep careful records of both your sales and purchases. Most state sales tax agencies require that you keep:

- books or computer files recording your sales and purchases
- bills, receipts, invoices, contracts, or other documents (called "documents of original entry") that support your books, and
- schedules and working papers used in preparing your tax returns.

In addition, if you conduct business in more than one county, city, or other local tax district, you may need to keep separate records of sales made in each area.

Finally, your records should show all sales your business makes, even sales that aren't taxable.

Remember that sales taxes are often a combination of state, county, and city sales taxes. For example, an 8.5% sales tax may actually break down into a 5% state tax, a 2% county tax, and a 1.5% city tax. So, if you conduct taxable sales in more than one tax district, you may end up paying several different rates. Conveniently, many states allow businesses to file just one state tax return that includes all taxes for all applicable districts. The return will usually ask you to identify where your sales were made so that the state can allocate the fair share of taxes to each tax district.

Businesses that have been issued a seller's permit will often receive their state sales tax return package automatically, along with an account number, due date, and filing instructions. Depending on your sales volume, you'll need to submit your sales tax return yearly, quarterly, or monthly. Contact your state agency for details.

Filling out the sales tax return is generally fairly straightforward, though as with other tax filing requirements, it's often a good idea to have a bookkeeper or an accountant help you with this task. If you're on a tight budget in the early days of your business and want to make a go of it yourself, consider getting one-time advice from a bookkeeper or an accountant to make sure you're on the right track. As your business grows, the task of filing and paying sales taxes will likely be handled by an in-house or outsourced bookkeeper or accountant.

Building Your Business and Hiring Employees and Other Workers

Depending on your business plan, you may plan to hire employees or contractors as an integral part of launching your start-up. Or you may be starting just by yourself, or perhaps with a partner, and see hiring staff as part of a later phase in growing your business—say, a year or two after launch (if at all). No matter when or why you hire staff, doing so is a big step for every small business owner—and often an exhilarating one as your business starts to take on a life of its own. But just as exciting as it can be to hire workers, it can also be stressful. Entrepreneurs (especially new ones) may have many concerns: Can I afford to hire staff? How do I choose the right people for the job? How much will I need to pay? And what about benefits? Is my space big enough (especially relevant if you're working from a home office)? How am I supposed to manage employees, and how much work will it involve? Would I be better off using independent contractors? What if I hire someone who doesn't work out? With all these considerations in mind and more, it's clear that hiring workers is a task that should be taken with care and proper planning.

That's where this chapter comes in. I'll take you through the process of hiring and managing staff (either employees or independent contractors) to help with the day-to-day operations of your business or to handle specific tasks, such as Web development. We'll start by explaining how to develop systems to ensure efficiency, consistency, and quality within your business (always important, but especially so if you are handing off tasks to staff). Next, I'll offer a methodical process for hiring and managing your staff, from figuring out what kind of help you need, to defining positions and developing employee review procedures—all essential before you interview or hire anyone.

In addition to the practical management issues involved in hiring one or more people to work for your business, we'll explain the important legal rules that apply to businesses with outside workers, including the difference between employees and independent contractors. This distinction is crucial. If the government considers your workers to be employees, you'll have to follow a number of state and federal laws and pay employment-related taxes. If, on the other hand, your workers meet the definition of independent contractors, you'll be spared many—but not all—of these tax and legal requirements.

Taking your business to the next level with employees

"I am lucky that Queen Bee has grown to the point that I have been able to hire excellent people to share some of the worry and burden of running the business on a daily basis. Ultimately, the buck still stops with me, but I have help with nearly all of the other aspects of the business, which goes a long way in helping me maintain better balance between personal and professional life. I can let go and trust that things are being taken care of, and I don't need to hover."

— **Rebecca Pearcy**

"The biggest mistake I see business owners make is thinking that you need to do it all. The belief that nobody can do it as good as you. The thought that you start a business and you're going to create the product, sell the product, package the product, ship the product, advertise the product, everything. That doesn't mean you need a million employees. But you need to realize that the more you lock yourself into being the worker, you will never be able to manage. You'll never be able to create new business. I know that right now. Because I don't have a strong enough salesperson right now, except for me, I'm locked into being the salesperson. For many years I believed that nobody could do anything better than me. Now I'm like, 'Yes, they can all do it better than me! Do it!' I'm fine with it. Really."

— **Kyle Zimmerman**

TIP

This chapter is useful to all entrepreneurs—even those of you planning to stay a one-woman operation. Professional consultants, contractors, and freelancers of all stripes have found success on their own terms as independent solo operators without any regular staff. In fact, over 20 million businesses (70% of all businesses in the United States) have no employees. That said, almost every business will usually benefit from occasionally hiring professionals (as independent contractors) to help manage specific aspects of your business—such as an accountant to prepare your business tax return or a technology consultant to build your website.

Most of the hiring and management advice we offer in this chapter applies to independent contractors and employees alike. For example, defining job responsibilities and interviewing candidates are important tasks whether you're hiring an employee or a contractor. And regardless of the worker's status as an employee or contractor, you'll need to manage the worker well once hired.

If you know you will not be hiring employees, you may skip the following sections: "Spell Out Employee Policies and Review Procedures," "Orient New Employees," and "Required Rules, Paperwork, Filings, and Taxes for Employees." The rest of the chapter should be useful whether you plan to hire employees or independent contractors.

Developing Systems to Run Your Business

Running a business involves many tasks—from the work involved in creating your products or providing your services, to marketing those products or services, to administrative tasks like bookkeeping and billing. Whether you're running your business on your own or with one or more co-owners, it's important to break down these and other important tasks, and structure them into efficient systems. By "system," we simply mean a methodical, clearly defined process to get things done consistently, efficiently, and correctly. Here are a few reasons why systems are so important.

- Consistency is a major factor in customer satisfaction and business success. Systems encourage consistency which helps build customer loyalty.
- When your business runs efficiently, you are more productive and profitable. Systems help you get more done with less stress and without having to work night and day.
- Solid systems will minimize embarrassing or costly errors, such as lost or incorrect orders, that can seriously damage your business's reputation.

Far too many entrepreneurs fail to create basic systems and operate more by the seat of their pants—or worse, in constant crisis mode. In addition to having a negative effect on your business success, the lack of systems is horrible for your mental health. If you've ever worked for a disorganized manager, you know full well how the lack of systems creates enduring chaos and inefficiency.

Establishing basic systems is especially important when you're considering hiring employees. Having ill-defined systems (or none at all) makes it near impossible to scope out job descriptions, too often resulting in fuzzy job boundaries, unclear responsibilities, and lack of accountability. In practice, this usually translates into more work for you, as you'll have to do more hands-on management to make sure things are running the way they should. There's no worse feeling than finding yourself tethered to the business even after you've gone through the trouble and considerable expense of hiring employees who should be taking care of business—but aren't.

Systems also are essential for any business aiming to grow, since expansion usually involves adding more employees and complexity. If you want to add dinner service to your breakfast and lunch cafe, take on more clients with your accounting business, add new services to your video postproduction firm, or produce more jewelry as a solo craftsperson, systems will smooth the way toward a larger operation.

> **EXAMPLE:** Sophia and Angelina opened their boutique hotel after many months of intense business planning focused on the financials of the business. They gave less attention to defining internal management systems, assuming that they would figure them out as they went. Unfortunately, this oversight had a nearly disastrous effect on the business. For the first few months after the hotel's grand opening, guest scheduling and intake was a nightmare. Employees who answered the phone weren't clear about what questions to ask while making a reservation, resulting in numerous errors. Guests were given rooms with the wrong number of beds; specific requests such as first-floor rooms or cribs weren't recorded and sometimes could not be honored; and, in some cases, reservations were lost altogether. Upon arriving, some guests were welcomed with a cup of tea and pool towels; others just received their key and were sent on their way. With all the constant errors and

inconsistencies, the vibe inside the hotel was anything but peaceful, and word started getting out that they didn't have their act together.

After a few months of this chaos, Sophia and Angelina realized they needed to take their guest management system seriously and they spent a week drafting clear procedures for every aspect of handling guests. A phone script was written to make sure that employees answering the phone would ask all the right questions when making reservations, and a list was included in the reservations book detailing all the amenities and features of each room. A list of what guests should be given upon arrival (their key, a map of the hotel and of the town, a cup of tea, and a pool towel) was included in an info sheet, and those items were clearly organized by the reception desk. Finally, Sophia and Angelina held a training with all the appropriate employees to make sure they understood the system.

Within a month, the hotel was running smoothly and the sense of panic passed. It took a few months to undo the damage to the hotel's reputation, but, eventually, it started getting rave reviews and people chalked up the early problems to the strains of start-up.

To get started in defining your systems, take a look at your business plan and make lists of all the tasks that need to be handled. You'll find that many tasks naturally fall together; some will be unique to your business and others are common to most businesses. For example, you'll need a system or procedure for how the business will provide its unique products or services, which may include things like ordering supplies, manufacturing products, tracking inventory, providing estimates to potential clients, or performing various services to customers. Other systems will be more standard, such as tracking and managing finances, tracking employees' time, handling marketing and public relations, and so on.

Refine your lists and write up step-by-step instructions for each system. Collectively, these instructions essentially become an operations manual for your business. Don't worry—I'm not talking about a 500-page manual here. For many small businesses, one or two pages of bullet-point instructions per system may well be adequate and the whole operations manual may total something like 20 pages, give or take. Of course larger, more complex businesses may need something longer, but most of you probably won't need a Russian-novel-length operations manual.

When systems have been successfully implemented—ideally, with procedures and policies put into a written operations manual—the business starts to operate more like a machine. This, in turn, reduces the burden on the business owner and on any managers, who won't need to be around as much or to manage as intensely as would be necessary in the absence of solid systems.

When you have sketched out a system for each of the essential tasks of your business, your needs for one or more employees or independent contractors will come into sharper focus. For example, you may decide that some of the legwork involved in your kitchen design business—such as ordering cabinet and flooring samples, setting up displays in your showroom, and making appointments—could be handled by a part-time administrative assistant, freeing you up to market your business and bring in more clients. Or you may decide you really need to offload certain tasks that you hate doing—say, bookkeeping or market research—giving you time to do the more people-oriented work you love.

Streamlining management and operations with systems

"For us, managing staff involves having enough systems so that people understand what they're doing here and how the place operates, and balancing that with being laid-back. You want the balance, you don't want to overwhelm people with rules—but at the same time, anytime we've had a big problem with morale or a problem with lack of responsibility or professionalism, it's been because there haven't been enough systems in place. So then we've reined it in. Right now, we're in a really good spot with that; it seems like we've found a good balance."

— **Elissa Breitbard**

"One thing systems-wise that's been helpful is actually realizing that I had a cap on my own ability to produce, and that there were some things that I could delegate. I had a part-time employee who worked for me for three years. She took care of things like multiple expense reports for different clients; she helped with photo sourcing for magazine projects; she did some light writing and editing. That was something that I had to learn, that I couldn't just do it all by myself. There were some things that I did need to delegate, and some things that I could delegate and I could afford to pay somebody, and that was a great thing to do."

— **Emily Esterson**

"Creating systems has been a really big theme over the past few years. I am not the most organized person in the operation (again, I'm the creative person) so I have hired and relied on others to help make things run even more smoothly. Manufacturing is a messy and chaotic type of business to be in. There is a lot of ordering raw goods of many different types, and storing and tracking those materials as they move through the production process. Managing incoming orders and tracking them also requires a lot of organizing efficiency. It makes sense to ask the people who are doing the work and using the systems to give input about what would work for them, or what kind of systems to create, in order for them to best perform their jobs."

— **Rebecca Pearcy**

"We didn't have systems until we had kids. That's what forced us to stop and say, 'Okay, now we need to implement these things.' We called it a workflow, some call it a system, but it's the same thing. When I stepped out for maternity leave, Jeff had to figure out what to do without me for a few months, and how employees could run it. I wanted him to be home more, and we wanted more family time. So that's when we started to figure out some structure, where before it was kind of a free-for-all. If we didn't have kids, to be honest with you, I don't think we would have ever reached this point. They forced us to get to where we are now, with systems so the business runs itself a little bit."

— **Sabrina Habib Williams**

"You have to have systems. I spent a couple years working on it nonstop. Bringing in different people to help me, different kinds of people involved in organizing, people involved in management, all kinds of different people who helped me work on those documents and those processes. I've got binders and I've got protocols—everything is outlined. That was probably about four or five years ago that we worked on those. Today, we don't really look at them much unless I have a new hire. And then I pull that book out and make photocopies, and it's kind of good! We can refer back to that. And every once in a while we have to go back in—for example when we switched from film to digital, everything changed. Everything in our paperwork had to change. Every process, every system, because now it all happened differently. So you have to be able to change and grow with how you do it differently."

— **Kyle Zimmerman**

Do I Need to Define Systems for My Freelance Business?

Many small businesses may have a tiny number of people (sometimes just one, as in you) to handle the systems and tasks that have been defined. There's nothing wrong with that—and in case you're wondering, it's not a waste of time to develop systems, even for a one-woman operation. Having those systems in place will help even the smallest businesses stay efficient and consistent, which not only will save you valuable time in running your business, but will result in a more professional operation, which is sure to boost your reputation. And if you hope to grow your business, having well-defined systems are essential so you can easily "plug in" additional staff and scale up the operation.

Hiring employees can be scary!

"It was just the two of us for the first five years. In the fifth year, we were working so much that we were losing sight of the vision we'd had when we started the business, which was to enjoy a sane and healthy work life that allowed us the time and freedom to have rich lives outside of work. People had been telling us for a long time we should hire employees, but we were afraid—afraid on several levels. We worried it was financially risky; we feared the changes it would bring to both the relationship between the two of us as well as our relationship with our clients; and we feared that the quality of our work might suffer if we didn't find the right person. We mitigated these risks by hiring a part-time, contract employee for a three-month stint, and by advertising (and interviewing) for a detail-oriented, meticulous coder—and that's exactly who we found. In the end, after the three-month contract was up, we rehired him as a permanent, full-time employee and we've never looked back.

"The financial piece took care of itself, because in our typically worry-wart fashion, we had calculated the risks but not the rewards. Having another pair of hands improved our bottom line almost instantly, because our turnaround time got faster, and our cash flow sped up just as quickly, because we were able to bill our clients more quickly. We've tried to remember those lessons each time we've expanded our ranks since. It never stops feeling risky, but over time our perspective has shifted, and nowadays one of our strongest motivators for growing our business is creating a company that can sustain a thriving staff of fabulous people."

— Lauren Bacon and Emira Mears

Hiring and Managing Staff

When asked to name the most challenging aspect of running a small business, entrepreneurs consistently rank hiring and managing employees at or near the top. From finding good candidates to making smart hiring decisions to managing your team well, there's nothing easy about building or maintaining an effective staff. The good news is that a few simple strategies and practices can make a huge difference in the quality and effectiveness of your team. By using a methodical approach to hiring and managing employees, you'll not only make the management job easier, but you'll also reap the benefits of having a well-trained and organized staff of workers.

In a nutshell, in order to hire and manage staff effectively, you'll need to create clearly defined positions with clear job descriptions for each, establish an efficient staff structure, implement a review process to evaluate performance, create an employee handbook, and train and orient your new hires appropriately. Let's look at these elements in more detail.

Create Job Positions

If you've done the crucial work involved in defining systems for your business, you'll be well positioned to define the job positions that will be necessary to execute those systems and hire the appropriate people. Depending on the size of your business, each system may correspond to one or more positions, such as office manager, marketing director, or products manager; for large businesses, systems might be handled by what might be considered a "department." You also might determine that a position seems more appropriate for an outsourced contractor instead of an in-house employee.

Consider some examples:

- A small business might assign duties related to financial management to one full-time position which it calls "financial director."
- A large business may have an accounting department with 15 employees (ten full time and five part time), each with their own job position and title.
- A one-person business might dispense with individual titles and simply call herself "director" or "principal" (though having well-defined task breakdowns and systems will still be very helpful; see "Do I Need to Define Systems for My Freelance Business?" above).
- A small or medium-size firm might realize that website maintenance would be best managed by an outside contractor.

How you define specific positions for your business will depend on many different factors, an important one being your budget for staff. Use your business plan and the financial projections within it to guide you in figuring out how many and what type of job positions you need to handle the various systems you've defined.

It's not uncommon for a small start-up business to hire just one key employee to handle a wide range of tasks such as running the store, answering phones, doing data entry, and updating the website. In this situation it's crucial to be crystal clear about the responsibilities assigned to this position, and to spell them out in a written job description, as we discuss next.

TIP

A little structure goes a long way toward ensuring the efficient operation of any organization. Progressive-minded folks sometimes look at staff hierarchies as undemocratic or somehow oppressive. If your business will have five or more regular employees, it's important to take the time to designate clear lines of authority and accountability. In small businesses, this often means that everyone reports to one of the business owners. As the business grows, you'll probably want to add a second layer of managerial accountability—for example, to require marketing associates to report to the sales and marketing manager, not directly to the business owner.

Delegate your way to success

"One key to success is knowing when to step back—meaning, a lot of entrepreneurs are very good entrepreneurs, but they're not very good at the day-to-day stuff. The successful ones acknowledge that and are able either to delegate or step away from the day-to-day and maintain their energy in the creative element of it, and delegate the more tedious work to a general manager or something like that. I think that's really key."

— Emily Esterson

Write Job Descriptions

Before advertising for a particular position, it's important to write out a formal job description that spells out the responsibilities, skills, and experience required for the job, pay, hours, and anything relevant (such as working weekends). Job descriptions are important both for regular employees and independent contractors; in both cases, you want a written record of the specific responsibilities of the job.

TIP
Co-owners should also have clear descriptions of their responsibilities. Assuming that you and any other co-owners will actively work in the business, you should define jobs for yourselves as if you were any other employee, making sure the tasks and responsibilities of your position(s) are clear. For more on working with co-owners, including choosing them wisely, see Chapter 1.

Note that in some cases, when you are looking to hire an independent contractor they may submit a written proposal that contains a detailed breakdown of the job (often called "scope of work" or something similar). If so, the proposal and the contract can serve as the job description.

Creating a job description for each position not only will help in the hiring process but will also manage expectations —for example, applicants for an administrative assistant position will clearly understand that the main job is to do mundane office tasks such as managing the customer database, and that helping write your newsletter or do market research are secondary parts of the job. Think about what works for you, not necessarily what your employee wants to do. A clear job description is also valuable when it's time to review an employee's performance. Fortunately, writing job descriptions should be easy if you have created the position from a task-based to-do list; the job description can simply restate the list in slightly more polished form.

> ### Written job descriptions keep everyone on track
>
> *"Anytime we have a big problem with managing staff, I just pull out my favorite document, 'Who Does What At Betty's' and explain clearly, 'This is your job, and this is your job,' and go down the list of what everyone is doing here and how do they function together."*
>
> **— Elissa Breitbard**

RESOURCE

Resource on writing job descriptions. *The Job Description Handbook*, by Margie Mader-Clark (Nolo), has everything you need to write an effective job description. For details and a sample chapter from this book, see www.nolo.com.

Decide How Much You'll Pay

Obviously, pay will be a key issue you'll need to consider early on. Look to your business plan for guidance on what you can afford. If you're hiring an employee, you'll need to pay at least minimum wage and comply with overtime rules (see the section below on laws and taxes that apply to employers). If you know your field well, you'll probably have a good idea of the going rates for various types of positions, from entry level to professionally qualified. If you need more guidance, ask people in your network, especially owners of similar businesses, for their ideas on pay for a particular position. Also look at classified ads for the same type of job to see what they pay.

In my opinion, paying a bit more than the going rate (if you can afford to do so) will more than pay off by attracting higher quality candidates. Hiring a less skilled worker who takes lots of your time to manage and supervise can really drag your business down. And underpaying employees tends to result in low morale and underachieving workers. If you can't afford to pay at least the going rate, consider other perks that might attract good employees, such as flexible hours or telecommuting (but only if these work for you). The opportunity for advancement and the chance to get in on the ground floor of a growing business can also attract employees willing to work for less pay. Many small businesses have found that allowing employees to bring their dogs to work is a huge plus (often worth lower pay).

Spell Out Employee Policies and Review Procedures

Even if you're hiring just one employee, we recommend you prepare an employee handbook (even if it's just a few pages) of important information about the job and workplace policies, including hours and flex time; benefits, such as sick and vacation leave; policies on workplace behavior (including discrimination and harassment); performance review and grievance procedures; termination; and anything else relevant to your business. Spelling out the rules employees must follow and procedures your business will use in dealing with workers will help ensure that your employment practices are sound. And compiling these policies in a guidebook promotes positive staff relations by demonstrating your business's commitment to fair treatment for all workers, according to the same set of rules.

TIP

Every business should implement an evaluation procedure before hiring anyone (ideally, it will be outlined in your employee manual). That way, new employees know what to expect from the very first day. The review procedure needn't be complex; it might simply identify who will participate in reviews, when they will occur (say, every six months or at a minimum once per year), and the criteria by which staff will be measured. Once again, having a well-written job description is a big asset here as it will form the basis for the review criteria. (Of course, the review process should not be a one-time thing: Keep good communication open, so you don't surprise an employee with a laundry list of complaints six months into the job.)

An employee handbook is also a powerful way to minimize the risks posed by anyone who works for your business. Unfortunately, a business's potential risk of a liability or contract lawsuit goes way up as soon as you hire even one employee. Not only can that worker potentially harm someone and expose the business to a lawsuit, but he or she also could sue the business for a host of discrimination, wrongful termination, or other claims. By offering clearly stated expectations and procedures for treating employees consistently, an employee handbook will go a long way toward minimizing these risks and provide a powerful deterrent to future workplace trouble.

Lots of new business owners find the prospect of creating a staff handbook too overwhelming in their harried early days. While this is understandable, it's a good idea to tackle the task earlier than later—it will be easier to create a handbook before the staff grows large and complex. It's simply unwise to have more than a few employees without a written set of policies.

RESOURCE

Resource for creating your employee handbook. *Create Your Own Employee Handbook*, by Lisa Guerin and Amy DelPo (Nolo), takes you step by step through creating an employee handbook, explaining the issues, and offering sample language you can modify to fit your workplace. For details and a sample chapter from this book, see www.nolo.com.

TIP

You're the boss, not a best friend. While you should certainly strive to treat your employees well, be careful not to confuse the employer/employee relationship with friendship. To start, don't hire people that seem really likable or with whom you instantly feel a good rapport, unless they truly have the skills for the job. Once they're hired, be careful to keep the relationship professional to ensure that you are able to manage them and maintain your expectations of them without personal friendships clouding the waters. For example, if you become close pals with your assistant and her job performance starts slipping, you might feel awkward about addressing the issue and let things slide. This can be a particular problem if you have multiple employees and other workers feel you favor certain workers. It's great to have friendly relationships with employees, but don't let friendships get in the way of effective and fair management.

The challenges of being the boss

"It can be a challenge to manage sales teams, to be willing to be strong with your people and guide them in the right way. Sometimes I have a tendency to be very nice towards my employees and it can be a tough call. You have to find a balance in how you work."

— **Nicola Freegard**

"Becoming and being an employer is probably the hardest thing I have done in my business. I really didn't know what I was doing from the beginning, so I made a lot of mistakes that I have learned from. I didn't have any experience managing other people, and it's not my forte. I started off by just accepting volunteer help from friends. Over the years, I learned that for myself it is best not to hire friends. Or, be very careful and mindful when hiring friends. Things can get sticky and I've learned that I would rather have my friends as friends and not employees. It took me a while to establish a good boundary with employees and coworkers, one that is friendly and approachable, but professional. I think that consistency, providing clear structure and policies (such as an employee handbook), is to the benefit of your staff. And that people really appreciate a boss that is approachable and steady in their nature."

— **Rebecca Pearcy**

CAUTION

Be careful when monitoring employees' activity on social media. There is a lot of legislative activity in this area. Federal laws prohibit employers from discriminating against an employee or applicant based on information they glean from social media related to the individual's race, color, national origin, gender, age, disability, or immigration status. More specific laws regarding employers' access to or use of social media information about employees or applicants exist at the state level. Several states have passed laws prohibiting employers from requiring passwords or log-in information from employees for their social media accounts. Laws vary a great deal from state to state, so if you have any plans to track your employees' or applicants' social media activity and use that information in hiring or termination decisions, be sure to learn your state's laws. One good source of updated information is the National Conference of State Legislatures website at www.ncsl.org.

Find, Interview, and Screen Job Applicants

Many entrepreneurs rely heavily on their personal network of colleagues, family, and friends to find good employees. Social media, which can vastly extend your networking reach, can also be a great way to get out the word about job openings. Depending on the specific job, you may also need to advertise. What works best depends on the position you're seeking to fill. Common resources for finding employees include craigslist (www.craigslist.com), researching LinkedIn (www.linkedin.com), industry-specific newsletters or websites, local college career placement offices, and local print media such as your city's daily or weekly newspapers.

Drafting a "help wanted" ad is simple if you've already written out a job description; you'll often need to edit it for length, but you'll want to include the main responsibilities in the ad to ensure you attract the right candidates. You may want to include qualifications in the ad, which you probably didn't include in the job description. For example, if you'll consider only candidates with a college degree, a particular certification, or a certain number of years' experience in the field, state these requirements in the ad.

To save time interviewing unqualified people, prescreen applicants over the phone before you arrange to meet anyone in person. Always check references (even if it's the cousin of your best friend), and run a credit report if the employee will be handling money. And be sure you comply with antidiscrimination laws (discussed below).

TIP

Take your time hiring. Make sure you are hiring the right person for the job—someone who's clear about the position and has the necessary skills, experience, and personality to work closely with you. You don't want to waste your time training someone who can't handle the details of the job or is unhappy with the work and quits after a few months.

> ### Consider a trial run
>
> *"For hourly staff, consider doing one or two paid 'test' shifts. In the kitchen especially, it's important for both the employee and the employer to see that everyone works well together. No interview is going to provide as much information as a trial run."*
>
> — **Catherine Oddenino**

Orient New Employees

When employees come on board, it's important to take some time to introduce them to your world. For efficiency's sake, it's a great idea to create a standard orientation process—it could be a short meeting and video shown in a conference room, a walk-through of the office, or a get-together at your house—to explain the ins and outs of working for the business. If and when you have several employees coming on board at once, you can save time by orienting them as a group.

All new hires should receive basic information about the business, but you'll want to provide a more extensive orientation for higher-level positions. For example, you may want to spend a significant amount of time with a general manager—say, a series of meetings over a few days—explaining the business and how you want it to be run. This might include discussing the business's history and any past problems that you do not want to see repeated. For regular employees, on the other hand, this much information would be overkill. The point here is to keep those whom you are orienting in mind when deciding what information to include in your orientation sessions.

A good starting point is to provide each new employee with a copy of your employee handbook and operations manual. Beyond that, the type of orientation may well depend on how many staffers are involved. If you're starting out with just a handful of employees, perhaps a couple of hours of orientation followed by lunch might work. As your staff grows, you may want to have new hires attend presentations by a manager or supervisor. Pairing new employees with experienced ones for a mentorship period is also a good way to bring newcomers on board.

Hire carefully

"Your business is only as good as the people who are in your business. I think a lot of people make a lot of mistakes in hiring, especially as they get bigger. They hire people for the wrong reasons—they're not clear what the job is supposed to be or what the expectations are. I've been doing work for an HR consulting firm and one of the things I just did a report on was job profiles, which are even a little bit more than job descriptions. I thought these were a great tool. They're the job description but they also profile the kind of person—without breaking any equal employment laws—that thrives in that kind of position. There's an old parable that you can't teach a bunny to fly. The bunny keeps coming to work, and the boss says 'You've got to learn to fly,' and the bunny says, 'Okay,' and tries to flap his ears. You just have to accept, this bunny's going to hop, and he's going to be really good at hopping, and that bird is going to fly. You can't put people in jobs where they're fundamentally not cut out for them."

— **Emily Esterson**

RESOURCE

Resources on hiring and managing staff. The "Employment Law Center" at nolo.com has lots of useful articles on the legal and practical rules involved in hiring employees and independent contractors, covering everything from wage and hour to antidiscrimination laws. *The Employer's Legal Guide*, by Fred S. Steingold (Nolo), covers a full range of legal and practical issues for hiring employees.

Nolo also publishes a variety of other employment books covering specific topics, such as creating an employee handbook and writing job descriptions (titles mentioned in the relevant sections above); managing employees; preventing and handling workplace discrimination and harassment; understanding federal employment laws, including family and medical leave; establishing policies such as employee email privacy; conducting performance appraisals; dealing with problem employees; and more. For details and sample chapters of Nolo titles, see www.nolo.com.

Using Technology to Manage Staff

Managing your staff doesn't just mean making sure they're doing their jobs well—it also involves administrative tasks such as tracking their hours, vacation and sick time, and often more. These are no small tasks, even if your staff is small. At a minimum, it's obviously important to have accurate information to correctly calculate paychecks (not to mention payroll taxes). And since tracking this type of information is an ongoing responsibility, it's essential not to fall behind.

The key to handling employee-related administrative tasks is—you guessed it!—to implement a clear system and use it consistently. Even if you use a bookkeeper to prepare employees' paychecks (which involves calculating and deducting the right amount of payroll taxes), you'll need a way to collect the hours' information. More often than not, this will involve some sort of digital technology such as spreadsheets and databases.

At the simple end of the technological spectrum, spreadsheet software such as Microsoft *Excel* allows you to keep sortable lists of employees and contract staff, along with important information about each individual, such as contact information, Social Security number, date of hire, and more. The spreadsheet will also allow you to enter their hours worked and pay rate, as well as keep a tally of vacation and sick time owed and used. You can easily create formulas that will make automatic calculations, such as multiplying the workers' hours by their pay rates to calculate their pay before taxes are deducted. A small business might implement a simple system in which employees enter their hours on a sign-in sheet, then at day's (or week's) end a manager or the business owner enters those numbers into the spreadsheet which acts as a master file for all employee hour information. Your bookkeeper can use the spreadsheet to prepare payroll each pay period.

Databases are similar to spreadsheets in that they store and organize information, but databases are generally more customizable than spreadsheets. In particular, databases are useful in generating reports from the data entered. For example, you could create custom reports showing how much of a project budget is being used by an employee each month, or what project milestones an employee has reached in a specific period of time. Of course, heavy customization will usually require that you hire a database consultant, which can get expensive. But if your business has the need and budget to track and monitor your workers, projects, and productivity closely, a highly customized database can be an incredibly powerful tool.

Instead of purchasing database software and customizing it to track your employee-related data, another option is to purchase a specific type of database product sometimes called employee relationship management (ERM) software. These applications are essentially databases at their core, but have been "precustomized" to focus on employee management, sometimes for specific industries.

Growing into the role of employer

"I think I was very naive in the beginning. I didn't really think about how hard it was going to be. I just knew I needed help. I needed support. And I found a few good people, I was really lucky, and I always had a good knack for picking the right people. As the years went by and we grew, and the business grew, and I had to have more and more staff, then I learned exactly what 'human resources' means. What it means to take care of people and all of the issues that are mixed in with that. Everything from boundaries to management, all of it. I just learned it a day at a time, just like everything else. For many years I have to say it wasn't the most fun part. It was sometimes the most painful part, dealing with the people. Because sometimes you have to let people go, and sometimes you have to discipline people, and it's never fun. I like being a friend; I didn't like being a boss! I think my strength, surprisingly enough now, is management. I think I'm pretty good at motivating a team and keeping the people who work with me inspired and happy. That's something I've grown into."

— **Kyle Zimmerman**

When figuring out the type and scope of system to use, bear in mind that generally speaking, it makes sense to track only the employee data that you actually plan to use. If, in the short term, all you want to accomplish is to track hours and vacation and sick time for payroll purposes, then you'll probably be fine with a relatively simple approach using a spreadsheet or minimally customized database. If, on the other hand, you want to generate detailed productivity reports, or to integrate project budgets along with employee hour information, you may want to invest in developing a more sophisticated database.

RELATED TOPIC

More info on spreadsheets, databases, and technology for project management. See "Using Technology to Manage Money, Inventory, and Projects" in Chapter 10.

Employees vs. Independent Contractors (ICs)

Anyone who works for your business (other than a business owner) is either an employee or an independent contractor (IC). In a nutshell, an employee is someone who works for you, on your site, with your tools and equipment, and according to your rules and procedures. Independent contractors, on the other hand, are in business for themselves; they work on their own time and with their own tools, and perform services for a number of different clients. Typical examples of ICs include accountants, interior decorators, attorneys, electricians, and Web developers.

The employee-IC distinction is not one to take lightly. Businesspeople who hire employees owe a number of employment taxes, such as payroll tax and unemployment tax, while those who hire only independent contractors do not owe these taxes, but still have some legal requirements to meet. The following sections cover the various rules and bureaucratic tasks for employees and ICs.

CAUTION

If you treat an employee as an independent contractor and fail to pay employment taxes, you risk a huge back-tax bill, plus interest and other state and federal penalties. More than a few businesses have been torpedoed and sunk into bankruptcy after making this mistake.

The Agencies That Matter

Because paying taxes is the main drawback to classifying workers as employees, it shouldn't surprise you to learn that the IRS takes a great interest in whether your workers are classified properly. At the federal level, the IRS will take swift and severe action if it finds out that you're treating a worker as an independent contractor when in fact that worker meets the criteria of being an employee. At the state level, there are rules for classifying workers that may be stricter than or otherwise different from the IRS rules. The penalties at the state level can be at least as harsh as those imposed by the IRS, so be sure you understand the rules in your state. The state agency in charge of worker status rules and enforcement is generally an employment agency, tax department, unemployment office, or other employment-related bureau.

RESOURCE

Resources for employers. IRS publications and forms are available online at www.irs.gov or by calling call 800-TAX-FORM. The IRS website also has a list of state agencies that cover employer issues, such as worker classification. Search "State Government Websites" at www.irs.gov and you'll find a state-by-state list broken down by category, such as "Employer Links."

IRS Criteria

The IRS's Publication 15-A, *Employer's Supplemental Tax Guide*, offers information and examples to help you determine whether a worker is in fact an independent contractor or an employee.

A worker should normally be considered an *employee*, not an independent contractor, when the following are true (note that no one characteristic is definitive; the IRS makes its determination based on a totality of circumstances). The worker:

- works only for you and not for any other business
- works on your premises (although you may allow the worker to work from home a day or two a week)

- uses your tools and equipment
- follows work hours you set
- follows your instructions on how to complete a job or task
- receives reimbursement for expenses incurred in doing a job
- supervises any of your other workers, or
- receives any employee benefits, such as holiday pay, vacation time, or health insurance.

On the flip side, a worker should probably be considered an *independent contractor* if the following are true (again, looking at the totality of circumstances). The worker:

- works for a number of different businesses or clients
- has a personal office, studio, garage, or other permanent place to work
- owns equipment and tools used for the work
- sets his or her own hours
- uses independent judgment as to how best to complete a job that you assign
- doesn't get reimbursed for expenses incurred in doing a job, or
- advertises services to the public.

You might hire a worker who displays some characteristics of both categories, which makes it harder to say for sure how this person should be classified. Ultimately, you'll need to consider these factors all together and weigh them against each other to decide whether a worker should be classified as an employee or as an independent contractor.

EXAMPLE 1: Renee is a bookkeeper with a major client, a local café. She works about 60 hours per month for the café, but also works for about five other local businesses. She always works in her home office (except for occasional visits to her clients), uses her own computers and software, manages her own hours, and receives minimal instructions as to how to do her work. Renee can probably be categorized as an independent contractor.

EXAMPLE 2: Virginia is a massage therapist and works primarily for a local wellness center, approximately 20 hours per week. She specializes in maternity massage, and occasionally takes clients at her home or at a booth she sets up at local festivals and fairs. She has regular hours at the wellness center and uses their massage tables and accessories when working there. She follows the operations manual at the wellness center and occasionally receives training in various therapeutic massage techniques. The government is likely to see Virginia as an employee. It would be risky for the wellness center to try to treat her as an independent contractor.

In borderline situations, it's safer to treat a worker as an employee than risk the penalties that may result if the IRS or your state decides you've misclassified an employee as an independent contractor. Keep in mind that the IRS and most state authorities tend to disfavor independent contractor status. They'd much rather see borderline workers classified as employees so that they can collect taxes on them.

If you can't decide how one of your workers should be classified, there are a few ways you can proceed. One is to consult a lawyer or an accountant who understands business tax laws. Another option is to go straight to the horse's mouth and ask the IRS or your state agency to tell you how they would classify a certain worker. You can file IRS Form SS-8, *Determination of Worker Status,* to request a formal ruling from the IRS on a worker's status. As already mentioned, however, don't be surprised if the IRS classifies your worker as an employee.

For a state determination, contact your state agency that governs worker classification and find out what procedure it uses. Like the IRS does, it's common for states to classify workers as employees rather than independent contractors. You'll have to decide for yourself whether it makes sense to leave the determination up to these agencies, or whether you feel confident enough to classify your workers on your own.

Required Rules, Paperwork, Filings, and Taxes for Employees

SKIP AHEAD

For businesses with independent contractors only. The rules in this section won't apply to you, and you can move on to "Rules for Hiring Independent Contractors," below. You may still want to read this section, however, for an overview of the regulations that apply to businesses with employees.

A raft of legal and tax requirements kick in when you hire your first employee. Not only will you have to pay a number of employment taxes, but you'll also need to register with several government agencies, buy certain types of required insurance, and comply with various federal and state laws, such as those requiring you to keep a smoke-free workplace and to post certain notices at your workplace.

Overview of Key Employment Laws

While the details of the many laws that apply to employers are beyond the scope of this book, the major requirements are listed below. If your needs can't be met by hiring an independent contractor and you must hire an employee, you'll need to consult additional resources to make sure you comply with the many state and federal laws governing employers. Relevant state and federal agencies and websites are listed below. See "Resources on hiring and managing staff," above, for a list of other useful publications.

In general, businesses with one or more employees are required to do the following:

- **Comply with federal, state, and local antidiscrimination laws.** These cover all aspects of the employee relationship, from hiring to firing. The exact rules depend on the number of your employees. See the U.S. Equal Employment Opportunity Commission (www.ceoc.gov) for details.

- **Comply with state and federal wage and hours laws.** The federal Fair Labor Standards Act establishes a federal minimum wage (currently $7.25 per hour) and rules for paying overtime. Many states also have their own wage and hour laws, and some impose a higher minimum wage (or more generous overtime rules) than the federal government. Check the U.S. Department of Labor website, www.dol.gov, for details.

- **Report all new hires to your state's employment department.** You must do this within 20 days of the employee's first day of work. The state uses this information to track down parents who owe child support.

- **Obtain workers' compensation insurance.** In addition, follow rules on notifying employees of their right to workers' compensation benefits. You may typically purchase this insurance from a state fund or from a private workers' compensation insurance company. For details, check www.workerscompensation.com.
- **Comply with state and federal job safety laws, administered by the federal Occupational Safety & Health Administration (OSHA) and the agency in your state that governs workplace safety.** Among other things, these laws require you to file an illness and injury prevention plan, report work-related injuries and illnesses that result in lost work time, and keep a log of all work-related injuries and illnesses. For information about OSHA regulations, see www.osha.gov.
- **Withhold federal income taxes and FICA taxes (Social Security and Medicare taxes) from employees' paychecks and periodically report and send these withheld taxes to the IRS.** See IRS Form 944, *Employer's Annual Federal Tax Return*, for details.

RESOURCE

IRS guide to reporting and withholding taxes. See IRS Publication 15, Circular E, *Employer's Tax Guide*, for details on withholding federal taxes and other IRS requirements discussed below.

- **Report wages and withholding to each employee and to the IRS with Form W-2 (*Wage and Tax Statement*).**
- **Pay the employer's portion of Social Security and Medicare tax for each employee, based on the employee's wages.** The employer's share is 7.65% of the employee's wages.
- **Withhold state income taxes (levied in most states) from employees' paychecks and periodically deposit them with your state income tax agency.**
- **Pay federal unemployment taxes.** It's the sole responsibility of the employer to pay the Federal Unemployment Tax (FUTA) directly to the IRS; you may not deduct it from employees' paychecks.

You must report FUTA taxes paid annually on IRS Form 940, *Employer's Annual Federal Unemployment Tax Return.*

- **Pay state unemployment taxes.** Most states require employers to pay unemployment taxes, which go into a state unemployment insurance fund. Generally, you can take a credit against your FUTA tax for amounts you paid into state unemployment funds. A list of state unemployment tax agencies is available on the U.S. Department of Labor website (www.workforcesecurity.doleta.gov/unemploy/agencies.asp).

- **Pay or withhold other employment-related taxes that may be required by your state, such as disability insurance.**

- **Have the employee complete USCIS Form I-9,** *Employment Eligibility Verification,* **and show you documents such as a passport, or a driver's license and birth certificate, which confirm the person's identity and eligibility to work in the United States.** See the website of the U.S. Citizenship and Immigration Services (USCIS, formerly the INS) at www.uscis.com for a copy of Form I-9. You don't have to file this form with the USCIS, but you must keep it for three years (or one year after an employee quits or is fired—whichever is later).

- **Put up required posters on employee rights.** See the Department of Labor's website, www.dol.gov, for details.

- **Comply with other federal, state, and local laws, depending on your business and number of employees.** For example, the Family and Medical Leave Act covers employers with more than 50 employees, and the Americans with Disabilities Act covers employers with more than 15 employees.

TIP
Trouble finding the relevant state agency? Search your state website (find yours at www.business.usa.gov), or check out the "Explore State and Local Resources" section at www.irs.gov.

Thinking twice about becoming an employer? There's no way around it: Hiring employees to your business undoubtedly makes running your business more complex. (And this is even without considering many other possibilities, such as providing optional benefits, such as health insurance or a 401(k) plan.) If there's a way to meet your needs with independent contractors rather than employees, it may be a much more practical road to take. At the very least, you shouldn't jump into hiring employees without having a clear reason to do so.

> ⚠ CAUTION
>
> **Make payroll taxes a top priority expense.** The owner of a cash-strapped small business might be tempted to put off paying payroll taxes for a quarter, or a year. "This happens all the time, but it is a huge mistake. It can lead to jail time," says David Rothenberg, a CPA. You must include payroll taxes in your cash flow planning and then pay those taxes regularly.

What About Employee Benefits?

By now you have probably heard that the Affordable Care Act (ACA) requires large employers, defined as businesses with more than 50 full-time equivalent (FTE) employees, to provide health insurance for these employees, or pay a per-month penalty, called the "Employer Shared Responsibility Payment," on their federal tax returns. Full-time equivalent means that an employer must count part-time employees who can "add up" to one FTE. (For more info on the definition of FTEs, go to www.irs.gov and search for "determining FTEs.")

This requirement, sometimes called the employer mandate, was originally set to begin in 2014, but was delayed until 2015. Since the political wrangling over this provision is intense (to say the least) and the details are likely to change before it is implemented, we'll leave the details for a future edition. It's worth noting, however that this mandate only applies to larger businesses and will not affect the vast majority of small startups that have nowhere near 50 FTE employees.

Legal mandates aside, providing a benefits package can be a major factor in attracting good employees, lowering turnover and absenteeism, and developing a loyal, motivated workforce. While providing health insurance or dental or vision coverage or other benefits is undoubtedly costly, your business can often deduct the business's contributions to benefit plans. In addition, you (the business owner) can take advantage of workplace benefits such as health insurance which may be more expensive or not as robust when purchased privately. (Purchasing health insurance for yourself is discussed in Chapter 1.)

Note that some states and local governments do require certain benefits (rules vary by size and type of business). Check IRS Publication 15-B, *Employer's Tax Guide to Fringe Benefits*, for more information. The IRS also has several other useful publications on different types of benefits, including Publications 560 (*Retirement Plans for Small Business*) and 969 (*Health Savings Accounts and Other Tax-Favored Health Plans*).

If you're seriously considering offering benefits, talk to a broker experienced in employee benefits for advice on your options and costs. As with finding other professionals, start with your personal network for broker recommendations, especially any colleagues in the HR field. A good broker should pull together proposals from insurance companies for you and help you pick one company (or a combination of companies) depending on the types of coverage you want (and your budget).

Rules for Hiring Independent Contractors (ICs)

Many small businesses do just fine hiring only independent contractors, or by supplementing their workforce with ICs (for example, for legal and financial services). While hiring independent contractors is generally much much simpler than hiring employees (and avoids several taxes), it does trigger some legal requirements. One of the main rules is that if you pay any independent contractor more than $600 in a year, you need to report those payments on Form 1099-MISC (*Miscellaneous Income*), which you must send to the worker and to the IRS. If the IC is doing business as a corporation, you don't have to file a 1099 (unless the IC has formed a medical corporation).

When hiring an IC, be sure to get basic information for your records, both for reporting purposes and to have on file as documentation in case of an audit. At a minimum, make sure you get the IC's business name, address, and federal taxpayer ID number. The easiest way to obtain this is to have the IC fill out and sign IRS form W-9, *Request for Taxpayer Identification Number and Certification*. You'll keep this form in your files; you don't have to submit it to the IRS. ICs who operate as sole proprietorships without any employees may simply use their Social Security numbers as their taxpayer IDs. Other ICs will have obtained employer identification numbers (EINs) from the IRS for their businesses. Either one is fine.

If you can't or don't obtain the IC's taxpayer ID number, you may need to withhold payments from the IC and deposit them to the IRS. Called "backup withholding," this is required if you do not have the IC's taxpayer ID number and you pay the IC $600 or more during the year. For more information on backup withholding, see the instructions for IRS Form 945, *Annual Return of Withheld Federal Income Tax*.

> **TIP**
>
> **Put your IC agreements in writing.** While it may not be legally required, it's always a good idea to use a written contract when you hire an IC. Besides helping to avert garden-variety conflicts over the terms of the job, having a contract in place will also help you prove that the worker is an independent contractor, not an employee. By stating in your agreement that the worker is an independent contractor, you are establishing an intent to create an independent contractor relationship. This may turn out to be helpful evidence in the case of an audit. If all other evidence demonstrates that the worker is an employee, however, that's how the IRS and your state will probably classify him or her. Remember, the only true test of a worker's status is how the worker is actually treated. If you treat workers as employees—require them to work on-site, define their hours, closely supervise their work, and so on—merely calling them independent contractors in your contracts won't magically change their status.
>
> For detailed information about hiring independent contractors and sample IC contracts, see *Working With Independent Contractors*, by Stephen Fishman (Nolo). For info on this book and a sample chapter, plus useful articles on various issues involving independent contractors, see www.nolo.com.

Hiring Your Kids and Other Family Members

Hiring your sister, a cousin, or another relative can be a great way to keep the business in trusted hands. But you need to be just as organized and professional when hiring family members as when hiring regular civilians—perhaps even more so, since your precious family relationships are on the line. To prevent major family conflicts, approach the hiring process methodically as described in this chapter. Make sure you have a detailed job description with responsibilities clearly outlined, and only hire a relative who is actually qualified to do the work. Keep track of time carefully and pay wages regularly, as you would with any worker.

If you're hiring your kids on a regular or an occasional basis to help run errands, answer phones, stuff envelopes, or other tasks, first make sure that you don't violate federal or state child labor laws. In general, these prevent hiring children younger than 18 years old for hazardous jobs, and establish numerous rules about allowable hours and mandatory breaks for different age ranges. For more details, visit the federal Department of Labor's website at www.dol.gov. Also check with your state's department of labor for any state rules, which may be more restrictive than the federal laws.

Tax rules can be complicated when you hire your spouse, a child, or a family member. *Tax Savvy for Small Business*, by Frederick W. Daily and Jeffrey A. Quinn (Nolo) has a detailed discussion of the topic.

RELATED TOPIC

Your spouse may volunteer for your business without being classified as an employee. See "Running a Business With Your Spouse" in Chapter 5 for details.

Lawyers and Accountants:
Building Your Family of Professionals

E very business needs to deal with legal and tax issues from time
to time—but, thankfully, for most small to medium-sized
businesses, serious legal issues don't come up that often. Many
legal tasks, such as filing LLC formation documents or signing a lease
for office space, are usually easy enough for you to handle on your own
(especially with the help of books like this one and the resources listed
throughout this book). But while you won't likely need in-house counsel
or a full-time accountant, you should aim to develop relationships with
legal and financial professionals for those times when you do need
guidance. When a question or a problem arises, you'll want to have an
established network of trusted people to turn to.

You might find yourself needing help from a lawyer if, for example,
you want to enter into a strategic partnership with another business and
don't know how to structure the relationship. Or perhaps a business
partner wants to cash out of the business and your partnership agreement hasn't spelled out terms for doing so. Maybe a customer is
threatening to sue you for an injury he sustained in your parking lot,
or a client is demanding a refund for a large custom order. If and when
these types of circumstances arise, the ideal situation is for you to have
an established relationship with a lawyer who knows your business and
whom you trust for good advice and possibly other services.

The same goes for an accountant. While you may have a full- or part-
time bookkeeper on staff or on contract, chances are you'll only use an
accountant a few times per year to do tax prep and answer questions
that come up outside of tax time. For example, you may want to consult
your accountant for advice on how to structure a health benefits package
so as to maximize tax savings. Your accountant may also be an excellent
adviser on questions of financial management and growth strategies.
And, of course, having a trusted accountant will be a godsend if you ever
get a notice from the IRS that you're being audited.

Finding lawyers and accountants who are a good fit for you and your
business can take some time, so it's smart to start looking early. Bear
in mind, your first choice might not work out—I tried two different
accountants before finding one I just adore and I know many other

businesswomen with similar experiences—so give yourself plenty of time. Ideally, you'll have some good relationships in place well before you have any pressing needs like a lawsuit or an audit. The better a professional knows you and your business, the better equipped she will be to provide the best advice and assistance for your specific situation.

This chapter offers strategies to help you find and hire a professional such as a lawyer or an accountant who's both competent and trustworthy. You'll find the advice useful in hiring other professionals, too, such as insurance brokers. In most cases, you will be hiring independent contractors, or ICs, (not employees). See Chapter 12 for legal rules for hiring ICs.

It pays off to get professional help

"It's key to know what your strengths and your skills are and then figure out ways to get help for the things that you don't do well. And pay for that help when necessary, whether that's tax help, or administrative help, or any other kind of help."

— **Emily Esterson**

"My bookkeeper works with me twice a week, for four hours a day, and then I have a tax accountant who I work with once a month, especially once a quarter and every year. It's not that expensive for what it saves me. I've had three or four bookkeepers over the ten years, and this is the first bookkeeper, that I've now had about six years, that has been amazing and I trust her."

— **Kyle Zimmerman**

"It is good to have a small group of trusted professionals—attorney, tax accountant, business consultant—that know your business well and that you can consult about any big decisions that you are making. I didn't have any of these people to talk with for many years, and just kind of fumbled through on my intuition. This approach worked to some extent for a while, but I am glad to have some others to talk with now."

— **Rebecca Pearcy**

Working With Lawyers

Having a good lawyer in your camp can give you a real sense of confidence in managing your business. Even if you don't call your lawyer very often, just knowing that you have a savvy ally to turn to for guidance is reassuring—and if you need to file or defend yourself against a lawsuit, your lawyer can help you avoid true disaster.

Some people find it difficult or intimidating to start the process of finding a lawyer, largely because they're not clear about what they're looking for or how to evaluate prospects. Here are some tips on finding and working with a lawyer, including typical billing arrangements.

What to Look for in a Lawyer

Look for an attorney who specializes in or at least has significant experience working with small businesses. Typically, this means skills and expertise in one or more of the following: business structures; contracts, leases, and negotiation; warranties; employment and human resources; regulations and permits; and intellectual property (copyright, trademark, and so on).

Even better than finding a garden-variety small business lawyer is finding one who has experience with your specific type of small business. The legal issues facing restaurants, for example, are largely different from those facing real estate agents or marketing consultants. Ideally, you'll find a lawyer who knows the legal terrain of your specific field.

Be aware that some lawyers are not litigators, meaning that they don't handle actual lawsuits. Since most businesses don't face lawsuits (either filing or defending against one) very often, it may be fine to hire a lawyer with significant business expertise in your field, but little litigation experience. It's preferable, however, that the attorney at least has some litigator contacts to refer you to if the need arises so you don't have to start a search from scratch. When you're talking with attorney prospects, ask if they have litigation experience and if not, whether they would be able to refer you to a good litigator (either an associate or an outside firm) in case you ever face a lawsuit.

In addition to finding a lawyer with the skills and experience relevant to your situation, it's important that you and the lawyer get along on a personal level. If an otherwise perfect lawyer—smart, experienced, and trustworthy—is condescending, rude, or slow in returning your emails or phone calls, you should keep looking for someone with better personal skills.

Finally, you may want to make a special effort to find a lawyer who is willing to work with you collaboratively on routine legal issues that you can handle at least partially on your own, such as amending your partnership agreement or executing a contract for services. If you'd like to be more involved with your business's legal matters and minimize the attorneys' fees you'll owe, be sure to ask the lawyer directly whether he or she is willing to have this kind of working relationship with you. (See "Using a Lawyer as a Coach," below.)

Starting Your Search

The best way to find a good lawyer is to get a referral, ideally from someone whose opinion you value and who runs a small business. Once again, tapping into your personal network (especially owners of businesses that are similar to yours) will be of tremendous help in finding good legal professionals. Book publishers, for instance, face different types of legal issues than do auto repair shops, and would be best served by lawyers familiar with legal areas such as copyright and other intellectual property issues.

If you just can't find anyone who can give you an enthusiastic referral, dig in a little deeper with your research (sorry, combing the yellow pages doesn't count). Keep your eyes and ears open for names of attorneys who have worked on cases in your field. For example, your local paper might have an article about a recent lawsuit involving a business similar to yours that mentions the names of the attorneys or the firm working on it. Also try contacting trade organizations, such as your local chamber of commerce. They can often direct you to lawyers who have worked in your industry. Your banker or accountant may also be a good source of attorney referrals.

Once you get some names, try calling these lawyers and asking if they're available. If not, there's a good chance they will know someone else who might be able to help you.

RESOURCE

Looking for a lawyer? Asking for a referral to an attorney from someone you trust can be a good way to find legal help. Someone looking to hire a lawyer, even if only for consultation, can also try these excellent and free resources:

- **Nolo's Lawyer Directory.** Nolo has an easy-to-use online directory of lawyers, organized by location and area of expertise. You can find the directory and its comprehensive profiles at www.nolo.com/lawyers.
- **Lawyers.com.** At Lawyers.com, you'll find a user-friendly search tool that allows you to tailor results by area of law and geography. You can also search for attorneys by name. Attorney profiles prominently display contact information, list topics of expertise, and show ratings—by both clients and other legal professionals.
- **Martindale.com.** Martindale.com offers an advanced search option that allows you to sort not only by practice area and location, but also by criteria like law school. Whether you look for lawyers by name or expertise, you'll find listings with detailed background information, peer and client ratings, and even profile visibility.

Making Contact With Prospects

When contacting your prospects, ask to speak with each lawyer personally. You can probably get a good idea of how an attorney operates by paying close attention to the way your call is handled. Is the lawyer available right away, and, if not, is your call promptly returned? Is the lawyer willing to spend at least a few minutes talking with you to determine whether the two of you are a good fit, and is there a fee for this consultation? When you talk, ask about the attorney's experience working with small businesses like yours. Do you get a good feeling from your conversation? How you're treated during your initial call can be a good indicator of how the lawyer treats clients in general. If you have a strong preference for email communication instead of phone, or vice versa, ask the attorneys whether they work the same way. Some old-school attorneys might be slow returning emails, or may not be very savvy with electronic documents, which will drive you nuts if that's the way you prefer to work.

Always ask a potential lawyer to provide client references, preferably two or three. When you've narrowed your list to just a few prospects, get in touch with the references and ask them about their experiences with each lawyer: Did they find the lawyer to be competent? Was the lawyer's advice and service useful? Did the lawyer return phone calls and emails promptly? Were the fees reasonable? Feedback from others can be of major help in making your final decision.

Using a Lawyer as a Coach

It's probably not a stretch to assume that most of you reading this book are do-it-yourself types, as most entrepreneurs tend to be. For us take-charge folks, it can be frustrating—not to mention expensive—to hand over full control of simple legal tasks to a lawyer, which is the traditional way attorneys have provided services. In many circumstances, the legal tasks involved may be straightforward enough for you to largely handle on your own—but you'll need to find a lawyer who is willing to work collaboratively with you, which may take a little extra searching.

In this relatively new model of legal services, sometimes called "legal coaching" or "unbundled legal services," the lawyer will provide only the services that you want, allowing you to do some of the work on your own. For example, if you want legal help in drafting a contract, you may want to arrange a short consultation with a lawyer to get answers to general questions, draft the contract on your own, then send it to the lawyer, who will review it and suggest any necessary revisions. Or, if you want to represent yourself in small claims court, you might use a lawyer to help prepare for hearings but otherwise pursue the case independently.

For a small business owner, using a lawyer as a coach can be especially useful. More often than not, the legal issues that arise in the course of business are relatively simple, and—with a bit of good legal advice— most businesspeople can handle them. Many times, you'll need nothing more than some guidance through the bureaucratic maze that small businesses need to navigate. For instance, facing a zoning conflict, you may be perfectly served by a five-minute explanation from a legal coach on the process of appealing a planning commission's decision. Rather than hiring an attorney for upwards of $1,000 to deal with the problem, using a coach might cost $100 and enable you to handle the zoning problem yourself.

Despite the good sense to this approach, it might be challenging to find a lawyer who is willing to be just a coach. To find one, use the same strategies discussed above (referrals from your business and personal contacts, for example), but take the extra step of asking the lawyer directly whether she is willing to help you in your efforts to solve your own legal problems. If you don't find someone willing to work this way with you right away, be persistent. In today's increasingly competitive legal marketplace, it's becoming easier to find lawyers who are willing to be flexible in the services they offer.

Legal Fees and Billing Arrangements

Before you hire any lawyer, be sure you fully understand how your fees will be calculated and the basics of your billing arrangement. Ask who's responsible for paying for things such as court fees, copy fees, transcription costs, and phone bills; these costs aren't trivial and can quickly send your otherwise affordable bill into the keep-you-awake-at-night range.

Lawyers generally use one of the following methods of calculating fees for their services.

- **Hourly fees.** This arrangement works just like it sounds: You pay the attorney's hourly rate for the number of hours the attorney spends on your case. Simple as this system is, there are some details to consider. First, find out what hourly increments the lawyer uses for billing. For instance, if an attorney bills in half-hour increments, you'll be charged for a full half-hour even if you talk for just five minutes. That can easily total $100 or more for a five-minute phone call. You'd be better off if your lawyer uses ten- or 15-minute periods, though not all attorneys break down their time into such small increments.

Another issue to ask about is whether all time spent on the case—even if the attorney isn't doing the work—is billed at the attorney's regular rate. For example, it's reasonable to expect a lower rate for time spent by the attorney's administrative staff on making copies or organizing paperwork. Make sure that the hourly fee for the attorney applies only to the work of the actual attorney.

Hourly fees for attorneys typically range from $100 or so to over $400 per hour. High rates may reflect a lawyer's extensive experience or high degree of specialization—or they might reflect nothing more than the attorney's expensive tastes. Don't pay the highest rates unless you feel the lawyer's expertise is worth it.

- **Flat fees.** For some types of cases, attorneys will charge a flat fee for a specific task, such as negotiating a contract or drafting and filing LLC formation documents. As long as the job goes as expected, you'll pay only the agreed price, regardless of how many hours the lawyer spent on the job. If the lawyer hits a snag, however, or if the case becomes convoluted for some reason, the price may go up. Be sure you and the lawyer are on the same page regarding the situations that may result in a higher fee. Also, find out if any expenses, such as court costs or copy fees, are charged in addition to the flat fee.

- **Contingency fees.** In a contingency fee arrangement, you pay an attorney's fee only if the lawyer wins money for you through a court judgment or a negotiated settlement. In that case, the fee you'd pay would be a percentage of the monetary award, usually one-third to one-half. In contingency fee arrangements, you need to be especially careful of costs such as travel expenses, transcription fees, and phone bills. If you lose your case, you won't owe attorneys' fees (because your lawyer didn't recover any money)—but you will often be responsible for the lawyer's out-of-pocket expenses.

Small business matters don't typically require contingency fee arrangements. This payment method is usually used in personal injury cases and others in which a plaintiff sues someone in hopes of winning a large money award.

- **Retainers.** Sometimes you can hire a lawyer to be more or less "on call" by paying a regular fee (usually monthly) called a retainer. This type of arrangement is useful when you have ongoing legal needs, such as contract review or negotiation. Based on your expected needs, you and the lawyer settle on a mutually acceptable monthly fee. Then you simply have the lawyer take care of any routine legal matters that arise. If you run into a sudden, complex legal dispute, or if your problems escalate greatly, you'll likely have to execute a separate agreement and pay additional fees. For this type of arrangement to work, it's important that you and the lawyer have a clear understanding of the routine services that you expect. Unless and until your legal needs are regular and predictable, a retainer arrangement is probably not your best option.

Get It in Writing

State laws may require a fee agreement to be in writing—for example, if your lawyer estimates the total cost of legal services to be more than $1,000, or if you have a contingency fee arrangement. Even if it's not legally required, it's always a good idea to get your fee agreement in writing, covering what work will be done, how much you'll pay, and on what basis (such as hourly fee or flat rate), and when you must pay the lawyer. A written agreement will help prevent disputes over billing and is the best way to avoid getting gouged.

Doing Your Own Legal Research

Some of the legal questions you may run into won't warrant an expensive consultation with an attorney but may be beyond the scope of a self-help book. For instance, you may need to look up specific consumer protection regulations on warranties, or find out your state's rules on terminating an employee. If you don't want to call your lawyer every time you have a question, you might consider doing a little legal research yourself.

Finding basic small business law is usually not difficult—much of the information you'll need can be found on the Internet. Here are some websites that offer helpful information on small business and tax law (we provide more resources on specific topics throughout this book):

- **Nolo (the publisher of this book) at www.nolo.com.** Nolo has many free resources for small businesses in its "Free Legal Information Section." Start by checking under the "Small Business," "Business Formation: LLCs & Corporations," and the "Employment Law" tabs to see if your question has already been covered in these sections, or to get some background information or a summary of state-by-state laws in the area of the law that interests you. Also, check out the "Legal Research" section of nolo.com for guidance in researching a particular business legal problem. Learning how to use legal resources online or at the law library will teach you to take care of a wide range of simple, everyday matters yourself, rather than paying someone else to handle them. And if you come across strange phrases like "illusory promise," "naked option," or "yellow-dog contract" in your legal meanderings, and you just know there's got to be a legal meaning behind them, try looking them up in Nolo's Free Dictionary of Law Terms and Legal Definitions, also available at nolo.com. In addition to all these free resources, Nolo publishes books, online apps, and software programs of special interest to entrepreneurs (we recommend many of them throughout this book).

- **Business.USA at www.business.usa.gov.** This is the U.S. government's official website for small businesses and provides access to federal, state, and local laws and information, including links to relevant agencies.

- **Official state and local websites (you can find your state's site at www.business.usa.gov).** Also, check out the "State Government Websites" section at www.irs.gov for specific state agencies. State sites often offer valuable information for small businesses, such as start-up registration requirements, state tax rules, laws on corporations and LLCs, downloadable forms, and much more. Keep in mind that there's a lot of variation from state to state in how much (and the quality of) info you'll find but, in general, the states have been rapidly improving their online information systems and making their sites more useful and accessible for citizens. The same is true for city and county sites.

- **National Federation of Independent Business at www.nfib.com.** This site tracks news and developments regarding small business legal information, offers links to state resources for small businesses, and publishes a wide range of other small business resources and practical information.

- **Internal Revenue Service at www.irs.gov.** The IRS site offers downloadable forms and instructions as well as a wide range of publications (including many that are referenced in this book) that do a fairly good job of explaining the tax laws. The "Small Businesses & Self-Employed" section is especially useful for finding resources on business tax issues.

- **The Library of Congress site at congress.gov.** This official source for federal legislative information offers a searchable database of small business bills pending in Congress, as well as laws that have recently been adopted. It replaces Thomas.gov.

- **Other business-oriented sites (such as trade associations relevant to your particular business) or the Small Business Administration.** We provide lots of URLs throughout this book, depending on the particular topic you're researching.

With bookkeepers, referrals are a must

"It's very important when you find a bookkeeper that it's somebody that is absolutely trustworthy and knows their stuff. You can't afford to just get 'someone' to do your books. You need to know that that person is qualified. Make sure that many, many people that you respect know and trust that person."

— **Kyle Zimmerman**

Working With Accountants, Bookkeepers, and Tax Professionals

Many of the issues that small business owners face can be solved by professionals other than lawyers. Accountants and other tax professionals are often indispensable in helping you manage your business's finances, particularly so as to minimize your tax bill and avoid mistakes that can result in costly penalties. In fact, tax advice is so essential to a successful small business that you really should consult with a tax expert like an accountant at least once a year.

This section discusses what money- and tax-related professionals you should consider and how they might fit within your business operations.

Which Professional Do You Need?

For routine maintenance of your books, you probably don't need the experience—or expense—of an accountant (certified or otherwise). An experienced bookkeeper will be able to put in place an effective system of tracking your income and expenses and staying on top of your important bills, including payroll and the various taxes your business will owe. Depending on the complexity of your business, you may even decide to do your own bookkeeping—a job that's undoubtedly easier these days with the availability of accounting software. As your business grows, however, an experienced bookkeeper will likely become a valuable investment.

If you find yourself seeking specific tax advice or encountering a tricky financial problem, you may need to go up a step on the professional ladder and hire an accountant who's intimate with tax laws. At the top rung are certified public accountants (CPAs), who are licensed and regulated by the state. Uncertified accountants, called public accountants (PAs), may also be licensed (depending on your state). Because the licensing requirements for CPAs are more stringent, they are considered to be the most experienced and knowledgeable type of accountants and, accordingly, will be the most expensive.

In addition to bookkeepers and accountants, there are other professionals out there who specialize in tax preparation. The main thing to keep in mind is that some are licensed and some are not. An enrolled agent (EA) is a tax professional, licensed by the IRS, who can answer tax questions and help you prepare your returns. Others who simply use the title "tax preparer" or "tax return preparer" may not be licensed at all (or have no experience handling taxes for businesses). If a tax professional doesn't have a license as an EA, PA, or CPA, it may mean that the "professional" has no official qualifications whatsoever.

The bottom line is that you should hire the person who is best equipped to meet your needs. Obviously, you shouldn't pay a CPA to do day-to-day bookkeeping entry, nor should you use a bookkeeper for preparing complex tax returns. You'll need to decide for yourself what kind of professional to hire for your financial tasks.

Choosing a Qualified, Trustworthy Candidate

The strategies discussed above for finding a lawyer are equally useful in finding financial and tax professionals. Getting a referral from a business or personal associate is the best way to find someone you can trust. Referrals from businesspeople in your field are particularly valuable. Since virtually every business has consulted a tax pro at one point or another, it shouldn't be too hard to get a decent list of names.

As with attorneys, choose a tax professional carefully, with an eye to developing a long-term relationship. Don't be shy about asking questions and checking references. Find out about the person's experience with small businesses similar to yours and knowledge of bookkeeping methods, the tax code, the IRS, or anything else that's relevant to the work you want the professional to do for you.

Also be sure you understand the professional's fee structure up front, before any work is done. Most charge hourly fees, which vary a great deal depending on the person's qualifications. You might find a bookkeeper to do simple work for $25 an hour, while most accountants will charge more in the $100 per hour range. Like your attorney fee agreement, your fee agreement with a tax professional should be in writing to reduce the possibility of disputes over the bill.

How to Use the Interactive Forms on the Nolo Website

This book comes with eforms that you can access online at **www.nolo.com/back-of-book/WBIZ.html**

To use the files, your computer must have specific software programs installed. Here is a list of types of files provided by this book, as well as the software programs you'll need to access them:

- **RTF.** You can open, edit, save, and print these form files with most word processing programs, such as Microsoft *Word*, Windows *WordPad*, and recent versions of *WordPerfect*.
- **PDF.** You can view these files with Adobe *Reader*, free software from www.adobe.com. Government PDFs are sometimes fillable using your computer, but most PDFs are designed to be printed out and completed by hand.
- **XLS.** You can open, edit, print, and save these spreadsheet files with Microsoft *Excel* or other spreadsheet programs that read XLS files.

Editing RTFs

Here are some general instructions about editing RTF forms in your word processing program. Refer to the form instructions in this book for help about what should go in each blank as described here.

- **Underlines.** Underlines indicate where to enter information. After filling in the needed text, delete the underline. In most word processing programs you can do this by highlighting the underlined portion and typing CTRL-U.
- **Bracketed and italicized text.** Bracketed and italicized text indicates instructions. Be sure to remove all instructional text before you finalize your document.
- **Optional text.** Optional text gives you the choice to include or exclude text. Delete any optional text you don't want to use. Renumber any numbered items, if necessary.
- **Alternative text.** Alternative text gives you the choice between two or more text options. Delete those options you don't want to use. Renumber any numbered items, if necessary.

- **Signature lines.** Signature lines should appear on a page with at least some text from the document itself.

Every word processing program uses different commands to open, format, save, and print documents, so refer to your software's help documents if you have questions about using your program. Nolo cannot provide technical support for questions about how to use your computer or your software.

CAUTION

In accordance with U.S. copyright laws, the forms provided by this book are for your personal use only.

List of Forms and Interviews Available on the Nolo Website

To download any of the files listed on the following pages go to:
www.nolo.com/back-of-book/WBIZ.html

The following word processing file is in Rich Text Format (RTF):

Form Name	File Name
Partnership Agreement	Partnership.rtf

The IRS Form SS-4 and its instructions are in Portable Document Format (PDF) and the form can be filled in on your computer:

File Name	Form Name
IRS instructions for Form SS-4	iss4.pdf
IRS Form SS-4	fss4.pdf

The following transcripts of interviews with women entrepreneur contributors to this book are in Portable Document Format (PDF):

File Name	Form Name
Elissa Breitbard Interview	Elissa_Breitbard.pdf
Emily Esterson Interview	Emily_Esterson.pdf
Isabel Walcott Draves Interview	Isabel_Walcott_Draves.pdf
Jennifer Cantrell Interview	Jennifer_Cantrell.pdf
Kyle Zimmerman Interview	Kyle_Zimmerman.pdf
Lauren Bacon & Emira Mears Interview	Lauren_Bacon_Emira_Mears.pdf
Leila Johnson Interview	Leila_Johnson.pdf
Nicola Freegard Interview	Nicola_Freegard.pdf
Rebecca Pearcy Interview	Rebecca_Pearcy.pdf
Sabrina Habib Williams Interview	Sabrina_Habib_Williams.pdf

The following business planning spreadsheets are in Microsoft's *Excel* format (XLS). Instructions for the spreadsheets are provided in Portable Document Format (PDF):

File Name	Form Name
Billable Rate Calculator	BillableRate.xls
Break-Even Analysis Worksheet	BreakEven.xls
Cash Flow Projection Worksheet	CashFlow.xls
Profit/Loss Forecast Worksheet	ProfitLoss.xls
Billable Rate Instructions	BillableRate_Instructions.pdf
Break-Even Instructions	BreakEven_Instructions.pdf
Cash Flow Instructions	CashFlow_Instructions.pdf
Profit/Loss Instructions	ProfitLoss_Instructions.pdf

Index

⚖️ NOLO | *Online Legal Forms*

Nolo offers a large library of legal solutions and forms, created by Nolo's in-house legal staff. These reliable documents can be prepared in minutes.

Create a Document

- **Incorporation.** Incorporate your business in any state.
- **LLC Formations.** Gain asset protection and pass-through tax status in any state.
- **Wills.** Nolo has helped people make over 2 million wills. Is it time to make or revise yours?
- **Living Trust (avoid probate).** Plan now to save your family the cost, delays, and hassle of probate.
- **Trademark.** Protect the name of your business or product.
- **Provisional Patent.** Preserve your rights under patent law and claim "patent pending" status.

Download a Legal Form

Nolo.com has hundreds of top quality legal forms available for download—bills of sale, promissory notes, nondisclosure agreements, LLC operating agreements, corporate minutes, commercial lease and sublease, motor vehicle bill of sale, consignment agreements and many, many more.

Review Your Documents

Many lawyers in Nolo's consumer-friendly lawyer directory will review Nolo documents for a very reasonable fee. Check their detailed profiles at **Nolo.com/lawyers**.